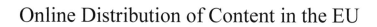
Online Distribution of Content in the EU

Online Distribution of Content in the EU

Edited by

Taina Pihlajarinne

Faculty of Law, University of Helsinki, Finland

Juha Vesala

Faculty of Law, University of Helsinki, Finland

Olli Honkkila

Faculty of Law, University of Helsinki, Finland

 Edward Elgar
PUBLISHING

Cheltenham, UK • Northampton, MA, USA

Published by
Edward Elgar Publishing Limited
The Lypiatts
15 Lansdown Road
Cheltenham
Glos GL50 2JA
UK

Edward Elgar Publishing, Inc.
William Pratt House
9 Dewey Court
Northampton
Massachusetts 01060
USA

A catalogue record for this book
is available from the British Library

Library of Congress Control Number: 2018959289

This book is available electronically in the **Elgar**online
Law subject collection
DOI 10.4337/9781788119900

ISBN 978 1 78811 989 4 (cased)
ISBN 978 1 78811 990 0 (eBook)

Printed and bound in Great Britain by TJ International Ltd, Padstow

Contents

List of contributors   vii

PART I   INTRODUCTION

1   Introduction   2
     Taina Pihlajarinne, Juha Vesala and Olli Honkkila

PART II   COPYRIGHT AND ONLINE DISTRIBUTION –
           ON A PATH TO FRAGMENTATION?

2   The DSM Directive: a package (too) full of policies   5
     Martti Kivistö

3   Linking and copyright – a problem solvable by
     functional-technical concepts?   25
     Taina Pihlajarinne

4   Neighbouring rights: in search of a dogmatic foundation. The
     press publishers' case   40
     Valentina Moscon

5   Meet the unavoidable – the challenges of digital second-hand
     marketplaces to the doctrine of exhaustion   62
     Péter Mezei

6   Extended collective licensing and online distribution –
     prospects for extending the Nordic solution to the digital realm   79
     Anette Alén-Savikko and Tone Knapstad

7   Liability and access to contact information: striking the
     balance when service is used to distribute copyrighted digital
     content   97
     Katja Weckström Lindroos

PART III   EMERGING TECHNOLOGIES FOR ONLINE
             DISTRIBUTION – MORE FRAGMENTATION
             IN THE FUTURE?

8   AI-generated content: authorship and inventorship in the age
      of artificial intelligence   117
      Rosa Maria Ballardini, Kan He and Teemu Roos

9   Winds of change: conceptualising copyright law in a world
      of 3D models and 3D design files – a perspective from the UK   136
      Dinusha Mendis

10   Different aspects of trade mark confusion with respect to
      distribution of CAD files in the era of 3D printing   153
      Taina Pihlajarinne and Max Oker-Blom

PART IV   DIGITAL SINGLE MARKET, COMPETITION
            AND REGULATION

11   Digital Single Market, digital content and consumer
      protection – critical reflections   172
      Katri Havu

12   Allowing online content to cross borders: is Europe really
      paving the way for a Digital Single Market?   188
      Giuseppe Mazziotti

13   Achieving a Digital Single Market for online distribution of content:
      when would extending the Geo-blocking Regulation be justified?   204
      Juha Vesala

14   Protecting domestic online content distribution in the EU: the impact
      of geo-blocking and open Internet rules on non-EU Over-The-Top players   223
      Marta Cantero

15   The Internet access provider's commercial practices under the EU
      rules on open Internet   240
      Olli Honkkila

PART V   CONCLUDING REMARKS

16   Concluding remarks   261
      Taina Pihlajarinne, Juha Vesala and Olli Honkkila

Index   266

Contributors

Anette Alén-Savikko	Post-doctoral Researcher, University of Helsinki, Faculty of Law
Rosa Maria Ballardini	Senior Lecturer in Intellectual Property Law, University of Lapland
Marta Cantero	Post-doctoral Researcher, University of Helsinki, Faculty of Law
Katri Havu	Associate Professor, University of Helsinki, Faculty of Law
Kan He	Doctoral Candidate in Intellectual Property Law, University of Munich
Olli Honkkila	Doctoral Candidate, University of Helsinki, Faculty of Law
Martti Kivistö	Doctor of Laws, University of Helsinki, Faculty of Law
Tone Knapstad	Doctoral Candidate, University of Helsinki, Faculty of Law
Katja Weckström Lindroos	Professor of Commercial Law, UEF Law School at the University of Eastern Finland
Giuseppe Mazziotti	Associate Professor, Law, Trinity College Dublin
Dinusha Mendis	Professor of Intellectual Property & Innovation Law, Co-Director, Centre for Intellectual Property Policy and Management (CIPPM), Bournemouth University
Péter Mezei	Associate Professor, University of Szeged, Faculty of Law and docent, University of Turku, Faculty of Law
Valentina Moscon	Senior Research Fellow, Max Planck Institute for Innovation and Competition
Max Oker-Blom	Docent, Hanken School of Economics, Finland

Taina Pihlajarinne   Professor, University of Helsinki, Faculty of Law

Teemu Roos   Associate Professor in Computer Science, University of Helsinki

Juha Vesala   Post-doctoral Researcher, University of Helsinki, Faculty of Law

PART I

Introduction

1. Introduction

Taina Pihlajarinne, Juha Vesala and Olli Honkkila

This book examines current issues raised by online distribution of content in the European Union (EU) – ranging from questions relating to copyright infringement and enforcement to competition and protecting the interests of consumers. These issues are highly topical, especially since the European Commission has proposed measures to create a Digital Single Market (DSM) for digital content and online content services. In particular, the Commission is seeking to ensure market conditions amenable to investing in creation of content and innovation in services, while also promoting EU-wide access and competition. To these ends, the Commission has proposed legislation in the fields of copyright, internal market and communications law that seek to tackle obstacles currently impeding cross-border and EU-wide online activities.

These ambitious Commission objectives require careful balancing of the various interests involved to ensure that measures in several fields of law achieve the aim of a DSM. In addition, several online content distribution issues are of utmost importance for developing online content markets beyond the DSM proposal. These issues also require careful analysis, whether by European or national courts, enforcement agencies or legislators. A major question is whether the proposed solutions – some of which have already been adopted – will lead to a more coherent or more fragmented legal framework at both EU and Member State levels.

This book consists of five parts including this introduction (Part I) and concluding remarks at the end (Part V). Part II focuses on copyright and other protection of content distributed online. In copyright and other areas of intellectual property (IP) law, ever-changing circumstances in online content distribution raise multiple issues. With a focus on ongoing endeavours to address problems such as what constitutes copyright or other IP infringement within diverse means of online distribution, Part II starts off with Dr Martti Kivistö painting an overall picture of the proposed Directive on copyright in the DSM and its potential impact. Professor Taina Pihlajarinne examines linking as a method that can in some cases be compared to content distribution, while Senior Research Fellow Valentina Moscon analyses the proposed related right of press publishers to digital use of their material and Associate Professor Péter Mezei provides an in-depth analysis of the doctrine of exhaustion from the perspective of digital second-hand marketplaces. Possibilities to facilitate online content distribution by using (extended) collective licensing arrangements are discussed by Post-doctoral Researcher Anette Alén-Savikko and Doctoral Candidate Tone Knapstad, and the balance between data protection and enforcement of copyright is explored by Professor Katja Weckström Lindroos.

Part III deals with IP issues relating to emerging technologies and methods of online content distribution. Senior Lecturer Rosa Maria Ballardini, Doctoral Candidate Kan He and Associate Professor Teemu Roos examine authorship issues concerning creations involving artificial intelligence. Professor Dinusha Mendis analyses 3D printing as a challenge to IP laws, particularly copyright law, while Professor Taina Pihlajarinne and Docent Max Oker-Blom continue discussion on 3D printing with a focus on trademark infringements. Although seemingly mere fledgling issues, protecting the subject-matter of these technologies raises novel questions that are highly relevant in terms of distribution online – for example, files for 3D-printing goods.

Part IV deals with competition law, consumer law and regulatory aspects relating to online distribution. This part examines issues closely related to practices of copyright holders, platforms and other companies operating at the various levels and aspects of content distribution. Their conduct may threaten innovation and creation, competition and consumer interests in various ways that may need to be addressed in competition law, consumer law and other regulation. In this part Associate Professor Katri Havu examines new consumer protection and other EU legislative efforts applicable to digital content distributed online. Next, three chapters examine from distinct perspectives attempts by the European Commission to facilitate EU-wide and cross-border supply of copyright-protected content. Associate Professor Giuseppe Mazziotti analyses the impact of new EU regulations concerning geo-blocking and portability of content services on cross-border, EU-wide online content distribution. Post-doctoral Researcher Juha Vesala then examines whether and under what conditions extending the geo-blocking regulation could achieve an EU-wide market in online content services. Post-doctoral Researcher Marta Cantero examines geo-blocking-related issues in combination with the open internet rules of the EU through the lens of their impact on non-EU services. Finally, questions regarding net neutrality and the open internet rules of the EU – as issues underlying the preconditions for online distribution of content – are examined in a chapter by Doctoral Candidate Olli Honkkila.

PART II

Copyright and Online Distribution – on a Path
to Fragmentation?

2.   The DSM Directive: a package (too) full of policies

Martti Kivistö

1.   INTRODUCTION

On 14 September 2016, the European Commission (the Commission) published a proposal for the so-called DSM Directive.[1] Ever since, this document has been the subject of heated debate not only within the European Parliament and the Council of Member States, but also among various interested parties, including rightholders, industry lobbies, non-governmental organisations, and consumer representatives. In addition, many academics have analysed the proposal in recent blogs, articles and seminars.

At the time of this writing in May 2018, the legislative procedure in the EU institutions is approaching its final stages. However, the contents of the instrument are still open in many respects because profound amendments have been submitted to the Commission draft. Against this backdrop, I prefer to focus on the original Commission proposal rather than try to anticipate the outcome of an unfinished and somewhat unforeseeable process.[2]

So far in the debate, scholars have tended to single out individual provisions or sections of the draft for their analyses. However, much less attention has been devoted to the instrument as a whole. In this chapter, I will choose

---

[1]   Proposal for a Directive of the European Parliament and of the Council on copyright in the Digital Single Market. COM(2016) 593 final.

[2]   In the Council, the Estonian and Bulgarian Presidencies had elaborated on a number of compromise proposals as of September 2017. The Permanent Representatives Committee (Coreper) agreed on a common position on 25 May 2018. In the European Parliament, the leading JURI Committee voted on the proposal on 20 June 2018 and adopted a compromise text prepared by the rapporteur, MEP Axel Voss. However, on 5 July 2018 the plenary rejected the JURI proposal by a margin of 318 to 278. Consequently, the decisive vote was postponed to the plenary session on 12 September 2018 where the modified text was adopted by 438 votes to 226, with 39 abstentions. This opens the way for the trilogue between the Commission, the Council and the Parliament.

a somewhat different approach and examine the DSM Directive also as a frame for a number of individual norms. My intention is to look at the proposal from two perspectives, that is, both as a normative and as a policy-making instrument, and to study the interdependence between these levels or dimensions.

I argue that for the Commission, and for many stakeholders, the DSM Directive is first and foremost a tool for achieving pivotal policy goals in the expanding digital domain. At the same time, however, it is a legal document, a future piece of the Union's copyright *acquis*, and as such, in the longer run no longer dependent on the policy objectives it was originally intended to serve. I am interested in the sustainability of the proposed directive. In particular: could it work as a remedy against the apparent fragmentation of copyright law or does it rather contain the makings of another step towards an increasingly disconnected and incoherent copyright system?

In order to understand the whole, one must first study the particles it is made of. I will therefore concentrate on the level of rules by examining the main substance of each article and by explaining their policy goals as laid out by the Commission. This reading will also serve as an overview of the contents and structure of the DSM Directive. Because of the extent and complexity of the draft, this introductory method leaves little space for analysis and discussion. However, observations and comments raised in recent academic debate have been indicated where relevant. My conclusions will be presented in the final section of this chapter.

2.   BACKGROUND AND GENERAL FRAMEWORK

The idea of a new regulatory instrument designated to tackle the special characteristics inherent in or generated by the digital domain was first launched by Jean-Claude Juncker, candidate for the Presidency of the European Commission, in his political guidelines addressed to the European Parliament in July 2014.[3] Under the heading 'A Connected Digital Single Market', Mr Juncker declared that 'we must make much better use of the great opportunities offered by digital technologies', meaning that 'we will need to have the courage to break down national silos', for example in copyright legislation. He also envisaged that 'by creating a connected digital single market, we can generate up to EUR 250 billion of additional growth in Europe', thereby creating many new jobs and 'a vibrant knowledge-based society'.

---

[3]   A New Start for Europe: My Agenda for Jobs, Growth, Fairness and Democratic Change. Political Guidelines for the next European Commission Opening Statement at the European Parliament Plenary Session Strasbourg, 15 July 2014.

With a view to achieving these goals, Mr Juncker promised that, within the first six months of his mandate, he would take 'ambitious legislative steps towards a connected digital single market', notably by – for example – 'modernising copyright rules in the light of the digital revolution and changed consumer behaviour'. The first step was taken in May 2015 when the Commission communication on a Digital Single Market Strategy for Europe was published.[4] This document included a specific chapter on 'better access to digital content', which laid out the basic elements of 'a modern, more European copyright framework'. Another, more detailed communication followed in December 2015.[5]

An extensive Impact Assessment was published in conjunction with the proposal.[6] In the next three sections, key contents of the proposed DSM Directive will be laid out, accompanied by the main arguments presented for each provision. The Impact Assessment gives a detailed picture of the markets and problems that the directive is intended to address and of the policy options that the Commission contemplated for each target area. Additionally, in formal terms the Impact Assessment is a disciplined and well-structured document that can serve as a solid foundation for this examination.[7]

---

[4] Communication from the Commission to the European Parliament, the Council, the European Economic and Social Committee and the Committee of the Regions: A Digital Single Market Strategy for Europe. COM(2015) 192 final.

[5] Communication from the Commission to the European Parliament, the Council, the European Economic and Social Committee and the Committee of the Regions: Towards a modern, more European copyright framework. COM(2015) 626 final.

[6] Impact Assessment on the modernisation of EU copyright rules. SWD(2016) 301 final (14.9.2016), part 1/3 (Impact Assessment). Parts 2 and 3 consist of various preparatory materials, including results of stakeholder consultations, market studies, and overviews of current Member State regulatory frameworks.

[7] Hence, Titles II, III and IV of the draft directive are the focus of this examination. Title I includes definitions, which will be dealt with in their own contexts of application. Title V lays down amendments to existing directives, rules on application in time, and other administrative provisions not relevant to this review.

3.   ADAPTING EXCEPTIONS TO THE DIGITAL AND CROSS-BORDER ENVIRONMENT

3.1   Text and Data Mining

Article 3 requires Member States to provide for an exception to the reproduction rights provided for in the InfoSoc Directive[8] and the Database Directive[9], and also in the proposed DSM Directive pertaining to press publishers' exclusive right in Article 11(1) 'for reproductions and extractions made by research organisations in order to carry out text and data mining of works or other subject-matter to which they have lawful access for the purposes of scientific research'. Text and data mining (TDM) is defined in Article 2(2) as meaning 'any automated analytical technique aiming to analyse text and data in digital form in order to generate information such as patterns, trends and correlations'.

The Commission explains that TDM refers to automated processing of large volumes of text and data to uncover new knowledge or insights. In this capacity TDM can be a powerful tool for analysing masses of text and data such as scientific publications or research datasets. As TDM may often involve copying, this means that reproduction rights and exceptions thereto as well as licensing practices followed by scientific, technical and medical (STM) publishers are of the essence. In the Commission's view, current research exceptions in EU law are not fully adapted to TDM, while national TDM exceptions, where available, are fragmented in scope. Moreover, even as regards subscription publications lawfully accessed by researchers, variation and obscurity exists as to whether TDM is included in such licences. All this results in a situation where the issue of whether prior authorisation for TDM is required or not must be assessed on a case-by-case basis.[10]

The preferred option is one of four examined. The concept of a 'research organisation' has been given a very specific meaning in Article 2(1): it is

> 'a university, a research institute or any other organisation the primary goal of which is to conduct scientific research or to conduct scientific research and provide educational services: (a) on a not-for profit basis or by reinvesting all the profits in its scientific research; or (b) pursuant to a public interest mission recognised by a Member State; in such a way that the access to the results generated by the scien-

---

[8]   Directive 2001/29/EC of the European Parliament and of the Council of 22 May 2001 on the harmonisation of certain aspects of copyright and related rights in the information society [2001] OJ L 167/10.

[9]   Directive 96/9/EC of the European Parliament and of the Council of 11 March 1996 on the legal protection of databases [1996] OJ L 77/20.

[10]   Impact Assessment 104–106.

tific research cannot be enjoyed on a preferential basis by an undertaking exercising a decisive influence upon such organisation'.[11]

In the Impact Assessment, the chosen option was intended to cover research projects carried out in the framework of public-private partnerships which may have an ultimate commercial outcome, but to exclude scientific research by commercial operators alone. Beneficiaries of this exception would be research organisations operating on a not-for-profit basis or pursuant to a public interest mission.[12] The definition adopted in the proposal is more extensive in three respects: first, research organisations with educational functions are also covered; second, the concept of 'not-for-profit' has been given a broader meaning; and third, the notion of 'public interest' is more clearly separated from the not-for-profit condition and accompanied by a rather obscure require-ment on non-exclusive enjoyment of the results generated. These changes suggest that the TDM exception has been elaborated towards a direction allow-ing its applicability to a broader sphere of uses and beneficiaries.[13]

3.2 Digital and Cross-border Teaching Activities

Article 4 requires Member States to provide for an exception or limitation (i) to the right of reproduction and that of communication and making available to the public provided for in the InfoSoc Directive, (ii) to the rights of repro-duction, extraction and re-utilisation provided for in the Database Directive, (iii) to the rights of reproduction, alteration and distribution provided for in the Software Directive,[14] and (iv) to press publishers' rights-to-be of repro-duction and making available to the public provided for in the forthcoming DSM Directive, 'in order to allow for the digital use of works and other

---

[11] See Christophe Geiger, Giancarlo Frosio and Oleksandr Bulayenko, 'The EU Commission's Proposal to Reform Copyright Limitations: A Good but Far Too Timid Step in the Right Direction' (2018) 40 EIPR 4 (eg questioning the non-applicability of the exception to unaffiliated individuals and researchers and criticising the condi-tion of purpose-specific TDM), and Martin Senftleben, 'EU Copyright Reform and Startups – Shedding Light on Potential Threats in the Political Black Box' (2017) http://www.innovatorsact.eu/wp-content/uploads/2017/03/Issues-Paper-Copyright-Directive-2.pdf, accessed 12 May 2018 (eg contemplating the impact of TDM exception on startups).

[12] Impact Assessment 109.

[13] See Benjamin Raue, 'Free Flow of Data? The Friction Between the Commission's European Data Economy Initiative and the Proposed Directive on Copyright in the Digital Single Market' (2018) 49 IIC 379 (eg regretting non-applicability of the TDM exception to commercial research and envisaging the impact of this policy choice).

[14] Directive 2009/24/EC of the European Parliament and of the Council of 23 April 2009 on the legal protection of computer programs [2009] OJ L 111/16.

subject-matter for the sole purpose of illustration for teaching, to the extent justified by the non-commercial purpose to be achieved'. In addition, such use must take place 'on the premises of an educational establishment or through a secure electronic network accessible only by the educational establishment's pupils or students and teaching staff', and it must be 'accompanied by the indication of the source, including the author's name, unless this turns out to be impossible'.

This rather complex set-up is designed to solve problems caused by the legal uncertainly that teachers and students face when they use protected content in digitally supported teaching practices, and in particular across borders. The Impact Assessment points out that the existing exceptions related to illustration for teaching, incorporated in the InfoSoc and Database Directives, may also cover digital uses. However, they have been implemented restrictively in some Member States and, on the whole, in a heterogeneous manner with a view to cross-border applicability. Collective licensing schemes are in place but not in all areas and not necessarily for digital and/or cross-border uses, thus generating significant licensing costs for educational establishments. This legal uncertainty is apt to negatively impact further development of digitally supported educational practices in primary and secondary education. But it is likely to affect higher education institutions even more strongly because their use of digital resources is more pervasive and development of cross-border and online education is rapid.[15]

The primary legal tool is to put in place an appropriate exception. However, the proposal gives some leeway to Member States, which – according to paragraph 2 – may provide that such an exception does not apply generally or as regards specific types of content, provided that adequate licences authorising the acts described in paragraph 1 are easily available in the market. This is justified by the presumption that such a mechanism would allow a favourable approach to licensing of those resources that are primarily intended for the educational market.[16]

The desired cross-border effect when teaching through secure electronic networks would be achieved by creating a 'legal fiction' in paragraph 3. This implies that use of protected content in compliance with adequate provisions of national law would be deemed to occur solely in the Member State where the educational establishment is established.[17] The same legal fiction would

---

[15]   Impact Assessment 87–90.

[16]   ibid 101. See Geiger et al (n 11), arguing eg that introduction of a voluntary scheme would work against harmonisation and therefore suggesting deletion of Art 4(2).

[17]   A similar solution was adopted in Art 4 of Regulation (EU) 2017/1128 of the European Parliament and of the Council of 14 June 2017 on cross-border portability of online content services in the internal market [2017] OJ L 168/1.

be applicable to equivalent licensed uses, too.[18] Finally, paragraph 4 enables Member States to introduce a system of fair compensation for harm incurred by rightholders due to use of their content under this exception.

3.3   Preservation of Cultural Heritage

Article 5 obligates Member States to provide for an exception (i) to the right of reproduction provided for in the InfoSoc Directive, (ii) to the rights of reproduction, extraction and re-utilisation provided for in the Database Directive, (iii) to the right of reproduction provided for in the Software Directive, and (iv) to the rights of reproduction and making available to the public to be provided for in the DSM Directive[19], permitting cultural heritage institutions to make copies of any works or other subject-matter that are permanently in their collections in any format or medium, for the sole purpose of the preservation of such works or other subject-matter and to the extent necessary for such preservation. Article 2(3) defines a cultural heritage institution (CHI) as 'a publicly accessible library or museum, an archive or a film or audio heritage institution'.

Again, legal uncertainty faced by CHIs when performing their preservation duties is a cause for action by the Commission. Member States do provide for exceptions to the right of reproduction for preservation purposes but their applicability to digital environments and works in digital form varies and can also be limited, unclear in scope, or both. Where no exception is available, the transaction costs for CHIs when trying to obtain relevant licences can be prohibitive. In the Commission's view, lack of timely preservation of works is primarily a cultural and social concern. But from an efficiency perspective, divergent legal frameworks can also be a barrier to the possibility, for instance, of sharing among CHIs the technical infrastructure utilised when storing digital copies.[20]

---

[18]   Impact Assessment 93.
[19]   A general reference to Art 11(1) also raises an exception to the making available right, which must not have been the purpose considering the scope of Art 5.
[20]   Impact Assessment 120–123. See Geiger et al (n 11), eg on the scope of this exception. Art 6 refers to Arts 5(5) and 6(4) of the InfoSoc Directive. These provisions apply to the exceptions and limitation in Title II.

4.　　ENSURING WIDER ACCESS TO CONTENT

4.1　　Out-of-commerce Works

This Chapter with three articles is the most extensive and complex in the proposal. According to Article 7(2), 'a work or other subject-matter shall be deemed to be out of commerce when the whole work or other subject-matter, in all its translations, versions and manifestations, is not available to the public through customary channels of commerce and cannot be reasonably expected to become so'.

Article 7(1) provides for an extended collective licence solution for licensing out-of-commerce works. Member States must ensure that – when a collective management organisation (CMO),[21] on behalf of its members, concludes a non-exclusive licence for non-commercial purposes with a CHI for the digitisation, distribution, communication to the public or making available of out-of-commerce works or other subject-matter residing permanently in the collection of the institution – the non-exclusive licence may be extended or presumed to apply to rightholders of the same category as those covered by the licence who are not represented by the CMO (the so-called 'extension effect'). In addition, (i) on the basis of mandates from rightholders, the CMO must be broadly representative of rightholders in the category of works or other subject-matter and of the rights which are the subject of the licence; (ii) equal treatment must be guaranteed to all rightholders in relation to the terms of the licence; and (iii) all rightholders must at any time have the right to object to their works or other subject-matter being deemed to be out of commerce and exclude application of the licence to their works or other subject-matter.

The problem this Chapter of the proposal is set to resolve relates to the rights clearance that CHIs need to conduct before they can digitise out-of-commerce works held in their collections and disseminate them to the public online, as well as across borders. Typically, in mass digitisation projects involving out-of-commerce works, transaction costs in licensing are high while the current commercial value of the works involved is inherently low.[22]

The Commission recognises that collective licensing by CMOs, where available, can provide a clear answer to the transaction costs problem. However, collective management is not available for all types of works and CMOs may

---

[21]　See Art 4(4) of Directive 2014/26/EU of the European Parliament and of the Council of 26 February 2014 on collective management of copyright and related rights and multi-territorial licensing of rights in musical works for online use in the internal market [2014] OJ L 84/72 (CRM Directive).

[22]　Impact Assessment 65. See note 192 on page 67 for an extensive list of unusual types of works.

only grant licences for the rights mandated to them by the rightholders that they represent. Given the nature of the out-of-commerce works involved, it is quite common that some rightholders are not represented in the relevant CMOs, which leaves individual rights clearance as the only solution for many works. Consequences of the clearance problems in this domain are two-fold: projects tend to be skewed towards the public domain or newer collections, or out-of-commerce work collections remain unavailable beyond CHI premises and not accessible across borders. Hence, the societal and economic benefits of the digitisation and dissemination of digitised cultural heritage are missed.[23]

The Commission contemplated two policy options. The first would focus on out-of-commerce books and learned journals only, while the second – which became the preferred option – covers all types of out-of-commerce works.[24] This choice is a considerable extension of scope and adds to the complexity of execution of the proposed out-of-commerce regime. However, as regards books and learned journals, the Commission trusts that, given the widespread use of collective management for these types of works, the costs for rightholders and CMOs related to developing licensing schemes for digital exploitation by CHIs would be limited. In certain other areas – for instance in the audiovisual sector – collective licensing structures would have to be developed or consolidated, which would entail some one-off costs for rightholders and CMOs. All in all, the Commission considers the preferred option most effective and efficient in that it applies to all types of works.[25]

Paragraph 3 of Article 7 relates to publicity measures that Member States are obliged to take in regard to the out-of-commerce status of works and other subject-matter, the licence and its extension effect, and the possibility of rightholders to object as referred to in Article 7(1). Paragraph 4 includes rules on the applicable points of attachment for different types of works and subject-matter vis-à-vis the competent CMO in each case, whereas paragraph 5 excludes application of the entire out-of-commerce regime to third-country nationals, with the exception of cases where some of the points of attachment incorporated in paragraph 4 are present.[26]

Article 8(1) provides for cross-border applicability of the proposed out-of-commerce regime by ruling that works or other subject-matter covered by a licence granted under Article 7 may be used by the CHI in accordance with the terms of the licence in all Member States. Paragraph 2 lays down a duty for

---

[23] ibid 67–69.
[24] The Impact Assessment does not mention other subject-matter – ie objects of neighbouring rights protection – in this context whereas those objects are encompassed by Art 7(1). See also rec 25 of the proposal for the Commission's reasoning.
[25] Impact Assessment 75–79.
[26] See rec 26 of the proposal.

Member States to see that information on the identification of content covered by out-of-commerce licences and the possibility of rightholders to object to their works and other subject-matter being deemed out of commerce is made publicly accessible in an online portal which, under paragraph 3, is to be established and managed by the EU Intellectual Property Office.

Article 9 concludes the Chapter on out-of-commerce works by requiring Member States to set up sector-specific stakeholder dialogues between representative users' and rightholders' organisations and other relevant stakeholder organisations. These dialogues are meant to foster the relevance and usability of licensing mechanisms for out-of-commerce works, ensure the effectiveness of safeguards for rightholders – notably as regards publicity measures – and, where applicable, assist in establishing the requirements referred to in the second subparagraph of Article 7(2).[27]

4.2   Access to and Availability of Audiovisual Works on VoD Platforms

Article 10 provides for a negotiation mechanism which each Member State must establish. This procedure must be available in view of situations 'where parties wishing to conclude an agreement for the purpose of making available audiovisual works on video-on-demand platforms face difficulties relating to the licensing of rights'. Then, the parties in question may rely on the assistance of an impartial body with relevant experience which will provide assistance with negotiation and help reach agreement.

The need for such a facilitating tool stems from the fact that access to and availability of EU audiovisual works on video-on-demand (VoD) platforms is still limited although these platforms are likely to become essential in terms of access to audiovisual works. First, there are contractual blockages linked to exclusive licensing practices and the release windows system. These may relate, for instance, to rightholders being disinterested in licensing or seeking maximum profits from the release windows preceding the VoD market. Second, clearance of rights for VoD exploitation may be complex in terms of

---

[27]   This subparagraph includes a rather ambiguous obligation for the Member States to ensure, in consultation with stakeholders, 'that the requirements used to determine whether works and other subject-matter can be licensed in accordance with paragraph 1 do not extend beyond what is necessary and reasonable and do not preclude the possibility to determine the out-of-commerce status of a collection as a whole, when it is reasonable to presume that all works or other subject-matter in the collection are out of commerce'. This provision has not been elaborated on in the recitals to the proposal. Presumably, the intention is to encourage taking up streamlined and comprehensive licensing solutions.

tracking down the owner of digital rights or ensuring that all relevant rights have been cleared. Third, there is no efficient licensing model for online exploitation rights. This is a result of the low level of expected revenues from, and the high level of transaction and technical costs related to, VoD markets.[28]

In the Commission's view, these obstacles can explain why some European audiovisual works, in particular small productions, are not available on VoD platforms. The Commission's mission, therefore, is to address specifically licensing problems and difficulties in acquisition of rights limiting the availability of European audiovisual works on VoD platforms. By contrast, the Commission stresses that any options imposing obligations that would restrict stakeholders' contractual freedom were discarded because their practical implementation and real impact on the market remain unclear.[29]

5.   ACHIEVING A WELL-FUNCTIONING MARKETPLACE FOR COPYRIGHT

5.1   Rights in Publications

Two separate rights are established in this Chapter. First, according to Article 11(1), Member States are to provide publishers of press publications with the rights of reproduction and of making available to the public provided for in the Infosoc Directive for the digital use of their press publications.[30] A definition of press publication is incorporated in Article 2(4) where it means

> a fixation of a collection of literary works of a journalistic nature, which may also comprise other works or subject-matter and constitutes an individual item within a periodical or regularly-updated publication under a single title, such as a newspaper or a general or special interest magazine, having the purpose of providing information related to news or other topics and published in any media under the initiative, editorial responsibility and control of a service provider.

---

[28]   Impact Assessment 52–54.

[29]   ibid 55, 57. The preferred option in the Impact Assessment included both a stakeholders' dialogue and an obligation for Member States to set up a negotiation mechanism. For some reason the stakeholder dialogue was not taken on board. See Impact Assessment 64.

[30]   See Taina Pihlajarinne and Juha Vesala, 'Proposed Right of Press Publishers: A Workable Solution?' (2018) 13 JIPLP 220 (eg examining the scope of the proposed right of making available to the public in the light of CJEU case law and raising concerns about the broad scope of protection in view of free dissemination of information) and the references in note 1 of Chapter 4 in this volume by Valentina Moscon for the debate on Art 11.

Paragraph 4 sets the term of protection for these exclusive rights at 20 years after publication of a press publication, calculated from the beginning of the following year.[31] Paragraph 3 refers to Articles 5 (exceptions and limitations), 6 (obligations as to technological measures), 7 (obligations concerning rights-management information) and 8 (sanctions and remedies) of the Infosoc Directive and to the Orphan Works Directive,[32] which will apply *mutatis mutandis* in respect of the rights referred to in paragraph 1.

A backdrop to the proposed new rights is the ongoing shift from print to digital which the publishing industry is experiencing in the form of declining print circulation of daily newspapers. Despite the growing success of publishers' content online, the increase in publishers' digital revenues has not made up for the decline of print. The Commission recalls that press publishers have traditionally made available online large proportions of their content for free. With the decline of print, they have become increasingly dependent on monetisation of their digital content, which is not always happening today. Freely available content is still crucial to press publishers as it attracts advertising revenues indispensable to their digital revenues. However, much of this content has also favoured the emergence of online service providers, such as social media and news aggregators, which base their business models in full or in part on reusing or providing access to press publishers' original content. [33] The Commission notes that press publishers have attempted to conclude licences with online service providers and sought to participate in the advertising revenues generated by their content on third parties' websites. However, they have generally not managed to do so, despite the fact that these services often engage in copyright-relevant acts.[34]

Second, Article 12 leaves at Member States' discretion whether they 'provide that where an author has transferred or licensed a right to a publisher, such a transfer or a licence constitutes a sufficient legal basis for the publisher to claim a share of the compensation for the uses of the work made under an exception or limitation to the transferred or licensed right'.

The Impact Assessment clarifies that the problem with online revenues does not affect publishers other than press publishers to the same extent because of the different nature of their products and business models. A more specific

---

[31]   Three scenarios for different terms of protection were tentatively examined: medium (between 10 and 50 years), short (between 5 and 10 years), and very short (between 1 and 5 years). See Impact Assessment 162.

[32]   Directive 2012/28/EU of the European Parliament and of the Council of 25 October 2012 on certain permitted uses of orphan works [2012] OJ L 299/5.

[33]   See Moscon, Chapter 4, Section 2 in this volume, for the undermining effect of social media platforms and technology companies on press publishers' business model.

[34]   Impact Assessment 155–157.

problem which affects all publishers, in particular book and scientific publishers, relates to their ability to obtain compensation for uses of their publications under exceptions. Publishers currently face legal uncertainty in this respect, which has recently been manifested in the *Reprobel* ruling[35] of the CJEU.[36]

The justification for the proposed publishers' rights is the discrepancy between their important role in assembling, editing and investing in content across different sectors, comparable to that of film and phonogram producers in their respective industries, and the fact that publishers are not identified as rightholders under EU copyright rules. The Commission argues that the gap in the current EU rules further weakens the bargaining power of publishers – who are obliged to rely on authors' rights transferred to them – in relation to large online service providers.[37]

Under the preferred option, press publishers would still need to obtain authors' consent to publish their contributions in a newspaper or a magazine, as they do today. The relationship between authors and publishers would thus remain untouched.[38] However, the Commission emphasises that a self-standing right will provide press publishers with substantial added value in terms of licensing out their publications for online uses by third parties.[39] It allows press publishers to benefit from (i) more efficient licensing mechanisms by providing them with a clearer position; (ii) more efficient enforcement of rights by enabling them to enforce their own rights, not only transferred rights; and (iii) stronger incentives for online services to seek licences for reuse of press publishers' content. In addition, the proposed entitlement to claim compensation for uses under an exception would have a positive impact on all types of publishers, in particular on book and scientific publishers, whose publications are often used, for instance, for private copying.[40]

---

[35] Case C-572/13 *Hewlett-Packard Belgium SPRL* v. *Reprobel SCRL* [2015] OJ C 16/3, paras 46–49.

[36] Impact Assessment 158.

[37] ibid 159–160. See Senftleben (n 11) and Christophe Geiger, Oleksandr Bulayenko and Giancarlo Frosio, 'The Introduction of a Neighbouring Right of Press Publishers at EU Level: The Unneeded (and Unwanted) Reform' (2017) 39 EIPR 202 (challenging the Commission's arguments). See Thomas Höppner, 'EU Copyright Reform: The Case for a Publisher's Right' (2018) IPQ 1 (supporting the Commission's proposal).

[38] This is reflected in Art 11(2) of the proposal.

[39] See Pihlajarinne and Vesala (n 30) for eg possibilities of technical control over the use of news content and the need to differentiate between various types of news utilisation.

[40] Impact Assessment 166, 170.

5.2   Certain Uses of Protected Content by Online Services

Article 13(1) is not an obligation directed to Member States, but to information society service providers (ISSPs) referred to in Article 2(b) of the E-commerce Directive.[41] This provision stipulates that ISSPs that store and provide to the public access to large amounts of works or other subject-matter uploaded by their users must, in cooperation with rightholders, take measures to ensure the functioning of agreements concluded with rightholders for the use of their works or other subject-matter or to prevent the availability on their services of works or other subject-matter identified by rightholders through cooperation with service providers. Those measures, such as use of effective content recognition technologies, must be appropriate and proportionate. ISSPs must provide rightholders with adequate information on the functioning and deployment of measures, as well as, when relevant, adequate reporting on the recognition and use of works and other subject-matter.

This condensed provision aims to solve the problem caused by the fact that rightholders have no or limited control over use of and remuneration for use of their content by the ISSPs in question. This is a result of a progressive shift from ownership to access-based models in the online content marketplace. Today, access to online content often takes place at the end of a process in which several parties participate. The rise of interactive services, including such participatory networks, has led to increasing amounts of content being accessed through content-sharing platforms that make available protected content uploaded by their users without involvement of rightholders. In addition to giving access to content, such user-uploaded content (UCC) platforms provide functionalities such as categorisation, recommendations, playlists or ability to share content.[42] These services use copyright-protected content in order to attract and retain users of their websites, thereby increasing the value of their services. However, rightholders are not necessarily able to enter into agreements with these platforms for use of their content.[43]

In the Commission's view, the negotiating position of rightholders is affected by the fact that they are not in a position to keep their content away from UCC platforms. They can only ask the platforms to take down infringing content in each individual case. In turn, this leads to significant costs for them

---

[41]   Directive 2000/31/EC of the European Parliament and of the Council of 8 June 2000 on certain legal aspects of information society services, in particular electronic commerce, in the Internal Market [2000] OJ L 178/1.

[42]   See Impact Assessment 138 notes 407–410, where YouTube, Daily Motion, Vimeo, SoundCloud, Pinterest and MySpace are given as examples of UCC platforms. See rec 38 of the proposal about the relevant acts and the role played by UCC platforms.

[43]   Impact Assessment 137–138.

and additionally appears to them insufficient, given the large scale of uploads. The problem described above also has an impact on online content service providers who acquire a licence from rightholders and distribute protected content directly to end users. This puts them at a competitive disadvantage: they negotiate and conclude licences with rightholders while UCC platforms have no or very limited content acquisition costs.[44]

The preferred option manifested in Article 13(1) builds on an obligation for service providers that store and provide access to large amounts of copyright-protected content to put in place measures – such as content identification technologies – to allow rightholders to better determine the conditions for use of their content, though leaving the 'large amounts' criterion to be determined on a case-by-case basis. Cooperation with rightholders will be required for the functioning of measures, meaning that rightholders should provide the data that are necessary for UCC services to identify the content whereas the services would be obliged to provide adequate information to rightholders on the deployment and functioning of the technologies.[45] The Commission stresses that the suggested obligations will be without prejudice to liability regimes applicable to copyright infringements and application of Article 14 of the E-commerce Directive. In particular, the obligation to put in place content identification technologies would not take away the safe harbour, provided that the conditions of Article 14 of the E-commerce Directive are fulfilled.[46]

5.3 Fair Remuneration in Contracts of Authors and Performers

This Chapter includes three articles. In line with Article 14(1), Member States are to ensure that

> authors and performers receive on a regular basis and taking into account the specificities of each sector, timely, adequate and sufficient information on the exploitation of their works and performances from those to whom they have licensed or transferred their rights, notably as regards modes of exploitation, revenues generated and remuneration due.

Article 15 includes a so-called 'bestseller clause'. This obligates Member States to ensure that 'authors and performers are entitled to request additional,

---

[44] ibid 140–141.

[45] Art 13(2) stipulates a redress mechanism for users.

[46] Impact Assessment 146–147. See Senftleben (n 11) and Martin Senftleben et al, 'The Recommendation on Measures to Safeguard Fundamental Rights and the Open Internet in the Framework of the EU Copyright Reform' (2018) 40 EIPR 149 (signed by 59 academics concerned about Art 13 from a fundamental rights perspective).

appropriate remuneration from the party with whom they entered into a contract for the exploitation of the rights when the remuneration originally agreed is disproportionately low compared to the subsequent relevant revenues and benefits derived from exploitation of the works or performances'.

Article 16 includes an obligation for Member States to provide that 'disputes concerning the transparency obligation under Article 14 and the contract adjustment mechanism under Article 15 may be submitted to a voluntary, alternative dispute resolution procedure'.

The reason for this intervention is the Commission's finding that authors and performers face a lack of transparency in their contractual relationships as to exploitation of their works and their performances and as to what remuneration is owed for exploitation. What constitutes appropriate remuneration depends, for example, on the nature and scope of the use of works but creators may lack access to that information. Transparency is also affected by the increasing complexity of new modes of online distribution, variety of intermediaries and difficulties in measuring actual online exploitation. This is ever more crucial since online distribution is expected to become the main form of exploitation in many content sectors.[47]

The main underlying cause of the weaker bargaining power of authors and performers in contractual negotiations is related to a market failure: a natural imbalance favours the counterparty. Additionally, creators are often dependent on their contractual counterparties and unwilling to challenge them or to request further information for fear of the possible consequences. In addition, transparency or reporting obligations in Member States, where imposed, are either too generic or only apply in certain sectors. Due to lack of information, creators run the risk of not being able to negotiate appropriate remuneration for their rights, to verify their receipts or to enforce their claims for remuneration effectively. Further, on the internal market creators are unable to effectively compare deals and offers, including across borders, whereas their contractual counterparties face a fragmented situation between different Member States. Those differences may also create legal uncertainty and lead to greater transaction costs and 'jurisdiction shopping' by transferees.[48]

Having studied the impact of three policy options, the Commission preferred the option imposing transparency obligations on the contractual counterparty of creators, supported by a contract adjustment right and a dispute resolution mechanism. The Commission argues that transparency measures would rebalance contractual relationships between creators and their contractual counterparties by providing creators with the information necessary to assess whether

---

[47] Impact Assessment 173–175.
[48] ibid 176–177.

their remuneration is appropriate in relation to the economic value of their works and, if their remuneration is deemed inappropriate, a legal mechanism in order to seek renegotiation of their contracts.[49]

6. SOME CONSIDERATIONS ON THE PROPOSAL

The existing directives in the copyright domain were passed mainly to address individual legal problems or combinations thereof in order to neutralise differences considered prejudicial in terms of the internal market. Unlike those, the proposed DSM Directive sets out to tackle a bundle of policy problems generated by digital technologies. This, of course, resonates well with Mr Juncker's declaration that kicked off the project. But in terms of the nature of the proposal as a legal instrument, the result is somewhat out of tune as to form, coherence and impact. These aspects will be dealt with in more detail in the following.

6.1 Choice of Instrument: Not Thoroughly Examined?

In the preparatory works, very little attention has been devoted to the choice of instrument. The main reason given in the Impact Assessment for using a regulation to put in place rules that deal with online exploitation of broadcast programmes was to ensure that the new rules apply in all Member States at the same time and to allow uniform application of the rules in the EU.[50] For the other topics, the Commission deemed a directive a more suitable instrument as it would allow Member States to determine the technical or practical aspects complementing the EU harmonised rules and to take into account existing national legislative frameworks.[51] The explanatory memorandum to the draft directive states that the choice of a directive is adequate because, when appropriate and taking into account the aim to be achieved, it leaves a margin of manoeuvre for Member States while ensuring that the objective of a functioning internal market is met.

Leaving aside the transitional time factor, the Commission's arguments when distinguishing between a regulation and a directive are not very convincing. First, the abundance of minutiae in the definitions and in many of the

---

[49] ibid 190. See Agnès Lucas-Schloetter, 'European Copyright Contract Law: A Plea for Harmonisation' (2017) 48 IIC 897 (review of the proposed provisions).

[50] Subsequently, Proposal for a Regulation of the European Parliament and of the Council laying down rules on the exercise of copyright and related rights applicable to certain online transmissions of broadcasting organisations and retransmissions of television and radio programmes. COM(2016) 594 final (14.9.2016).

[51] Impact Assessment 195.

articles suggests that in practice Member States will have very little margin for manoeuvre when transposing these provisions into domestic law. Hence, the Commission's 'targeted approach' will result in de facto uniform application, close to that of a regulation.[52] Second, the substance of several important concepts has been left open, including 'not-for-profit', 'non-commercial', and 'public interest mission'. In the transposition stage this is apt to give Member States leeway to adopt solutions that do not necessarily serve a functioning internal market in an optimal fashion.

Surely, other avenues for law-making would have been available. For instance, the InfoSoc Directive could have been amended by adjusting the present exceptions in Article 5 and by introducing press publishers as a new category of beneficiaries in Articles 2 and 3. The substance of the proposed out-of-commerce regime would easily build up a separate – and probably more readable – directive, comparable to the Orphan Works Directive. For the remainder, regulations, even recommendations, on targeted areas could have been an option, too. However, from a tactical perspective such a decentralised approach might have been politically too low profile in relation to Mr Juncker's grandiose vision and, more seriously, it would mean opening up existing directives, which the Commission is presumably reluctant to do.

6.2   Grand Visions Do Not Guarantee High-quality Legislation

On the level of policies, the DSM Directive testifies to a broad horizontal perception of the pervasive impact of digitalisation, be it on commerce, education, research or the functioning of cultural memory organisations. The proposal indicates that the Commission is determined not only to address and resolve the problems caused by this upheaval, but also to make digital technologies serve a wide array of interests and expectations of individuals and organisations across the EU.

But on the level of rules and rights this all-embracing cohesive force is less evident. Within the frame of one legislative instrument, a set of utmost complex and controversial copyright-related problems have been put together to form clusters of provisions with no apparent systemic interrelations or thematic proximity. In terms of internal consistency, the draft directive therefore fails to give the impression of an integrated, robust and polished construction. Rather, the (over)abundant compilation of facts, norms and policies makes one perplexed, to say the least. In this case, a targeted approach seems to equal a fragmented approach.

---

[52] National transpositions of the also highly detailed CRM Directive provide evidence to this effect.

In Article 1, the subject-matter of the directive is characterised as 'further harmonising the Union law applicable to copyright and related rights in the framework of the internal market, taking into account in particular digital and cross-border uses of protected content'. As mentioned above, the existing directives tend to focus their harmonising efforts around one topic or legal problem. In terms of systematisation, this is conducive to understanding the *raison d'être* of regulating that particular area and the role of that particular instrument in the European legal order. But what will be the position and idiosyncrasy of the DSM Directive in the copyright *acquis*? An appendix to the InfoSoc Directive? Or a regulatory 'buffet' where over time some parts develop their independent nature while the rest fall into oblivion? All in all, the guidance given in Article 1 is probably too broad and superficial to be very useful in this sense.

6.3   To Induce or to Impose, That is the Question

My final remarks relate to market dynamics. The Commission's manifesto on the DSM reflects an underlying observation that the market is not developing rapidly enough and not necessarily in the direction envisaged by the Commission. Hence, the DSM Directive conjures up a clockwork-like piece of machinery where various stakeholders in their respective target areas are expected to assume their dedicated roles and act accordingly. However, one may with good reason ask whether the market or its players actually work like this in real life.

To function properly, markets need frames and rules and, when necessary, control and corrective measures, but it is as important to give them sufficient room for manoeuvre to develop innovative and efficient solutions. However, the meticulous and teleological nature of the proposed directive suggests that the Commission does not fully rely on the markets to do the right things in the right way. One cannot help thinking that by imposing this regulation the Commission is trying, at least in places, not only to induce the players to produce the desired end results but also to steer the functioning of the market in itself. But this may prove to be difficult.

In relation to market behaviour, the Commission's problem is two-fold. First, in situations where an interface between private and public interests is present, say – for instance – when adjusting TDM vis-à-vis licensing practices or making out-of-commerce works available to the public through collective rights management, one should find ways to persuade the private parties to do their job in complex 'high cost, low return' business cases in order to accomplish policy goals. Second, in cases with dominantly private and adverse interests, such as negotiating on VoD rights or ensuring fair remuneration to rightholders, the Commission is walking on thin ice when trying to push for certain types of solutions in fields that typically belong to the core area of contractual freedom. Indeed, most suggested measures are of a supporting nature and the only direct intervention in the negotiation mechanism relates to the obligation of ISSPs performing an act of communication to the public to conclude licensing agreements with rightholders.

7.   CONCLUDING REMARKS

In the introduction to this chapter I set out to examine whether the DSM Directive could work as a remedy to curb fragmentation or whether, on the contrary, it is prone to accelerate that development. An in-depth study of the draft indicates that the directive consists of detailed regulation with many built-in specificities relating to technology, concepts, circumstances, beneficiaries, purposes of use and the like. There are few, if any, generic rules or provisions that are meant to or could be applicable beyond their immediate context as imposed in the directive. It is perhaps also fair to say that as a legal instrument the directive is not very principled but rather pragmatic and technical. All this points to the conclusion that it is difficult to accept the DSM Directive as a serious attempt to counteract fragmentation. On the contrary, in many respects the directive is the epitome of fragmentation *par excellence.* As argued above, visionary policies do not effortlessly turn into first-class legal systems.

3. Linking and copyright – a problem solvable by functional-technical concepts?

Taina Pihlajarinne

1.　INTRODUCTION

Linking as such is nothing new in copyright discussion – a discussion that started in the early 1990s. However, the Internet, its business models and linking activities as part of those models has undergone thorough changes. Indeed, as opposed to early discussion that concerned linking in its simple form in an undeveloped Internet, nowadays it is questionable whether linking can be discussed as a single, discrete phenomenon. Moreover, the role of a link has changed: while its immediate function is to deliver information on the location of a particular entity's web address, in a broader perspective the claim might be made that linking is also in certain cases used as a tool for de facto content distribution.

In this connection, it seems that the Court of Justice of the European Unions's (CJEU) endeavour to create clear and predictable rules on linking, which as such is understandable, has unfortunately led to a failure to differentiate various linking situations. This, in turn, might have contributed to the attempt to resolve some of the problems on linking-related business models with a solution of a very straightforward nature, that is to say, the proposed new related right.

Press publishers have accused news aggregation services of free-riding on publisher-produced news content. As publishers did not obtain the response they wished for through CJEU practice on linking – they could not defeat this long-term battle by interpretations of linking as an act of communication to the public – they instead managed to convince the European Commission through arguments that news aggregation services threaten the functioning and vitality of the press sector. The Commission has proposed that press publishers would be granted a related right under Article 11 of the proposal for a Directive on copyright in the Digital Single Market (DSM) (see in more detail Chapter 4 in this volume by Valentina Moscon). While the proposal does not directly affect the legal status of linking,[1] it is clearly directed at the activities of news aggregation services. However, the proposal incorporates many serious problems: the proposed right could unnecessarily obstruct other legitimate interests such as freedom of expression as it does not take into consideration the divergence of online services. In fact, introducing a new related right would only further complicate and fragment EU copyright law.[2] Could this kind of one-eyed policymaking be avoided if more nuanced solutions were adopted in considering linking[3] – by distinguishing between linking for loyal and disloyal purposes: for instance, paying more attention to commercial or uncommercial, systematic or occasional nature of linking, as well as whose acts are decisive in selection of linked material, and whether links are genuinely used to imply the location of certain material, or as tools for de facto distributing the works of others? At the same time, evaluation of linking should be based on flexible

---

[1]   According to Art 11, the exclusive right would cover reproduction and making available to the public of press publications to the extent that digital uses are concerned. Rec 33 of the proposal for a Directive on copyright in the DSM states that the new 'protection does not extend to acts of hyperlinking which do not constitute communication to the public'. Commission, 'Proposal for a Directive on copyright in the Digital Single Market' COM(2016) 593 final.

[2]   It is also doubtful whether the proposal can address concerns about the weak bargaining position of news publishers, as similar national rights have proved failures. See for more on the problems relating to the proposal, for instance, C. Geiger, O. Bulayenko and G. Frosio, 'The Introduction of a Neighbouring Right for Press Publishers at EU Level: The Unneeded (and Unwanted) Reform' (2017) 39(4) EIPR 202, 208–209; T. Pihlajarinne and J. Vesala, 'Proposed Right of Press Publishers: A Workable Solution?' (2018) 1 Journal of Intellectual Property and Practice 220, 220–228.

[3]   As to details, many aspects of the CJEU's linking practice have provoked criticism. For instance, Mezei expected that the CJEU would have sought an internal rebalance in its *GS-media* and *Filmspeler* cases. This assessment would have weighed copyright concepts and social norms against each other more carefully. Mezei suggested introduction of new concepts such as 'innocent dissemination'. In this way, the need for time-consuming legislative procedures could have been avoided. P Mezei, 'Enter the Matrix: The Effects of CJEU Case Law on Linking and Streaming Technologies' (2016) 10 Journal of Intellectual Property Law and Practice 778, 794. Leistner has pointed out that the CJEU's practice on linking to legal sources has gone too far: for instance, it is problematic that the CJEU also allows embedding and therefore individual content can be placed almost freely in a new context. On the other hand, Leistner states that the presumption of knowledge in practice of linking to illegal sources causes a danger that courts will not limit the presumption in a realistic way. In addition, changes which are not easy to identify might occur in terms of the legal status of linked material. A consequence might be a continuous monitoring duty. M. Leistner, 'Closing the Book on the Hyperlinks: Brief Outline of the CJEU's Case Law and Proposal for European Legislative Reform' (2017) 39(6) EIPR 327, 329–332.

guidelines, since future artificial intelligence (AI)-based digitality will challenge the feasibility of any standpoints that are currently relevant.

We cannot know for sure. While it is possible that the answer is affirmative, another option is that there is nothing that could have hindered rightholders from creating the political pressure that led to the Commission proposal. However, in this chapter I will assess what alternative solutions might be available.

2.   DIVERSITY OF LINKING AND LEGITIMATE INTERESTS

As a remarkable challenge for legal assessment, linking situations do not form any kind of homogeneous group in terms of assessing their functions and impacts. Commercial linking includes a wide scope of situations with different impacts and divergent interests, as indeed does linking by private persons. These need to be recognised and the interests evaluated further.

News aggregation is one example of this diversity. It is a highly contradictory issue whether news aggregation services, by serving as substitutes, might negatively affect rightholders' advertising incomes and disadvantage them on pricing advertising space – because the aggregator does not have to invest in content production – or whether aggregation solely benefits online news producers.[4] However, it is probable that great diversity exists as to effect between the types of news aggregation services. For instance, those news aggregation services that include only collections of simple hyperlinks are inclined to increase the number of visitors to the news publisher's site since the only way for a user to read more than only the headline of a news article is to click the link and to go to the publisher's site. In that case, news aggregation services are probably beneficial purely for press publishers. In contrast, services in which a substantial part of news items are available directly on the news aggregation providers' site might have a significant effect on rightholders' incomes on the basis of operating as a substitute for news publishers. In that case, the news aggregation service provider might collect advertising income at the expense of the press publisher's potential revenues. This might mean free-riding, at least to some extent. However, one guideline could be that only clear cases of systematic free-riding should be noteworthy, since free-riding as such should

---

[4]   On this discussion, see, eg, E. Rosati 'Neighbouring Rights for Publishers: Are National and (Possible) EU Initiatives Lawful?' (2016) 5 International Review of Intellectual Property and Competition Law 569, 569; M. Stanganelli, 'Spreading the News Online: A Fine Balance of Copyright and Freedom of Expression in News Aggregation' (2012) 34(11) EIPR 745, 746–747; F. Mukaddam 'Online News Aggregation S ervices: The Dispute' (2013) 15(2) E-Commerce Law & Policy 3, 3–5.

be tolerated to some extent in society.[5] Therefore, only free-riding that has a disturbing or damaging effect on the fundamental goals of the intellectual property rights system, such as maintaining incentives for creative work, should be recognised in any assessment.

In addition, while some aggregation services are only collections of simple hyperlinks, others may use linking as a factual tool for content distribution. An extreme case here might be services forming news collections that look like individual, virtual magazines. Here, new personal products are generated by utilising copyright material. Moreover, evaluation is not made any easier if we factor in the variable that, besides the type of news aggregation service, the type of news publisher might also result in crucial differences. Small and lesser-known publishers might find aggregation more beneficial than bigger ones since aggregation makes their websites far more visible for users.

A remarkable diversity is present in terms of the effects of freedom of expression when assessing linking in various situations. Very often the ultimate purpose of linking is purely to deliver information on the location of a particular entity's web address. Additionally, linking for business-oriented purposes covers a broad range of situations. For instance, in some services, content consists solely of links to others' copyrighted material, while some services include other material as well. Displaying links to copyrighted works in social media services might, for instance, awaken political discussion that resorts to the core of freedom of speech due to its essential importance to democracy.

It is of the utmost importance for the free flow of information that services that are equivalents to search engines are not restricted without due reason.[6] Therefore, when evaluating reading and aggregation services we should also assess to what extent these services are genuine tools for searching and processing information or whether they are instead comparable to distributing others' copyright-protected work. In addition, without some of these services,

---

[5]   Eg, Cooper Dreyfuss states that the intellectual property system is not aimed at preventing free-riding. Free-riding is a part of everything: in principle, it is free-riding to learn from a colleague's teaching techniques or a merchant who benefits from a rival's actions that raise interest in a product category. R. Cooper Dreyfuss, 'Reconciling Trademark Rights and Expressive Values: How to Stop Worrying and Learn to Love Ambiguity'. In G. Dinwoodie and M. Janis (eds), *Trademark Law and Theory. A Handbook of Contemporary Research*. Edward Elgar Publishing 2008, 261, 285.

[6]   On various Internet platforms and their relationship with freedom of speech, see B.J. Jütte, 'The Beginning of a (Happy?) Relationship: Copyright and Freedom of Expression in Europe' (2016) 1 EIPR 11, 11–22 and A. Murray, *Information Technology Law*. Oxford University Press 2010, 110–124. On the freedom of speech argument in the context of news aggregation services, see Stanganelli (n 4) 748–750.

information would be impossible to find whereas some services only make control of material easier for users.

These differences make it hard to find any consistent and unambiguous basis for assessing the impacts of linking. Due to divergent situations and interests, consideration of linking in copyright cannot be based on simple and straightforward rules. Instead, a case-sensitive means of weighing and balancing those interests is needed.

3. PROBLEMS IN THE NATURE OF KEY COPYRIGHT CONCEPTS: HISTORICAL DEVELOPMENTS

The basic concepts in copyright are the outcome of historical development. In this context, Johannes Gutenberg's introduction of the printing press in Europe in 1439 is a crucial benchmark. The Renaissance period was characterised by an increasing number and wide variety of intellectual creations, which created an attitude of ownership of these creations and a gradual need for copyright protection. Growing printing activity in the 15th century was associated with Venice being granted the first printing privileges and thereafter the expansion of printing privileges elsewhere in Europe during the 16th century. This meant the possibility to obtain permission for a printer's exclusive monopoly to print a particular text in order to secure the printer's investment, which in turn was extensive because of the expense of printing.[7] In England, the first law to create a modern-type copyright, the Statute of Anne in 1710, recognised the right of authors to print books but not for printers.[8] The area of exclusivity under the Statute of Anne covered printing, reprinting and importing books.[9] When considering the scope of exclusivity, the Act was mainly focused on printing of books, that is to say, one particular form of reproduction. However, the Act recognised importing books as a relevant act – which is today considered as a particular method of distributing copies of works to the public.

---

[7]   Printing required investment in very expensive specialist equipment. This new business model of publishing, in other words producing books for sale, involved risks. See I. Gadd, 'The Stationers' Company in England before 1710'. In I. Alexander and H.T. Gómez-Arostegui (eds), *Research Handbook on the History of Copyright Law.* Edward Elgar Publishing 2016, 81, 82–83.

[8]   However, it is unclear whether the ultimate purpose of the Statute of Anne was to benefit authors, booksellers or the public in general. See further, B. Lauriat, 'Copyright History in the Advocate's Arsenal'. In Alexander and Gomez-Arostegui (n 7) 7, 22–24.

[9]   See further, I. Alexander 'Determining Infringement in the Eighteenth and Nineteenth Centuries in Britain: A Ticklish Job'. In Alexander and Gomez-Arostegui (n 7) 174, 175–177.

After that, a similar development took place elsewhere in Europe and the United States. Gradual development and expansion made these rights more extensive. Finally, pressure for enhanced international copyright protection was the reason for introducing the first drafts of the Berne Convention in 1886.[10] In many countries, exclusive rights were centred around the right of reproduction, though also including provisions on different forms of making a work available to the public. Nevertheless, the original version of the Convention did not include explicit provisions on general exclusive rights of reproduction or the right to make available. However, the original Convention contained several references to reproduction.[11] A general exclusive right of reproduction was adopted in the Berne Convention ('in any manner or form', Article 9) as late as 1967 (Stockholm Act). Historically, the right to distribute copies of a work emanated from gradual development of being separated from the right of reproduction and recognised as an individual exclusive right in Member States' copyright Acts. The general right of distribution was adopted in the World Intellectual Property Organization (WIPO) Copyright Treaty in 1996 (Article 6).[12]

Exclusive rights, and concepts as their building blocks, have been under continuous re-evaluation and expansion. In the early stages of digitalisation, in the 1990s, the general focus of discussion on international copyright conventions seems to have been on ascertaining that exclusivity based on traditional copyright concepts also covers digital acts.[13] For instance, due to digital change,

---

[10]   See, eg, N. Koutras, 'History of Copyright, Growth and Conceptual Analysis: Copyright Protection and the Emergence of Open Access' (2016) 2(2) Intellectual Property Quarterly 135, 138–147; F. Makeen, *Copyright in a Global Information Society. The Scope of Copyright Protection Under International, US, UK and French Law*. Kluwer Law International 2000, 1–10.

[11]   Eg, according to Art 10, '[t]he following shall be specially included amongst the illicit reproductions to which the present Convention applies: unauthorized indirect appropriations of a literary or artistic work, of various kinds, such as adaptations, musical arrangements, etc., when they are only the reproduction of a particular work, in the same form, or in another form, without essential alterations, additions, or abridgments, so as not to present the character of a new original work'. The adaptation right tacitly included the right to reproduction. Similarly A. Dixon, and M. Hansen, 'The Berne Convention Enters the Digital Age' (1996) 18(11) EIPR 604, 604. There was also a provision concerning an exception to a reproduction right in Art 7 (articles from newspapers or periodicals could be reproduced in the original or in translation in the other countries of the Union, unless explicitly forbidden by authors or publishers).

[12]   On historical development, see Dixon and Hansen (n 11) 609–610.

[13]   For instance, one aim of the development that subsequently led to the WIPO Copyright Treaty (a proposal for a protocol of the Berne Convention in 1996) was to reaffirm that the reproduction right is not limited to tangible or permanent copies of a work, by stating that both permanent and temporary acts of reproduction constitute

in the WIPO Copyright Treaty the exclusive right of 'making available' was extended to digital transmissions on the Internet, since the traditional way of defining communication to the public adopted in the Berne Convention does not encompass such means of utilising works.[14] However, these developments have not changed the core nature of concepts which still have their roots in the business model of printing and selling books.

Essentially, economic rights in modern copyright consist of two basic pillars: the right of reproduction on one hand and an exclusive rights to, for instance, distribute copies and communicate the work to the public on the other hand.[15] Of these fundamental concepts, the right of reproduction is perhaps the least suitable for the digital environment as new methods and practices of reproduction fundamentally challenge the general doctrines of copyright.[16] Communication to the public right might be somewhat easier to adapt to the new technological and economic environment. One indication of such adapt-ability might be the CJEU's efforts to introduce and develop the notion of a 'new public'.[17] However, this ease emerges only in comparison with the adapt-ability – or in fact, the inadaptability – of the concept of reproduction. Like the notion of reproduction, 'communication to the public' is functional-technical by its very essence. The difference is that communication to the public and

---

an act of reproduction. See Dixon and Hansen (n 11) 608–609. The Agreed Statements concerning the WIPO Copyright Treaty stated that 'the reproduction right, as set out in Article 9 of the Berne Convention, and the exceptions permitted thereunder, fully apply in the digital environment, in particular to the use of works in digital form. It is understood that the storage of a protected work in digital form in an electronic medium constitutes a reproduction within the meaning of Article 9 of the Berne Convention.'

[14] Eg, H. Saito, 'Significance of the Making Available Right'. In G. Karnell et al (eds), *Liber Amicorum Jan Rosén*. eddy.se 2016, 709, 710–716; Makeen (n 10) 289–294 and Dixon and Hansen (n 11) 610.

[15] The relationship between the concepts of 'communication to the public' and 'making available to the public' is not completely clear. However, the CJEU has stated in the *C More Entertainment v. Linus Sandberg*, C-279/13 that the concept of 'making available to the public' used in Directive 2001/29 forms part of the wider 'communica-tion to the public' right.

[16] See for more on problems relating to the concept of reproduction and on alternative solutions, T. Pihlajarinne, 'Should We Bury the Concept of Reproduction – Towards Principle-based Assessment in Copyright Law?' (2017) 8 International Review of Intellectual Property and Competition Law, 953, 953–976.

[17] The CJEU has concluded that the work must be directed at a new public, that is to say, at a public that was not taken into account by the copyright holders when they authorised the initial communication to the public (eg, *Svensson, Sjögren, Sahlman, Gadd v. Retriever Sverige AB*, C-466/12; *Sociedad General de Autores y Editores de España (SGAE) v. Rafael Hoteles SA*, C-306/05; and *Organismos Sillogikis Diakhirisis Dimiourgon Theatrikon kai Optikoakoustikon Ergon v. Divani Acropolis Hotel and Tourism AE*, C-136/09).

making available to the public leave the door slightly more open for interpretation than reproduction. This is because the notion of 'public' is vaguer and more abstract than 'reproduction', which directly refers to copying of any kind. Nevertheless, communication to the public also involves evaluation through technical-functional lenses rather than consideration of legitimate interests. This is also demonstrated by the very detailed formulation of 'communication to the public' under the InfoSoc Directive (Article 3(1)) and the WIPO Copyright Treaty (Article 8): 'by wire or wireless means, including the making available to the public of their works in such a way that members of the public may access them from a place and at a time individually chosen by them'.

The ultimate problem is the same as in reproduction: the nature of the concept of communication to the public inevitably leads the interpreter to assess certain actions per se. Actions as such do not necessarily indicate what kind of effect they have on relevant interests. A certain level of vagueness and openness to interpretation is needed to achieve a capability of genuine adaptation. A second important factor is that, while surrounding reality is faced with an accelerated dematerialisation process, the concept of reproduction is inevitably tied to fixation. This contradiction underlies the problematic nature of the concept of reproduction in the digital age – whereas communication to the public as such is more neutral because the 'public' as a concept, for instance, is more technology neutral. Therefore, in comparison to reproduction, communication to the public is a concept that leaves slightly more space for creating new doctrines and weighing and balancing interests. The CJEU's preliminary rulings, which will be discussed next, demonstrate that difference.

4.   TWO LINES OF CASES – IS IT SO SIMPLE?

During the past few years, the CJEU has issued several preliminary rulings on linking as an act of communication to the public. The first case that could be described as a landmark case was *Svensson*,[18] where the CJEU held that a provision on a website of clickable links to works freely available[19] on another website does not constitute an act of communication to the public since there is

---

[18]   *Svensson et al v. Retriever Sverige AB*, C-466/12.

[19]   However, when a link circumvents restrictions on public access to the work that are aimed at restricting access only to subscribers, eg, there is a new public, and linking constitutes an act of communication to a new public (see *Svensson*, para 31).

no new public.[20] In the next case, *BestWater*,[21] the Court concluded that creating links to copyrighted work freely available on the Internet using a framing technique cannot be classified as communication to the public if the work is not transmitted to a new public. In both cases, the linked material was submitted as being freely available on the Internet with the rightholder's permission.

Subsequently, two more cases were decided, *GS Media*[22] and *Filmspeler*.[23] These form the second part of the CJEU's linking saga so far. In *GS Media*, the court assessed whether linking to material freely available without the rightholders' consent was an act of communication to the public. The court concluded that an assessment must be made as to whether links are provided without pursuit of financial gain by a person who did not know or could not reasonably have known of the illegal nature of the publication of those works on that other website or whether, on the contrary, links are provided for that purpose, a situation in which that knowledge must be presumed. In *Filmspeler*, the court held that the sale of a multimedia player for which pre-installed add-ons contained hyperlinks to websites freely accessible to the public, on which copyright-protected works were made available to the public without the consent of the rightholders, amounted to communication to the public. The court referred to *GS Media* and stated that in *Filmspeler* it was evident that there was full knowledge of the add-ons containing hyperlinks that gave access to works published illegally on the Internet. In addition, the multimedia player was supplied with a view to profit, the price for the multimedia player being paid in particular to obtain direct access to protected works available on streaming websites without the consent of the copyright holders.

There is indeed a clear division between the two lines of cases. *Svensson* and *Bestwater* are 'cold' cases in which the CJEU did not open the various interests relating to the range of linking situations, such as freedom of speech and economic arguments asserted in those cases. This is surprising since *Svensson*, in particular, is a case with a strong basis in freedom of expression.[24] However, in

---

[20]   For more about the case, see, eg, Emanuela Arezzo, 'Hyperlinks and Making Available Right in the European Union – What Future for the Internet after Svensson?' 2014 (5) International Review of Intellectual Property and Competition Law 524, 524–555.

[21]   *BestWater International GmbH v. Michael Mebes and Stefan Potsch*, C-348/13.

[22]   *GS Media BV v. Sanoma Media Netherlands BV et al.*, C-160/15.

[23]   *Stichting Brein v. Jack Frederik Wullems (Filmspeler)*, C-527/15.

[24]   Jütte notes that although the CJEU did not address the freedom of expression dimension in *Svensson*, freedom of expression is nevertheless a crucial part of the case. Jütte (n 6) 18. A similar approach can also be seen in the ruling *TV Broadcasting Ltd ym. v. TVCatchup Ltd*, C-607/11, where the CJEU stated that when communication to the public is to be considered, the profit-making nature of the acts assessed or competitive relationships between the parties are irrelevant.

GS Media and *Filmspeler*, the economic interests are at some level taken into account, even though only indirectly, as part of the assessment of awareness of the illegal nature of material. Of course, a substantive division between these two sets of cases is natural because of the crucial division between whether – or not – linked material was on a site with the rightholder's permission.

In cases of legal material being linked, the immediate question of an implied licence arises. The implied licence notion is based on the idea that, when uploading copyrighted material on the Internet, a carefully operating rightholder can be expected to be familiar with the special characteristics and conduct codes of the Internet.[25] In the context of linking, a rightholder who delivers material via the Internet presumably agrees to the material subsequently being linked. While an implied licence is not explicitly mentioned by the CJEU in *Svensson*, the *ratio* behind the case is closely related to the formulation behind the implied licence construction, since the CJEU seems to have adopted an interpretation that places responsibility on rightholders to clearly control access to copyrighted works.[26] The reason why the CJEU has not directly referred to an implied licence might be that copyright contract law is not harmonised. The legal framework for assignments and waivers has been left to national legislative discretion since these legal acts depend on national law.[27] The notion of an implied licence goes hand in hand with the doctrine of exhaustion, a doctrine originally based on the idea of an implied licence.[28] Moreover, in some jurisdictions the idea that a buyer can use a product in any way they choose after purchase is directly based on the concept of an implied licence.[29] The approach adopted by the CJEU is therefore inevitably close to the construction of exhaustion, and the CJEU's decisions have been asserted as

---

[25] Eg, J. Ungern-Sternborg, 'Schlichte einseitig Einwilligung und treuwidrig widersprüchliches Verhalten des Urheberberechtigten bei Internetnuzungen' (2009) 3–4 Gewerblicher Rechtsschutz und Urheberrecht 369, 370.

[26] Similarly S. Karapapa, 'The Requirement for a "New Public" in EU Copyright Law' (2017) 42 ELR 63, 74.

[27] Similarly, C. Geiger and F. Schönherr, 'The Information Society Directive, Article 5'. In I. Stamatoudi and P. Torremans (eds), *EU Copyright Law. A Commentary*. Edward Elgar Publishing 2014, 458–459. However, in general, the need for the EU to harmonise on copyright contracts has been discussed. See, eg, A. Strowel, 'Towards a European Copyright Law: Four Issues to Consider'. In Stamatoudi et al (above) 1137–1138.

[28] See, eg, A. Kur, 'Completely Exhausted or Just Relaxed? Some Thoughts on the CJEU's "New Exhaustion Principle" in Internet Linking Cases'. In Karnell et al (eds) (n 14) 443, 443, with references therein.

[29] Eg, the House of Lords decision in *United Wire Limited v. Screen Repair Services (Scotland)* 20.7.2000.

establishing de facto exhaustion of the right of making available to the public, while exhaustion should concern only the right of distribution.[30]

Naturally, the implied licence type of *ratio* is not applicable when illegal material is linked. Awareness of material being illegal is a natural doctrinal basis for liability in those cases.[31] In addition, profit-motivated activity can be considered as a circumstance creating a presumption of such knowledge since such an actor can be considered as having a duty to act with an extra standard of care. Consequently, the division between these two lines of cases might undermine the diversity of interests in linking to material that is available with the author's consent. While a positive new element in *GS Media* and *Filmspeler* was that the economic interests were indirectly taken into consideration in the assessment of linking, it is hard to see why the relevance of assessing the commercial nature of linking should be limited to situations of linking to illegal material.[32]

Furthermore, a fresh look could be taken into the concept of 'communication to the public' by adopting a doctrine where the focus is more on weighing and balancing legitimate interests rather than on single-lensed functional aspects. It would be feasible for the CJEU to construct several lines of inter-

---

[30] It is explicitly stated in Art 3(3) of the Infosoc Directive that a right to communication to the public shall not be exhausted by any act of communication to the public or making available to the public. As to this problematic see, eg, Mezei (n 3) 788–789. Kur takes a deeper perspective by stating that exhaustion as a technical legal term should not be assessed but instead a conflict between exclusive rights and fundamental freedoms. Therefore, a prerequisite is that the specific subject-matter of a right cannot be disproportionally affected. Kur (n 28) 452.

[31] However, the issue is complex since general liability issues are not harmonised in the EU. In principle, the alternative would have been to conclude that setting a link was unlawful, but due to the absence of negligence or required intention no liability arose. But this would have indicated a clash with the Member States' liability standards, typically setting strict liability for direct copyright infringements. P. Savola, 'EU Copyright Liability for Internet Linking' (2017) 8 JIPITEC 139, 143.

[32] Mezei states that even though the line between commercial and private linking might be obscure and they might also involve similar consequences, nevertheless policy-related reasons might exist to distinguish between commercial and private linking. Mezei (n 3) 792. Kur, in her 'specific subject-matter approach' states that framing is not necessarily compatible with the principle of proportionality. However, she stresses that the mere fact that linking might reduce a rightholder's profits or that business models might be based on linking does not amount to sufficient reasons to consider linking as covered by copyright: Kur (n 28) 458. Also the report by the Association Littéraire et Artistique Internationale, 'ALAI Report and Opinion on a Berne-compatible reconciliation of hyperlinking and the communication to the public right on the Internet' is based on the distinct legal status granted to cases of hyperlinking, and, on the other hand, to cases of deep-linking and framing. See http://www.alai.org/en/assets/files/resolutions/201503-hyperlinking-report-and-opinion-2.pdf.

pretation instead of two, based on a more comprehensive analysis of economic and freedom-of-speech-related interests.

5.   A POSSIBLE SOLUTION…?

In the context of assessing the feasibility of the concept of reproduction, I have proposed that in an imaginary world where international conventions would not create obstacles for revising the area of copyright exclusivity instead of reproduction, more attention should be paid to whether utilisation of a copyrighted work affects, or is liable to affect, the legitimate interests of the rightholder, or alternatively, whether utilisation follows honest practice in the particular sector of the creative industry.[33] Again, in the context of linking and communication to the public, the feasibility of similar kinds of general balancing mechanisms could be assessed, while no major obstacles should exist for creating lines of interpretation taking account of such general objectives.

Therefore, one solution might be to build lines of interpretation to differentiate various situations in the context of linking of legal material. One possibility here is to try to draw a distinction between loyal and disloyal purposes. As part of this assessment, a distinction might be needed between whether linking is commercial or without the intention to gain an economic advantage. Additionally, in the case of commercial linking, an important aspect is whether a service utilising linking is based completely on systematic linking or whether linking is occasional in nature. Finally, another aspect that should be paid more attention to is whether linked material in commercial services is selected mainly by acts of the service provider or by acts of the user instead. This criterion might be important in drawing the distinction between genuine search services and services using linking techniques as tools for de facto distributing the works of others. In the latter case, links are not genuinely used only in order to imply the location of certain material on the web. However, these criteria should only serve as guidance in the overall assessment of loyalty, which should always be connected to the development of the Internet and its business models.[34]

---

[33]   See Pihlajarinne (n 16) 953–976.

[34]   Adoption of this kind of legislation was, some years ago and before the CJEU's preliminary rulings, under active consideration in Finland. The Finnish Copyright Commission, chaired by professor Niklas Bruun from the University of Helsinki, published its final report 'Report of the Copyright Commission: Solutions to challenges of the digital age, Reports of the Ministry of Education and Culture, Finland 2012:2' on 26 January 2012 (available with English abstract at http://www.minedu.fi/OPM/ Julkaisut/2012/Tekijanoikeustoimikunnan_mietinto.html?lang=en). One of the several themes discussed in the report was commercial linking. The Copyright Committee

6.   ...BUT HOW ABOUT THE FUTURE?

Linking itself, as well as the interests behind it, are under constant development. One remarkable factor is automatisation and AI (by which is usually meant machine learning, where a machine teaches itself) in content production, which is already being used in editorial processes of news articles.[35] This will undoubtedly have an impact on the issue of news aggregation, for instance. It is clear that many news items created with the assistance of AI are original enough to be copyrighted works.[36] However, the crucial question is: who should hold the copyright for news created by AI, or should anybody? Many parties are involved in the process: the programmer(s) and journalists who set guidelines on issues that are important in each topic (for instance, when writing an article on elections by utilising automation, the success of political parties is more interesting than that of individual candidates) and

---

decided to commission a study on commercial linking from the author of this chapter. The study assessed the feasibility of the various possibilities of setting rules concerning commercial linking. As a conclusion, the possibility considered the most promising was to adopt the kind of presumption rule – as discussed in this chapter – concerning an implied licence for linking. In addition, eg, using collective licence arrangements could be considered especially for news aggregation services. After discussion of the options, the Copyright Commission decided not to propose any linking-related revisions to Finnish copyright law in the current situation. The Commission stated, however, that the study would give guidance to courts for assessment of linking-related copyright cases. In this assessment, a crucial factor should be – instead of linking techniques – the impact of linking on the legitimate interests of rightholders' and users' possibilities to gain valuable content in electronic form. These conclusions in the report have impacted assessment of linking cases in Finland by the Finnish Copyright Council (Copyright Council Decisions 2013:22 and 2014:14). The copyright Council is an organ appointed by the Finnish government for, eg, issuing statements on the application of the Copyright Act in individual cases. It could be described as a soft-law type of dispute resolution mechanism because its statements do not have binding effect but rather they have the nature of recommendations. Nonetheless, they have great practical relevance as the number of court decisions in the copyright area is very limited.

[35]   The reasons behind increasing interest in using automation in journalistic work are financial difficulties faced by news publishers combined with increased input in terms of news – since previously non-public data is to an increasing degree published openly in digital format – and demands for localisation and personalisation of news. See L. Leppänen, M. Munezero, S. Sirén-Heikel, M. GranrothWilding and H. Toivonen, 'Finding and Expressing News From Structured Data'. In Proceedings of AcademicMindtrek' 17, Tampere, Finland, 20–21 September 2017, 1, 1. Available at https://www.cs.helsinki.fi/u/ljleppan/pub/leppanen2017finding.pdf.

[36]   It is evident that, by utilising AI, works can even be created that could be characterised as a piece of art, including literary art such as poetry. See, eg, J. Dickenson, A. Morgan and B. Clark, 'Creative Machines: Ownership of Copyright in Content Created by Artificial Intelligence Applications' (2017) 39(8) EIPR 457, 457.

rules on what kind of expressions can be used. The role of the AI user, such as a journalist, might be creative to some extent. Additionally, in developed AI systems, a distance might exist between the engineering of AI and work created by AI.[37] While some analogies might be found from rules on copyright to apply to computer-generated works,[38] this alone is not sufficient since they do not take account of the special characteristics of more advanced and sophisticated AI in the future.[39] It is also possible that no human needs an incentive in these situations. Another option is that in copyright assessment in the era of AI the role of investment will attract substantially more attention than today.

However, it is evident that utilisation of AI has the potential to revolutionise the ecosystem of incentives behind news production. If the investment needed for creative work by humans is essentially reduced on the part of news producers, if there is a tendency to consider programmers as authors instead of journalists, or if there is no copyright holder since nobody needs a utilitarian-sense incentive, then the question of linking might need careful reassessment. This is a relevant issue not only when considering news aggregation, but also in terms of linking any material created by AI. Naturally, the guidelines established by the CJEU should be open to rapid change if needed to reflect changes in society or business logic.

7.   CONCLUSIONS

From the perspective of legal fragmentation and overprotection, the DSM proposal on related rights for press publishers follows an unfortunate path in EU copyright. Continuous expansion of the area of exclusivity, especially creation of new related rights due to political pressure, is one problem. Moreover, this has been done by adopting new directives and narrow provisions, instead of amending existing ones and trying to create more flexible and principle-oriented rules. In order to avoid complicating EU copyright, problems that emerge should primarily be resolved whenever possible via CJEU case law instead of new directives. In areas with continuous impact of

---

[37]   Similarly Dickensen et al (n 36) 458.

[38]   For instance, the UK copyright Act (CDPA) s. 9.3 stipulates that in the case of a literary, dramatic, musical or artistic work which is computer generated, the author shall be taken to be the person by whom the arrangements necessary for the creation of the work are undertaken. In the case of algorithms, this might indicate that a copyright owner would be the one who created them, that is to say, a software engineer. However, the provision dates back to the time when the problems of AI had not yet arisen, while the provision might not be directly applicable to works created by AI. See Dickenson et al (n 36) 458.

[39]   On machine learning, see M. Hildebrandt, 'Smart Technologies and the End(s) of Law'. Edward Elgar Publishing 2016, 35–36.

emerging technologies, problem-solving via CJEU case law could provide a mechanism equipped with the adaptability to respond when technical developments cause shifts in the economic or cultural basis of evaluation.

In considering linking on the one hand and the DSM Directive proposal on the other, it is possible that instead of adopting a related-rights approach based on an overprotective attitude, some issues of news aggregation could have been solved by fine-tuning the case law on linking. Of course, it is equally possible that even in the case of such a solution, pressure for related rights would still have arisen.

The answer to the question contained in the headline of this chapter could be the following: yes, it is as such possible to solve the problem of linking and copyright by functional-technical concepts – but not solely by those concepts. One solution is for the CJEU to build more lines of interpretation, based on enriched argumentation concerning legitimate interests and recognition of the diversity of linking situations, possibly by utilisation of new auxiliary concepts. Of course, this would not serve those who favour simplistic solutions. However, flexibility and the possibility to re-evaluate assessment of legitimate interests and possible auxiliary concepts due to technical developments would be needed since development of AI and deep learning might fundamentally change the basis of how linking should be evaluated. The same applies to related rights, for instance – but the fundamental difference is that, once created, a related right is extremely difficult to revisit.

4. Neighbouring rights: in search of a dogmatic foundation. The press publishers' case

Valentina Moscon

1. INTRODUCTION

The European Commission proposal for new copyright related rights for press publishers[1] comes in the wake of a general trend of creating new 'neighbouring rights'. Article 11 of the proposed Directive on Copyright in the Digital Single Market – widely criticized for various reasons in the literature[2] – reflects

---

[1]   The proposed neighbouring right is included in the Proposal for a Directive of the European Parliament and of the Council on copyright in the Digital Single Market COM (2016) 593 final.

[2]   C Geiger, O Bulayenko and G F Frosio, 'The Introduction of a Neighbouring Right for Press Publisher at EU level: the unneeded (and unwanted) reform' (2017) 39(4) EIPR 202; V Falce and M L Bixio, 'Verso un nuovo diritto connesso a favore degli editori on line. Brevi note su recenti derive (iper)-protezionistiche' (2017) http://www.dimt.it/wp-content/uploads/2016/09/Paper-Ancillary-copyright.pdf; A Peukert, 'An EU Related Right for Press Publishers Concerning Digital Uses. A Legal Analysis' (2016) Research Paper of the Faculty of Law, Goethe University Frankfurt am Main No. 22/2016, https://ssrn.com/abstract=2888040; M Senftleben, M Kerk, M Buiten and K Heine, 'New Rights or New Business Models? An Inquiry into the Future of Publishing in the Digital Era' (2017) 48(5) IIC 538; R M Hilty and V Moscon (eds), 'Modernisation of the EU Copyright Rules. Position Statement of the Max Planck Institute for Innovation and Competition' (2017) Max Planck Institute for Innovation and Competition Research Paper No. 17-12, http://pubman.mpdl.mpg.de/pubman/item/escidoc:2470998:11/component/escidoc:2479390/E-Book%20-%20Hilty%20-%20Moscon%20-%2018.09.2017.pdf; R Xalabarder, 'Press publisher rights in the new copyright in the digital single market draft directive', CREATe Working Paper 2016/15; E Rosati, 'Neighbouring Rights for Publishers: Are National and (Possible) EU Initiatives Lawful?' (2016) IIC 569; L Bently and M Kretschmer, 'Strengthening the Position of Press Publishers and Authors and Performers in the Copyright Directive' (2017) Study for the Policy Department for Citizens' Rights and Constitutional Affairs, http://www.europarl.europa.eu/thinktank/en/document.html?reference=IPOL

the lack of a solid dogmatic foundation in dealing with neighbouring rights. Invoking these rights as a panacea for various issues without a sound understanding of both legal problems and solutions may increase uncertainties which impact on the European *acquis*, causing further fragmentation of EU copyright law. The increasing recourse to neighbouring rights for the protection of different subject matters, including organization of sporting events, [3] calls for careful reflection on the legal nature of such rights and their relation to copyright. The Commission proposal represents a case study, analysis of which adds more general background to the question when it would be appropriate to introduce new neighbouring rights.

The issue of news protection in the interest of press publishers first arose in different historical times; both copyright and neighbouring rights have been considered as means of protection. However, during the Berne Convention (BC) negotiations and subsequently in the debate prior to adoption of the Rome Convention in 1961 the international legislator excluded news protection from the copyright and neighbouring rights area.[4] This historical record

---

_STU%282017%29596810; R Danbury, 'Is an EU Publishers' Right a Good Idea?' (2016) *Report on the AHRC project*; T Pihlajarinne and J Vesala, 'Proposed Rights of Press Publishers: A Workable Solution?' (2017) 13(3) JIPLP 220–228; F Zuleeg and I Tasheva: 'Rewarding quality journalism or distorting the Digital Single Market? The case for and against neighbouring rights for press publishers' (2017) European Policy Centre – Discussion Paper; A Ramalho, 'Beyond the Cover Story – An Enquiry into the EU Competence to Introduce a Right for Publishers' (2017) 48(1) IIC 71; C Caron, 'Legal analysis with focus on Article 11 of the proposed Directive on Copyright in the Digital Market' (2017) Briefing paper for the JURI Committee, http://www .europarl.europa.eu/thinktank/en/document.html?reference=IPOL_BRI(2017)596834; M van Eechoud, 'A publisher's intellectual property right: Implications for freedom of expression, authors and open content policies' (2017) OpenForum Europe, 32 http://www.openforumeurope.org/wp-content/uploads/2017/01/OFE-Academic-Paper -Implications-of-publishersright_FINAL.pdf.

[3]   A new Article 12a protecting sport event organizers was introduced at a late stage by the European Parliament on 12 September 2018. See, Proposal for a directive on copyright in the Digital Single Market (COM(2016)0593 – C8-0383/2016 – 2016/0280(COD)). According to Article 12a 'Protection of sport event organizers Member States shall provide sport event organizers with the rights provided for in Article 2 and Article 3 (2) of Directive 2001/29/EC and Article 7 of Directive 2006/115/ EC'. The text was adopted by the European Parliament on September 12, 2018.

[4]   International Convention for the Protection of Performers, Producers of Phonograms and Broadcasting Organisations (Rome, 26 October 1961), 496 UNTS 43, which entered into force on 18 May 1964. This treaty was adopted under the auspices of three international organizations: the World Intellectual Property Organization (WIPO, formerly the United International Bureaux for the Protection of Intellectual Property), the United Nations Educational, Scientific and Cultural Organization (UNESCO) and the International Labour Organization (ILO).

offers some guidance for wide-ranging reasoning on the object and purpose of neighbouring rights. The aim is to investigate whether protection of press publishers' investment in producing and circulating news may be a task for neighbouring rights. The chapter is structured as follows: the next section focuses on the positioning of press publishers against the currently multifaceted digital background. Against this backdrop, Section 3 looks at the Commission proposal, focusing in particular on the subject matter of protection of the proposed neighbouring right. Section 4 undertakes a historical perspective, clarifying the reasons for excluding copyright protection for news. The preparatory work before the BC states that the subject falls into the area of competition law. Thus, the distinction between intellectual property law and competition law is taken into account for assessing whether the subject matter of protection of the proposed neighbouring right for press publishers is attributable to the area of intellectual property law or competition law (Section 5). Finally, after concluding that neighbouring rights are inadequate legal instruments for press publishers' investments (Sections 6 to 8), Section 9 focuses on four legal instruments which may safeguard the interests of press publishers, at the same time enhancing news circulation through multiple channels and the quality of the information made available to the public. Finally in Section 10 some conclusions will be drawn.

2.   A MULTIFACETED BACKGROUND

[T]he digital journalism produced by many news organizations has become less and less meaningful. Publishers that are funded by algorithmic ads are locked in a race to the bottom in pursuit of any audience they can find – desperately binge-publishing without checking facts, pushing out the most shrill and most extreme stories to boost clicks. On some sites, journalists who learned in training that 'news is something that someone, somewhere doesn't want published' churn out 10 commodified stories a day without making a phone call. 'Where once we had propaganda, press releases, journalism, and advertising,' the academic Emily Bell has written 'we now have content'. Readers are overwhelmed: bewildered by the quantity of 'news' they see every day, nagged by intrusive pop-up ads, confused by what is real and what is fake, and confronted with an experience that is neither useful nor enjoyable.[5]

These words mirror a complex background. Social media platforms and technology companies are having a greater effect on press publishers than even the shift from print to digital and the growth of the commercial Internet. The

---

[5]   Katharine Viner, 'A mission for journalism in a time of crisis, The long read', *The Guardian* (16 November 2017) https://www.theguardian.com/news/2017/nov/16/a -mission-for-journalism-in-a-time-of-crisis accessed April 2018.

transition from print to digital did not initially change the basic business model for many news publishers – that is, selling advertisements to fund the journalism delivered to readers. For a time, it seemed that online audiences might potentially compensate for the decline in print readers and advertisers. But that business model is currently facing a crisis, which is partly related to the powerful rise of third-party market players such as social media platforms and technology companies including Google and Apple,[6] which have influenced the news market.[7] These companies are much more than mere distribution channels. They can control what audiences see, who gets paid for their attention and what format and type of journalism succeeds. In particular, social media platforms and search companies lead the distribution and presentation of news as well as the monetization of publishing and their relationship with the audience. Indeed, many platforms actively select, rank and classify news publications with the aim of getting as many people as they can to use their platforms. This has incentivized the spread of low-quality content provided that it attracts readers. At the same time, the rapid adoption of smartphones has transformed news consumption, turning technology companies with their apps and operating systems into the gatekeepers of information.[8]

Therefore, the distribution and presentation of news, the monetization of publishing and the relationship with the audience, in the forms briefly mentioned above, tend to be concentrated in the hands of a few companies. For example, Facebook owns WhatsApp and Messenger, the two most popular messaging apps, along with Instagram, which has been incorporating many of Snapchat's most popular features. Alongside Google, the company has acquired and is maintaining enormous power over the discovery and distribution of content, including news.[9] This concentration is partly related to companies' ability to collect and use data on readers' habits and preferences.

Against this multifaceted background, news publishers are struggling to understand whether and how to rethink their processes and structures. Reactions have hitherto been different, also depending on the market they

---

[6]   Globally there are over 40 different social media sites and messaging apps through which news publishers can reach segments of their audience. As shown by empirical studies such as the one reported in Reuters Institute Digital News Report 2017 [available at https://reutersinstitute.politics.ox.ac.uk/] the news and technology industry is partly different in the US and Europe.

[7]   See Emily Bell, Taylor Owen et al, 'The Platform Press. How Silicon Valley Reengineered Journalism, Columbia Graduate School of Journalism', 2017, available at http://towcenter.org/wp-content/uploads/2017/04/The_Platform_Press_Tow_Report_2017.pdf, accessed December 2017.

[8]   See Reuters Institute Digital News Report 2017 (n 4) 10.

[9]   See Reuters Institute Digital News Report 2017 (n 4) 12.

cover.[10] Various methods have been used to give new life to press publishing; refocusing on quality of journalism that perhaps people would be prepared to pay for and focusing on audience engagement are some trends, though these are not universal.

Groups of press publishers are seeking help from the legislator. They argue that the new ways of consuming content facilitate free-riding by third parties that would profit from using content in a variety of ways without sharing the value generated from them, thereby preventing publishers from receiving market compensation for their production activities. In some European countries – Germany[11] and Spain[12] are examples – press publishers have managed to procure special laws within national copyright regimes, while similar laws have been proposed without success in other countries – for example, in Austria,[13] Italy,[14] Sweden,[15] and France with respect to images.[16] In other European countries, pressure from publishers has brought about negotiated

---

[10]   Viner (n 3).

[11]   Section 87f–g Copyright Act of 9 September 1965 (Federal Law Gazette Part I, 1273) as last amended by Section 8 of the Act of 1 October 2013 (Federal Law Gazette Part I, 3714). This provision gave rise to many criticisms, which are summarized, among others, in M Stieper, 'Abschnitt 7. Schutz des Pressverlegers', in G Schricker and U Loewenheim (eds), *Urheberrecht. Kommentar* (5th edn, C.H. Beck 2017) 2096–2121.

[12]   See Boletín Oficial de las Cortes Generales, Congreso de los Diputados, Informe de la Ponencia: Proyecto de Ley por la que se modifica el Texto Refundido de la Ley de Propriedad Intelectual, aprobado por Real Decreto Legislativo 1/1996, de 12 de Abril, y la Ley 1/2000, de 7 de enero, de Enjuiciamiento Civil, No. 81-3 (22 July 2014) http://www.congreso.es/public_oficiales/L10/CONG/BOCG/A/BOCG-10-A-81-3.PDF. Comments on this law in R Xalabarder, 'The Remunerated Statutory Limitation for News Aggregation and Search Engines Proposed by the Spanish Government; Its Compliance with International and EU Law' (*infojustice.org*, 2014) http://infojustice.org/archives/33346; ibid., 'Press Publisher Rights in the New Copyright in the Digital Single Market Draft Directive' (2016) CREATe Working Papers 2016/15, 20.

[13]   Urheberrechts-Novelle 2015, available at https://www.ris.bka.gv.at/Dokument.wxe?Abfrage=Begut&Dokumentnummer=BEGUT_COO_2026_100_2_1102902. See Tom Hirche, 'Surprising Turn in Austria', available at http://ancillarycopyright.eu/news/2015-06-15/surprising-turn-austria.

[14]   Decree Law 3 October 2006 no. 262 – cancelled upon conversion – proposed a change to Art 65 of Law no 633 of 1941 (Italian Copyright Act). See, Falce and Bixio (n 1).

[15]   See, Greg Sterling, 'Sweden the Latest to Consider Google "Link Tax" For Newspapers', 10 November 2014, available at https://searchengineland.com/sweden-latest-consider-google-link-tax-207706.

[16]   Brad Spitz, 'Thumbnails: French proposal for payment of royalties by search engines', Kluwer Copyright Blog (28 April 2014), http://kluwercopyrightblog.com/2014/04/28/thumbnailsfrance/.

solutions, as in Belgium, France and Italy.[17] Negotiated solutions appear to be the preferred approach for press publishers in the US.[18]

3.   THE EUROPEAN COMMISSION'S PROPOSAL

3.1   Content

In heeding press publishers' claims, the European Commission – following the German model – has proposed a new neighbouring right for press publishers. Article 11 of the proposed Directive on copyright in the Digital Single Market states that 'Member States shall provide publishers of press publications with the rights provided for in Article 2 and Article 3(2) of Directive 2001/29/EC for the digital use of their press publications'.[19] Articles 2 and 3(2) of Directive 2001/29/EC provide for exclusive rights of reproduction and the right of making available to the public.

The press publication to be protected is defined by the Commission as a 'fixation of literary works of a journalistic nature, which may also comprise other works or subject matter and constitute an individual item within a periodical or regularly updated publication under a single title'. In addition, this publication must have 'the purpose of providing information related to news or other topics and published in any media under the initiative, editorial responsibility and control of a service provider' (Article 2(4)). Pursuant to Article 11(4), the proposed right will expire 20 years after issuance of the press publication.

Recitals 31 and 32 of the proposed Directive explain that a free and pluralistic press is essential to ensure the quality of journalism and citizens' access to information, and that the organizational and financial contribution of publish-

---

[17]   The Italian, Belgian and French solutions are compared in M L Bixio, 'Google-Fieg, tregua per l'info-mediazione' (*dimit*, 2016) http://www.dimt.it/index .php/it/notizie/15166-28google-fieg-tregua-per-l-info-mediazione.

[18]   See D Chavern, 'Protect the News From Google and Facebook. A Partial Exemption from Antitrust Laws Would Help Publishers and Readers', *Wall Street Journal* (25 February 2018) https://www.wsj.com/articles/protect-the-news-from -google-and-facebook-1519594942; M Purdue, 'Newspapers Want Anti-trust Pass to Handle Facebook, Google', *USA TODAY* (10 July 2017) https://www.usatoday.com/ story/tech/news/2017/07/10/newspapers-want-anti-trust-pass-handle-facebook-google/ 465379001/; D Chavern, 'How Antitrust Undermines Press Freedom', *Wall Street Journal* (9 July 2017) https://www.wsj.com/articles/how-antitrust-undermines-press -freedom-1499638532; J Rutenberg, 'News Outlets to Seek Bargaining Rights Against Google and Facebook', *New York Times* (9 July 2017) https://www.nytimes.com/2017/ 07/09/business/media/google-facebook-news-media-alliance.html?_r=0.

[19]   Both the European Parliament and the Council of the European Union have proposed some amendments to Article 11, however both share the Commission approach.

ers must be recognized and rewarded so that the industry can be sustainable. According to the Commission, the introduction of a new neighbouring right in favour of press publishers would grant remuneration to press publishers for the services they provide to the general public. The Impact Assessment on the modernization of EU copyright law accompanying the proposal gives two other reasons for introducing new neighbouring rights:[20] (1) to strengthen press publishers' bargaining position vis-à-vis online platforms;[21] and (2) to facilitate licensing and enforcing their rights against online infringement.

3.2 A Case Study

Over recent years the tendency has been to resort to intellectual property for protection of intangible assets which are not attributable to the traditional catalogue of intellectual property rights. Some 'atypical' exclusive rights are ascribed to the category of neighbouring rights despite the fact that the neighbourhood of these rights to copyright is difficult, if not impossible, to determine. This is the case, for example, with exclusive rights recognized by some European countries – and at a late stage introduced by the European Parliament within the amendments adopted on 12 September 2018[22] – in favour of organizers of sporting events.[23]

The French legislature enacted a specific provision for organizers of sporting events in Law no. 84-610 of 16 July 1984[24] on the organization and promotion of sporting and physical activities, subsequently amended and now codified in Article L. 333-1 of the French Sports Code.[25] Article L. 333-1 of the Sports Code establishes that sports federations and organizers of sporting events are proprietors of the exploitation rights of the sporting events or com-

---

[20] Commission, 'Staff Working Document, Impact Assessment on the Modernisation of EU Copyright rules, accompanying the Proposal for a Directive on Copyright in the Digital Single Market and the Proposal for a Regulation on the exercise of copyright and related rights applicable to certain online transmissions of broadcasting organisations and retransmissions of television and radio programmes', SWD (2016) 302 final, 156 and Annex 3A (Impact Assessment).

[21] See Impact Assessment, 160.

[22] See Note 3.

[23] On the protection of sporting events in the EU, see T Margoni, 'The Protection of Sports Events in the EU: Property, Intellectual Property, Unfair Competition and Special Forms of Protection' (2016) 47(4) IIC – International Review of Intellectual Property and Competition Law 386–417.

[24] See Loi n. 84-610 du 16 Juillet 1984 relative à l'organisation et à la promotion des activités physiques et sportives, Art 18-1.

[25] See Code du Sport, created by Ordonnance n. 2006-596 du 23 Mai 2006 relative à la partie législative du code du sport, as amended.

petitions they organize. The nature of this right is not explicitly defined by the law. However, while some sources classify it as a property right,[26] others refer to it as a type of neighbouring right to copyright.[27] Although the reasons advanced for protection emphasize principled arguments (such as promoting sporting and physical activity), as a matter of fact, the subject of protection are economic investments as such.[28]

Similarly, in Italy a new neighbouring right was introduced in 2007 by a legislative decree amending the Italian Copyright Act and creating a new Article 78-*quater* entitled 'audio-visual sports rights'.[29] Audio-visual rights are defined as exclusive rights lasting 50 years from the date of the event covering the fixation and the live or delayed, temporal or permanent reproduction, in any manner or form, of the event, its communication and making available to the public, distribution to the public, rental and lending, and the fixation, elaboration or reproduction of the broadcast of the event. According to Article 3 Sports Decree, the competition and event organizers are joint owners of audio-visual rights to a sporting event.

In this context, the Commission proposal creating new copyright related rights for press publishers – which has opened the way to the European Parliament amendment introducing a new neighbouring right for sport event organizers – appears to be just the tip of the iceberg, to be observed as a case study for a general reflection on neighbouring rights.

3.3   Undefined Subject Matter of Protection

According to Article 2(4) of the proposed Directive, the press publication to be protected is a 'fixation of a collection of literary works of a journalistic

---

[26]   See the Report to the French National Assembly of 2009, http://www.assemblee -nationale.fr/13/pdf/rapports/r1860.pdf at 312; Cour d'Appel de Paris, Arrêt du 14 Octobre 2009, 08/19179 (*Unibet Int. v. Federation Francaise de Tennis*) at 4.

[27]   Michel Vivant and Michel Bruguière, *Droit d'auteur et droits voisins* (2nd edn, Dalloz 2012) 1053 ff; André Lucas and Henri-Jaques Lucas, *Traité de la propriété littéraire et artistique* (4th edn, Litec 2012) 934 ff.

[28]   See Conseil d'État (France), 5ème et 4ème sous-sections réunies, 30 Mars 2011, 342142, http://www.juricaf.org/arret/FRANCE-CONSEILDETAT-20110330-342142.

[29]   The new neighbouring right is based on Legge 19.07.2007 n. 106, 'Diritti tele-visivi sugli eventi sportivi nazionali: delega per la revisione della disciplina', and on the decrees implementing the framework act, mainly the legislative decree 'Sport e diritti audiovisivi', Decreto legislativo 09.01.2008, n. 9. For a detailed account see L Ferrari, 'Rights to Broadcast Sporting Events under Italian Law' (2010) I-II The inter-national Sports Law Journal 65–73. For a critical analysis see V Zeno Zencovich, 'La statalizzazione dei diritti televisivi sportivi' (2008) XXVI Il diritto dell'informazione e dell'informatica 6, 695–710; G Resta, *Diritti esclusivi e nuovi beni immateriali* (1st edn, Kluwer 2010).

nature which may also comprise other works or subject-matters'.[30] However, such definition remains rather obscure. One may first wonder whether the provision refers to arranging a particular layout.[31] But, if that were the case, the provision would be poorly worded. Also, if the protection of the layout were the objective of Article 11, it would be worth considering whether and to what extent this may be covered by the trademark law as an element of the publisher branding.

Also, one might wonder whether fixation may be intended as the transfer of the work onto carriers. However, a distinction between text or images and their fixation is hardly feasible.[32] Fixation is made in the first instance by the author, who fixes the work during writing, drawing or photographing. And it is fixation by the author – assuming grounds for protection exist – that enjoys copyright protection. Press publishers can hardly be compared with phonogram producers: a recording made by the producer – which consists in fixation of performance of the musical work on the carrier – is distinguishable from the work which incorporates it. In fact, musical works can be performed and recorded multiple times, resulting in different phonograms. Indeed, the fixation of musical works on the carrier is just one of the possible uses and exploitation channels of works. Musical works may be enjoyed without being fixed in a phonogram.

Furthermore, in most European legal systems newspapers enjoy copyright protection as collective works. Therefore, even assuming that the European Commission with the definition at hand refers to the selection and editing of articles, the new right for press publishers overlaps copyright protection. For example, Article 3 of the Italian Copyright Act[33] – similarly to German,[34]

---

[30] The Commission proposal has been amended during the legislative procedure. In particular, up to now the text of the negotiating mandate that Member States agreed on in Council has been available since 25 May 2018. The amendments provided for by the Council with regard to Article 11, however, do not amend conceptually the Commission's proposal. The Council has deleted the word 'fixation', defining in Article 2(4) press publication as 'a collection composed mainly of literary works of journalistic nature ...'. Such amendment does not change the weaknesses of the proposal as described below with regard to the subject matter of protection. The European Parliament has left substantially unchanged the definition proposed by the Commission.

[31] In some countries, e.g. the UK, the publisher will also have copyright in the published edition, the typographical arrangement of the publication – design, layout and typeface.

[32] On this, see A Ohly, 'Ein Leistungschtutzrecht für Pressverleger' (2012) Wettbewerb in Recht und Praxis 41.

[33] Law No 633 of 22 April 1941, for the Protection of Copyright and Neighbouring Rights.

[34] German Copyright Act of 9 September 1965. See, eg, T Dreier, '§ 4 Sammelwerke und Datenbankwerke', in Gernot Schulze and Thomas Dreier (eds), *UrhG* (5th edn, C.H. Beck 2015) § 4, paras 8–15.

French[35] and Spanish[36] laws – states that 'Collective works..., shall be protected as original works...'. According to the Italian Copyright Act the author is the person who organizes and directs creation of the collective work. In addition, Article 38 states that publishers have the right to use the work, unless otherwise stipulated.[37] Moreover, needless to say, in most cases press publishers acquire authors' rights by direct individual contract being therefore in the position to claim effective protection as derivative rightholders. The conclusion is that press publishers, according to most of the national European legislation, are already protected by copyright law to a far-reaching extent.

Yet the proposal seems to differentiate the objectives of the proposed neighbouring right from that of copyright; recital 32 states that Article 11 intends to protect press publishers for their 'organizational and financial contribution'. This purpose however did not find expression in the text of the legislation rendering it difficult a common understanding (and therefore a common implementation) of this provision at national level. The misalignment between objectives and text of the provision only renders any interpretation substantially uncertain. At the same time, the Commission does not impose any protection requirements. If the 'organizational and financial contribution' of press publishers – that are publishers' investment – were in fact the intended subject matter of protection, this should be made clearer by the European legislators and requirements of protection should be stated alike. Without the definition of the threshold of protection even minimal or insignificant investments may be sufficient enough to provide publishers with an exclusive right.

In this context a parallel can be drawn with the *sui generis* right for databases. First, although objectionable from several perspectives,[38] *sui generis* database protection has been specified by EU legislators as for the purpose, subject matter and threshold requirements of protection.[39] The *sui generis* right explicitly aims at protecting the investment of the database producer. In order to be protected under the *sui generis* database right pursuant to Article 7(1) of the Database Directive, a database qualitatively and/or quantitatively requires a substantial investment in obtaining, verification or presentation of

---

[35]   See Article L113-2 of the French Intellectual Property Code.

[36]   See Article 12 of the Spanish Royal Legislative Decree No. 1/1996, of 12 April 1996.

[37]   According to the majority of commentators, this right is subsequent to the original one of the author; parties can indeed differently agree on the use of rights. See B Cunegatti, 'Le rassegne stampa on-line tra esclusive d'autore e divieti di concorrenza sleale' (2007) *Dir. Internet*, 3.

[38]   See, Peter K Yu, 'The Political Economy of Data Protection' (2010) 84 Chicago-Kent Law Review 777–801.

[39]   Dir 97/9/EC (Database Directive).

the content. Second, the achievement of the investor is precisely identified in the database Directive. Moreover, assuming that the subject matter of protection of the proposed right is the investment of the publisher, there may be an overlap between *sui generis* database protection and the new neighbouring right. Press publications might be considered databases within the meaning of the database Directive when requirements of protection are met.

4.   PUBLIC INTERNATIONAL LAW AND NEWS PROTECTION

4.1   Premise

The right proposed by the European Commission falls into the category of neighbouring rights and as such within the scope of rights regulated by international treaties outlining regimes that are collectively called 'intellectual property'.[40] The establishment of new neighbouring rights must therefore be consistent with international intellectual property regimes to be interpreted – as stated by Article 31 of the Vienna Convention on the Law of Treaties (VCLT) – 'in their context and in the light of its object and purpose'.[41] According to Article 32 VCLT, the preparatory work for the treaty and the circumstances of its conclusion provide relevant support for any possible interpretation of treaties.

The starting point for the issue at hand is the Berne Convention (BC),[42] which states in Article 2(8): 'The protection of this Convention shall not apply to news of the day or to miscellaneous facts having the character of mere items of press information.' This wording has been part of Article 2 since the Stockholm Revision of 1967,[43] but the issue was discussed at national level even before the first BC of 1886.[44]

---

[40]   See S Ricketson, 'The Public International Law of Copyright', in I Alexander and H T Gomez-Arostegui (eds), *Research Handbook on the History of Copyright Law* (Edward Elgar Publishing 2016).

[41]   Vienna Convention on the Law of Treaties (with annex). Concluded at Vienna on 23 May 1969.

[42]   See Berne Convention for the Protection of Literary and Artistic Works (Paris, 4 May 1896), 1161 UNTS 3, which entered into force on 5 December 1887, as revised in Paris on 24 July 1971, as amended on 28 September 1979 (Berne Convention).

[43]   See Berne Convention for the Protection of Literary and Artistic Works (Paris, 4 May 1896), 828 UNTS 221, which entered into force on 5 December 1887, as revised in Stockholm on 14 July 1967 (Stockholm Act).

[44]   S Ricketson, and J C Ginsburg, 'Intellectual Property in News? Why Not?', in S Ricketson and M Richardson (eds), *Research Handbook on Intellectual Property in Media and Entertainment* (Edward Elgar Publishing 2016).

4.2 News Stories and Press Publishers' Investments: an Old Issue

Legal proposals for 'property rights' in news circulated in the Australian colonies as early as the 1870s.[45] The growing popularity of newspapers in this period was linked to the advent of the telegraph, which made communication of news from one place to another overseas easier and quicker than before. However, protection of news included in telegrams was difficult to achieve under both imperial copyright and Australian copyright. The inference drawn was that there was no copyright in the news itself, but there may have been copyright in its mode of expression.[46] In this context, the Australian Associated Press pressured the legislators of the Australian colonies to establish property rights in news, though obtaining success only in some colonies.[47]

A similar debate took place in the US, where, until the middle decades of the 1800s, newspapers were partisan organs mostly supported by political sponsors and government subsidies. Towards the end of the 19th century technological changes narrowed the lead-time advantage that newspapers traditionally had and exposed them to competition from which they had previously been geographically isolated. Therefore, news companies began pressuring legislatures[48] and courts, obtaining protection only from the latter. The issue was debated in *International News Service v. Associated Press*,[49] which has now lost its importance as a precedent in the US[50] but deserves to be mentioned as the court stated two relevant principles: (1) the majority opinion recognized that the information found in the Associated Press news was not copyrightable and free access to and use of information per se cannot be called into ques-

---

[45]   Lionel Bently, 'Copyright and the Victorian Internet: Telegraphic Property Laws in Colonial Australia' (2004) 38 Loyola of Los Angeles Law Review 71.

[46]   *Walter v. Steinkopf* (1892) 3 Ch. 489 (Eng.).

[47]   See, Lionel Bently, (n. 47).

[48]   The one serious attempt in Congress took place in 1884. On 4 March 1884, Senator John Sherman of Ohio introduced 'A Bill Granting Copyright in Newspapers', S. 1728, 48th Cong., see Cong. Rec. 1578. Six days later, representative John Randolph Tucker of Virginia introduced an identical bill in the House: H.R. 5850, 48th Cong., see 15 Cong. Rec 1758. The story is reconstructed in detail in Robert F Brauneis, 'The Debate Over Copyright in News and Its Effect on Originality Doctrine', in Robert F Brauneis (ed), *Intellectual Property Protection on Fact-based Works. Copyright and Its Alternatives* (Edward Elgar Publishing 2009) 39–74, at 54 ff.

[49]   248 U.S. 215 (1918). On the situation in the US, see E Easton, 'Who Owns the First Rough Draft of History? Reconsidering Copyright in News' (2004) 27 Colum. J.L. & Arts 561.

[50]   This decision is considered as an experiment in common-law protection of intellectual property. It has not spawned a broad jurisprudence of common-law intellectual property, but has been given a narrow reading, limited to 'hot news' misappropriation. And as a matter of federal court jurisdiction it has been repudiated.

tion;[51] and (2) regulation of the news market does not concern the field of copyright, but rather the area of law which regulates relations among competitors. The Associated Press was entitled to an injunction against International News Service because its use of news copied from bulletin boards and early editions of the Associated Press member papers constituted misappropriation, a kind of unfair competition. The majority opinion described the defendant's interest in its news as 'quasi-property', which, however, is good only for a short period (less than one day) and only against a direct competitor of the plaintiff. This doctrine 'postpones participation by complainant's competitor in the processes of distribution and reproduction of news that it has not gathered, and only to the extent necessary to prevent that competitor from reaping the fruits of complainant's efforts and expenditure'.[52]

4.3 The Line Between Copyright and Other Regulatory Tools in the Berne Convention

As mentioned above, Article 2(8) BC denies copyright protection to 'news of the day' or 'miscellaneous facts' provided that such articles have the character of mere news items. Provision in that form has been part of Article 2 since the Stockholm Revision of 1967.[53] The Stockholm study group report made clear, first, that the provision did intend to exclude facts from copyright protection but not the copyrightable articles in which facts were contained. The study group highlighted further that this provision works as a reminder of the freedom of information and constitutes the expression of a principle from which legislation and jurisprudence can take their lead by excluding mere facts or information from copyright protection. This principle suggests something similar – albeit limited to the press – to the idea/expression dichotomy that was later developed and expanded by international legislators in Article 9(2) TRIPS[54] and Article 2 of the 1996 WIPO Copyright Treaty.[55]

Second, according to the study group the provision fixes the line of demarcation between copyright and other means of protection. This point had

---

[51]   248 U.S. at 234.

[52]   248 U.S. at 241.

[53]   WIPO, *Records of the Intellectual Property Conference of Stockholm* (Stockholm Intellectual Property Conference 1971) vol 1, 115.

[54]   Agreement on Trade-Related Aspects of Intellectual Property Rights (Marrakesh, 15 April 1994), Marrakesh Agreement Establishing the World Trade Organization, Annex 1C, The Legal Texts: The Results of the Uruguay Round of Multilateral Trade Negotiations 321 (1999), 1869 UNTS 299, 33 ILM 1197 (1994), which entered into force on 1 January 1995 (TRIPS).

[55]   WIPO Copyright Treaty (Geneva, 20 December 1996), 2186 UNTS 121, 36 ILM 65 (1997), which entered into force on 6 March 2002.

already been raised in the context of the Berlin revision[56] where it was stated that the commercial interests of press publishers do not fall within the province of copyright. According to the Berlin working group, commercial questions regarding news reproduction are to be regulated in the field of competition law.[57] The issue was debated during the Paris Convention but various attempts to introduce a provision in the Convention that could guarantee effective protection of news all failed.[58] The international debate on the issue offers guiding principles for national states.[59]

5. INTELLECTUAL PROPERTY AND COMPETITION LAW

From an economic perspective two main (interrelated) arguments form the basis of intellectual property exclusive rights. On the one hand exclusive rights are intended to create incentives for production of intellectual works; on the other hand, these rights serve to avoid potential market failure. Given the role played by intellectual property in market regulation, contemporary commentators recognize that intellectual property performs functions complementary to competition law, which is by nature devoted to regulating competitor relations.[60] Although legal approaches protecting intellectual property and competition are to be considered as a whole,[61] it is important not to lose sight of the particularities of each field.[62]

---

[56] Berlin Act (no 20) Art 9(3). See further, International Union for the Protection of Literary and Artistic Works, *L'Union internationale littéraire et artistique, 1886–1936: sa fondation et son développement* (Berne 1936) 249 ff.

[57] *Actes de la Conférence* 1908 (no 27) 251–252.

[58] For a historical reconstruction, see Ricketson and Ginsburg (n 42).

[59] See Stephen P Ladas, 'Patents, Trademarks, and Related Rights: National and International Protection' (2nd edn, Harvard University Press 1975) vol 3, 1724–1725.

[60] Among others, see A Kur, 'Funktionswandel von Schutzrechten: Ursachen und Konsequenzen der inhaltlichen Annäherung und Überlagerung von Schutzrechtstypen', in Gerhard Schricker, Thomas Dreier and Annette Kur (eds), *Geistiges Eigentum im Dienst der Innovation* (Nomos 2001) 23–50; id, 'A New Framework for Intellectual Property Rights – Horizontal Issues' (2004) 35(1) IIC 1–21; R H Weber, 'Dritte Spur zwischen absoluten und relativen Rechten?', in H Honsell, W Portmann, R Zäch and D Zobl (eds), *Aktuelle Aspekte des Schuld- und Sachenrechts, Festschrift für Heinz Rey* (Schulthess Juristische Medien 2003) 583–595.

[61] See Reto M Hilty, 'The Law Against Unfair Competition and Its Interfaces', in Reto M Hilty and Frauke Henning-Bodewig (eds), *Law Against Unfair Competition. Towards a New Paradigm in Europe? MPI Studies on Intellectual Property, Competition and Tax Law, 1* (Springer 2007) 1–52.

[62] See, Reto M Hilty, 'Gedanken zum Schutz der nachbarrechtlichen Leistung-einst, heute und morgen' (1991) 116 UFITA 35 ff.

In most national competition law systems, subject matter worthy of protection consists of investments in products and services to be marketed. However, competition law does not protect investments as such, at least not unconditionally. The requirements for and characteristics of protection vary to a significant extent in the various states, but generally speaking protection of investments is related to the behaviour of the competitor taking over the investment.[63] It must be asked whether the behaviour of a competitor taking over investments is likely to squeeze the original competitor out of the market and whether this leads to market failure in the long run.[64] Moreover, competition law is normally based on 'liability' rules and on the technique of balancing of interests: competition as such is not prohibited or penalized – but the methods used by competitors may be. Presumptions of liability may be applicable in some cases, but this does not change the nature of things, namely that the legal protection places itself in the domain of competition law (i.e. tort law).

Intellectual property focuses instead on the result of the investment (such as a work or a patent) which will be given protection based on an exclusive right. In fact, although intellectual property protection (whatever theory one may follow) results in market regulation, the aim of protection goes further than mere market regulation and further than protection of investments.[65] Intellectual property law is mostly related to the quality of the product which is the result of an investment. The question is not whether an investment should be protected with the only objective of avoiding a distortion of competition. The key element of intellectual property law is that the subject matter of protection has special characteristics. Intellectual property laws reveal indeed requirements of protection in particular in qualitative terms.[66]

---

[63]   ibid, 16–19.

[64]   See Hilty (n 63); a similar argument has been made by G Resta, 'Nuovi beni immateriali e *numerus clausus* dei diritti esclusivi', in G Resta (ed), *Diritti esclusivi e nuovi beni immateriali* (Kluwer 2010) 3–25.

[65]   S Ricketson, 'Rights on the Border: The Berne Convention and Neighbouring Rights', in R L Okediji (ed), *Copyright Law in the Age of Limitations and Exceptions* (CUP 2017) 342–374.

[66]   See Hilty (n 63), p. 23.

6.   NEIGHBOURING RIGHTS IN INTERNATIONAL LAW

6.1   Neighbourhood with Copyright Law

In the first half of the last century an attempt was made at protection of news as a copyright-related right[67] as part of a broader international debate about the introduction of special rights for subject matter such as sound recordings, broadcasts and live performances that, for different reasons, do not meet the requirements for copyright protection.[68] Separate rights, analogous to those of authors but outside authors' rights regimes altogether, emerged as 'neighbouring rights'. This first occurred in the Rome Convention of 1961 granting protection to sound recordings, broadcasts and live performances. A further development of these rights was established in the 1990s by Article 14 TRIPS and the WIPO Performances and Phonograms Treaty (WPPT). These rights – whose legal character appears to be not yet entirely clarified – have been considered 'neighbouring', as each of them is connected, albeit in different ways, with the exploitation of authors' rights. With regard to 'press news', a neighbouring right for press publishers was proposed in the 'Samedan draft' but the degree of 'neighbourhood' with copyright law was ultimately considered very low or non-existent.[69] Thus, protection of press information was seen as unconnected to authors' rights but rather connected with concepts of unfair competition. Even the Post-Samedan history suggests that press publishers' rights to news were not a subject that could be located in a neighbouring-right formulation and more generally in the 'norm formulation agenda of WIPO'.[70]

6.2   Taxonomy of Rights

There are cases in which no conflicts of interest arise from the relationship between copyright and neighbouring rights: first, when the performances,

---

[67]   The most thorough and accessible account of the work of the Samedan Committee is to be found in the October, November, and December 1940 issues of Le Droit d'auteur, DA 109–111, 121–125, 133–138. The minutes of the meeting are recorded as being in the UNIDROIT archives. 'Maggiori informazioni su questo tentativo normativo' in Ricketson and Ginsburg (n 42) 12–13.

[68]   See Ricketson (n 62); R Fleischer, 'Protecting the Musicians and/or the Record Industry?' (2015) 5(3) Queen Mary Journal of Intellectual Property 327–343; S Ricketson and J G Ginsburg, *International Copyright and Neighbouring Rights* (2nd edn, OUP 2006) vol 2, 1205 ff.

[69]   Ricketson (n 62) 366.

[70]   ibid.

recordings or broadcasts of works are not protected by copyright, having fallen into the public domain and second, when no work in the copyright sense is involved. However, in the majority of cases works are involved and here the question is whether the neighbouring rights conflict with those of the authors. According to Article 1 Rome Convention and Article 1(2) WPPT neighbouring rights must leave intact and in no way affect protection of copyright. Indeed, while assuring protection for the contribution of performers, phonogram producers and broadcasters, the drafters at the various meetings sought to achieve a taxonomy of rights that kept authorship at the centre. A hierarchy of interests is involved, with the starting point being creation of works, which accordingly has the largest claim to recognition.[71] Performers, phonogram producers and broadcasters build on these initial contributions, either through performance or interpretation, in the case of performers, or through fixation and dissemination in the case of phonogram producers and broadcasters.

7.   IN SEARCH OF A SYSTEMATIC APPROACH FOR NEIGHBOURING RIGHTS

International law does not preclude nation states from including in their own legal systems new neighbouring rights which indeed have been introduced to protect different subject matters. States are also free to determine the legal concept by which beneficiaries are enabled to prevent unauthorized exploitation of their achievements.[72] While it is known that there are two different approaches in the common law and civil law systems,[73] neighbouring rights – when adopted – replicate to a large extent copyright protection. It is not the aim of this work to carry out a comparative analysis of national implementations of neighbouring rights. However, in general terms, the three main drivers of these rights can be summarized as follows.[74]

The first driver concerns achievements which, although close to works protected by copyright, differ from them in that they lack a minimum gradient of creativity.[75] Falling into this category might be critical or scientific editions of works in the public domain, theatrical sketches, photographs or engineering

---

[71]   ibid, 372–373.

[72]   A Peukert, 'Related Rights', in J Basedow, K J Hopt and R Zimmermann (eds), *The Max Planck Encyclopedia of European Private Law*, 2 vols (OUP 2012) 1443–1446.

[73]   ibid, 1445.

[74]   V Falce, *La modernizzazione del diritto d'autore, Giappichelli Editore* (Giappichelli 2012) 68–71.

[75]   A Musso, *Diritto d'autore sulle opere dell'ingegno letterarie e artistiche* (Zanichelli 2008) 299.

projects. A special role is played in Europe by non-creative databases for which qualitatively and/or quantitatively substantial investments are made in either obtaining, or verifying or presenting the contents. This right is often dealt with separately from other neighbouring rights due to the fact that – unlike the neighbouring rights mentioned above – the protected subject matter is the investment in a database. Nevertheless, it seems reasonable to include *sui generis* rights on a database in this group since protection concerns a specific achievement, which is the non-creative database. If the database is creative, it would be a copyrighted work.[76] The second driver has to do with performances which, despite their artistic character, do not result in works. Performances make works available to the public and allow them to be marketed. The third driver refers to phonograms, videograms, and radio and television broadcasts. These neighbouring rights are triggered by specific investments from market players who develop their business models mostly based on pre-existing works. Those investments are indeed functional to full exploitation of the work in question.[77] This connection attracts this protection of entrepreneurs' achievements within the field of intellectual property law.

8. DOES THE PROPOSED NEIGHBOURING RIGHT FOR PRESS PUBLISHERS FIT INTO THE 'SPIRIT' OF INTERNATIONAL INTELLECTUAL PROPERTY REGIMES?

The BC, 'Samedan' and 'Post-Samedan' history suggests that copyright law and neighbouring rights are not adequate legal tools to protect publishers' investments in producing news items. This history further indicates that the protection of the organizational and financial contribution of publishers – whenever needed – does not fall within the area of intellectual property, whilst it might be covered by unfair competition regimes. The legal and systematic foundation of neighbouring rights has not been developed as it has in the case of copyright and other intellectual property rights. However, as mentioned above, they are considered and treated as intellectual property rights. Thus nation states when considering the introduction of new neighbouring rights to protect investments from market players as such should consider that a conjunction ring with the area of intellectual property is needed. Indeed, from a systematic perspective, where points of contact between investments

---

[76] P B Hugenholtz, 'Directive 96/9/EC (Database Directive)', in T Dreier and P B Hugenholtz, *Concise European Copyright Law* (2nd edn, Wolters Kluwer 2016) 379 ff.
[77] Ricketson and Ginsburg (n 64) 1206.

protection and intellectual property are missing, it appears difficult to qualify exclusive rights protecting investments as intellectual property rights.

Further, in the case at issue (also given the unclear definition of the subject matter of protection) a potential conflict between press publishers' neighbouring rights and copyright of authors (who play a central role in creating news stories) cannot be excluded. And the taxonomy of rights outlined by international law may be jeopardized. For example, a journalist may have an interest in having an article found and linked by a search engine content aggregator, however the decision whether this can be done might remain in the publishers' hands if the neighbouring right on the 'fixation of a collection of literary works of a journalistic nature' was exclusively attributed to publishers. In fact, merely stating that this right should not be exercised against the interests of the authors and other rightholders – as established in the Impact Assessment of the European Commission – does not resolve the possible conflict of interests. One may argue that, even in the current situation where authors transfer their right to press publishers, authors' interests might be negatively affected by those of publishers. In fact, publishers as copyright rightholders might potentially act against the interests of authors. However, this is a question of copyright contract law and might be solved by regulating this matter, fostering synergies between authors and press publishers.

9.   FOUR COMPLEMENTARY DRIVERS FOR A HOLISTIC APPROACH

In order to evaluate both the *an* and the *quomodo* of any legal intervention, at least two dimensions should be considered: on the one hand, the economic perspective concerning market functioning; on the other, the regulatory perspective inspired by social values. Dealing with both dimensions requires adopting a holistic approach based on the consistent and complementary application of four legal instruments: copyright law, *sui generis* database protection, competition law and trade mark law.

For copyrighted news, press publishers enjoy copyright as subsequent rightholders. In this respect, the position of press publishers might be strengthened, focusing on publishers' need to easily license, enforce their rights and participate in the statutory remuneration for copyright permitted uses, rather than on creating new rights. With regard specifically to the European context, the legislator could amend Article 5 'Presumption of authorship or ownership' of Directive 2004/48/EC[78] to create the presumption that a press publisher

---

[78]   Directive 2004/48/EC of the European Parliament and of the Council of 29 April 2004 on the enforcement of intellectual property rights.

must be regarded as entitled to enforce copyright in any item if that publisher's name appears in the news publication.[79]

Furthermore, *sui generis* database protection might play an important role. Digital publishing might be encouraged towards developing new business models based on a content platform.[80] Indeed, the value of a business model based on developing content platforms that allow users to benefit from added value compared to a mere online magazine is connected to the functionality of the platform and the organization of content.

The third instrument to focus on is competition law. The expression 'competition law' is used in this context by reference to its substantive and broad meaning concerning market regulation. Although EU harmonization so far mostly concerns antitrust law and consumer protection law, harmonized solutions for unfair competition with press publishers would be preferable to avoid fragmentation of the press publishing market.[81] Different national legal conceptions and regulations as to what is permissible and non-permissible commercial activity under unfair competition law may threaten the uniform internal market. Various forms of regulation within the competition law area might be introduced. In this regard it is worth mentioning, as a possible approach, Article 101 of the Italian Copyright Act. Although placed in the Copyright Act it contains a provision that is clearly about competition law by specifying a general ban on unfair competition, which is regulated in Italy by Article 2598 of the Civil Code. According to Article 101, reproduction and distribution of news are free (if not protected by copyright), as long as they are not conducted in ways that go against the honest use of journalistic news.[82]

---

[79] Alexander Peukert, 'An EU Related Right for Press Publishers Concerning Digital Uses. A Legal Analysis' (20 December 2016). Research Paper of the Faculty of Law, Goethe University Frankfurt am Main No. 22/2016, https://ssrn.com/abstract= 2888040.

[80] Senftleben et al (n 1) 538–561.

[81] See Protocol no 27 on Internal Market and Competition annexed to the Treaty on European Union, which states that 'THE HIGH CONTRACTING PARTIES, Considering the Internal Market as set out in Article 3 of the Treaty on European Union includes a system ensuring that competition is not distorted, Have agreed that: To this end, the Union shall, if necessary, take action under the provisions of the Treaties, including under Article 352 of the Treaty on the Functioning of the European Union'. Moreover, Article 3(1)(b) TFEU states that one of the areas in which the Union has exclusive competence is 'The establishing of competition rules necessary for the functioning of the Internal Market'.

[82] On this point see P G Marchetti and L C Ubertazzi (eds), *Commentario breve alle leggi su proprietà intellettuale e concorrenza* (Wolters Kluwer 2016) 1897–1901; Cass. civ. 10 maggio 1993, n. 5346 with commentary by M Fabiani, 'Sui limiti di protezione delle notizie e informazioni di stampa', in (1994) Dir. Aut., 76. See also, Cunegatti (n 34) 251.

The fourth path to enhance the value of press publishers' services should aim at promoting branding and the quality of press publishing by means of trademark law. A brand can be a publisher's key asset in strengthening its position in the market. In following this path, press publishers are called upon to work on their own business models to create added value for their products,[83] promoting the quality of the service. At the same time, advertisers might prioritize investing in more attentive and responsible platforms, thereby promoting a virtuous circle of growth.

Finally, as in many other areas of the digital economy, a significant role in digital press publishing is played by accessibility to data as 'digital resources'.[84] It is not the aim of this work to dissect the issues of a complex subject that stands at the centre of academic and legislative debate.[85] However, it is enough to highlight in this context that data are fundamental digital resources in a data-driven economy: all companies, including publishers, compete over data.

10.   CONCLUSION

Although the European proposal is anchored to the social value attributed to press publishers' activities, the chosen method of regulation is barely justifiable on a systematic and policy level. First, the creation of new neighbouring rights for press publishers does not fit properly within the 'spirit' of international intellectual property law. As has emerged from the historical development of international law, copyright and neighbouring rights have been expressly excluded as means of legal protection for news items and press publishers interests. The debate leading up to this exclusion suggested that the subject fell outside the scope of intellectual property law. The commercial interests of press publishers, it was stated, fall under the scope of competition law.

While considering the issue at hand, international legislators have therefore traced a path indicating a demarcation line between intellectual property and competition law. In fact, the rationale for protecting competitors in the market is primarily the functioning of the market and therefore differs from

---

[83]   See Senftleben et al (n 1) 538–561.

[84]   See Gintare Surblyte, 'Data as a Digital Resource' (6 October 2016) Max Planck Institute for Innovation & Competition Research Paper No. 16-12. https://ssrn.com/abstract=2849303 or http://dx.doi.org/10.2139/ssrn.2849303*t*.

[85]   Ibid.; Josef Drexl, et al, 'Position Statement of the Max Planck Institute for Innovation and Competition of 26 April 2017 on the European Commission's "Public consultation on Building the European Data Economy"' (26 April 2017) Max Planck Institute for Innovation & Competition Research Paper No. 17-08 https://ssrn.com/abstract=2959924 or http://dx.doi.org/10.2139/ssrn.2959924.

the rationale behind intellectual property law. Intellectual property mostly focuses on the quality of the achievement (e.g. the creative work) rather than the investment itself.

In the proposed neighbouring right for press publishers the subject matter of protection has not been openly identified by the European Commission. However recital 32 states that Article 11 intends to protect press publishers for their 'organizational and financial contribution'. This purpose however did not find expression in the text of the provision. If the 'organizational and financial contribution' of press publishers – that are publishers' investment – were in fact the intended subject matter of protection, this should be made clearer by the European legislators and requirements of protection should be stated alike.

This clarification is a cornerstone even from a systematic perspective allowing for an interpretation of the legal instruments that is consistent with the objectives pursued by legislators. Conversely, an unclear definition of the legal instruments may cause legal uncertainty and undesirable effects on both market functioning and the social values pursued by the legal system.

Moreover, only in few cases neighbouring rights aim to protect business 'investments' as such, and in those cases reasons of 'connection' with copyright law, and in particular functionality to the exploitation of works, draw protection of those investments into the scope of intellectual property. This connection is not apparent in the case at issue.

Therefore, rather than improperly relying on neighbouring rights, a holistic approach would be recommendable. This should be inspired by market-functioning needs, but also by values such as diversification of information channels and quality of information. In enhancing digital press publishing, a proper regulation should aim at promoting development of new business models triggered by the quality of services and content offered. To these ends, the interplay among four complementary key drivers – copyright law, *sui generis* database protection, competition law and trademark law – may be enhanced in the digital environment.

5. Meet the unavoidable – the challenges of digital second-hand marketplaces to the doctrine of exhaustion

Péter Mezei

1. A CENTURY-OLD DOCTRINE

The doctrine of exhaustion, or the first sale doctrine, is both a fundamental principle of copyright law and an utmost guarantee for lawful owners of cultural goods to exercise their interests stemming from the right of property. Under this doctrine, the rightholder must accept that copies, or the originals of copyrighted works, and other subject matter lawfully placed into circulation by or with the authorization of the rightholder, through sale or in any other form of transfer of ownership, are subsequently distributed by the lawful owner of those copies or originals, if the rightholder received proper remuneration for the initial distribution. This chapter addresses mainly the question whether this doctrine might be applied for the online redistribution of works and other protected subject matter.

Anglo-Saxon academia and case law have often stressed that the doctrine stems from the common law's refusal to permit restraints on the alienation of chattels,[1] but the earliest direct reference to *Erschöpfungslehre* in copyright law is found in Joseph Kohler's monograph published in 1880.[2]

Regardless of the precise origins of the doctrine, both the US Supreme Court and the Supreme Court of the German Reich confirmed the validity of this concept, at similar times and in cases with comparable fact patterns.[3] The

---

[1] *Supap Kirtsaeng v. John Wiley & Sons, Inc.*, 133 S.Ct. 1351 (2013) 1363.
[2] Joseph Kohler, *Das Authorrecht – Eine zivilistische Abhandlung* (Verlag von Gustav Fischer 1880) 139.
[3] The foundations of the doctrine were first set by court decisions in the United States, commencing from the mid-1880s. See *Clemens v. Estes*, 22 Fed. Rep. 899 (1885).

Königs Kursbuch[4] and the *Bobbs-Merrill*[5] cases both concerned the resale of books which were originally put into circulation by their respective publishers at a fixed price, yet subsequently, in some instances, were resold at a lower price. Both rulings were based on the premise that a rightholder that had received fair remuneration for the first sale had no right to control further resale of the given copies. This is known as *Belohnungstheorie* (EN: reward theory) in the German legal system and as reward theory in Anglo-Saxon jurisprudence.

Following the above two rulings from 1906 and 1908, respectively, the doctrine has been developed for many decades exclusively on a national level. The exact content of the doctrine varied in light of countries' divergent socio-economic backgrounds and their differing policy considerations. Most developed countries with large economic potential, strong domestic markets and the capacity to export cultural goods (such as the United States or Germany) were interested in national exhaustion. In contrast, countries that relied heavily on the importation of cultural goods as well as being developing and small market countries in general, such as the Netherlands, Switzerland, Japan, Australia and New Zealand, were interested in international exhaustion. As a third option, regional protection of copyright law has been developed through CJEU case law. Indeed, several rulings, particularly on the free movement of goods and services, have played a pivotal role in the evolution of copyright law within the EU.[6] This approach was later codified via the EU copyright directives.

For a long time, international interest in further development of the doctrine was absent as this would inevitably have required surrender of domestic solutions. The Agreement on Trade-Related Aspects of Intellectual Property Rights (TRIPS Agreement), adopted in 1994, was the first international agreement on intellectual property that touched upon the copyright aspects of exhaustion. Nevertheless, as the contracting parties failed to reach a compromise on an independent right of distribution,[7] the TRIPS Agreement introduced no new substantive obligations on the doctrine of exhaustion. Instead, it granted absolute freedom to the signatories on the issue of regulation, 'whether enacted by statute, articulated in judicial opinions, or formulated in agency

---

[4] RG 10.06.1906 (Rep. I. 5/06).

[5] *Bobbs-Merrill Company v. Isidor Straus and Nathan Straus*, 210 U.S. 339 (1908).

[6] The earliest preliminary ruling of the ECJ in this matter was Case 78/70 *Deutsche Grammophon Gesellschaft mbH v. Metro-SB-Großmärkte GmbH & Co. KG* [1971] ECR 487.

[7] Jörg Reinbothe and Silke von Lewinski, *The WIPO Treaties 1996 – The WIPO Copyright Treaty and the WIPO Performances and Phonograms Treaty, Commentary and Legal Analysis* (Butterworths Lexis Nexis 2002) 80.

regulations or rules',[8] and whether regulation should have national, regional or international reach. The TRIPS Agreement approached the doctrine from a neutral perspective, stressing that '[f]or the purposes of dispute settlement under this Agreement, subject to the provisions of Articles 3 and 4 nothing in this Agreement shall be used to address the issue of the exhaustion of intellectual property rights'.[9]

The two World Intellectual Property Organization (WIPO) Internet Treaties of 1996 showed a clear progression of the norms of exhaustion. For the first time in international copyright law, these treaties allowed for a general right of distribution. At the same time, signatories of the treaties should comply with specific substantive provisions on exhaustion, while remaining free to develop their own regulations in other aspects.[10] The WIPO Copyright Treaty (WCT) and the WIPO Performances and Phonograms Treaty (WPPT) allowed signatories to choose whether to introduce domestic, regional or international exhaustion, as well as leaving open the option to leave the issue unregulated.[11] Additionally, the treaties required that affected copies should be lawfully sold, or ownership over them should otherwise be transferred.[12] The expression 'nothing in this Treaty shall affect' makes it clear that no further provisions of the treaty, including the three-step test,[13] create an obstacle for signatories to regulate on exhaustion.[14] In practice, this means that the freedom of lawful acquirers to dispose of property in a copy is absolutely in accordance with the law. Resales do not, per se, conflict with the normal exploitation of works, nor do they unreasonably prejudice the legitimate interests of the author.[15] The Agreed Statement attached to Article 6 of the WCT and Article 8 of the WPPT makes clear that '[a]s used in these Articles, the expressions "copies" and "original and copies", being subject to the right of distribution and the right of rental under the said Articles, refer exclusively to fixed copies that can be put into circulation as tangible objects'.

A partial and certainly not surprising conclusion might be drawn at this point. The more than a century-old history of the doctrine makes clear that when introduced it was designed to affect tangible copies of protected subject

---

[8]   Shubha Ghosh, *The Implementation of Exhaustion Policies – Lessons from National Experiences*, Issue Paper 40 (International Centre for Trade and Sustainable Development 2013) 3–4.

[9]   TRIPS Agreement Art 6.

[10]   See Art 6(2) of WCT and Art 8(2) of WPPT.

[11]   Reinbothe and von Lewinski (n 7) 85.

[12]   ibid at 86–87.

[13]   WCT Art 10; WPPT Art 16.

[14]   Reinbothe and von Lewinski (n 7) 87.

[15]   Silke von Lewinski, *International Copyright Law and Policy* (OUP 2008) 453, para. 17.65.

matter. This is well evidenced by the fact that the statutory endorsement of the doctrine stems from the analogue age. Further, the WIPO Internet Treaties (as well as their European implementation norm, the InfoSoc Directive) expressly refer to the tangible nature of copies that might be subject to lawful resale.

Problems associated with the doctrine of exhaustion have, however, grown concurrently with the emergence of digital technologies, in particular with development of the Internet. The question as to whether the doctrine of exhaustion is applicable to the online distribution of digital files has become pressing since shortly after protected subject matter (especially software, audio and audiovisual content, e-books) has been predominantly (or at least significantly) sold online. This dilemma challenges the pre-existing set of economic rights, freedom to provide services, free movement of goods, and the traditional business models of the copyright industry. Courts have faced legal disputes more often following the Millennium, and undoubtedly disputes surrounding the idea of digital exhaustion are far from over. Indeed, the digital redistribution of lawfully acquired copies of works can have a significant and direct effect on the fate of consumption of cultural goods in general.

Following these introductory remarks, the present chapter is separated into two main sections. First, it summarizes the key elements of the *UsedSoft* and the *ReDigi* rulings (Section 2). Second, it collects the pros and cons regarding possible introduction of a digital exhaustion doctrine. I argue that the traditional positivist approach is a dead end, whereas a constructive realistic approach can convincingly serve as the basis for application of the doctrine in the digital age (Section 3).

2.   *USEDSOFT* AND *REDIGI*

2.1   The *UsedSoft* Case

UsedSoft was the first major decision to shed light on digital exhaustion. In this case, Oracle sued UsedSoft for reselling used software licences. Eighty-five per cent of Oracle's clients downloaded the software from the Internet. The respective section of Oracle's End User Licence Agreement (EULA) provided as follows: '[w]ith the payment for services you receive, exclusively for your internal business purposes, for an unlimited period a non-exclusive non-transferable user right free of charge for everything that Oracle develops and makes available to you on the basis of this agreement'.[16] Oracle similarly offered so-called volume licences, under which 25 end-users had the

---

[16]   Case C-128/11 *UsedSoft GmbH v. Oracle International Corp.*, ECLI:EU:C: 2012:407, para. 23.

right to use the computer programs. UsedSoft acquired parts of the volume licences, where the original licensee had not installed the computer program in the available number offered by Oracle. UsedSoft directed its clients to Oracle's website to download the respective program from Oracle's web page. UsedSoft launched an Oracle special offer in October 2005. It offered up-to-date software licences for resale, where the maintenance agreement was also in force. The company testified to the validity of the original purchase of the licence key by a notarial certificate. Oracle initiated court proceedings to stop UsedSoft's special offer, and the case finally reached the Court of Justice of the European Union (CJEU).[17]

The CJEU provided a bright-line rule on exhaustion of the software distribution right. The Grand Chamber recalled that under Article 4(2) of the Software Directive the right of distribution exhausts if a copy of the computer program is sold within the European Economic Area by or under the authorization of the rightholder.[18] Consequently, the issue to decide was whether conclusion of a EULA and download of the computer program from Oracle's website led to a first sale of the program.[19] Since the Software Directive does not refer to Member States' law in terms of sale, the CJEU interpreted this term in an independent and uniform way.[20] The CJEU concluded that '[a]ccording to a commonly accepted definition, a "sale" is an agreement by which a person, in return for payment, transfers to another person his rights of ownership in an item of tangible or intangible property belonging to him'.[21] Further, the CJEU noted that downloading the computer program and concluding the EULA form an indivisible whole. Downloading a copy of the computer program (the source code) from the data carrier or from the Internet to the user's computer and concluding a EULA remain inseparable from the point of view of the acquirer. Moreover, Oracle's EULA allowed for permanent use of the software in exchange for payment of a fee that corresponded to the economic value of the computer program. As a result, the principle of exhaustion could not be evaded merely by renaming the contract a licence.[22]

The CJEU rejected the claim by Oracle and of the Commission that offering a computer program for download on a website represents making that program available to the public, as long as the contract leads to a sale, as in this case the right of distribution applies.[23] The CJEU also discussed whether the

---

17 On the facts of the case *see* ibid. at paras 20–26.
18 ibid at para 36.
19 ibid at para 38.
20 ibid at paras 39–41.
21 ibid at para 42.
22 ibid at paras 44–49.
23 ibid at paras 50–51.

doctrine of exhaustion applies to intangible copies of computer programs, or only to physical/tangible copies. The CJEU noted that the Software Directive refers to the first sale of a computer program without specifying the form of the copy sold. Therefore, the doctrine of exhaustion covers the sale of both tangible and intangible copies of computer programs, including works that were downloaded from the Internet.[24] Here, the CJEU argued that the Software Directive operates as a *lex specialis*. Therefore, interpretation of Article 4(2) should be independent of international and other EU norms.[25]

The CJEU used two policy arguments. First, it claimed that '[t]he on-line transmission method is the functional equivalent of the supply of a material medium'.[26] Second, limiting the doctrine of exhaustion to copies sold on a tangible medium 'would allow the copyright holder to control the resale of copies downloaded from the internet and to demand further remuneration on the occasion of each new sale, even though the first sale of the copy had already enabled the rightholder to obtain an appropriate remuneration'.[27]

The CJEU accepted Oracle's argument on the partial resale of volume licences. The judges held that volume licences are sold as a block by Oracle. An original purchaser who wants to get rid of parts of that must deactivate the remaining copies of the computer program as well. Finally, the CJEU provided a joint answer to the first and third questions. It concluded that the second (and any later) purchaser of the licence key should be deemed a lawful acquirer, who has the right to refer to the doctrine of exhaustion as a limitation on the right of distribution. Nevertheless, a reseller of a computer program must make the original copy installed on their computer unusable and the rightholder is allowed to ensure deactivation by all technical means.[28]

Taking into account all reformatory arguments of the CJEU, the result of the procedure for the preliminary ruling is most appropriately summarized by Sven Schonhofen as 'facts plus policy = results = doctrine'.[29] Christopher Stothers also noted that '[FAPL and UsedSoft] will become fundamental decisions on the interaction between intellectual property rights and the European single market in the online world, in the same way that Consten and Grundig

---

[24] ibid at paras 53–59.
[25] ibid at para 60.
[26] ibid at para 61.
[27] ibid at para 63.
[28] ibid at paras 69–71. The preliminary ruling was later confirmed almost in its entirety by the German Federal Supreme Court. See BGH 17.07.2013 (I ZR 129/08) 264–272.
[29] Sven Schonhofen, 'UsedSoft and its Aftermath: the Resale of Digital Content in the European Union' [2015] Wake Forest Journal of Business and Intellectual Property Law 277.

and Deutsche Grammophon set the current framework in relation to physical goods in the 1960s and 1970s'.[30]

2.2   *Capitol Records v. ReDigi*

In *ReDigi*, 'the world's first and only online marketplace for digital used music'[31] was sued shortly after launching its service in October 2011. ReDigi's original version allowed registered users to upload their legally purchased sound recordings to ReDigi's Cloud Locker via the company's Media Manager program. Media Manager detected the uploader's computer and built a list of eligible files, which were lawfully purchased on iTunes or from another ReDigi user. This feature technically guaranteed that 'pirate' copies of music files could not be entered into the system. Simultaneously with the uploading of the file to the Cloud Locker, the content was erased from the source computer. This process was generally termed as 'migration' or 'atomic transaction' of the file. The other function of Media Manager was to continuously double-check whether users retained any copy of the resold files on their computer's hard drive or on any portable devices synchronized with the computer. If Media Manager detected any file of that kind, users were warned to erase the copies. Users who failed to comply with the warning had their account terminated by the company.

After uploading the files to the Cloud Locker, users had two options: they either accessed their music for personal use or sold it to other users. In the latter situation, the files were stored in the same location in the Cloud Locker. However, the 'file pointers' of the content were transferred. Accordingly, the new purchaser could exclusively access the sound recording. Users paid with credits purchased from ReDigi for each resale. ReDigi earned a transaction fee on every sale: it retained 60 per cent of the price, while 20 per cent was allocated to the seller and 20 per cent was retained in an escrow fund for the respective artist.[32]

In its partial summary judgment in March 2013, the district court accepted Capitol's claims. First, the district court noted that sound recordings are undeniably protected under US copyright law and Capitol owned copyrights on several recordings that were transferred via ReDigi's system. Second, sound recordings are fixed in phonorecords and these constitute material objects in which sounds are fixed and 'from which the sounds can be perceived, repro-

---

30   Christopher Stothers, 'When is Copyright Exhausted by a Software Licence?': UsedSoft v. Oracle' [2012] EIPR 790.
31   *Capitol Records, LLC. v. ReDigi Inc.*, 934 F.Supp.2d 640 (2013) 644.
32   ibid at 644–646.

duced, or otherwise communicated, either directly or with the aid of a machine or device'.[33] Finally, sound recordings are reproduced every time they are fixed in a new material object.

Based on this logic, the district court stuck rigidly to the case law on P2P file-sharing,[34] noting that 'when a user downloads a digital music file or "digital sequence" to his "hard disk", the file is "reproduce[d]" on a new phonorecord within the meaning of the Copyright Act'.[35] Migration of the file was deemed irrelevant by Judge Sullivan, as moving a file from the user's computer to the ReDigi server was declared to represent reproduction.[36]

The court also noted that the electronic file transfer fell within the meaning of the right of distribution.[37] Thus, ReDigi's users infringed both the right of reproduction and the right of distribution when they used the company's service. The only chance to escape liability was to rely on the fair use or first sale doctrines. ReDigi failed to successfully rely on either defence,[38] yet I believe the fair use analysis of the district court was mistaken. Judge Sullivan found ReDigi directly liable for the reproduction and distribution of Capitol's sound recordings as it willingly allowed the upload of content to the Cloud Locker.[39] However, it was not ReDigi but users that uploaded, migrated, sold, purchased and finally downloaded files. If ReDigi was liable for these acts in any way, its liability should be based on secondary liability doctrines. The fair use doctrine only applies to direct infringements, that is, to acts by users, rather than by ReDigi. Elsewhere, the Second Circuit confirmed that 'space-shifting' digital content, that is, reproduction of sound recordings from computers to portable devices and vice versa, is fair use.[40] In that situation, it is users rather than service providers that create copies in the cloud.[41]

The district court further said that ReDigi's system was capable of interfering with the legitimate primary markets of the rightholders.[42] The Second Circuit could confirm that the doctrine of exhaustion is not bound by the three-step test and that resale of copies of works by lawful acquirers should be

---

[33] USCA §101.

[34] See especially London-Sire Records, Inc. v. John Doe 1, 542 F.Supp.2d 153 (2008).

[35] *Capitol v. ReDigi* (n 31) 649.

[36] ibid at 650.

[37] ibid at 651.

[38] ibid at 652–654.

[39] ibid at 657.

[40] *Recording Industry Association of America v. Diamond Multimedia Systems, Inc.*, 180 F.3d 1072 (1999).

[41] *Cartoon Network LP, LLLP, et al. v. CSC Holdings, Inc., et al.*, 536 F.3d 121 (2008) 132.

[42] *Capitol v. ReDigi* (n 31) 654.

accepted, even if it is against the primary economic interest of the rightholders. In sum, if the fair use doctrine applies to the upload and download of sound recordings by private users, the main argument of the district court would become pointless.

The district court's reasoning on the first sale doctrine is also contradictory. Judge Sullivan noted that ReDigi users must have produced a new phonorecord on the ReDigi server when they uploaded the files to their Cloud Locker. Consequently, users could not sell that 'particular' copy via ReDigi.[43]

There are some concerns that the district court's reasoning on 'particular' and 'that' copy are correct. Music files sold via iTunes are marked with a Persistent ID number that individually identifies the content. The migration of the file via Media Manager and the Cloud Locker therefore leads to duplication and transfer of an entirely identical file marked with the same ID number. From this perspective, content sold via ReDigi is exactly 'that particular copy'.

Finally, ReDigi tried to satisfy the court that Capitol's interpretation of the first sale doctrine would provide broader protection to the company than envisaged by Congress. The district court rejected this argument and stressed that it is up to Congress and not the courts to change the scope of the first sale doctrine.[44]

On 4 April 2016, shortly before the trial for damages was scheduled, the parties settled the remedy portion of the case. The district court endorsed a stipulated final judgment on 3 June 2016 and provided for stipulated damages and injunctive relief.[45] However, since the defendants reserved their right to appeal the summary judgment of the district court, the procedure continued to second instance. As of 31 January 2018, the appeals procedure is still pending.

3.   THE FATE OF DIGITAL EXHAUSTION

3.1   Traditional Positivism: a Dead End

Yves Gaubiac noted as early as 2000 that dematerialization of works and the advancement of online uses make it necessary to appropriately categorize dissemination of digital content via the Internet.[46]

---

[43]   ibid at 655.

[44]   'It is left to Congress, and not this Court, to deem them outmoded.' See ibid at 655–656.

[45]   *Capitol Records, LLC. et al. v. ReDigi, Inc.*, 2017 WL 2131544 (Brief for Plaintiffs-Appellees) 7.

[46]   Yves Gaubiac, 'The Exhaustion of Rights in the Analogue and Digital Environment' [2002] Copyright Bulletin 10.

Several leading international and regional copyright norms try to rectify this problem. The Agreed Statement to Article 6 of the WCT stressed that copies of protected works might be subject to distribution (and consequently exhaustion) if they are fixed and can be put into circulation as tangible objects. Recitals 28–29 of the InfoSoc Directive expressly exclude from the scope of the doctrine of exhaustion intangible copies, services (especially online services) and tangible copies produced with the help of services and online services. Similarly, the E-Commerce Directive categorizes online sale of goods as services,[47] and the VAT Directive also declared supply of services as 'any transaction which does not constitute a supply of goods',[48] whereas supply of goods means 'the transfer of the right to dispose of tangible property as owner'.[49]

Nevertheless, many have criticized the ambiguities of the InfoSoc Directive's language. AG Bot found that 'the distinction as to whether the sale takes place remotely or otherwise is irrelevant for the purposes of applying that rule'.[50] Andreas Wiebe took the view that uncertainties in this field stem from the fact that the doctrine of exhaustion and the goods-versus-services dichotomy serve different purposes in law.[51] He claimed that the emphasis in respect of goods and services was misplaced in EU copyright law. The WCT/WPPT excluded online sale of copies from the scope of the doctrine of exhaustion as no physical copy is provided by the seller to the purchaser. EU law generally (and unnecessarily) treated these transmissions as services. However, Wiebe argued that 'the assumption that online transmissions always involve a service is flawed'.[52] Accordingly, it is not the goods-versus-services dichotomy that leads to exclusion of the doctrine of exhaustion in cases of electronic supply of

---

[47]   Directive 2000/31/EC of the European Parliament and of the Council of 8 June 2000 on certain legal aspects of information society services, in particular electronic commerce, in the Internal Market, rec 18. On the concept of sale in the digital domain see further Chapter 11 in this volume by Havu.

[48]   Council Directive 2006/112/EC of 28 November 2006 on the common system of value added tax, Art 24(1).

[49]   ibid at Art 14(1). The ECJ also classified the supply of e-books as electronically supplied services. See Case C-479/13 *European Commission v. French Republic*, ECLI:EU:C:2015:141, para 36.

[50]   Case C-128/11, *Opinion of the Advocate General, Axel W. Bierbach, administrator of UsedSoft GmbH v Oracle International Corp.*, ECLI:EU:C:2012:234, para 76.

[51]   Andreas Wiebe, 'The Principle of Exhaustion in European Copyright Law and the Distinction between Digital Goods and Digital Services' [2009] Gewerblicher Rechtsschutz und Urheberrecht Internationaler Teil 115.

[52]   ibid.

content, but rather the fact that the seller is not obtaining control over a physical/tangible copy of the work in question.[53]

The present author takes the view that the goods-versus-services dichotomy leads to a stalemate for the doctrine of exhaustion, while the status quo relating to the doctrine of exhaustion is outdated in that it fails properly to reflect the economic, social and technological realities of our age.

3.2   Constructive Realism: the Economic, Social and Technological Effects of the Digital Exhaustion Doctrine

The idea of a digital exhaustion doctrine, coupled with the concept of virtual property, perfectly illustrates how twenty-first-century copyright law should keep pace with social realities. This is what ReDigi, UsedSoft and other digital second-hand marketplaces[54] noticed when they launched their novel business models.

The following paragraphs will show that a digital exhaustion doctrine is completely realistic: it reflects the technological, social and legal *Zeitgeist*, as well as providing for a more balanced treatment of competing interests between users and rightholders.

The digital exhaustion doctrine should also respect the interests of rightholders. Digital exhaustion should not make downstream commerce of digital copies easier than the first sale doctrine generally allows for resale of tangible copies. Technological measures, as well as legal guarantees, should be put in place to guarantee protection of rightholders.

3.2.1   Pros and cons
Many commentators routinely proclaim that digital copies represent an equivalent of the originals and that they can be illegally reused over and over again.[55] Therefore, downstream commerce of digital copies would decrease the need

---

53   ibid at 115–116.
54   This chapter uses the expression 'second-hand marketplaces' purely as a reference to those service providers where lawfully acquired copies of works and other subject matter are offered for resale/redistribution.
55   Herbert Zech, 'Vom Buch zur Cloud – Die Verkehrsfähigkeit digitaler Güter' [2013] ZGE/IPJ 394; Ole-Andreas Rognstad, 'Legally Flawed but Politically Sound? Digital Exhaustion of Copyright in Europe after UsedSoft' [2014] Oslo Law Review 17; Marco Figliomeni, 'The Song Remains the Same: Preserving the First Sale Doctrine for a Secondary Market of Digital Music' [2014] Canadian Journal of Law and Technology 232–233; Nils Rauer and Diana Ettig, 'Can e-books and Other Digital Works Be Resold?' [2015] Journal of Intellectual Property Law & Practice 715–716.

for originals and would harm the interests of rightholders and intermediaries.[56] This can negatively affect rightholders' incentives to innovate.[57]

Similarly, the White Paper 2016 of the Internet Policy Task Force concluded that acceptance of a digital exhaustion doctrine would have a negative effect on the primary markets of rightholders; it would exclude the possibility of rightholders to develop their own flexible business models and technologies; forward-and-delete technologies could not provide complete protection against potential infringements; and, finally, no convincing evidence exists on the potential advantages of introducing a digital exhaustion doctrine.[58] Equally, the reform proposals of the European Commission on the Digital Single Market were also silent on application of the doctrine of exhaustion to the digital environment.[59]

The reluctance of legislatures and academia to accept the practicality of a digital exhaustion doctrine can be refuted by several counter-arguments.

First, the WCT makes it clear that the three-step test should not affect resales covered by the doctrine of exhaustion. Consequently, the form of sale is not decisive. Indeed, should the form be relevant, rightholders would be able to unilaterally exclude others from downstream commerce and would gain an unfair monopolistic advantage in this field.

Second, downstream commerce is *per definitionem* 'cheaper' than traditional marketplaces. This has numerous advantages for purchasers who are willing to pay for content but who are unable to afford higher-priced originals.

Third, resale of digital goods could be useful for the whole economy as it would lead to reinvestment in the copyright ecosystem.[60] Physical data carriers (e.g., CDs and DVDs) have almost totally vanished from the marketplace and in their place is a constantly growing group of users who have subscribed

---

[56] Nakimuli Davis, 'Reselling Digital Music: Is There a Digital First Sale Doctrine?' [2009] Loyola of Los Angeles Entertainment Law Review 370–371.

[57] Wolfgang Kerber, 'Exhaustion of Digital Goods: An Economic Perspective' [2016] ZGE/IPJ 161.

[58] The Department of Commerce – Internet Policy Task Force, *White Paper on Remixes, First Sale and Statutory Damages – Copyright Policy, Creativity, and Innovation in the Digital Economy*, January 2016 (http://www.uspto.gov/sites/default/files/documents/copyrightwhitepaper.pdf) 51–66.

[59] *Communication from the Commission to the European Parliament, the Council, the European Economic and Social Committee and the Committee of the Regions – Towards a modern, more European copyright framework*, COM(2015) 626 final, Brussels, 9.12.2015.

[60] Theodore Serra, 'Rebalancing at Resale: ReDigi, Royalties, and the Digital Secondary Market' [2013] Boston University Law Review 1777; Sarah Reis, 'Toward a "Digital Transfer Doctrine"? The First Sale Doctrine in the Digital Era' [2015] Northwestern University Law Review 196.

to paid streaming services. It is still plausible that many consumers would continue purchasing digital copies if they were to acquire the right to later resell them, and so they could retrieve some of their investment in the copies. This is aptly demonstrated by Aaron Perzanowski and Chris Jay Hoofnagle's empirical "MediaShop study", which convincingly evidences that end-users are 'term optimists', in other words they 'expect a contract to contain more favourable terms than it actually provides'.[61] This finding evidences that consumers understand contracts on the acquisition of digital files (clicking on the 'Buy Now' button) as a sale of content.[62]

Fourth, the doctrine of exhaustion allows rightholders to be remunerated for distribution of their works only once, after the first sale of copies or originals. This logic has been followed in *UsedSoft*[63] and in *Tom Kabinet*.[64] There is no valid reason to limit the functioning of reward theory in the digital domain.

Fifth, the negative effects of downstream commerce might be eased by voluntary remuneration systems. Stretching the limits of the exhaustion doctrine this way represents the good faith of service providers and a more balanced treatment of rightholders' economic interests.

Sixth, George Orwell, when talking about the introduction of 'cheap' ('sixpenny') Penguin books in the first half of the twentieth century, noted that cheap books hurt trade as a whole.[65] The history of the book industry has evidenced that members of this industry can and do survive, even if the price of items decreases. It is more – rather than less – plausible that introduction of a digital exhaustion doctrine would not kill traditional forms in the copyright industry either. Indeed, businesses would respond with new business models.

Finally, Göbel has convincingly argued that the advance of lawful digital secondary markets would lead to an increase in prices of used copies and a decrease in prices of originals[66] since investing more money in market expansion, advertising, or strengthening company goodwill would undoubtedly raise retailers' expenses. On the other hand, rightholders could opt for a price reduc-

---

[61] Aaron Perzanowski and Chris Jay Hoofnagle, 'What We Buy When We Buy Now' [2017] University of Pennsylvania Law Review 321.

[62] ibid at 337.

[63] *UsedSoft v. Oracle* (2012) para 63.

[64] Court of Appeal of Amsterdam, *Nederlands Uitgeversverbond and Groep Algemene Uitgevers v. Tom Kabinet*, 200 154 572/01 SKG NL:GHAMS:2015:66, 20 January 2015, [2015] Computer Law Review International 48.

[65] Milton Friedman, *Price Theory* (4th edn, Transaction Publishers 2008) 349.

[66] Alexander Göbel, 'The Principle of Exhaustion and the Resale of Downloaded Software – the UsedSoft v. Oracle case [UsedSoft GmbH v. Oracle International Corporation, ECJ (Grand Chamber), Judgment of 3 July 2012, C-128/11]' [2012] European Law Reporter 228–229.

tion in order to make original copies more attractive or to use their existing goodwill to entice consumers back.

The second significant aversion of rightholders to a digital exhaustion doctrine is that it can lead to rearrangement of market powers as downstream commerce should necessarily be dominated by new, competing service providers. Not surprisingly, dominant content distributors, such as Amazon or Apple, have taken immediate steps to patent their own forward-and-delete technologies. Amazon also introduced Kindle Unlimited in 2014. Rightholders should be cautious, however, as monopolizing the market and preventing new actors from entering the market could potentially breach competition law.[67]

A third classic argument against the digital exhaustion doctrine is based on the premise that digital content can be reproduced infinitely at zero cost and without loss of quality.[68] Any such claim is implicitly based on the assumption that members of society are willing to copy protected materials for free.[69] There is nothing surprising in users reproducing works if they can. Indeed, humans have a deep-rooted desire for possession of culturally valuable goods – a desire that exists independently of the form of protected content.

However, differences between copying analogue or digital content have largely vanished since the spread of digital technologies. There is no greater danger in reproducing digital goods than analogue ones. Further, digital content also degrades over time, although markedly differently from analogue copies. The evolution of information technology inevitably makes file formats obsolete or files become useless for lack of proper software or hardware.[70] This type of evolution is surprisingly faster than degradation in the quality of tangible copies.

Therefore, the problem does not start here. It is more problematic when the costs of producing the original copies, that is, investment by rightholders,

---

[67] Mario Cistaro, 'The Interface Between the EU Copyright Law and the Fundamental Economic Freedoms of Trade and Competition in the Digital Single Market: From the FAPL Case to the Decision in UsedSoft' [2016] Queen Mary Journal of Intellectual Property 146–151.

[68] Victor F. Calaba, 'Quibbles 'n Bits: making a Digital First Sale Doctrine Feasible' [2002] Michigan Telecommunications and Technology Law Review 7–9, 29; Ellen Franziska Schulze, 'Resale of Digital Content Such as Music, Films or eBooks under European Law' [2014] EIPR 13; Wolfgang Kerber, 'Exhaustion of Digital Goods: An Economic Perspective' [2016] ZGE/IPJ 161.

[69] Tomasz Targosz, 'Exhaustion in Digital Products and the "Accidental" Impact on the Balance of Interests in Copyright Law'. In: Lionel Bently, Uma Suthersanen and Paul Torremans (eds), *Global Copyright – Three Hundred Years Since the Statute of Anne, from 1709 to Cyberspace* (Edgar Elgar Publishing 2010) 347.

[70] Aaron Perzanowski and Jason Schultz, *The End of Ownership – Personal Property in the Digital Economy* (The MIT Press 2016) 181.

cannot be refunded in the chain of commerce. However, this is not the case in a balanced digital exhaustion scenario.

Further, exhaustion covers all future resales of lawfully sold copies of protected subject matter. No internal limitation applies regarding the exact number of future resales of the same copy. A rightholder who fears the prospect of unlimited resales of copies of his works should apply a pricing strategy that reflects that very situation. Furthermore, it is not a prerequisite for applying the doctrine that resold copies should be inferior in quality to the originals. The fact that such inferiority was present in the analogue age should not automatically exclude digital copies from having a quality identical to the originals.

3.2.2   A balanced approach for a digital exhaustion doctrine

In 2001 Joseph Liu argued that the right to transfer a digital copy is a bundle of interests under digital copy ownership.[71] Liu correctly saw that an unlimited right to transfer digital copies would clearly undermine the incentives of rightholders.[72] He therefore named two distinct measures that are capable of balancing the different interests at stake. First, without using a precise expression, he noted that a fully automated forward-and-delete technology would be necessary for the functioning of the right to transfer a digital copy. This technology would prevent creation of a new permanent copy and, at the same time, it would guarantee that the original file is deleted simultaneously.[73] Second, this solution could also be backed by a bright-line fair use ruling.[74]

The present author maintains that a balanced digital exhaustion doctrine can be achieved by a combination of technological measures and legal guarantees.

The first technological measure should be a unique ID number that is inserted in the metadata of each digital file sold lawfully by the original seller. Only digital files tagged with a unique ID number would be eligible for resale. The privilege of tagging files should be reserved to rightholders and authorized retailers. This would guarantee that content is sold and acquired only through reliable sources.

The second measure should involve application of a workable forward-and-delete technology that is capable of managing unique ID numbers; to validate that a given file is not an illegal copy of protected subject matter; to control transfer of files between parties; and to guarantee that no copies are retained by the reseller.

---

[71]   Joseph P. Liu, 'Owning Digital Copies: Copyright Law and the Incidents of Copy Ownership' [2001] William and Mary Law Review 1349–1360.

[72]   ibid at 1351 and 1355–1356.

[73]   ibid at 1353.

[74]   ibid at 1358–1359.

Alternatively, blockchain technology could be used to facilitate conclusion of smart contracts for the sale of digital goods. The most significant advantage of blockchain is that it can record all data relating to a particular transaction in chronological order and all this data is stored and periodically synchronized on every computer that forms part of the network.[75] Such smart contracts guarantee that all transactions are valid and that former transactions cannot be invalidated.[76]

The combination of a unique ID number and forward-and-delete or blockchain technologies could guarantee that end-users can acquire and resell content that was first lawfully marketed by the rightholder or any authorized retailers and that files can be effectively traced in downstream commerce. These could effectively guarantee that copies of works are resold in a visible and controlled way that forecloses unlawful duplication of content.

Workable forward-and-delete technologies are available on the market and numerous service providers sell media with unique ID numbers. Likewise, blockchain is already used, for example, by OpenBazaar to resell tangible goods over the Internet. No technological obstacles exclude extension of the use of smart contracts to resale of digital files.

If digital second-hand markets are legalized, we could immediately be swamped by millions of digital files. However, it is unimaginable that this would generally destroy original marketplaces. First, it is plausible that only a limited number of works will be offered for sale via these systems as end-users would most probably upload only their unused files and would keep the rest of their content for future enjoyment. Second, any broadening of the supply side would require lawful acquisition of further original copies by end-users. If no one purchases new files, then there would be nothing to resell either. Third, a significant number of end-users would continue to acquire cultural goods from original dealers rather than from downstream commerce as these services will be far less viral than well-known brands such as iTunes or Amazon. Fourth, this model would not open the floodgates to unauthorized copies downloaded from illegal services. It would similarly be impossible for end-users to resell content ripped from their lawfully purchased CDs or DVDs as the files stored on these data carriers have never been assigned a unique ID number. Finally, some might question why any rightholder or intermediary would tag content sold by them with a unique ID number since that would allow for later resale of those files. Doing so would be absolutely logical for

---

[75] Aaron Wright and Primavera De Filippi, 'Decentralized Blockchain Technology and the Rise of Lex Cryptographia' (manuscript, available at SSRN: https://ssrn.com/abstract=2580664) 6–7.

[76] ibid at 7.

at least two reasons. First, this way the unique ID number would work as electronic rights management information. Any attempt to remove or alter the unique ID number would lead to legal remedies under Article 12 of the WCT. Second, nothing prevents rightholders/intermediaries from launching their own digital second-hand markets. If societal demand exists for a given service (here, resale of used digital files), it is still a better option to remain in the whirlwind, rather than staying out of the business.

If a lawful user intends to sell a copy on digital marketplaces then the operator of the market should effectively guarantee that the digital file is removed from the seller's computer and any connected devices. The seller is required to erase all permanent copies they created on external data carriers (including, but not limited to external hard drives, memory sticks, mp3 players or mobile phones). If the latter devices are used in offline mode, it is hard to prove the existence of unauthorized copies. Most probably this situation lasts only for a limited period. If the user synchronizes the device with a computer connected to the digital marketplace, the forward-and-delete technology applied by the operator's software should detect the unauthorized copy. In such a case the operator should notify the user to expeditiously remove the given copy. If the end-user fails to comply with the notice, the operator should be entitled to block or at least limit access to the end-user's account.

The digital exhaustion doctrine should be regulated by national or international norms as well. These norms should explicitly refer to the transferability of intangible copies of protected subject matter; the requirement of lawful acquisition of the given copy; and the obligation of the reseller to erase a copy sold via digital marketplaces.[77]

The above system balances the interests of rightholders and end-users in downstream commerce. End-users, like property owners, are allowed to control the fate of the copies they acquire, and their private sphere is not unreasonably intruded on. In contrast, recurring but ad hoc control of synchronized data carriers is a necessary way of protecting the interests of rightholders. Similarly, a balanced approach to the digital exhaustion doctrine is cost-effective and restricts an influx of pirated copies to downstream commerce.[78]

---

[77]   Targosz (n 69) 351.
[78]   Calaba (n 68) 26–27.

6. Extended collective licensing and online distribution – prospects for extending the Nordic solution to the digital realm

Anette Alén-Savikko and Tone Knapstad

1. INTRODUCTION

This chapter addresses whether the Nordic extended collective licensing (ECL) scheme might resolve some of the challenges arising from online distribution, such as mass digitization and fragmentation of rights. Indeed, online distribution has created new possibilities for making works available in digital format as well as storing them. However, rights clearance can prove complicated, while works must often be used on a mass scale. This chapter provides an overview of ECL and analyses the opportunities and drawbacks of ECL as a solution for the digital realm, while also presenting some current use cases. The focus is on online distribution in particular, as opposed to digital media in general. However, ECL is not without its problems in terms of EU law and the international framework for copyright, or the cross-border nature of the online environment. Moreover, ECL has been developed in the specific socio-cultural environment in the Nordic countries.

Not limited to a Nordic perspective, ECL appears as a flexible and appealing solution that might solve some of the problems copyright is currently facing, especially in terms of mass licensing and digitization, including online uses. Simultaneously, however, ECL must be viewed in light of important preconditions at both the EU and international level.[1] Historically, ECL was developed in the Nordic countries as a solution to copyright mass licensing in the

---

[1]   Felix Trumpke, 'The Extended Collective License – A Matter of Exclusivity?' (2012) 3 NIR 264, 294; Thomas Riis and Jens Schovsbo, 'Extended Collective Licenses and the Nordic Experience: It's a Hybrid but is it a Volvo or a Lemon?' (2010) 33 Colum. J.L. & Arts 471, 497.

context of broadcasting, while, subsequently, it has been put to use in various situations of mass use. Regarding terminology, instead of a uniform 'Nordic model', a common core exists: ECL essentially means that by force of law all works in a particular area are covered by a freely negotiated licence between a representative organization and a user. The core thereby includes both the conditions for representation and the effect on outsiders or non-members.[2]

Basically, ECL provisions make up a scheme where a user and a rightholder organization agree on the mass use of all works in a given field for a specific purpose on specified terms, while the organization is also responsible for distributing remuneration. As to requirements concerning collective management organization (CMO), the Nordic countries have opted for somewhat differing solutions over the years.[3] Currently, in Finland, the organization in question must be approved by the Ministry of Education and Culture pursuant to section 26(1) of the Finnish Copyright Act (FCA). The organization must represent numerous authors in a relevant field, but the law also deems the organization in question a representative of other authors in the given field (non-members, outsiders) with regard to a specific licence. However, in specific ECL use cases, the law may allow outsiders the right of refusal, while they are entitled to personal compensation even in cases where the members are not (§ 26(5) FCA).

At first glance, the online environment, digitization, and digital distribution appear to be potentially fertile ground for ECL since use cases are often complicated and of a mass nature, involving numerous rightholders and fragmentation of rights. Technological development and new business models, such as those taking advantage of online distribution, are apt to create tension between rightholders, users and other stakeholders. Indeed, digital uses may be disruptive in nature but nonetheless involve legitimate public interest. Thus, not only must workable solutions be found, but also solutions which are balanced and comply with existing legal frameworks. In order to discuss and analyse the potential of ECL as a solution for the digital realm, first, two Finnish use

---

[2]   Ole-Andreas Rognstad, 'Avtalelisens som nordisk løsningsmodell – Noen refleksjoner, særlig knyttet til avtalelisensens legitimitet i utlandet' (2012) 6 NIR 620, 621, 623; Jan Rosén, 'Den nordiska avtalslicensen – karaktäristika, kvaliteter och tillkortakommanden Extended Collective License' (2017) 6 NIR 242. For the history of ECL, Gunnar Karnell, 'Avtalslicenskonstruktionen, principiella och praktiska frågor' (1981) 4 NIR 255, 255–6; Astri M. Lund, 'The Nordic Extended Collective Licence – Particular Aspects' (2017) 6 NIR 553; also Riis and Schovsbo (n 1) 495; also Johan Axhamn and Lucie Guibault, 'Cross-border extended collective licensing: a solution to online dissemination of Europe's cultural heritage?' (Final report prepared for EuropeanaConnect. Amsterdam, the Netherlands 2012) 25–44, 70, https://www.ivir.nl/publicaties/download/292 (accessed 10 February 2018).
[3]   Rognstad (n 2) 621–30.

cases are discussed: the first involves ECL provisions for media archives; the second concerns network personal video recorder (NPVR) services. Then, the findings are analysed inductively with a view to drawing conclusions for the use of ECL in digital distribution on a general level. Moreover, both EU and international preconditions are discussed as important factors framing the use of ECL. Finally, some conclusions are drawn on the possibilities and problems related to the promise of ECL for digital distribution, in particular in the online environment.

2.   RECENT USE CASES FROM FINLAND

To digitize and distribute works often involves exclusive rights to reproduce and to communicate a work to the public. These are acts which require consent of the copyright holder. When use is on a mass scale, this would mean numerous rightholders and high transaction costs. Furthermore, individual rightholders might be difficult to reach or they might create a hold-up problem in declining to license their work. For example, broadcasts comprise several types of protected subject matter with various rightholders and collecting societies. Indeed, this was the original field of application for ECL in the Nordic countries. However, ECL has found new ground in the digital realm as well. For example, the FCA has been amended over the last couple of years in order to facilitate digital distribution of copyright subject matter in two distinct situations. These are discussed in more detail below: media archives and network video recording services. Both situations have been resolved by means of ECL provisions.

In late 2013, Section 25g of the Copyright Act on reuse of media content was updated and extended in scope: previously limited to retransmission of archived television programmes, the provision came to include communication to the public in general, also in the online environment, while radio, newspapers and periodicals were included as well.[4] Thereby, by virtue of ECL, broadcasters may reproduce and distribute their archived television or radio programmes and works included therein. The provisions cover works included in programmes produced or commissioned by the broadcaster in question and transmitted prior to the beginning of 2002. Publishers enjoy similar opportunities provided the works were included in a newspaper or periodical before 1999. However, authors have the possibility to opt out, in which case their works cannot be used. The new provisions aim to enable re-utilization of archives by the initial broadcasters and publishers themselves where con-

---

[4]   Anette Alén-Savikko, 'New Provisions on Extended Collective Licence for Archives' (2014) 2 IRIS 17.

tracting on an individual basis would be impossible or require disproportionate investment.[5] Other Nordic countries had similar provisions for broadcasters. In Denmark, the digitization of the public service broadcaster's archives, among other cultural heritage, also paved the way for a general ECL provision, discussed in more detail below. The concept refers to the possibility to render any agreement between users and relevant collecting societies a licence with extended effect.[6]

In 2014, core industry stakeholders – that is, major national broadcasters, teleoperators and collecting societies – negotiated a solution to legislate on NPVR services in Finland. A government bill (HE 181/2014 vp) forwarding that solution was passed the same year and new provisions were introduced in the form of section 25l of the Copyright Act. The provisions allow providers of online recording services, by virtue of ECL, to reproduce works within programmes and make them available to the public. However, since authors may have assigned the relevant rights to broadcasters, the provisions are non-applicable in such cases (§ 25l(2)). Furthermore, where producers have acquired relevant rights, they may decline use (§ 25l(3)).[7] The Finnish model relies on ECL combined with direct contracting: ECL covers those rights which are not licensed by broadcasters in granting permission for their own and acquired rights, alongside agreeing on practical execution of the services. Broadcasters also need to license their signal, which is protected by a related right. ECL was chosen since direct contracting was deemed basically impossible, while mere collective licensing would have left 'holes' in rights clearance.[8] After section 25l of the Copyright Act entered into force, the Ministry of Education and Culture approved four rightholder organizations, namely

---

[5] Government, *Government bill on Acts amending the Copyright Act and on the use of orphan works* (HE 73/2013 vp); Education and Culture Committee, *Report on the Government bill on Acts amending the Copyright Act and on the use of orphan works* (SiVM 6/2013 vp); Copyright Commission, *Report of the Copyright Commission – Solutions to challenges of the digital age* (Reports of the Ministry of Education and Culture 2012:2).

[6] Riis and Schovsbo (n 1) 476–7.

[7] For an overall analysis, see Anette Alén-Savikko, 'Copyright-proof Network-based Video Recording Services? An Analysis of the Finnish Solution' (2016) 23 Javnost – The Public 204. Also Jorma Waldén, 'The Development of the Copyright Protection in Finland since 2015' (2017) 6 NIR 521, 522; Government, *Government bill on Act amending to the Copyright Act* (HE 181/2014 vp); Education and Culture Committee, *Report on the Government bill on Act amending to the Copyright Act* (SiVM 26/2014 vp). NPVR services refer to digital online services that allow recording of, eg, TV. They may be provided via open internet or using Internet Protocol television (IPTV).

[8] Government (n 7); Education and Culture Committee (n 7). Also Copyright Commission (n 5).

Kopiosto, Teosto, Tuotos and Gramex,[9] to license NPVR use, while Kopiosto acts as a one-stop-shop for practical reasons. The terms apply to all domestic free-to-air TV channels on the antenna network so as to allow viewing for a maximum of two years against a graded fee. Service providers must also ensure that no other use is possible and report monthly to Kopiosto.[10]

With regard to EU law, at the time of drafting the Finnish solution to NPVR services, some frameworks are noteworthy. For its part, the private copying exception in Article 5(2)(b) of the InfoSoc Directive[11] had been noted as excluding commercial activities by third parties.[12] Moreover, in *ITV Broadcasting et al*, the Court of Justice of the European Union (CJEU) found that 'communication to the public' within the meaning of the InfoSoc Directive also covered third-party streamed retransmission of works included in a terrestrial television broadcast in a situation where subscribers are within the area of reception of the original broadcast. With regard to multiple uses of a work, the intention of the EU legislature was to safeguard authorization for each transmission using a specific technical means.[13] Subsequently, developments in case law have occurred at the EU level. In *VCAST*, the CJEU concluded that Article 5(2)(b) of the InfoSoc Directive prohibits national law 'which permits a commercial undertaking to provide private individuals with a cloud service for the remote recording of private copies of works protected by copyright, by means of a computer system, by actively involving itself in the recording, without the right holder's consent'.[14] Determining factors thus seem to be the active role of the service provider in facilitating the activity.

---

[9] Kopiosto represents authors and publishers and also licenses retransmission of TV channels. Teosto represents composers and lyricists, and Tuotos and Gramex AV and music producers respectively. The organizations carry mandates and oversee transferred rights, whereas representation of foreign rightholders occurs via reciprocal arrangements. Interestingly, Tuotos and Kopiosto had a dispute over sharing funds collected for domestic productions. The Market Court of Finland found it had no competence in the matter, which was not based on the Copyright Act but rather was linked to the law of property or obligations or contract law (MAO:149/17).

[10] Kopiosto, 'TV-ohjelmien verkkotallennuspalvelut', http://www.kopiosto .fi/kopiosto/teosten_kayttoluvat/Verkkotallennuspalvelut/fi_FI/Tv_ohjelmien _verkkotallennuspalvelu/ (accessed 1 February 2018).

[11] Directive 2001/29/EC on the harmonisation of certain aspects of copyright and related rights in the information society (InfoSoc Directive) [2001] OJ L 167/10.

[12] António Vitorino, 'Recommendations Resulting from the Mediation on Private Copying and Reprography Levy' (31 January 2013) 5, http://ec.europa.eu/internal _market/copyright/docs/levy_reform/130131_levies-vitorino-recommendations_en .pdf (accessed 1 February 2018).

[13] Case C-607/11 *ITV Broadcasting et al v TV Catch Up Ltd* [2013] EU:C:2013: 147, paras 19, 24–6.

[14] Case C-265/16 *VCAST Limited v RTI SpA* [2017] EU:C:2017:913.

Furthermore, while the private copying exception covers only reproduction for private use, the architecture of services may also amount to distribution. In Finland, views were expressed, by teleoperators in particular, on the need to include not only reproduction but also the act of communication to the public in the NPVR provisions.[15]

3.   EU AND INTERNATIONAL LEGAL FRAMEWORK

3.1   EU Developments Around ECL

Although EU legislation on copyright does not set up specific ECL rules, several examples from the EU acknowledge the existence and use of ECL in the Member States. Already in the Satellite and Cable Directive,[16] the EU established the possibility of using ECL for broadcasting rights. According to Article 3(2) of that Directive, under certain circumstances national law may provide an extension of a collective agreement to 'right holders of the same category who are not represented by the collecting society'. Further, Article 9(1) stipulates that only CMOs may authorize cable retransmission, while a CMO managing the same category of rights 'shall be deemed to be mandated' also to manage cable retransmission rights of non-members (Article 9(2)). The aim of these provisions has been to prevent hold-up problems and to establish mandatory collective management for retransmission, which is difficult to manage individually. The traditional reasoning in the Nordic countries, however, was based on transaction costs.[17] Furthermore, a type of nonchalance towards ECL solutions in the Member States can be found in the preambles to

---

[15]   Government (n 7) 44. Indeed, § 25l(1) is formulated as follows: 'A provider of online recording services may make a copy of a work included in a programme transmitted on the television by virtue of extended collective licence, in compliance with section 26, to be used for making available to the public ...'. Unofficial translation by the Ministry of Education and Culture, https://www.finlex.fi/fi/laki/kaannokset/1961/en19610404.pdf (accessed 14 August 2018).

[16]   Directive 93/83/EEC on the coordination of certain rules concerning copyright and rights related to copyright applicable to satellite broadcasting and cable retransmission (Satellite and Cable Directive) [1993] OJ L 248/15. The Satellite and Cable Directive will be complemented by a new Regulation currently at the proposal stage.

[17]   Riis and Schovsbo (n 1) 478; Rognstad (n 2) 624. Also Johan Axhamn, 'The Consistency of the Nordic Extended Collective Licencing Model with International Copyright Conventions and EU Copyright Norms' (2017) 6 NIR 563, 576–7.

the InfoSoc Directive, the Collective Management Directive and the Orphan Works Directive.[18]

The EU has kept ECL on its legislative agenda, and although a positive attitude has been expressed towards such a solution, it has been clear that the Commission would not unconditionally accept ECL.[19] In particular, protection of authors' rights and avoiding unreasonable prejudice to their commercial interests has been emphasized.[20] As part of the Digital Single Market (DSM) strategy, in 2015 the Commission also set out to modernize the EU copyright rules to fit the digital age as one of the objectives. To carry out the DSM strategy, several new legislative actions have been set in motion. Two new legislative proposals make use of an extension effect. First, the proposed Broadcasting Regulation[21] complements the existing Satellite and Cable Directive and aims to increase cross-border access to TV and radio programmes by simplifying copyright clearance.[22] Article 3 stipulates that retransmission rights can only be exercised by CMOs as they 'shall be deemed to be mandated to manage the right on behalf of' rightholders who have not transferred the management rights. The wording indicates a mandatory collective management solution. Second, Article 7 of the proposed DSM Directive[23] entails a more general obligation for the Member States to provide an extension effect or presumption for certain agreements between CMOs and cultural heritage institutions.

---

[18] InfoSoc Directive, preamble (18); Directive 2014/26/EU on collective management of copyright and related rights and multi-territorial licensing of rights in musical works for online use in the internal market [2014] OJ L 84/72, preamble (12); Directive 2012/28/EU on certain permitted uses of orphan works [2012] OJ L 299/5, preamble (24). Then again, the absence of 'prejudice' in specific legal instruments in the field of copyright does not mean that ECL would be categorically exempted from EU law in general (eg, discrimination). Riis and Schovsbo (n 1) 478–9; Axhamn (n 17) 575–6.

[19] Riis and Schovsbo (n 1) 479 with further references.

[20] Commission, 'Creative Content in a European Digital Single Market: Challenges for the Future' (Reflection Document) (22 October 2009) 14, http://ec.europa.eu/internal_market/consultations/docs/2009/content_online/reflection_paper%20web_en.pdf (accessed 11 February 2018).

[21] Commission, 'Proposal for a Regulation laying down rules on the exercise of copyright and related rights applicable to certain online transmissions of broadcasting organisations and retransmissions of television and radio programmes' COM(2016) 594 final.

[22] Commission, 'Digital Single Market – Proposal for a Regulation laying down rules on the exercise of copyright and related rights applicable to certain online transmissions of broadcasting organisations and retransmissions' (14 September 2016) https://ec.europa.eu/digital-single-market/en/news/proposal-regulation-laying-down-rules-exercise-copyright-and-related-rights-applicable-certain (accessed 11 February 2018).

[23] Commission, 'Proposal for a Copyright in the Digital Single Market Directive' COM(2016) 539 final.

Deliberations on the Directive were still in progress in the autumn of 2017, when a new chapter (1a) 'to facilitate collective licensing' was introduced.[24] This would establish ECL as one of the European-wide models for streamlined collective licensing.[25] Moreover, at the national level and outside the Nordic EU Member States, several others have adopted various forms of ECL for specific uses of mass-communication. For example, both Poland and Germany have adopted ECL solutions for out-of-commerce works and most recently the UK implemented ECL into their Copyright Act.[26]

The CJEU decision in *Soulier and Doke*[27] discusses the legitimacy of national legislation that grants an approved collecting society the right to authorize digital reproduction and communication of works to the public to which the authors or their successors have not objected. An amendment to the French law on intellectual property enabled digitization of out-of-print books published in France before 1 January 2001, provided they were no longer com-mercially distributed by a publisher or currently published in print or digital form.[28] The collecting society SOFIA was granted the right to authorize use of the books six months after they were added to a database. The law allowed the authors or their successors to object before use began, but within six months of registration in the database.[29] The evaluation focused on Articles 2(a) and 3(1) of the InfoSoc Directive, according to which Member States must provide authors with the exclusive right to authorize or prohibit reproduction and communication to a new public. The Court stressed that the provisions are pre-ventive in nature, and that any act by a third party requires prior consent.[30] This prompted the question how the author's consent can be given. Unlike Advocate General (AG) Wathelet in his Opinion, the Court did not require consent to be explicit, therefore also allowing tacit consent in line with previous EU case

---

[24] Council of the European Union, 'Proposal for a Directive of the European Parliament and of the Council on copyright in the Digital Single Market – Consolidated Presidency compromise proposal' (30 October 2017) 13842/17. Also Rán Tryggvadottir, 'The European Union's Proposed Measures to Improve Licensing Practices and Ensure Wider Access to Content in Cultural Heritage Institutions and their Compatibility with the Nordic ECL System' (2017) 6 NIR 615.

[25] Jukka Liedes and Tone Knapstad, 'Extended Collective Licences and Other Extension-Based Solutions Outside of the Nordic Countries' (2017) 6 NIR 591.

[26] Polish Act on Copyright and Neighbouring Rights, Act No. 83 (1994), Art 35; Law concerning the use of orphan and out of commerce works and a further amendment of the Copyright Law of Germany (UrhGuaÄndG) (2013) BGBI. I.S. 3728 (nr 59), Art 13(d); Copyright, Designs and Patents Act of the UK, (1988) c. 48, s. 116B.

[27] Case C-301/15 *Marc Soulier and Sara Doke v Premier ministre and Ministre de la Culture et de la Communication (Soulier and Doke)* [2016] EU:C:2016:878.

[28] ibid, para 17.

[29] ibid, para 24.

[30] ibid, para 33.

law.[31] For implicit consent not to be purely hypothetical and deprive the effect of the principle of author's prior consent, authors must actually be informed of the intended use of their works and the means to prohibit use if they so desire.[32] The Court pointed out that French legislation does not ensure that each author is actually and individually informed of the envisaged use so that the authors' wish to redistribute out-of-commerce works might rightly be questioned.[33] The interpretation of consent in AG Wathelet's Opinion would be problematic for ECL regardless of whether the rightholder is a member of the contracting CMO or not. Accordingly, *Soulier and Doke* might have challenged the legitimacy of the Nordic countries' ECL mechanism, or indeed the more recent ECL solutions adopted in EU Member States.[34] Although potentially interfering with the use of ECL, it would seem more reasonable to read the judgment as stressing protection of authors and the need to inform them effectively and individually of use of their works.[35] However, the ruling sends a strong signal that the European judiciary is a guardian of the conditions for exercising the exclusive right enshrined in the InfoSoc Directive.[36]

Another topical issue in the EU that has again brought up discussion on ECL is the Europeana project. This is a digital platform intended to function as a common access point for Europe's cultural heritage. The digitization and dissemination of larger parts of collections by European cultural institutions was difficult due to transaction costs relating to clearance of copyright and related rights.[37] Both multi-territory licensing and the ECL model were thoroughly discussed as solutions for mass digitization.

---

[31] *Soulier and Doke* (n 27) Opinion of AG Wathelet EU:C:2016:536, paras 38–9; *cf* Soulier and Doke, paras 35–6.

[32] *Soulier and Doke* (n 27) paras 37–9.

[33] ibid, para 43.

[34] Caterina Sganga, 'The Eloquent Silence of Soulier and Doke and its Critical Implications for EU Copyright Law' (2017) 12 JIPLP 321, 328. On the case, see also Axhamn (n 17) 577–9.

[35] In this direction, eg, Axel Paul Ringelhann and Marc Mimler, 'Digital Exploitation of Out-of-print Books and Copyright Law: French Licensing Mechanism for Out-of-print Books under CJEU Scrutiny' (2017) 39 EIPR 190, 193; Florence-Marie Pirou, 'The Ruling of the Court of Justice in Soulier Revisited' Kluwer Copyright Blog (2 October 2017) http://copyrightblog.kluweriplaw.com/2017/10/02/ruling-court -justice-soulier-revisited/ (accessed 11 February 2018).

[36] Pirou (n 35).

[37] Axhamn and Guibault (n 2) 2–3; Tryggvadottir (n 24).

3.2   International Issues

While the use of ECL is well established and the concept is viewed as a good solution in the Nordic countries, extended use of ECL might raise issues with the international framework for copyright. In this regard, the Berne Convention[38] and the TRIPS Agreement[39] in particular set international standards for evaluating ECL. Indeed, ECL provisions need to take into consideration exclusivity, the principle of national treatment and the ban on formalities, as well as the three-step test to comply with these international treaties.

With regard to exclusivity, there are sporadic debates relating to compliance of ECL with the rights stipulated in the Berne Convention. The Convention – the cornerstone of international harmonization of legal protection within the field of copyright – limits its signatories' leeway to restrict the rights of authors. Importantly, the Convention provides authors with the exclusive right to authorize reproduction of their works.[40] ECL as a default rule might become problematic in light of the Convention since ECL also directly impacts the exclusive rights of outsiders who are not members of the CMO in question.[41] Riis and Schovsbo argue that the possibility of opting out of the ECL agreement is central to preserving the exclusive nature of copyright under the Berne Convention. However, they also stress that lack of an opt-out possibility in some cases may solve hold-up problems, since one single rightholder cannot block use.[42] For example, the proposal for the Finnish NPVR provisions originally contained no right of refusal. However, during the legislative process, this right was deemed necessary. The reasoning behind that view was the risk of foreign film producers wanting to challenge the solution in the absence of a refusal right. In the eventual ECL provisions, the right to refuse use was channelled to be exercised via the producer.[43]

Although an opt-out mechanism is helpful, the ECL system itself does not ensure that rightholders are informed that their works are used under an ECL agreement and that they are entitled to remuneration.[44] This aspect makes accordance with the Berne Convention somewhat more uncertain, especially

---

[38]   Berne Convention for the Protection of Literary and Artistic Works, 9 September 1886.

[39]   Agreement on Trade-Related Aspects of Intellectual Property Rights, 15 April 1994 (TRIPS Agreement).

[40]   Berne Convention, Art 9(1).

[41]   Trumpke (n 1) 278–9.

[42]   Riis and Schovsbo (n 1) 482. Also Trumpke (n 1) 279.

[43]   Education and Culture Committee (n 5); Alén-Savikko (n 7) 208.

[44]   Riis and Schovsbo (n 1) 482–3. On different approaches in the Nordic countries, Lund (n 2) 556.

if the CMO in question does not have internal rules for notification, which in turn transfers the risk and responsibility to rightholders who are not members of a CMO. Even if they opt out, rightholders regain exclusivity from that point on and in the future, but not retrospectively.[45] However, non-members have the right to equal treatment and individual remuneration under the agreement.[46] The principle of national treatment enshrined in Article 5(1) of the Berne Convention also means that foreign authors enjoy the same rights as domestic authors both by national laws and under the rights granted by the Convention. Despite equal treatment of members and non-members under the ECL provisions, it may be difficult for foreign rightholders in practice to find out that their works are being exploited. Most members of a CMO are nationals of the country where it operates, while foreign rightholders on the whole are not members. Since undistributed remuneration is allocated to the organization and used for the collective benefit of its members, national rightholders are arguably treated more favourably.[47] Moreover, undistributed remuneration is also used for social purposes to facilitate development of the organization and of society as a whole.[48] Riis and Schovsbo raise the same concerns, arguing this should influence the institutional design of the ECL scheme, particularly taking into consideration the interest of rightholders to ensure that they 'receive remuneration on non-discriminatory terms and furthermore that they have an equal opportunity to exercise their rights'.[49]

Compliance of the ECL scheme with the Berne Convention – in that the exercise of copyright must not be subject to any formality (Article 5(2)) – might also be questioned since the opt-out demands action from the rightholder. However, rightholders covered by ECL agreements still clearly exercise their rights even when they do not opt out because the CMO in these cases has taken over the task of enforcing their copyright covered by the agreement with an associated claim against the CMO (as opposed to the user). Thus, it can be argued that the 'formality' in the ECL rules is of a different nature from those targeted in the Berne Convention.[50] On the other hand, exercise of an exclusive right entails being able to prohibit use of a copyrighted work,

---

[45]   Trumpke (n 1) 280.

[46]   ibid, 275, 278 with further references; Felix Trumpke, 'Effects and Potential of Extended Collective License Systems' in Kung-Chung Liu and Reto Hilty (eds), *Remuneration of Copyright Owners* (Springer 2017) 89; Riis and Schovsbo (n 1) 475–6, 482–3.

[47]   Zijian Zhang, 'Transplantation of an Extended Collective Licensing System – Lessons from Denmark' (2016) 47 IIC 640, 664; Axhamn (n 17) 567–8.

[48]   Zhang (n 47) 664.

[49]   Riis and Schovsbo (n 1) 491–2.

[50]   ibid, 483.

which rightholders in the case of ECL must opt out of to prohibit. Overall, it is unclear whether this formal prerequisite according to law violates Article 5 of the Berne Convention.[51]

Moreover, whether ECL fulfils the three-step test for limitations and exceptions set out in Article 9(2) of the Berne Convention might be called into question. For its part, Article 13 of the TRIPS Agreement has taken the test a step further, as it now applies to all economic rights guaranteed by TRIPS as minimum standards.[52] Thereby, limitations must be limited to 'certain special cases' and they cannot 'conflict with a normal exploitation of the work' nor can they 'unreasonably prejudice the legitimate interests of the author'. At the EU level, Article 5(5) of the InfoSoc Directive also contains a version of the test: compared to the original test, the Directive refers to application instead of legislation and the rightholder instead of the author. Indeed, the test has faced 'mutation', to use Geiger's term, when integrated into various instruments.[53] To be submitted to the test, there needs to be a limitation or exception. The nature of ECLs as such, and with it the applicability of the three-step test, is not clear. When an opt-out is possible, exclusivity is arguably not limited but economic rights may be enforced on behalf of rightholders by the CMO.[54] Then again, as Trumpke notes, the test might apply to every substantial restriction potentially harmful to the economic income of the rightholder. Moreover, foreign, outsider rightholders might outnumber rightholders who are members of the CMO when national CMOs license a world repertoire, which might lead to a limiting nature.[55] In case ECL rules do not offer an opt-out solution, it is more likely that these rules are seen as limitations or exceptions, with the consequence that the three-step test is applicable – even if the opt-out possibility were rather theoretical.[56] Indeed, with regard to the character of ECL, the FCA originally included ECL provisions under the heading of exceptions and limitations. Moreover, legal doctrine also acknowledged such a nature of ECL due

---

[51]   ibid, 484; Axhamn (n 17) 569.

[52]   P. Bernt Hugenholtz and Ruth L. Okediji, 'Conceiving an international instrument on limitations and exceptions to copyright final report' (2008) 20, http://www.ivir.nl/publicaties/download/937 (accessed 11 February 2018).

[53]   Christophe Geiger, 'From Berne to National Law, via the Copyright Directive: The Dangerous Mutations of the Three-step Test' (2007) 29 *European Intellectual Property Review* 486, 487–9.

[54]   Zhang (n 47) 666, with further references to Hugenholtz and Okediji (n 52) 20.

[55]   Trumpke (n 1) 285–6.

[56]   Zhang (n 47) 650–1, 666; Trumpke (n 1) 285. About the test, also Lund (n 2) 554; Axhamn (n 17) 570–2.

to the extended effect, while ECL was also compared to a compulsory licence for non-members.[57]

Traditionally, the ECL rules found in the Nordic countries have been considered to be in accordance with the test. ECL's relation to the Berne Convention has also been taken into consideration when applying the law. An example is provided by the *Norwaco* case, where the Norwegian Supreme Court showed reluctance to interpret the scope of a retransmission right under an ECL scheme wider than indicated in the preparatory works for the provisions in question.[58] However, although the (specific) ECL rules mainly have a quite clearly defined and narrow scope, it could be questioned whether all of these rules 'add up', not making them certain special cases but more of a default.[59] Furthermore, it is not only the ECL provisions that decide the terms for use of copyright-protected works. An ECL agreement is freely negotiated between licensee and licensor (the CMO), and establishes the rules and conditions under which copyrighted works can be exploited. The licence thus narrows down the scope – but still it might be a question of possibilities under the provisions, whereby in particular the concept of a general ECL might be challenged.[60] In any case, the legitimacy of the agreement arises from the principle of contractual freedom. For its part, adoption of a general ECL in Denmark could seem problematic in terms of becoming a default rule, where the parties can define the specific area of use by agreement.[61] However, this general provision is subsidiary, meaning that it is only to be applied in cases where it is (almost) impossible to obtain consent from rightholders individually or through their representative organizations.[62] This use of a general ECL is intended to relieve the legislator from the burden of constantly amending national legislation because of rapid technical development.[63] Still, the actual terms of the agreement, the principle of equal treatment, the right to individual remuneration, and (where available) an opt-out possibility also protect outsiders here.[64] In his categorization, Trumpke points out that, unlike permitted uses (for example, quotation), ECL allows for some reliance on exclusive rights, while a statutory licence (for example, private use) allows use without

---

[57] Pirkko-Liisa Haarmann, *Immateriaalioikeus* (Talentum 2014) 98; Mogens Koktvedgaard and Marianne Levin, *Lärobok i immaterial rätt* (Norstedts Juridik 1992) 32.

[58] Norwegian Supreme Court decision HR-2016-562-A *Norwaco*, para 52.

[59] Riis and Schovsbo (n 1) 487–8.

[60] Trumpke (n 1) 273.

[61] Danish Copyright Act, Art 50(2). For the Swedish and Norwegian perspective, Lund (n 2) 557–8.

[62] Axhamn and Guibault (n 2) 34.

[63] ibid, 34.

[64] ibid, 34–5.

negotiation (but with an indispensable right to remuneration), in contrast to an ECL scheme. Both compulsory licences and ECL rely on contracts – the former on an individual (and compulsory) basis and the latter on a collective basis. Mandatory collective management (for example, cable retransmission) and ECL share the element of collectivization. For outsiders, unlike members of a CMO, the outcomes of ECL may be similar to mandatory collective management or a statutory licence (that is, they are left with a claim for remuneration).[65] Overall, ECL as a whole is a complicated scheme with a 'two-tiered structure' (provisions/licence) and multiple impacts, as noted by Trumpke. Therefore, different groups of rightholders must be viewed separately, that is, members and non-members.[66]

4.   ECL IN THE DIGITAL REALM: SOME PROMISES AND PROBLEMS

The ECL scheme is referred to as a solution that meets not only the 'original' rationales of copyright law, that is, balancing of interests and providing incentives in particular, but also (some of) the current needs in light of digital uses.[67] For their part, the Nordic countries already use ECL as a solution for many mass uses, including in the digital realm as shown by the Finnish use cases discussed above. However, what is more interesting is the possibility of implementing ECL on a supranational level or on a national level in other countries (so-called exportation or 'transplantation').[68] Indeed, awareness of ECL has grown across the globe, especially in situations related to mass licensing and digitalization; examples outside Europe include the USA and Canada.[69] And, as at the dawn of ECL, it is broadcasting that is in need of workable solutions. For example, the European Broadcasting Union (EBU) has placed hopes on ECL in also favouring the model from a public server broadcaster perspective

---

[65]   Trumpke (n 1) 273–8, 286. For a comparison of rights clearance mechanisms, Olav Stokkmo, 'The Extended Collective Licensing Agreement, or the Extension of Voluntary Licensing Agreements around the World' (2017) 6 NIR 594.

[66]   Trumpke (n 1) 278.

[67]   Riis and Schovsbo (n 1); Trumpke (n 1).

[68]   Riis and Schovsbo (n 1) 496; *cf* Günther Teubner, 'Legal Irritants: Good Faith in British Law or How Unifying Law Ends up in New Divergences' (1998) 61 Modern L. Rev. 11.

[69]   Trumpke (n 1) 265; Riis and Schovsbo (n 1) 479–81. Also Daniel Gervais, 'The Purpose of Copyright Law in Canada' (2005) 2 U. Ottawa L & Tech. J. 315; Pamela Samuelson, 'Legislative Alternatives to the Google Book Settlement' (2011) 34 Colum. J.L. & Arts 697.

and noting that ECL should be promoted as 'an optional model for clearing rights' in the audio(visual) sector, including for on-demand services.[70]

With regard to the original rationales, it is questionable whether ECL provisions truly provide for 'balanced solutions'. Nonetheless, the Finnish solution to NPVR services was expressly hailed as a 'balanced' way of reconciling the interests of all stakeholders, that is, service providers, broadcasters, rightholders and consumers.[71] Indeed, the original objectives behind ECL provisions include both those related to public interest or fundamental rights and those related to profit and development.[72] These objectives are certainly among the core goals to be pursued in the digital realm. Moreover, according to the Final Report of EuropeanaConnect, more specific rationales for expanding ECL to new areas in the Nordic countries have included the following:

- the existence of (legitimate) public interest in a mass use situation;
- the impossibility of direct contracting either on an individual or a collective basis due to high transaction costs; and
- the non-desirability of *ex lege* exceptions or compulsory licences coupled with remuneration and the potential incompatibility of these with international/EU law.[73]

These criteria also apply to digital use cases as shown by the Finnish use cases discussed above. However, a few important issues remain to be taken into account in extending the scope of ECL or turning it into a law-making technique – alongside the important international and EU-level legal frameworks discussed above and noted in the criteria. First, ECL has been developed in the Nordic countries in specific socio-cultural circumstances. ECL is a living tradition with a context – that context arguably lying behind the success of ECL.[74] Therefore, it would arguably not be a simple task to adopt ECL elsewhere, and that task could be wider than merely introducing ECL rules.[75] Then again, taken simply as a technique, one possible benefit of ECL is its relative efficiency and speed in light of technological developments and the incentive function.[76] Second, in the digital realm, national borders in mass licensing schemes such

---

[70] EBU, 'EBU Copyright White Paper. Modern copyright for digital media. Legal analysis and EBU proposals' (March 2010) https://www.ebu.ch/files/live/sites/ebu/files/Publications/Position%20Papers/EBU-Position-EN_Copyright%20White%20Paper.pdf (accessed 1 February 2018).

[71] Government (n 7) 24; Alén-Savikko (n 7) 209–10.

[72] Eg, Mikko Huuskonen, *Copyright, Mass Use, and Exclusivity. On the Industry Initiated Limitations to Copyright Exclusivity* (University of Helsinki 2006) 246–7.

[73] Axhamn and Guibault (n 2) 28–9; Axhamn (n 17) 566–7.

[74] Riis and Schovsbo (n 1) 497.

[75] Eg, Riis and Schovsbo (n 1) 496.

[76] Eg, the example in ibid, 472 fn 2.

as ECL might be problematic. For their part, the Finnish use cases discussed above only apply within Finland. Indeed, with regard to digitization of archives, Riis and Schovsbo point to the risk of a national ECL creating 'a de facto copyright haven', whereas worldwide availability online of the works in question would create additional problems with regard to non-members and thus negatively affect the usability of the service.[77] For example, in 2012 the Norwegian mass-digitization project *Bokhylla* aimed to make literature published in Norwegian available online,[78] and, by means of ECL, the agreement was extended to cover rightholders who are not represented by Kopinor.[79] Making use of the ECL mechanism has seemingly contributed to efficient digital dissemination of works. A Norwegian IP address is needed to access the online resource, but the National Library 'may on concrete requests give other users access for distinct purposes, mainly for research and educational purposes, on terms defined more closely by the parties'.[80] Similar problems relate to TV broadcasts. While, for instance, NPVR services as part of internet protocol television (IPTV) schemes would be limited within national borders, over-the-top (OTT) services would not if no technical restrictions apply. As pointed out in the context of EuropeanaConnect, cross-border dissemination would require an additional solution. For its part, the country-of-origin principle could override territoriality but deprive rightholders in the receiving country of their exclusive right. Multi-territorial licensing, in turn, would offer a pan-European licence for online distribution and could rely on mandatory mandates between CMOs.[81]

Third, ECL provisions are not always practical or principled. In specific use cases, they may offer seemingly practical solutions, while the underlying principles and problematic concepts remain untouched: for example, the Finnish ECL provisions did not solve the question of what is 'private' in the digital realm.[82] The actual practicality may also be questionable especially due to the underlying complexity and rights of refusal. Finally, individually tailored

---

[77]   ibid, 498.

[78]   Kopinor, 'Bookshelf contract' (2012), Section 1 available at http://www.kopinor .no/articles/bookshelf-contract (accessed 11 February 2018).

[79]   ibid, Section 3, with further reference to Section 16a of the Norwegian Copyright Act, *cf* Section 36.

[80]   Bookshelf contract (n 78) Section 4; Kopinor, 'Bokhylla er fullført' (1 February 2018) available at http://www.kopinor.no/nyheter/bokhylla-er-fullfort (accessed 11 February 2018).

[81]   Axhamn and Guibault (n 2) 72. For a project on cross-border digital library and the possibility of a global solution, Jerker Rydén, 'Extended Collective Licensing and Aspects of Territoriality. Is a Global Library a Vision or Utopia?' (2017) 6 NIR 629, 632–3.

[82]   Alén-Savikko (n 7) 211, 215.

ECL provisions might not endure in the speedily changing digital realm due to their casuistic nature. Indeed, general ECL provisions could provide a more technology-neutral solution – but be simultaneously problematic in their 'generality' or flexibility from the perspective of an EU and international legal framework, as discussed above.[83] In any case, lack of technological neutrality (despite the ambition to achieve it) in copyright law, whether specific ECL provisions or exceptions and limitations, seems to be a frequent problem in light of technological developments. Outside Europe, the issue is noted, among others, by Key-Matuszak in analysing the Australian case (*Optus*)[84] around so-called copyright 'time-shifting' provisions, allowing for recording of TV programmes, and a cloud-based personal video recorder service. To Key-Matuszak, the assumptions behind the relevant copyright provisions had become obsolete: 'time shifting' was also enabled via a commercial service with shared control (user and service provider) – not only as the previously 'user-controlled good'. However, copyright law did not allow an interpretation in favour of technological neutrality since it would have gone against the express wording and legislative intention of the law.[85]

5.   CONCLUSION

ECL suits the Nordic countries in cases of traditional and digital uses, in particular in the online environment. Moreover, it might also provide answers to some challenges related to digital distribution outside the Nordic countries, especially within the EU and regarding online use. With the rapid development of new technologies and mass digitization of works, ECL has proven an efficient and flexible measure. Furthermore, it contributes to legal certainty for users, which in turn stimulates use. However, the use of ECL must be carefully assessed and prepared. ECL does not provide a quick-fix technique for rendering all types of mass use legal, nor is it without problems from the perspective of EU and international copyright law. One of the main concerns for export of ECL internationally or within the EU is whether the possibility to opt out sufficiently preserves exclusivity, especially when outsider rightholders are not notified of use of their works. There is thus scepticism, especially with regard to the role of foreign rightholders and non-members. National borders and

---

[83]   Riis and Schovsbo (n 1) 479; Trumpke (n 1) 286.

[84]   Federal Court of Australia, *National Rugby League v Singtel Optus* [2012] FCAFC 59. The case is also discussed in Alén-Savikko (n 7) 210–11.

[85]   Peter Key-Matuszak, 'Time Shifting after *NRL v Optus*: A Need for Amendments' (2012) 35 EIPR 439, 444. Sampsung Shi Xiaoxiang, 'Time Shifting in a Networked Digital World: Optus TV Now and Copyright in the Cloud' (2012) 34 EIPR 519, 532.

Table 6.1   Requirements for ECL features

ECL FEATURE	EU		International	
	Legislation	CJEU	Berne	TRIPS
Effect on outsider rightholders			Art 9(2)	
Effect on foreign rightholders			Art 5(1)	
Opt-out	Art 5(5)		Art 9(2)	Art 13
	InfoSoc Dir		Art 5(2)	
Specific ECL	Art 5(5)		Art 9(2)	Art 13
	InfoSoc Dir			
General ECL	Art 5(5)		Art 9(2)	Art 13
	InfoSoc Dir			
Representation by CMO		*Soulier and Doke*		

territoriality also pose significant restraints in the online environment.[86] The requirements for ECL features in light of EU law and international framework are shown in Table 6.1.

With regard to fragmentation of rights, ECL schemes may provide solutions from the perspective of complex rights clearance and potentially high transaction costs. In this regard, ECL solutions bring also outsider rightholders within the scope of the relevant provisions and enable, for instance, online re-utilization (on a mass scale) of pre-existing material, such as in the case of media archives. However, the legal position of outsider rightholders cannot be overlooked as noted above. Moreover, the representation of different rightholders for various subject matters must be safeguarded (including related rights), which may require multiple CMOs also across the field, such as in the case of NPVR services.

One important note is that different types of ECL models exist, each with somewhat differing concerns. Whereas a general ECL scheme might serve the ideals of technological neutrality, it comes with additional concerns due to its potential for being considered a default rule and flexibility in terms of scope. In any case, overly casuistic provisions should be avoided in light of rapid technological development, not least because they would undermine some of the benefits of applying ECL in the digital realm, including in the online environment. With regard to online distribution, the opportunities for cross-border solutions would appear particularly worthy of further consideration.

---

[86]   Riis and Schovsbo (n 1) 492, 496, 498.

7. Liability and access to contact information: striking the balance when service is used to distribute copyrighted digital content

Katja Weckström Lindroos[1]

1. INTRODUCTION: PRESUMPTIVE FRAGMENTATION

This chapter discusses illegal distribution of exclusive copyrighted content online outside the designated platforms for on-demand digital content services. It addresses fragmentation caused by legal intervention in cases regarding unauthorized access to digital content. Fragmentation is present in two ways. First, Lessig's famous statement 'code is law'[2] is used to question whether in essence (1) technological fact dictates law (code is law), (2) legal norms dictate technology (law is code) or (3) legal questions can be addressed by legal tools (law is law). This theoretical framework is applied to a series of cases decided by the Finnish Market Court (MAO) seeking to define a standard of liability for 'significant distribution of unauthorized digital content'.[3] The cases, involving pre-release file-sharing of high demand TV series, boiled down to intricate technological evidence to establish liability. Has law lost its bearings against the digital 'it could have been anyone' defence, or can courts rely on established legal doctrine to establish personal liability? It is argued that courts have not lost discretion to assess credibility of defences merely due to a technological setting preventing absolute certainty of fact.

---

[1]   The author would like to thank the participants at the Online Content Distribution Conference in Helsinki for valuable comments on an earlier draft of this chapter. Research Assistant Kaarina Leppänen has provided invaluable support for completion of this chapter.
[2]   L Lessig, *Code and Other Laws of Cyberspace* (Basic Books, 1999) at 24.
[3]   This concept embodies a balance of constitutional values in the Finnish Copyright Act, discussed in section 3.2.

The second broader issue of fragmentation links to democratic and constitutional values. If law is law, thus nationally flavoured, how do we address the question of fragmentation based on territoriality? The issue relates to differences in compensation cultures for digital copyright infringement in Finland and abroad. Pressure is put on teleoperators to release contact information of Internet service users. Consequently, the MAO has balanced competing interests in several decisions. The MAO indirectly addressed the issue of scope of liability by establishing infringement of Nordic, not global rights. The court was reluctant to grant the rightholder access to information that could be used against Finnish defendants in other jurisdictions. First, if law is subordinated to code, it escapes Finnish jurisdiction, because technology is global. Second, if code is subordinated to copyright law, it escapes Finnish constitutional values, because development of copyright law is international. Third, if local democratic and constitutional values may influence actual liability for digital copyright infringement, rightholders may not abuse court procedures to bring suit in forums with higher punishment or compensation cultures.[4] These silent legal cultures,[5] whether national, regional or global, have great impact on balancing interests in practice.

The Finnish market for digital content is booming, and on-demand services are acquiring a market footing. The demand for access to popular exclusive series is soaring. Copyright enforcement is aggressive since supply of unauthorized copyrighted digital content is plentiful.[6] This chapter analyses the principles set forth relating to access to information, as well as navigating complex evidentiary issues[7] in establishing infringement for sharing copy-

---

[4]   The US courts have exercised jurisdiction on the Internet in cases of illegal file-sharing. For a thorough account see J Hörnle, 'The Jurisdictional Challenge of the Internet' in L Edwards and C Waelde, *Law and the Internet* (3rd edn, Hart Publishing, 2009) 121–158, at 144–145.

[5]   Lessig talks of architecture that constrains social and legal power. I argue that silent legal cultures form legal architecture that restricts power to protect core values. National legal cultures may have subcultures originating in conflicting national or international soft law, or national or international social norms.

[6]   In 2013–2017 the MAO released contact information relating to 198,552 IP addresses. A working group delivered its report suggesting guidelines for cease-and-desist letters and out-of-court settlement of disputes. *Hyvät käytännöt yksityishenkilöihin kohdistuvassa kirjevalvonnassa* (Opetus- ja kulttuuriministeriön julkaisuja 2018:2, ISBN:978-952-263-543-3).

[7]   For a more thorough account of the intricacies of criminal prosecution and preliminary injunctions see K Weckström, 'Fundamental Rights Conflicts in the Context of Prosecuting Internet Crime' in G Calcara et al, *Cybercrime, Law and Technology in Finland and Beyond* (Finnish Police Academy, forthcoming 2018) and K Weckström, 'Preliminary Injunctions Against Intermediaries for Trademark and Copyright Infringement' in K Weckström (ed), *Governing Innovation and Expression*

right content. It is argued that fragmentation of legal rules may constitute a positive cap on liability connecting digital infringement to similar standards used in assessing real world liability, thus revealing silent legal cultures in decision-making.[8]

2.   CODE IS LAW, LAW IS CODE, OR LAW IS LAW

In Code, Lessig identifies an architecture that structures and constrains social and legal power to the end of protecting fundamental values. These shared values are principles and ideals reaching beyond the compromises of ordinary politics.[9] A balance securing liberties and freedom is the result of conscious and continuous effort in everyday implementation. This effort combats every-day attempts at derailing freedom for the sake of self-serving control asserted by state, political or private enterprise. Similarly, Adams and Prins recognize that shared values underpin Western conceptions of democracy without necessarily realizing the same normative outcome when applied in similar conditions.[10] When regulating the Internet the result is the outcome of existing social, economic and technological relationships.[11] Like Lessig, they recognize technology as a tool that merely plays a part in a dynamic interplay between multiple processes, interests and actors.[12] Technological tools can enhance or lose their value for democracy depending on how well they are optimized towards achieving legitimate outcomes.[13] Similarly, regulation, or conceptual tools, may also lose their value for democracy or upholding the rule of law if viewed too narrowly through traditional conceptual lenses.[14] A coherent and neatly hierarchical system of law flowing from an ideal of one state law may be debilitating in both a normative and practical setting.[15] Pure state law hardly exists in practice anymore since the reality is too complex and norms

---

New Regimes, Strategies and Techniques (University of Turku Faculty of Law, 2013) at 213–238.

[8]   M A Gollin, *Driving Innovation Intellectual Property Strategies for a Dynamic World* (CUP, 2008) at 308–309.

[9]   Lessig (n 2) at 5.

[10]   M Adams and C Prins 'Digitalization Through the Lens of Law and Democracy' in C Prins, C Cuijpers, P Lindseth and M Rosina (eds), *Digital Democracy in a Globalized World* (Elgar Online 2017) at 5.

[11]   Gollin (n 8) at 54.

[12]   Adams and Prins (n 10) at 7.

[13]   Cuijpers in Prins et al (eds) (n 10) and R Weill, 'Election Integrity: the Constitutionality of Transitioning to Electronic Voting in Comparative Terms' in Prins et al (eds) (n 10) at 142.

[14]   Gollin 2008 (n 8) at 20.

[15]   Adams and Prins (n 10) at 17.

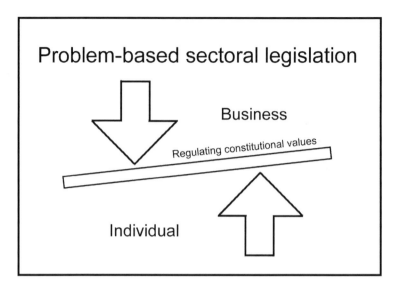

Figure 7.1   Problem-based sectoral legislation – limited discretion

too intertwined in practice. Fragmentation and polycentricity of law may be a pragmatic solution for problem-based regulation. However, legal fragmentation and polycentricity as a tool for Internet regulation may enhance or lose its value for democracy, depending on how well it is optimized towards achieving legitimate outcomes.

Figure 7.1 shows the limited discretion to consider constitutional values within the confines of problem-based sectoral legislation. Sectoral legislation rarely allows revisiting constitutional values in a manner that disrupts the status quo between vested interests.

When values cross the borders of established legal fields, modern law – especially in the civil law tradition – struggles with releasing itself from rules of systematization attributable to the nation state.[16] This applies to the division between public and private law, but also between, for example, the law of obligations and property law.

To illustrate, the European Union (EU) telecommunications sector is divided between 'reserved' and 'liberalized' sectors, which has its roots in regulating national monopolies in securing services of general interest; an exception to the free movement of services and the obligation to provide

---

[16] R Zimmerman, 'Europeanization of Comparative Law' in Mathias Reimann and Reinhard Zimmerman (eds), *The Oxford Handbook of Comparative Law* (OUP, 2006) 553–555 at 550.

market access. Likewise, 'electronic communications' refers only to services providing access or interconnection (networks), not to those providing content. Content regulation, then, is determined on the basis of the nature of the content and subject to sector-specific regulation. The same Internet service provider (ISP) is subject to separate regulation for access service and audiovisual media service, each with their own definitions, criteria and scope of application. However, for the regulatory framework to work, it is ideal that an ISP be either an 'electronic communications service',[17] an 'information society service'[18] or an 'audiovisual media service'.[19] Contemporary ISPs tend to fit into all or none of these definitions. Forcing the mould as tradition ties the hands of regulators and interpreters alike and reduces available options for problem-solving.

An increasingly ill-fitting mould should be remoulded to accommodate new developments and not be referred to in terms of absolutes for the sake of tradition. While states may not agree on the level of protection of specific fundamental values, I have argued elsewhere that Western states share an interest in protecting fundamental values.[20] Contemporary comparative legal scholarship tends to focus on comparing different solutions to any given legal problem instead of looking for shared fundamental values underlying similar solutions in different jurisdictions. The surface level legal solution is not significant, but whether the solutions are more similar than they are different.[21] Solutions in

---

[17] Telecommunications Framework. Directive 2002/21/EC of the European Parliament and of the Council of 7 March 2002 on a common regulatory framework for electronic communications networks and services (Framework Directive).

[18] E-Commerce and InfoSoc Directives Framework. Directive 2000/31/EC of the European Parliament and of the Council of 8 June 2000 on certain legal aspects of information society services, in particular electronic commerce, in the Internal Market (Directive on electronic commerce); Directive 2001/29/EC of the European Parliament and of the Council of 22 May 2001 on the harmonisation of certain aspects of copyright and related rights in the information society.

[19] Audiovisual Media Directives Framework. Directive 2010/13/EU of the European Parliament and of the Council of 10 March 2010 on the coordination of certain provisions laid down by law, regulation or administrative action in Member States concerning the provision of audiovisual media services (Audiovisual Media Services Directive).

[20] K Weckström, *A Contextual Approach to Limits of EU Trade Mark Law* (IPR University Center, 2011) and Weckström forthcoming 2018 (n 7).

[21] Tuori's multi-level model of law, where the base of the pyramid is labelled 'deep structure', from which a legal system's 'legal culture' and 'surface level activity' stems and into which it resonates back. He argues that the multi-layered nature of modern law is essential in solving the problems on limits and legitimacy of law. K Tuori, *Critical Legal Positivism* (Dartmouth Publishing 2002, 2011) at 147. The law's sub-surface levels must be understood as distillations from surface-level legal material, and consequently, legal culture and deep structure have their origin at the surface level; these levels also represent common features in surface-level legal material, which only

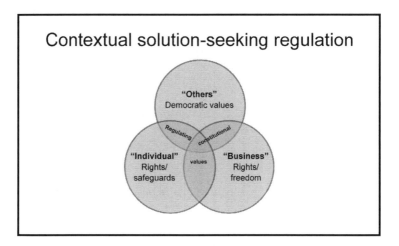

Figure 7.2   Contextual solution-seeking regulation: discretion to consider democratic values

new areas of law should build on fundamental similarity of goals as opposed to real or semantic differences in formal approach, institutional choice or interpretative result. Presumptive contextualism may be used as a tool to identify and balance competing interests in a new setting.[22]

Figure 7.2 shows that a contextual solution-seeking approach allows consideration of other implicated values alongside vested interests. This approach is useful in addressing issues arising in norm thickets and norm vacuums.

Law is generally viewed as territorially limited to the nation state and its subjects.[23] Only state sovereigns can voluntarily take upon themselves additional obligations and give force to foreign law within their jurisdiction.[24] Individuals may voluntarily subject themselves to foreign law by leaving the territorial jurisdiction of the home country to enter another. International law, as a theoretical concept, cannot exist without the procedural cooperation of

---

gradually (and relatively slowly) sediment into structures supporting the surface. Ibid at 201.

[22]   Weckström 2011 (n 20).

[23]   The principle of territorial sovereignty or principle of territoriality: Art 29 of the Vienna Convention on the Law of Treaties, UNTS 1155 UNTS 331, 8 ILM 679, entered into force 27 January 1980.

[24]   Regardless of whether they choose to recognize treaties or soft law in the form of institutional or commercial practice as officially or unofficially binding upon them.

state sovereigns in implementing or ratifying it.[25] The same rule upholds the global systematization of law as well as forming the foundation of jurisdiction in international law.[26] From the value-neutral perspective of legal tradition in Europe, the civil law tradition starts from a legal positivist view[27] of a hierarchy of norms and a shared recognition of specific legal sources[28] as generators of legal norms.[29] Thus, while many voices[30] challenge the existence of an international body of rules that would reflect a self-sustained binding shared interest in protecting fundamental values, the Member States of the EU have since the 1950s repeatedly and consistently subjugated themselves to the supremacy of international law on this matter.[31] From the perspective of legal tradition these norms have sedimented through to the deep structure of the individual legal systems that now also bind Member States from within their national legal orders as constitutional norms.

There is a substantive and procedural (systemic) aspect to the legal preoccupation with state sovereigns. The substantive aspect relates to the legitimacy of democratic governance that has persistently started and ended in the sovereign state to the detriment of other actors. A practical (procedural) consequence, however, relates to what Muir Watt calls the 'shadow of the nation state' and its profound systemic effect on legal interpretation:[32]

> The shadow of the nation state made itself felt nevertheless through the fact that the legal traditions under comparison were assumed to be coextensive with the territory

---

[25]   In the end, this is true also within the EU, where Member States ultimately decide whether to give effect to EU law (what they have agreed upon).

[26]   This is a practical systemic argument, not a theoretical, substantive or value argument.

[27]   There is a rich European discussion on the theoretical foundations of legal positivist theories. Here, positivism is used as a reflection of (civil law) tradition, not as a theoretical argument.

[28]   That are generated by legal institutions and legal practices.

[29]   Legal norms are rules and principles that govern interpretation, not to be confused with sector-specific statutory provisions.

[30]   Eg, proponents of the New Haven School, Critical Legal Studies movement and Law and Economics scholarship views of the (non-)binding nature of international law upon national decision-making. By contrast, it is routinely argued that Western values that are reflected in international law are binding upon non-Western nations. For an excellent summary of theories of international law, see A Boyle and C Chinkin, *The Making of International Law* (OUP, 2007) at 10–19.

[31]   Most notably by acceding to the European Convention on Human Rights and its institutions. Convention on the Protection of Human Rights and Fundamental Freedoms signed in Rome, 4 November 1950, as amended by Protocols Nos 11 and 14 and supplemented by Protocols Nos 1, 4, 6, 7, 12, 13.

[32]   H Muir Watt, 'Globalization and Comparative Law' in Reimann and Zimmerman (eds) (n 16) at 582.

of a given community to which they historically linked, while sources of law were in the main official sources, with judicial decisions in the fore as comparative legal studies began to flourish in the Anglo-American world ... Comparative law is faced ... with the issue of what makes up tradition disconnected from state or irreducible to the concept of a national 'legal system'.

...it remains the case that the representation of the object...as regards the various laws of nation states was still implicitly reproduced and reinforced. First, by philosophical representations as to the nature of law, perceived either as expressive and coextensive with the territorial power of the sovereign, or alternatively as constitutive of a 'system' whose *grundnorm* was to be found in a national constitutional norm, the state appeared as the ascendance of a form of individualized, formal, rationality. Second, on an epistemological level, a distinctive bias towards rule-based knowledge of the law indeed constitutes to a certain extent to push the emphasis in comparative work towards legal rules.[33]

While it may be a solution for comparative law to reject both assimilation between law and rules and law and state (contextualism), it could still be argued – as some neoliberalists[34] do – that law has been reduced merely to a product and has lost the ability to solve societal problems. However, contextualism can be anchored in law and traditional legal sources without the corresponding inflexibility and exclusiveness of the mindset of a nation state. Instead, a rule of persuasiveness in light of existing options could guide interpretation and selection of legal institutions that are applicable in a given circumstance.[35] Legal sources are merely a vehicle for legal argumentation and interpretation, an art of which legal jurists have a profound and well-developed understanding.[36] It is not the instruments but the skilled actors using them that constitute the essence of legal science.[37] Deference or defeatism to other disciplines according to the prevailing political climate resonates poorly with a thorough understanding of the dynamic regulatory state with changing legal and political preferences.

---

[33]　ibid, at 584.

[34]　The basic premise of law and economics scholarship is that judicial discretion should be reduced to ratifying market-produced efficient outcomes, as opposed to legitimately producing results based on other objectives (morals or societal-political preferences). Law is a source among many others, but not supreme. R Posner, *The Problematics of Moral and Legal Theory* (Harvard University Press 1999) at 3–8.

[35]　Weckström, *A Contextual Approach to Limits of EU Trade Mark Law* (n 20).

[36]　J Husa, 'Understanding Legal Languages: Linguistic Concerns of the Comparative Lawyer' in Jaap Baaij (ed), *The Role of Legal Translation in Legal Harmonisation* (Kluwer Law International, 2012) 161–181. Also available at http://papers.ssrn.com/sol3/papers.cfm?abstract_id=2326910. Citations to SSRN version (visited 12 February 2018) at 8.

[37]　Tuori (n 21).

A modern approach to law in a dynamic regulatory state:

1. recognizes patterns of dominance in society;
2. tests them against existing values as recognized in legal rules
3. voices concerns of those underrepresented or trampled[38]; and
4. proposes solutions to accommodate or safeguard them in law and in practice.

Lifting the shadow of the nation state allows comparison of stripped legal solutions to protecting values and filling norm vacuums in new areas of law based on the level of persuasiveness of the proposed solution instead of requiring inherent consistency with prior national systematization. This is especially preferable in EU law and international law since giving preference to national solutions may be politically difficult. National discretion shifts the final tailoring to Member States that are in a better position to fit the new solution within the national legal system. There is no apparent reason why the exercise of searching for optimal solutions to a specific legal problem should be limited to existing legal frameworks where the problem (or its attempted solution) may not yet have surfaced. The regulator may have to be reminded of the precise application of legal rules in new and unforeseen circumstances.[39] Upholding tradition in a legal sense constitutes respect for the law and the underlying values it seeks to protect without turning a blind eye to non-legal or semi-legal solutions or holding on to conservative means or solutions to the detriment of more efficient or appropriate ones. Legal judgment should focus on showing how different solutions protect competing values that are affected by a specific legal problem, and refrain from a judgment that gives preference to one over the other.[40] Instead, one should carefully examine ideological, political and cultural similarities and differences in order to ascertain whether different solutions are merely products of different legal cultures or whether they reflect ideological preferences.

Thus, legal solutions can be presented as viable alternatives on a given problem, which may or may not have legal support in the legal environment where it is proposed for inclusion. Alternatively, a combination of different solutions may be proposed. Deep analysis of the ideological and legal underpinnings of each solution offers a more nuanced view of available options in

---

[38] Gollin (n 8) at 55–56.
[39] Lessig is less sceptical but recognizes that ideally judges or institutions could perform this task. Lessig (n 2) at 22.
[40] The scholar should focus on making sense of the solution and discovering the *ultima ratio* of it or its context instead of measuring it against others. R Michaels, 'The Functional Method of Comparative Law' in Reimann and Zimmerman (eds) (n 16) at 363 and 365.

securing fundamental values and distinguishes the legal basis from political assumptions or preferences. Such a method would be based on comparing functionally equivalent legal solutions (for example, comparing cases on point), which would serve a constructive function[41] in presenting the relevant legal environment as it is presented to the relevant court without imposing the nation state bias through forced systematization. Unlike legislation or abstract legal rules, there are always two parties to a dispute that ideally present competing arguments. Moving from the specific case-setting to the general (legal institution, field of law, or legal system) as opposed to vice versa forces the judge to seek to understand the meaning of the case in its legal context. Presumptive contextualism allows recognition of competing interests and the effect of those interests depending on the outcome of the case.

Understanding and respecting differences does not prevent convergence of rules. Instead, it may lead to a fuller understanding of the law. Shared values may not take the same legal form or be capable of precise legal definition. However, deep scrutiny of different solutions may reveal agreement on substance despite disagreement on level, degree or form.[42] Framing the question to focus on shared values as opposed to differences or conflicting values may help in bridging grey areas or norm vacuums in new and underdeveloped areas of law.

3.   LAW IN ACTION – REVEALING SILENT LEGAL CULTURE

3.1   Legal Fundamental Values: Technology and Burden of Proof

The strong tradition of international intellectual property law-making and the sheer volume of decisions from the EU institutions, from which rules may be derived, in effect may lead national courts to ignore national rules and precedent in favour of resolving a particular issue based on EU sources of law. It is true that national courts increasingly look to the Court of Justice of the EU (CJEU) for guidance and tend to follow the body of preliminary rulings when interpreting national implementing legislation. Thus, 'law in action' may be less diverse or nationally flavoured than expected, and national courts could be

---

[41]   ibid, at 376–381.

[42]   R Zimmerman, 'Europeanization of Comparative Law' in Reimann and Zimmerman (eds) (n 16) at 550, referring to Hein Kötz's *European Contract Law*, which goes a crucial step beyond merely presenting laws, and provides 'an integrated account by adopting a vantage point situated beyond, or above, the national legal systems'. This ambitious approach establishes an intellectual framework for discussing, developing and teaching law in Europe.

viewed as passive receivers of EU Internet law, or semi-active interpreters of EU Internet law, but no longer as independent developers of national Internet law doctrine. Indeed, Internet law, as a field, is quick to adapt to international influences, and substantial international scholarship also raises issues quickly to international debate. In comparison, for example, to tax or criminal law, Internet law is internationally integrated within the Western world.

However, even the most pro-integrationist national judge is likely or able to set aside national rules of procedure when deciding a case. 'Law in action' will always be nationally flavoured because of the structure of decentralized decision-making to national courts in the EU, regardless of the relative amount of EU law ingredients used. Much as in a federal system, the structure of the court system by itself secures continuous development of both EU and national law. Thus, law in action at any given time may reflect the fact that national courts give preference to EU rules in many cases, but law in action is also a reflection of the silent legal culture, system and court structure in which national courts operate. This silent structure grows in importance when judges are faced with claims of liability in new settings that trigger interests that have not traditionally been protected in national or EU law. How national interpreters bridge this gap is the focus of 'law in action' in this chapter. The silent culture reflects ideological as well as national legal tradition.

The MAO has decided a cluster of cases relating to illegal file-sharing of copyrighted content to Finnish consumers.[43] Crystalis Entertainment (Crystalis) distributes movies, TV shows and TV formats worldwide. It holds an exclusive worldwide licence to distribute the *Black Sails* TV series online. Scanbox Entertainment (Scanbox) holds an exclusive licence to distribute the movie *A Walk Among the Tombstones* in Finland. In MAO 419/16, the defendant's contact information had been released by court order against the teleoperator in order to identify the subscriber of an Internet connection. The IP address was identified as having shared the plaintiff's content 82 times from 3 January 2015 to 29 March 2015 using BitTorrent technology. Crystalis sought compensation for sharing ten episodes of the TV series *Black Sails*. Scanbox sought compensation for sharing the movie from 2 February 2015 to 5 May 2015. The defendant denied using the Internet connection during the periods in question in his open Wi-Fi network. After receiving the plaintiff's cease-and-desist letter the defendant protected the network with a password.

---

[43] Markkinaoikeus (Market Court/MAO) 419/16, decision of 4 July 2016 (MAO 93/15, unpublished decision of 12 February 2015 and 170/15, unpublished decision of 10 March 2015); MAO 423/16, decision of 7 July 2016; MAO 424/16, decision of 7 July 2016; MAO 425/16, decision of 7 July 2016; MAO 55/17, decision of 7 February 2017.

Thus, the MAO had to assess evidence on:

1. whether the defendant had shared copyrighted content;
2. if and what the defendant was required to pay compensation for; and
3. the amount of reasonable compensation.[44]

The parties presented elaborate technical evidence on the functioning of BitTorrent technology, wireless Internet connections and open networks. The defendant presented counter-evidence relating to the technological randomness of BitTorrent technology, its sharing patterns and open networks.

BitTorrent protocol enables file-sharing in peer-to-peer (P2P) networks without a server. Anyone with an Internet connection and BitTorrent software[45] can use the network. P2P technology allows files to be split into packets at the source to allow for efficient transmission. Torrent files contain information on availability of specific content in the network. When tasked to do so by its user, Torrent software locates specific content based on the Torrent file. A complete file may consist of packets from different sources, which are randomly selected to optimize efficiency from all sources that carry the file. The packet contains data, which enables the network protocol (here, BitTorrent) to address it to the right location. The packet also contains data that identifies the content of the packet; that is the sequence of the requested content file, which the (BitTorrent) software extracts to compile the packets received into a complete content file. Thus, while the content is the same the actual file reconstructed for the user is not the same file that is available at any particular source. Technically, users may set their computers to receive packets ('Leech') or to distribute ('Seed') content already acquired. However, neither can control nor effectively remove content once it has been shared. For the purposes of copyright infringement, it is not possible to assert unlawful copying. Instead, the infringement is based on unlawful distribution to the public of copyrighted works without the rightholder's consent. The act of sharing copyrighted content without the rightholder's consent is clearly an act of infringement.[46] The randomness of the technology renders enforcement difficult, in particular relating to identifying the infringer; determining the scope of infringement; and determining the amount of reasonable compensation.

---

[44]   The details of assessing the amount of compensation cannot be discussed here.

[45]   The defendants in the Finnish cases had used less frequently employed software like qTorrent and Transmission. µTorrent software is one of the most frequently used worldwide. Today, P2P technology and software are predominately used for legal purposes, such as Ubuntu Linus and OpenOffice or mobile networks.

[46]   Hallituksen esitys (Government Bill) HE 28/2004 vp, at 77–78.

Table 7.1   *Questions of law and questions of fact*

Legal Requirement	Legal Threshold	Question of Law or Fact?
Identification	Not responsible for acts of others	Act of infringement – standard of proof
Scope of infringement	(1) Release of personal data requires significant infringement (2) Injunction or deterrent effect	(1) Territoriality and use of information in other cases against the same actor (2) Responsibility for random effect – possibility of control
Compensation	Right to reasonable compensation for 'use' of work	Actual harm or general harm? - effect of infringement, - adequate compensation, - generally reasonable?

Table 7.1 illustrates which subquestions are triggered at different stages of litigation. In reality cases may turn on whether a question is considered a question of fact, i.e. turns on evidence and burden of proof, or a question of law. Questions of law are subject to judicial interpretation. Discretion allows consideration of democratic values and a contextual solution-seeking approach to issues that arise in new technological settings and emerging markets.

First, as a matter of fact, it is not possible to prove the identity of the infringer without catching the perpetrator at the scene. As a matter of law, it is possible to find infringement without full proof that eliminates all doubt as to the identity of the infringer. The court has discretion to weigh evidence and determine whether the plaintiff has met its burden of proof. The standard of proof remains high, but how high? Need the plaintiff show high probability, or eliminate reasonable doubt as to the defendant's identity?

Second, as a matter of fact, it is not possible to determine the scope of infringement attributable to the infringer because of the nature of P2P technology. As a matter of law, consideration must be given to the ability of the infringer to control the effects of the infringement. Focus shifts to intent and disregard for the consequences of one's acts.[47] As a matter of (copyright) law, proof of intent is not required since file-sharing without the copyright holder's consent is illegal per se. Yet the teleoperator is only required to release the contact information for the subscriber of the Internet connection if infringement is significant. Need the plaintiff show general harm,[48] or specific harm, from the acts of the infringer?

---

[47]   KKO 2010:47.
[48]   Lost revenues for copyright owners from the black market in software, music and movies amount to 150 billion US dollars according to Gollin (n 8) at 53 and 313. Exact

Third, as a matter of fact it is not possible to determine the effect of the infringing acts because of the nature of P2P technology and the indirect effect of black markets on commercial markets. As a matter of law, it is possible to assess what is reasonable and take into account mitigating factors.[49] Yet the borderless nature of P2P networks, as well as legitimate markets for copyrighted content, makes it difficult to assess which acts and effects are linked to a specific territorial jurisdiction.

We focus on the threshold for reliable evidence in a reality of technological uncertainty. In all cases, the plaintiffs asserted that finding infringement is not dependent on technological fact, but on a question of law (probability). Compensation must, as a matter of law, be determined as a question of fact. Thus, the law dictates liability and use of technology (law is code). The defendants, on the other hand, relied on technological fact to determine the legal outcome. Thus, technology dictates liability for unlawful acts (code is law). Both parties relied on extreme measures:[50] full liability for results of technology or no liability because of technology. The law is clear on the question of liability and compensation for copyright infringement. Therefore, the cases turn on technology and fact-finding.

In the first case, the MAO dismissed the defendant's general claim of reported inaccuracies relating to contact details received from teleoperators in similar cases. Instead, it assessed the reliability of information given in the case at hand. The teleoperator's records unequivocally directed to the defendant's Internet connection at all times for which information had been requested.[51]

The MAO relied on expert statements and witnesses relating to the reliability of information gathered by NARS software, which attaches itself to swarms sharing illegal content with BitTorrent technology.[52] It targets IP addresses suspected of distributing copyrighted content, makes a trial download, and compares the acquired files with one supplied by the rightholder. It logs traffic to and from the IP address concerned, software and ports used as well

---

losses are contested, but nonetheless substantial. Loss of revenue for on-demand digital content services is not covered in these figures.

[49]   KKO 2010:47.

[50]   This is to be expected and follows common argumentation in contested intellectual property cases. Gollin (n 8) at 59.

[51]   MAO 419/16.

[52]   NARS (Network Activity Recording and Supervision). Swarms are randomly formed when torrent files identifying content files are shared in the network. If the same content is available from several IP addresses the technology randomly answers requests. It is not possible to limit or control sharing once the file has been made available to the network.

as descriptive data of the content files, such as info_hash values.[53] Experts opened the files to test the information for accuracy. The MAO relied on evidence relating to the software used (qBittorrent), the qBittorrent 3.1.0 version used, and the port used. The fact that the software was relatively rare (3.2 % of users) and that the three factors were all present at the various times when file-sharing had occurred implicated one person as opposed to any random users of an open Wi-Fi network. While it was technically possible for others to have used the Internet connection inside or outside the apartment, the defendant did not present evidence that anyone else had in fact used it. The MAO relied on the changes in traffic that occurred after the defendant received the cease-and-desist letter. The traffic data, the defendant's communication with the plaintiff's attorney and activity online rendered the claims by the defendant implausible. The course of events presented by the plaintiff's evidence was more likely an accurate reflection.[54]

However, the bulk of the evidence against the defendant was attributed to self-incrimination in online chat rooms.[55] This raises the question whether the case turned on fact or on law; would liability have been found had the infringer not been careless? In another case, the MAO was presented with that very conundrum.[56] Here the defendant had changed routers, used multiple IP addresses and claimed to have set the Internet connection as an open Wi-Fi network. The plaintiff relied on similar technical evidence identifying that all IP addresses used connected to the defendant's Internet connection used rare BitTorrent software (Transmission) and a rare port to connect to the network over the entire period of NARS technology surveillance. The MAO was convinced that there was only one – not multiple – infringers. However, the fact that the defendant owned similar hardware to that used did not convince the court since the defendant offered said hardware for independent expert inspection. According to expert testimony, no traces were found of the Transmission software or the copyrighted content, nor was there evidence of over-writing such records.[57] Likewise, while the plaintiff presented evidence to show that the defendant's Internet connection was closed and not open, the measurements had occurred five months later than the alleged infringements.[58] The defendant presented witness testimony that a visitor had accessed his

---

[53]   Info_hash values uniquely identify particular torrent files, including the file name and size of the file shared.
[54]   MAO 419/16, decision of 4 July 2016.
[55]   MAO 419/16, decision of 4 July 2016, at 45–51.
[56]   MAO 55/17, decision of 7 February 2017.
[57]   MAO 55/17, decision of 7 February 2017, at 80–83.
[58]   The case involved an elaborate technical detour relating to the range of routers and accuracy of GPS technology. MAO 55/17, decision of 7 February 2017, at 69–79.

network on numerous occasions during the times infringements occurred. Thus, the MAO found that the plaintiff had not met its burden in presenting evidence that the network was closed at the time of infringement.

In another case[59] by contrast, the MAO dismissed the defendant's evidence of a screenshot indicating the Wi-Fi network setting was open and user data because it could not be ascertained when the screenshot was taken and data was gathered.[60] Thus, if the plaintiff proves that there is only one infringer responsible for the infringing act using the defendant's Internet connection, the defendant must prove that it was not him/her.

In a third case[61] the quality of presented evidence was once again tested. There was uncontested proof that the defendant was not at home (within the range of the open Wi-Fi network) during the time that the alleged infringement occurred. The defendant, an IT expert, claimed to have only one device with Internet connectivity and this device, a work laptop, was with him at that time. The whereabouts of the defendant and the laptop did not convince the court as to whether the defendant was the infringer. The defendant did present evidence in rebuttal, including the possibility of other users and use of other IP addresses. Additionally, a technical inspection of the laptop had been carried out. However, the evidence was inconclusive, unreliable and not on point.

The MAO found that the plaintiff had met its burden of proving that the defendant was the likely infringer, and the defendant had failed to present credible or reliable evidence to the contrary. In addition to the technical data generated by NARS surveillance, the plaintiff presented evidence that the defendant used Pulsar software, which is software that provides subtitles to movies and TV series, and by default uses the same port that had been attached to the defendant's Internet connection at the time of the alleged infringements. While this port is not infrequently used, the site for download of the most frequently used BitTorrent software, μTorrent, actively discourages use of these ports. The choice of these ports indicated intentional use and a sophisticated user.

3.2   Cultural Fundamental Values: Procedural Safeguards and Territoriality

The infringer is required to pay reasonable compensation for unauthorized distribution of copyrighted works under section 57 of the Finnish Copyright Act. The Finnish legal system, like most European countries, does not recognize

---

[59]   MAO 419/16, decision of 4 July 2016, also involving distribution of episodes of *Black Sails* and the movie *A Walk Among the Tombstones*.

[60]   MAO 419/16, decision of 4 July 2016, at 57 and 59.

[61]   MAO 565/17, decision of 15 September 2017, also involving distribution of episodes of *Black Sails* and the movie *A Walk Among the Tombstones*.

punitive damages. General tort law follows the principle of full compensation.[62] Damages may be adjusted based on reasonableness. Adjustment is also possible in criminal cases when the full effect of the crime was unforeseeable.[63] Reasonable compensation cannot be adjusted since it is compensation for unauthorized use, not damages for harm.[64] Nevertheless, the Finnish Supreme Court has interpreted the term 'reasonable' in light of Finnish compensation culture when defining the harm attributable to the defendant.[65] The MAO decisions on determining compensation have been in line with precedent.[66]

Recent cases relating to ordering teleoperators to release contact information of subscribers connected to IP addresses identified by NARS surveillance suggests a possible shift in copyright enforcement. The procedural safeguard built into Section 60a of the Copyright Act limits access to contact information to cases of significant unauthorized distribution of copyright content.[67] Rightholders had requested release of contact information of all subscribers whose IP addresses had been linked to a swarm identified by NARS surveillance at the time when unauthorized use of copyrighted content occurred. The records identified approximately 1,000 swarm members when two movies were shared. The MAO relied on CJEU case law that requires courts to interpret all exceptions to the confidentiality of communications narrowly.[68] Narrowly tailored exceptions are restricted to what is absolutely necessary and proportionate to the goal sought. The MAO rejected the request as over-inclusive since the Copyright Act limits liability to concrete infringements by the defendant.[69] The teleoperator could not be ordered to release contact information without evidence that significant distribution of copyrighted content had occurred from the IP address in question.[70] Thus, proving significant demand for or access to content is not the same as proving significant distribution to the public.[71]

---

[62] Vahingonkorvauslaki (31.5.1974/412) Section 2:1.1.
[63] ibid, Section 2:1.2. KKO 2012:94.
[64] KKO 2010:47.
[65] KKO 2010:47. For an in-depth discussion of Finnish cases assessing compensation for copyright infringement see K Lindroos, 'Internet Commerce and Law' in GB Dinwoodie (ed), *Secondary Liability of Internet Service Providers* (Springer International Publishing, 2017) at185–212.
[66] MAO 419/16, MAO 55/17 and MAO 565/17.
[67] The Finnish term used is *merkittävissä määrin*.
[68] Joined Cases C-203/15 & C-698/15, *Tele2 Sverige and Watson et al.* EU:C:2016: 970; Case C-275/06 *Promusicae* EU:C:2008:54; and Case C-461/10 *Bonnier* EU:C: 2012:219.
[69] MAO 333/17, decision of 12 June, at 6.
[70] ibid, at 4–6.
[71] ibid, at 6.

In earlier cases[72] the MAO had found significant infringement and ordered teleoperators to release contact information when content had been in high demand, over 1,000 shares a day and up to 45,000 shares a day. Yet the release request concerned IP addresses that were linked to the swarm for a longer period. The teleoperator was not required to release information on all possible swarm participants based on a NARS log prematurely based on the risk for delayed enforcement.[73] The teleoperator is, however, required to secure the requested data (NARS log) pending release. In practice, the teleoperator may not delete or over-write the subscriber data in question while the plaintiff investigates and sends cease-and-desist letters.[74]

The MAO has also utilized other procedural safeguards to limit enforcement to Finland. Scanbox holds an exclusive licence to distribute content in P2P networks with subtitles in the Nordic language, and authorization to police unauthorized distribution, and therefore may apply for release of contact information. However, since the distributed files were not equipped with subtitles in the Nordic languages these files did not injure the exclusive right to distribute content in the Nordic languages. Hence, Scanbox lacked standing to request reasonable compensation.[75] Similarly, an exclusive licence to distribute in Finland and the right to police infringements in Finland limits the judgment to infringement in Finland.[76] Crystalis may only use the contact information for investigating and prosecuting infringement of rights under the Finnish Copyright Act in Finland and as a condition for the order committed to not surrendering information outside the European Economic Area.[77]

Recently the Supreme Court found that teleoperators may refuse to release data stored specifically for government authorities, and limit release of contact information to data stored for customer use.[78] Teleoperators store data for nine months for specific government authorities, while teleoperators generally store data for three months. In practice, the threshold of significant distribution requires copyright holders to act quickly and cannot rely on NARS technology snapshots of activity in BitTorrent networks.[79] The MAO has limited com-

---

[72]   MAO 419/16 and MAO 423-425/16.

[73]   MAO 333/17.

[74]   MAO 351/17.

[75]   MAO 55/17.

[76]   MAO 424/16.

[77]   MAO 423–425/16.

[78]   KKO 2017:85. Information Society Code (917/2014). Unofficial translation available at https://www.finlex.fi/en/laki/kaannokset/2014/en20140917.pdf (last visited 23 March 2018).

[79]   The Supreme Court granted leave to appeal in a recent unpublished decision of the Market Court (MAO 2016/402, 3.10.2016), where the teleoperator was ordered to

pensation claims to targeting seeds not leeches.[80] The procedural limitations on access to contact information limit the scope of private enforcement via cease-and-desist letters.

4.   CONCLUDING REMARKS ON PRESUMPTIVE CONTEXTUALISM AND LAW IN ACTION

The Finnish Market Court has successfully given voice to the ideological choices of the Finnish legislator by way of using its discretion to assess third-party interests in the context of specific cases. Despite technological uncertainty that inevitably affects fact-finding, the law has not lost its bearings finding and limiting liability in the online context. However, the silent legal culture of national legal systems may limit the scope of enforcement in practice. Silent legal cultures consist of both legal tradition and cultural tradition that reflect a specific ideological balance between competing interests in society. Presumptive contextualism allows the silent legal culture to visibly guide decision-making and balance fundamental rights in new legal settings, as required by EU law. Thus, fragmentation of legal rules may constitute a positive cap on liability connecting digital infringement to similar standards used in assessing real-world liability. Revealing silent national legal cultures in decision-making allows readjustment of piecemeal sectoral legislation to fundamental values embedded in the legal system.[81] This approach restores legitimacy of law and sets pace with rapid developments of technology in new legal settings. Presumptive contextualism reduces the risk of rendering law irrelevant and limits enforcement to appropriately recognize competing fundamental values. Presumptive contextualism is useful in navigating norm thickets created by overlapping legislation or norm vacuums between general and specific regulation. It is particularly appropriate for decision-making relating to tailoring liability rules that promote long-term innovation and development of digital infrastructures and services. It allows decision-making to shift from reactive to proactive regulation that develops future law rather than compromising new developments.

---

release information stored under Section 157 (VL 2018-13). KKO 2017:85 was decided on 8 December 2017.

[80]   MAO 419/16 at 7.

[81]   Gollin (n 8) at 308–309.

PART III

Emerging Technologies for Online Distribution
– More Fragmentation in the Future?

8. AI-generated content: authorship and inventorship in the age of artificial intelligence

Rosa Maria Ballardini, Kan He and Teemu Roos

1. INTRODUCTION

Predicting the future of technology is notoriously difficult. Indeed, predicting how law and regulation should be shaped to meet the needs of future technological developments is a task that might often lead to hilarious predictions.[1] The difficulty in predicting technological development is certainly reflected in the current debate about the future of artificial intelligence (AI). Within this framework, currently two extremes can be identified: those who view AI as a path towards 'superintelligence' that transcends humanity, and those who think AI is merely a glorified version of data analysis and statistical inference. In any case, it seems realistic to foresee that in the near future there will be an increase in machines that are able to perform more tasks in more efficient and autonomous ways than we can currently envision. These tasks include production of artistic, technological, and scientific innovations that might potentially be protectable via intellectual property (IP) laws. Because of the economic value of these innovations, there may be an interest in 'controlling' these intellectual creations via intellectual property rights (IPRs). In this context, a key question relates to how to interpret the concepts of 'authorship' (copyright) and 'inventorship' (patents) of creations and inventions generated by AI systems.

IPRs aim at protecting the fruits of the human mind. IPRs are a set of limited exclusive rights allocated to 'persons', either natural or legal. As such, both

---

[1]   Eg, the prediction by CONTU that '[Electronic distribution] may ease the problem which has been caused by the wide availability of photocopying machines capable of producing copies quickly and relatively inexpensively' (CONTU, United States 1979: 78).

copyright and patent laws in Europe have traditionally relied upon the concept of the author or inventor as a natural person. Indeed, that idea is reflected not only in the legal definitions of author and inventor, but also in concepts such as 'work' and 'invention', as well as in the requirements to be satisfied in order to acquire protection. By possibly allowing production of innovations in an 'autonomous' way, AI naturally challenges these well-established traditional legal notions. Can an AI-generated work or invention attract IPR protection under current rules? Is there a need to reshape our understanding and interpretation of authors and inventors as natural persons in view of the rapid expansion of AI? What would be the benefits and consequences of such a shift?

This chapter focuses on the concepts of authors and inventors for AI-generated innovations as prerequisites for copyright and patent protection. The issue is important not only because authors and inventors enjoy ownership rights in their copyright or patent, but also (and more fundamentally) because if there is no legitimate author or inventor, IPR might either not be granted in the first place or might be held invalid or unenforceable in court. Indeed, these clarifications are of fundamental importance for multiple industry sectors, especially for those operating in the digital environment, in order to promote legitimate distribution of digital content and, this way, foster further developments of digital markets.

The chapter begins by explaining some fundamental technological concepts concerning AI and by providing examples of AI-generated outputs that can potentially attract IPR protection. The next section explores copyright- and patent-related issues in the context of AI, with a focus on existing concepts of authorship and inventorship in European copyright and patent laws. The chapter then goes on to discuss the possible need to open possibilities to non-human authors or inventors, as well as the possible consequences of doing so. The whole discussion is contextualized and pondered within the framework of justifications for IPRs: we address the issue of authorship and inventorship rights on AI-generated innovations via a theoretical discussion about IPR protection and access. This allows us to argue in favour of a 'modernist' type of school, which follows a balanced approach between protection and access. We conclude in favour of a legal provision stating that only 'natural' persons can be deemed to be authors/inventors and that only the natural person(s) behind the arrangements necessary for the creation or invention involved should be considered as the author or inventor.

2.   WHAT DO WE MEAN BY 'AI-GENERATED'?

According to Russell and Norvig, AI is 'the study of agents that exist in an environment and perceive and act'.[2] Schalkoff defines AI as '[a] field of study that seeks to explain and emulate intelligent behavior in terms of computational processes'.[3] The latter definition highlights the importance of emulation and behaviour. In fact, when we observe the behaviour and products of AI systems without being aware of their internal working – as if they were 'black boxes' that we cannot open – we may often be tempted to use words such as 'perceive' and 'think'. Yet, when the workings of the systems are revealed to us in the form of an algorithm and code, or the principles underlying them, we may prefer to use more mechanical terms such as 'input' and 'process'.[4]

The distinctive feature of AI systems compared to other software systems is their higher degree of autonomy. To better explain the significance of this feature for the present discussion, let us first present some examples of tools familiar for artistic creation. A word-processing system, even if it is helpful in creating a novel, has very little to do with the end result (the novel) and the user of the system is the author of the novel. In other words, such a system is clearly a simple tool that can be compared to a paint brush. Different tools may be necessary for creating different products but the user (author) is still responsible for the creative contribution to produce any given result.

The opposite extreme is a system that allows the user to choose between a small set of possible outcomes. Consider, for example, systems used for creating avatars[5] on computer gaming platforms such as Microsoft Xbox or Sony PlayStation: the user gets to choose the height and weight of the avatar, as well as its gender, hairstyle, hair colour and various other features. The system basically involves a sequence of multiple choice questions, and even though different choices lead to markedly different outcomes, the creative contribution of the user is negligible compared to the contribution of the artists who design the visual appearance of the different elements such as body, face and clothing.

---

[2]   S J Russell and P Norvig, *Artificial Intelligence: A Modern Approach* (3rd edn, Pearson, 2010).

[3]   R Schalkoff, *Artificial Intelligence: An Engineering Approach* (McGraw-Hill, 1990).

[4]   Indeed, a third definition of AI is 'AI is whatever hasn't been done yet', quote attributed to Larry Tesler; see D Hofstadter, *Gödel, Escher, Bach: An Eternal Golden Braid* (Basic Books, 1979).

[5]   'In computing, an avatar is the graphical representation of the user or the user's alter ego or character', Wikipedia: Avatar (computing), retrieved 9 February 2018.

A continuous spectrum exists between tools in the paint brush category, including word-processing systems, and those in the 'avatar' category. Many AI systems fall somewhere in between these two extremes: they require significant user input but they also significantly guide and affect the outcome.

Yet another critical aspect in many AI systems, especially those based on machine learning, is data. Machine learning is a sub-discipline of AI that can be defined as the study of algorithms and systems that improve their performance in a given task as they are provided with more data.[6] The performance of AI systems based on machine learning relies critically on the quality of the data. Thus, the role of the data provider also needs to be acknowledged. To continue the avatar example, the system could extract the graphical elements that it uses to create avatars from a third-party data source such as photographs or paintings that were not necessarily originally intended to be used as parts of avatars.

Table 8.1 includes a set of examples of currently existing AI systems that are challenging the notions of author and inventor.

Overall, we argue that all the above examples are 'autonomous' only in a clearly constrained and limited scope and, as such, they can probably be handled within existing laws and regulations. However, the development of more advanced and more autonomous AI systems in the future may challenge existing notions in more fundamental ways.

3.   AI AND IPRS: AUTHORSHIP AND INVENTORSHIP

3.1   Copyright Law and Authors

Authors always form the starting point and centre of any discussion on copyright law. According to the labour theory developed by Locke, for instance, the intellectual labour of the author mixed with other resources justifies the author's right over the fruits of their labours. The personality theory by Hegel claims that a work belongs to or reflects the personality of its creator. Although utilitarian theory starts with the welfare of the public and society as a whole, the fact that copyright is considered as an incentive for authors to create cannot be denied. But who is to be conceived as the author of a work?

---

[6]   T. Mitchell, *Machine Learning* (McGraw Hill, 1997).

Table 8.1   *AI systems*

Name	Category of IPR	Description
Next Rembrandt[1]	Copyright	By analysing the statistical properties of known Rembrandt paintings on the level of high-resolution photographs and depth images, a new painting was produced by 3D printing. The painting had similar properties to the Rembrandt paintings but it was clearly a new painting in the sense that it was not a copy or a variant of an existing one, at least in any obvious way.
Poem machine[2]	Copyright	Text can be analysed in a similar fashion by estimating word co-occurrence statistics from a corpus (the input data that determines the style) and producing new text with matching statistics. The methods can also take into account rhyme and other constraints.[3] In a related project, the partially random choice of content was determined by using brain signals from users although the user had no conscious control of the outcome.[4]
Flow Machines[5]	Copyright	The Flow Machines tool can extract patterns from a music database and create new compositions in the style of a chosen genre or artist. Significant adjustment of (human) musicians is still needed to reach a satisfactory end result. This includes adding tracks, writing and producing lyrics, and mixing.
Invention machine	Patent	In principle, in order to optimize the design of, eg, an antenna, two things are sufficient: a 'goodness function' that assigns to each proposed design a value that is the higher the better the design, and an algorithm that explores possible designs to identify those that have high goodness values. This approach has been used successfully to find antenna designs and electrical circuits that have been awarded patents.[6]
Robot Scientists Adam and Eve	Patent	Adam and Eve are systems capable of independently carrying out experiments in molecular biology, guided by an AI algorithm that generates hypotheses about reaction pathways and chooses experiments to test them.[7] Adam was claimed to be the first machine to independently discover scientific knowledge.[8]

Notes
1   https://www.nextrembrandt.com.
2   https://runokone.cs.helsinki.fi/start.
3   J Toivanen, O Gross and H Toivonen, 'The Officer Is Taller Than You, Who Race Yourself!: Using Document Specific Word Associations in Poetry Generation', in S Colton, D Ventura, N Lavrac and M Cook (eds),(Jožef Stefan Institute, 2014).
4   A Kantosalo, J M Toivanen, P Xiao and H Toivonen. 'From Isolation to Involvement: Adapting Machine Creativity Software to Support Human-computer Co-creation', in Colton et al (above).
5   http://www.flow-machines.com/ai-makes-pop-music.

6   J R Koza, F H Bennett III, D Andre and M A Keane, 'Genetic Programming: Biologically Inspired Computation that Creatively Solves Non-Trivial Problems', in Laura F Landweber and Erik Winfree (eds),(Springer-Verlag, 2001).
7   R D King, K E Whelan, F M Jones, P G K Reiser, C H Bryant, S H Muggleton, D B Kell and S G Oliver, 'Functional Genomic Hypothesis Generation and Experimentation by a Robot Scientist' (2004) 427(6971)247–252.
8   http://www.cam.ac.uk/research/news/robot-scientist-becomes-first-machine-to-discover-new -scientific-knowledge.

3.1.1   'Author' in European copyright law

European copyright law comprises international copyright treaties to which the European Union (EU) is a signatory, EU legislation and cases from the Court of Justice of the European Union (CJEU), as well as national laws and cases. In this chapter we will only focus on the EU level.

The three major international treaties relevant to European copyright law are the Berne Convention,[7] the World Intellectual Property Organization (WIPO) Copyright Treaty[8] and the TRIPS Agreement.[9] Although the term 'author' is often mentioned and used in the text of the Berne Convention, it is not explicitly defined.[10] As Ricketson explains, the possible reason is that when the Berne Convention was under discussion, a similar understanding was shared among the Member States as to who is an author, so that further interpretation was not needed.[11] Later, in the revision of the Convention, divergences between national laws on other aspects of authorship have become more pronounced.[12] One of these divergences is the actual degree of intellectual creation required to meet the criteria of originality. Common law systems traditionally emphasize the degree of skill and labour involved, while continental law countries tend to put more weight on the level of creativity. Indeed, this issue may also indirectly concern the question whether an author has to be a natural or a legal person.[13] At the same time, however, the Berne Convention indirectly specifies one concept of author by stipulating that if the author's name is indicated, that person will be regarded the author of a literary or artistic work in the absence

---

[7]   Berne Convention for the Protection of Literary and Artistic Works as amended on 28 September 1979.
[8]   WIPO Copyright Treaty (WCT) 1996.
[9]   Agreement on Trade-Related Aspects of Intellectual Property Rights (Marrakesh, Morocco, 15 April 1994), Marrakesh Agreement Establishing the World Trade Organization, Annex 1C, THE LEGAL TEXTS: THE RESULTS OF THE URUGUAY ROUND OF MULTILATERAL TRADE NEGOTIATIONS 321 (1999), 1869 U.N.T.S. 299, 33 I.L.M. 1197 (1994) (TRIPS).
[10]   Jane C Ginsburg, 'The Concept of Authorship in Comparative Copyright Law' (2003) 52 DePaul. L. Rev. 1063, 1069.
[11]   Sam Ricketson and Jane C Ginsburg, *International Copyright and Neighbouring Rights: The Berne Convention and Beyond* (2nd edn, volume 1, OUP, 2005) 358.
[12]   ibid, 359–360.
[13]   ibid.

of proof to the contrary.[14] Rather than defining the author, though, this rule aims at offering some certainty and reducing the burden of proof for rightholders. It seems reasonable to argue that the author could then be a natural or legal person because both can exhibit their names on a work.

Both the WIPO Copyright Treaty and the TRIPS Agreement remain silent with regard to the definition of 'author', even though both treaties require compliance with the Berne Convention.[15]

As international treaties leave the definition of 'author' to the discretion of each national jurisdiction, the Member States of the EU could have stipulated different concepts of 'author' in their respective copyright laws. As diversity in the definition of 'author' could have increased fragmentation and hindered establishment of the internal market, EU lawmakers have harmonized certain key concepts. Especially relevant are the various Directives on cinematographic and audiovisual works, as well as on computer programs and databases.

Article 2(1) of the Computer Program Directive states that 'the author of a computer program shall be the natural person or group of natural persons who has created the program or ... the legal person designated as the right holder by that legislation'.[16] If literally interpreted, this clause seems to set up the general principle that the author should be a natural person, that is, the human being who created the program.[17] On the other hand, the use of 'right holders' rather than 'author' makes it unclear whether a legal person could be regarded as 'author'.

Legislative history tells us that this article follows the prevailing view in continental Europe,[18] where it is understood that only natural persons can accomplish an intellectual creation and, therefore, be authors.[19] The integration of 'legal person' tries to respect the common law tradition.[20] This is an exception to the basic concept.[21] Thus, it seems reasonable to say that a legal person cannot be an author but can be, rather, a rightholder.

---

[14] Art 15.1 Berne Convention.

[15] Art 1, WCT; Art 2(2) TRIPS.

[16] Art 2(1) Directive 2009/24/EC of the European Parliament and of the Council of 23 April 2009 on the legal protection of computer programs [2009] OJ L 111.

[17] Thomas Dreier and P Bernt Hugenholtz (eds), *Concise European Copyright Law* (2nd edn, Wolters Kluwer, 2016) 248.

[18] Michel Walter and Silke von Lewinski (eds), *European Copyright Law: A Commentary* (OUP, 2010) 5.2.2.

[19] ibid.

[20] Walter and von Lewinski (n 18) 5.2.6.

[21] ibid, 5.2.10.

The Database Directive follows this model in Article 4(1).[22] In addition, Article 2(2) of the Rental and Lending Directive[23] and Article 1(5) of the Satellite Directive[24] designate the principal director of a cinematographic or audiovisual work as the author. It is commonly accepted that the principal director is the natural person who takes the lead in making artistic decisions.

Indeed, some rules, such as those governing co-authorship – for instance in relation to other persons that contribute to a work, such as screenwriters, camera operators, editors and producers – might still interface with existing national concepts.[25] These types of leeway may leave some room for the Member States to designate a legal person as 'co-author' of a cinematographic or audiovisual work.

All in all, although these Directives offer some harmonized definition of 'author', as yet no uniform or common understanding of this concept is available in EU copyright law: on the one hand, the Directives define 'author' only for specific types of work, and, on the other, a clear answer is still awaited as to whether a legal person can be regarded as an 'author'.

3.1.2   Interpretation by the CJEU

Despite the fact that the CJEU has never decided directly on the concept of author, a definition can be derived from a cluster of decisions on the merit of the criteria of 'originality'.

The requirement of originality in European copyright law is defined in the Computer Programs Directive,[26] the Database Directive[27] and the Term Directive[28] as the 'author's own intellectual creation'. However, up until the *Infopaq* decision of 2009,[29] this interpretation of 'originality' applied only to specific categories of works, namely photographs, computer programs and

---

[22]   Art 4(1), Directive 96/9/EC of the European Parliament and of the Council of 11 March 1996 on the legal protection of databases [1996] OJ L 77/20.

[23]   Art 2(2), Directive 2006/115/EC of the European Parliament and of the Council of 12 December 2006 on rental right and lending right and on certain rights related to copyright in the field of intellectual property [2006] OJ L 376.

[24]   Art 1(5), Directive 93/83/EEC of the European Parliament and of the Council of 27 September 1993 on the coordination of certain rules concerning copyright and rights related to copyright applicable to satellite broadcasting and cable retransmission [1993] OJ L 248.

[25]   Walter and von Lewinski (n 18) 6.2.8.

[26]   Art 1(3), Computer Program Directive (n 16).

[27]   Art 3(1), Database Protection Directive (n 22).

[28]   Art 6(1), Directive 2006/116/EC of the European Parliament and of the council of 12 December 2006 on the term of protection of copyright and certain related rights [2006] OJ L 372.

[29]   Case C-5/08 *Infopaq International A/S v Danske Dagblades Forening* [2009] ECLI:EU:C:2009:465.

databases. *Infopaq* extended the interpretation of originality as the 'author's own intellectual creation' to all other categories of work. Based on the argument that the Information Society Directive[30] should be rooted in similar principles as other Directives, the CJEU held that copyright protection within the meaning of Article 2(a) of the InfoSoc Directive should apply only to subject-matter that is original in the sense that it is its author's own intellectual creation.[31] The CJEU further interpreted this concept in other key decisions, such as *Murphy*,[32] *Painer*[33] and *Football Dataco*,[34] stating that 'author's own intellectual creation' means that the author should 'stamp his personal touch or reflect his personality in the sense that he expresses his creative abilities in original manner by making free and creative choices'.[35]

Following this logic of extending interpretation of the concept of originality from specific categories of works (as the law dictates) to all categories of works (via case law interpretation), it seems reasonable to argue that the CJEU could extend the interpretation of 'author' as a natural or legal person from specific categories of cinematographic and audiovisual works, computer programs and databases, to all categories of works. Indeed, this is a suitable interpretation in view of the establishment of a harmonized legal framework for copyright in the EU. It is then reasonable to predict that, should the CJEU have to interpret the concept of 'author', it will extend to all categories of works the same interpretation already included in some EU Directives. Indeed, the emphasis on the 'personal touch' and 'personality' followed by the CJEU in interpreting the concept of 'originality' indicates the idea of the author as a natural person since only human beings can possess personality and a personal touch.

In sum, under current copyright laws and interpretations, a non-human or an entity with no legal personality, like an AI, is not eligible for authorship status of cinematographic and audiovisual works, computer programs and databases in the EU. Moreover, based on the line of reasoning followed by the CJEU in

---

[30] Directive 2001/29/EC of the European Parliament and of the Council of 22 May 2001 on the harmonisation of certain aspects of copyright and related rights in the information society [2001] OJ L 167.

[31] *Infopaq*, paras 36–37.

[32] Joined Cases C-403/08 and C-429/08 *Football Association Premier League Ltd et al v QC Leisure et al* [2011] ECLI:EU:C:2011:631.

[33] Case C-145/10 *Eva-Maria Painer v Standard Verlages GmbH et al* [2013] ECLI: EU:C:2013:138.

[34] Case C-604/10 *Football Detaco Ltd et al v Yahoo! et al* [2012] ECLI:EU:C: 2012:115.

[35] Kan He, 'The Concept of Originality in EU and China', in Nari Lee, Niklas Bruun and Mingde Li (eds), *The Governance of IP in EU and China* (Edward Elgar Publishing, 2016) 150.

key cases concerning originality, it seems unlikely that AI could qualify as the author of other types of works either.

3.2   Patent Law and Inventor

European patent law operates in a complex multi-level system consisting of national and regional patent laws. The European Patent Convention (EPC)[36] has largely harmonized the patent laws of the EU Member States at procedural and pre-grant stage, while leaving infringement-related post-grant litigation to national jurisdictions, along with exceptions and limitations to infringements.

As to defining 'inventor', the EPC states in Article 60(1) that '[t]he right to a European patent ... belong[s] to the inventor or his successor in title'. According to Article 60(3) EPC, '[f]or the purposes of proceedings before the [EPO], the applicant shall be deemed to be entitled to exercise the right to the European patent'. However, the inventor is always entitled to be mentioned as such before the EPO, regardless of who files the application.[37] The EPC and its Implementing Regulations clearly state that the application should mention the inventor (or its successor in title).[38] Finally, where the inventor is an employee the EPC refers to national law provisions.[39]

On the one hand, it is clear that if a patent does not mention an inventor it will not be accepted by the patent office on the grounds that it lacks formalities. On the other, however, neither the EPC nor its case law provides an explicit definition of the nature (human or not) of an inventor. Furthermore, in practice, the EPO never investigates whether the proposed inventor is indeed the 'true inventor'.[40] This is probably justified by the fact that the European patent system is based on the so-called 'first to file' approach to patent entitlement, according to which priority of claims depends purely on who is first to submit a complete application to the patent office.[41] This is opposed by the 'first to invent' approach followed in other countries (such as the USA before the American Invent Act), which requires a procedure that allows the stage where intervention actually occurred to be identified.

---

[36]   Convention on the Grant of European Patents of 5 October 1973 (European Patent Convention/EPC).
[37]   EPC Art 62.
[38]   EPC Art 60.
[39]   EPC Art 60.
[40]   EPC Implementing Regulations, Rule 19(2).
[41]   Art 60(2) EPC.

Moreover, the national laws of most EU Member States do not include a specific definition of 'inventor'.[42] That said, under European patent law the presumption is nevertheless that inventions are made by natural persons only. For instance, even though in Europe the right to a European patent may be transferred before the filing of an application (via human-centred acts such as contract, or inheritance, or according to the applicable national law on employees' rights),[43] the inventor has the right to be mentioned as such before the EPO. Moreover, designating an inventor requires, for example, a statement of 'the family name, given names and full address of the inventor', which seems to conceive the inventor as a human being. Another indication of this presupposition is that when referring to the inventor the law uses words like 'right', 'he' or 'his'.[44]

Joint inventors or co-inventors exist when a patentable invention is the result of inventive work by more than one inventor, even if they did not contribute in equal parts. Also in this case, however, it appears that only human beings (and only private persons) can qualify as 'co-inventors' under European law.

Indications that the EPC intended to refer to inventors as human beings can also be found in patentability requirements such as novelty, inventiveness and disclosure: these requirements are assessed based on the knowledge of a person skilled in the art (PSITA), who is 'presumed to be a skilled practitioner' (that is, a human being) 'who is possessed of average knowledge and ability with normal means and a capacity for routine work and is aware of what was common general knowledge in the art at the relevant date'.[45] The idea behind creating the imaginary figure of the PSITA is for the Office to make a fair judgment in comparison to the level of knowledge of the inventor at the time when the invention was made: were the inventor a non-human, that comparison would become unbalanced.

3.2.1 Interpreting 'inventor' – EPO and national case law

Currently, no EU or European-wide common forum is available for patent litigation. The most recent, yet still ongoing, post-grant patent law harmonization effort in the European context is the EU Unitary Patent Package. This is an initiative for a new Unitary Patent (UP) (allowing patent protection to be obtained in all EU countries by submitting a single request to the EPO) and a Unified Patent Court (UPC) within the EU (to offer users of the UP system

---

[42] 'Inventorship of multinational inventorship' (2015) AIPPI. Available at: http://aippi.org/library/?publication_title=inventorship+of+multinational+inventions&=&publication_categories%5B%5D=7&start_date_range=&end_date_range.

[43] Art 60(1) EPC.

[44] Art 62 EPC.

[45] Guidelines for Examinations (2017), G.VII.3.

a cost-effective option for patent enforcement and dispute settlement across Europe). As such, in terms of interpreting European patent law, cases passed down by the EPO Boards of Appeal, as well as national court interpretations of the EU Member States, are primary research sources.

Broadly speaking, both the EPO and national courts have interpreted 'inventorship' as being determined by 'contribution to the inventive concept'. To date, no case law has been handed down by EPO Boards on interpreting the concept of 'inventor'. However, some EU national courts have passed down a set of relevant court decisions on the matter.

The UK is among the only nations in Europe to somehow positively define 'inventor'. English law states that the inventor is the actual 'deviser of the invention'.[46] This provision has been interpreted by the courts as: 'whoever' has contributed to the inventive concept (understood as a whole) should be considered as an inventor. German law does not define 'inventor', but German case law has referred to 'inventor' as 'the person' that has creatively contributed to the subject-matter of the patent in view of the entire content of the patent application, including description and drawings (that is, on the basis of the patent application as a whole).[47] French law contains no legislative or regulatory provision that explicitly defines inventor. Case law explains that the concept of 'inventor' is assessed by reference to the means which constitute the invention. According to Paul Matéllyâ, '[w]hoever' conceives and makes the invention has the status of inventor. The invention consists in 'means which constitutes the invention'.[48]

Overall, it can be affirmed that thus far the concept of 'inventor' has not been given any particular focus either in legislation or case law in the EU area – the law remains silent in most cases. In particular, neither the EPC nor the national laws of most EU Member States explicitly define 'inventor'. Moreover, the case law is quite scarce: no case law from the EPO Boards and little jurisprudential material stemming from national courts.

Generally, however, it can be derived from the wording of the relevant provisions and their interpretations that, even though patent ownership can also be held by legal persons, only human beings can qualify as 'inventors'. Indeed, this way of reasoning is also reflected in a recent study conducted by the AIPPI organization, where several countries were asked their opinions about the need to develop a harmonized concept of 'inventor': all EU Member

---

[46]   S. 7(3) Patent Act 1997.

[47]   BGH decision X ZR 70/11 of 22 January 2013; BGH decision X ZR 53/08 of 17 May 2011 – *Atemgasdrucksteuerung*; BRG GRUR 1979 – 540 (541) – *Biedermeiermanschetten*; BRG GRUR 1978 – *Motorkettensäge*; BRG GRUR 1966 – *Spanplatten*.

[48]   AIPPI (n 50).

States interviewed favoured creation of a common definition of 'inventor' as a 'human being'.[49]

4. A THEORY OF EVOLUTION: BALANCING INCENTIVES AND ACCESS

The above analysis shows that under current interpretations non-humans, such as AI systems, are not entitled to either authorship or inventorship status in Europe. At the same time, however, the law per se is partly silent as to whether non-humans can qualify for authorship/inventorship, this way leaving the issue possibly open to judicial interpretation.

As technological developments in AI bring new challenges to these traditional concepts, the fundamental question arises whether there is a need to shape the law and/or its interpretations in order to promote rather than stifle technological developments. In other words, one could ask: is a system optimal if it either prevents copyright or patent protection on AI-generated innovations by prohibiting computer authorship or inventorship, or if it allows such IPRs only by permitting humans who have supported or discovered the work or invention of creative machines to be authors/inventors? Addressing this crucial and fundamental question requires us to take a step back and look at traditional theories that justify IPRs. We rely upon some major IP theories, namely utilitarian or economic theories of IP.[50]

Utilitarian theories justify protecting IPRs for the purpose of creating an incentive for innovative and creative activities. By awarding an exclusive right to the creator of an artistic work or the inventor of a technical innovation, the government provides the rightholder with *inter alia* the ability to hinder a competitor from utilizing that creation or invention. From an economic point of view, the rightholder obtains a temporary 'monopoly' limited in scope and enforceable for a specified period.

For patents, the justification is that, unless protection is provided, an inventor who is trying to cover the costs of R&D might face challenges when a new product is ready to be commercialized due to the ability of others to copy it. Because competitors are able to copy without having to bear R&D costs, the price of the product might drop and the inventor might not be able to cover the costs incurred. Ultimately, this might disincentivize development of further

---

[49] ibid.

[50] Peter S Menell, 'Intellectual Property: General Theories', in Boudewijn Bouckaert and Gerrit de Geest (eds), Encyclopedia of Law & Economics: Volume II (Edward Elgar Publishing, 2000); Robert P Merges, Peter S Menell, Mark A Lemley and Thomas M Jorde, *Intellectual Property in the New Technological Age* (Aspen Publishers, Inc., 1997).

inventions. Patents are also conceived positively in respect to secrecy because they allow disclosure of information: the inventor discloses information about the invention in exchange for being granted a temporary limited monopoly. Disclosure allows competitors to *inter alia* target how to direct their R&D resources, that is, how to 'invent around'.[51]

In the case of copyright, it is understood that creative activity usually includes a 'cost of expression' (a firm cost, corresponding to the time used to create the work) and a 'cost of production' (a running cost, dependent on the number of copies produced). In order to make creation of a work of art economically worthwhile, the estimated income from sales minus the cost of production should exceed or at least equal the cost of expression.[52] Even though several other factors can incentivize a creator, this economic argument is usually the most relevant.

Indeed, a balance needs to be sought in terms of protecting IP investments in order to promote innovations and creations, that is, between providing incentives and guaranteeing access.

How does all this, then, reflect on IPR regulation of AI with regard to authorship and inventorship? We answer this question by depicting three scenarios:

1. the Revolutionary School, with a 'property-centred' type of approach;
2. the Romantic School, with a 'non-property-centred' approach; and
3. the Modernist School, with a 'property-balanced' approach.

This method will guide us towards developing a holistic map of key factors to be considered by legislators and policymakers when trying to strike the balance between protection and access in the field of AI.

4.1   The Revolutionary School

One possibility for regulating AI-generated innovations could be to include in the law (or jurisprudence) an explicit provision that allows non-human authorship/inventorship. This solution would follow a 'property-centred' type of approach in the sense that it would allow IPR entitlement to any innovation produced by non-humans, as far as the other protectability requirements are met.

From a 'pure' legal perspective, a provision of this kind would have the consequence of attributing legal personhood to a non-human. In fact, both copyright and patent laws assume that the first author or inventor is also the

---

[51]   William Landes and Richard Posner, *The Economic Structure of Intellectual Property Law* (Harvard University Press, 2003) 294–402.
[52]   ibid, 37–165.

first owner of the IPR. In other words, opening the door for AI to become author/inventor would make a non-human a rightholder. Not only is this a much broader question than the one this chapter aims to address, but it is also a question that, for the time being, should be answered in the negative.

From the point of view of economic justifications of IPRs, increasing the reach of IP entitlements would indicate a policy focus on the need to provide incentives, rather than access. The question is then: who should we incentivize? Clearly, this mechanism does not aim at incentivizing a machine but, rather, the human stakeholders that are part of the innovation process. Generally, it could be argued that allocating IPRs this way – thus clarifying that any AI-generated output can attract IPRs in favour of some human beings (upon meeting the other requirements) – could either incentivize or disincentivize innovations in AI, depending on whom these IPRs are allocated to. For instance, assigning IPRs automatically to the owner of the AI machine would incentivize them to produce more AI systems, but it could disincentivize other stakeholders in the innovation process, such as data set providers or the like. One option could be to include a rule for assigning IP entitlement in favour of any natural person behind the arrangements necessary for the creation or invention involved. Even though this suggestion might be 'leaky' from multiple practical angles, it appears to us that the major problem of this solution is its heavy reliance on IPRs and an unbalanced expansion of the scope of protection very much in favour of IP holders.

Indeed, strengthening the reach and/or scope of IPRs has often been perceived as a suitable policy measure in the early phases of technological innovation. Previous examples include the extension of patentable subject-matter to allow protection for computer programs and DNA/gene-related inventions. At the same time, these same examples shed light on the negative side of regulating technology through law or regulation at too early a stage, with the US software industry being the most striking example: opening the doors to software and business methods patents has proven to have disastrous consequences for legal certainty and the entire US patent system.[53] Moreover, the European Parliament has already shown an eye for caution in terms of AI and IPRs in particular, by explicitly demanding a 'horizontal and technological neutral approach to intellectual property' with regard to AI, as well as a 'balanced approach to IPR ... that protect and at the same time foster innovation'.[54]

[53] RM Ballardini, 'Intellectual Property Protection of Computer Programs. Developments, Challenges, and Pressures for Change' (2012) 246 Economics and Society, https://helda.helsinki.fi/handle/10138/35504.

[54] Report with recommendations to the Commission on Civil Law Rules on Robotics (2015/2103(INL)), 27.01.2017: http://www.europarl.europa.eu/sides/getDoc.do?pubRef=-//EP//TEXT+REPORT+A8-2017-0005+0+DOC+XML+V0//EN.

In addition, mainstream scholarly literature has lately claimed that 'the main risk to advanced economies may not be that the pace of innovation is too slow, but that institutions have become too rigid to accommodate truly revolutionary changes'.[55]

In this light, creating new rules for AI and authorship/inventorship might not be justified either from a purely legal point of view or from an economic perspective as it might ultimately hinder rather than promote technological development.

4.2   The Romantic School

At the other extreme, a solution could be sought in a 'property-last' type of approach where no IPR entitlements would be conceived for creations or innovations made by non-humans.

From a legal point of view, the Romantic School follows the idea that the existing IPR framework should be interpreted so as to allow only natural persons to be authors/inventors in all categories. In addition, this approach would categorically deny IPR entitlement for non-human-produced innovations.

From the point of view of economic theories of IPR, securing IP protection on AI systems could arguably be sufficient to recoup R&D costs and investment and thus to incentivize new developments, while extending IPRs to the results produced by an automated system is not justified. As such, allowing innovations created by AI to fall into the public domain might ultimately benefit society more than assigning exclusive rights only to some.

This School, however, does consider several important factors, *inter alia* the fact that developers might actually build AI systems exactly for the purpose of creating artistic works or technical inventions in certain specific ways that, for instance, would not be achievable by human beings themselves. Indeed, in these cases, what incentivizes humans to develop AI systems is the prospect of having exclusive rights to the output. This could be even more true in cases where, for example, the AI machine per se would not be able to attract IPRs (because, for instance, the IPR requirements are not formally met) but the outcome could do so.

These situations might lead to an increase in the use of trade secrecy or contractual agreements as legal tools to protect AI-generated innovations. As previously mentioned, IPRs are usually conceived as better tools for promoting innovation than secrecy. Moreover, this system might ultimately create an

---

[55]   The Economist, 'Innovation Pessimism: Has the Ideas Machine Broken Down?', 22 (12 January 2013).

additional burden on patent or copyright offices, or ultimately courts, in terms of establishing whether a work or invention has been created by a human or not.

In the worst case scenario, the Romantic School approach might discourage rather than foster investment in and development of AI as a whole.

4.3 The Modernist School

Finally, one way to approach the issue could be to include in the law (or jurisprudence) a provision stating that only 'natural' persons can be authors/inventors and, at the same time, create a rule according to which the natural person(s) behind the arrangements necessary for the creation or the invention involved should be considered as the author/inventor. The Modernist School follows a similar approach that has been embraced in the UK with regard to computer-generated works, according to which, '[I]n the case of a literary, dramatic, musical or artistic work which is computer-generated, the author shall be taken to be the *person* by whom the arrangements necessary for the creation of the work are undertaken'.[56]

Indeed, a provision of this kind would leave no doubt that non-humans cannot be authors/inventors and that creations or inventions produced by non-humans cannot attract IPRs. Yet it would not remove possible problems and controversies about entitlement to IPRs. Indeed, in the AI context, several possibilities could exist for IPR entitlement, including, *inter alia*, assigning IPRs to (i) the designer(s) of the system, (ii) the data provider(s), and (iii) the user(s) of the system. On the other hand, though, a rule of this kind should be interpreted in light of the actual human contribution to the work or invention: obtaining the status of author/inventor would entail having contributed to the work or invention via inputting human intellectual creation or via sufficiently contributing to the inventive concept.

From the point of view of economic theories, one could ask whether a reason can be given for granting IPRs to the natural person that stands behind the innovation created, even where AI-generated innovations were not originally foreseen. On the one hand, even though the complexity of developing AI systems requires considerable upfront investment in R&D, such IPRs should be directed to the AI machine per se rather than to innovations generated by such AI. On the other hand, it is certainly undeniable that without human intervention no AI system could currently exist. But does this justify extending IPRs to AI-generated results as well?

---

[56] Copyright, Designs and Patents Act 1988, s. 9(3).

Under the Romantic School, we have already seen the potential negative effects of a system that forbids IPRs on non-human-generated innovations. In addition, an evident way to justify the Modernist School is that IPRs would arise only in cases where a sufficient human contribution to AI-generated innovation is found. In other words, unless the human contribution in the development of AI-generated output suffices for the purpose of showing the existence of a human's own intellectual creation or contribution to the inventive concept, no (human) author/inventor would be found. This approach also respects some already established and harmonized principles of European copyright and patent law and thus would avoid creation of unwanted fragmentations of the IPR framework. Indeed, it is likely that these questions would ultimately be addressed while assessing the originality of inventiveness of the innovations involved. To date, though, it is quite clear that creation of increasingly advanced AI systems will require immense efforts by humans even in the future because the problems are becoming ever harder. In the circumstances, it appears that the role of humans in the innovation process will remain crucial in the development not only of AI systems per se, but also of AI-generated output.[57]

5.   CONCLUSION

Traditionally, technological changes have generated tensions in the IP system. AI technology is no exception. With increasingly advanced AI, the roles of author/inventor are likely to become less clearly defined. This will challenge established notions of authorship and inventorship in copyright and patent laws. The Revolutionary and Romantic schools do not seem justifiable either from the perspective of legal traditions or from the standpoint of economic justification of IPRs. At one extreme, the Revolutionary School assigns legal personhood to AI, fundamentally contradicting our general understanding of the law. Moreover, even where AI is author/inventor, the need remains to incentivize human participants in the innovative process: such a determination might be highly complex and too challenging at this stage. The Romantic School categorically excludes the possibility of attributing IPRs to non-human-generated innovations. However, this solution neglects to provide proportionate incentives to the humans participating in developing AI systems and, potentially, AI-generated output. The Modernist School, as a compromise,

---

[57]   A similar approach seems to be followed in the USA. See, eg, Margot E Kaminski, 'Authorship, Disrupted: AI Authors in Copyright and First Amendment Law' (2017) 51(589) UC Davis Law Review and Jane C Ginsburg, 'People Not Machines: Authorship and What It Means in the Berne Convention' (2018) 49 IIC 131–135.

allows IPR entitlements to natural persons that have sufficiently contributed to AI-generated output. In that light, it may be a better fit to promote innovation in a world of AI-generated content. On the one hand, this does not distort commonly accepted legal principles, while, on the other, it offers a reasonable and proportionate incentive to human involvement in the innovation process that ultimately leads to AI-generated output.

9. Winds of change: conceptualising copyright law in a world of 3D models and 3D design files – a perspective from the UK

Dinusha Mendis

1. INTRODUCTION

> New technologies such as 3D printing seem likely…to create…widespread consumer-driven infringements, of the sort seen in other sectors that led to the collapse of intellectual property regimes…[1]

The above quote captures the disruption that additive manufacturing[2] – or 3D printing as it is more commonly known – can bring about. The concept, which can be traced back to a 1974 article,[3] led to a patent in 1977[4] and to the first commercial 3D printer in 1988.[5] Since then, the technology has come a long way and has paved the way for many opportunities in the medical, transport, food, toy and hobby, fashion and cosmetics industries, to name but a few.[6]

---

[1]   *Economic Review of Industrial Design in Europe* (MARKT2013/064/D2/ST/OP) (Europe Economics; 2015) 13.

[2]   Additive manufacturing refers to the production of end-use layer manufactured parts produced within a business-to-consumer supply chain. 3D Printing is used to refer to the manufacture of layer-manufactured products within the home or community.

[3]   D Jones, 'Ariadne' Column, 3 October 1974, *New Scientist*, 80.

[4]   Application no. 05/165042 filed 23 July 1971. US Patent 4,041,476 'Method, medium and apparatus for producing three-dimensional figure product' granted 9 August 1977.

[5]   Application no. 06/638,905 filed 8 August 1984. US Patent 4,575,330 'Apparatus for Production of Three-Dimensional Objects by Stereolithography' granted 11 March 1986.

[6]   European Parliament, Working Document on Three-Dimensional Printing, a Challenge in the Fields of Intellectual Property Rights and Civil Liability 23 November 2017 and and 26 June 2018. On 3 July 2018, the report by Joelle Bergeron was adopted by the European Parliament.

Moreover, this new technology has opened up doors to design freedom and the ability to create precise physical replication.[7]

This latter point, of creating precise physical replicas, has also raised a number of challenging questions in the context of intellectual property (hereinafter IP) laws. In particular, the recent introduction of home-based 3D printing has enabled consumers to engage in the manufacture of products using digital content bought or 'shared' online, circumventing much of the traditional manufacturing and retail value chain.[8] This has provided the potential for designing, sharing and reproducing physical objects[9] through the medium of design files, which in turn raises the question whether 3D printing has heralded a new type of 'file-sharing' – that is, from the online distribution of music, games and films to physical objects. Similar to previous technologies and online distribution platforms,[10] 3D printing and its associated elements such as object design files and online platforms are also universal in their reach. Yet the law is territorial. Therefore, as online distribution in the sphere of 3D printing begins to gather speed, it is imperative to consider the IP framework.

However, the position in relation to the technology as well as IP laws remains under-developed. For example, design barriers, such as lack of a straightforward 'print' button for 3D printing, means that at present 3D printing continues to be largely reserved for those with technical ability and technical knowledge.[11] Even so, the bigger obstacle to the '3D printing evolution' is that few consumers or designers have the ability to operate the software, which is used to render objects and turn them into files that can be printed and as such are reliant on existing designs. 'A lot of people are 3D printing other people's designs, but they can't yet model their own.'[12] This is further exacerbated by

---

[7]   H Lipson and M Kurman, *Fabricated: The New World of 3D Printing* (Indiana: John Wiley & Sons, Inc.; 2013) 20–24.

[8]   See, Innovate UK, Materials KTN: *Shaping Our National Competency in Additive Manufacturing* (September 2012) 4. As a digital technology, 'additive manufacturing' (more commonly called 3D Printing) is progressively being integrated with the internet, enabling consumers to engage directly in the design process, and allowing true consumer personalisation.

[9]   Lipson and Kurman (n 7) 7.

[10]   Eg, these include platforms which have engaged in illegal file-sharing such as Napster, Grokster and Pirate Bay amongst others, to legal platforms such as Spotify and Netflix.

[11]   *Economic Review of Industrial Design in Europe* (n 1)).

[12]   Ibid.

access to online sharing platforms,[13] which facilitate[14] the creation and dissemination of 3D object designs or Computer-Aided Design (hereinafter CAD) files for download and printing.[15]

This chapter will explore the challenges to IP laws, particularly copyright law, as a result of 3D printing. This analysis will be carried out from the perspective of the United Kingdom (UK) as informed by European Union (EU) law. Whilst the current political climate in the UK following Brexit has opened up uncertainties in relation to the future of IP law,[16] the discussion in this chapter will be considered from the perspective of a harmonised and Union-wide IP framework, which has informed UK law over the years.

As a starting point, the chapter will provide an account of the protection of 3D models in the UK and, in doing so, will draw a line through history to chart the development of artistic works. Through this narrative the chapter will offer an insight into the protection of engravings, sculptures and 3D models over the years. Thereafter the chapter will turn to consider the eligibility and protection of CAD files, and will question whether they can be protected as a copyright work, before moving on to consider the implications for copyright law of 3D scanning of 3D models and the modification of 3D object design files through online tools. Therefore, whilst 3D printing raises a variety of issues relating to IP rights,[17] this chapter will focus particularly on the implications for copyright law.

---

[13]   Online platforms for 3D printing include amongst others, Thingiverse, Shapeways Sculpteo, GrabCad, 123D, Cubify, Ponoko and Pirate Bay.

[14]   In the UK, under the Copyright, Designs and Patents Act 1988 (CDPA 1988) the law prohibits the 'authorisation' of infringement. 'Section 16(2) – Copyright in a work is infringed by a person who without the licence of the copyright owner does, or *authorises another to do,* any of the acts restricted by the copyright' (emphasis added).

[15]   D Mendis, D Secchi and P Reeves, *A Legal and Empirical Study into the Intellectual Implications of 3D Printing* (London: UK Intellectual Property Office; 2015) 6–7. Available at: https://www.gov.uk/government/publications/3d-printing -research-reports.

[16]   R Arnold, L Bently, E Derclaye and G Dinwoodie, 'The Legal Consequences of Brexit Through the Lens of IP Law' (15 February 2017) Oxford Legal Studies Research Paper 15/2017; University of Cambridge Faculty of Law, Research Paper, No 21/2017, available at https://papers.ssrn.com/sol3/papers.cfm?abstract_id=2917219.

[17]   For a discussion on the implications of 3D printing as it relates to various intellectual property laws, see D Mendis, '"Clone Wars": Episode I – The Rise of 3D Printing and its Implications for Intellectual Property Law: Learning Lessons from the Past?' (2013) 35(3) *European Intellectual Property Review* 155–169; and S Bradshaw, A Bowyer and P Haufe, 'The Intellectual Property Implications of Low-Cost 3D Printing' (2010) 7(1) *Script-ed,* available at www.law.ed.ac.uk/ahrc/script-ed/vol7-1/ bradshaw.asp.

2.   FROM ENGRAVINGS AND SCULPTURES TO 3D OBJECTS AND MODELS: THE CHANGING LANDSCAPE OF ARTISTIC WORKS IN THE UK

'Engravings' were first recognised under the Engravings Copyright Acts of 1735 (also known as Hogarth's Act)[18] and 1767 and gave protection to producers of engravings. Engravings were therefore the first 'artistic works' to be protected, giving the artist a monopoly on the *engraving and printing* of his or her work for a term of 28 years after first publication, provided the artist's name and the date appeared on the original prints.[19] This significant development in copyright law was followed by sculptures, which attracted copyright protection in 1798.[20] In accordance with the Act, the engraver (that is, the artist) was considered the owner of the original design, whether it was a historical print, portrait, landscape, architectural design, and so on. Conversely the artist was given the right to copy an existing design, provided consent had been acquired from the owner of the original print.[21] Either way, under the 1735 and 1767 Acts, the protection afforded to the value of engravings and sculptures was assessed by how closely they could reproduce the 2D print.[22] This, in turn, gave the engraver an exclusive licence to stop others from reproducing the same 2D print as an engraving, unless the print/design belonged to a public institution, in which case other engravings could be made from the same picture.[23]

However, the 1735 and 1767 Acts were repealed by the Copyright Act 1911, which defined 'engravings' as including 'etchings, lithographs, wood-cuts, prints, and other similar works, not being photographs'.[24] This definition of engravings, explicitly excluding photographs, is significant and represents a move away from faithful reproduction of works to works which reflect the

---

[18]   Named after William Hogarth (1697–1764), who is best known for his moral and satirical engravings and paintings. See S Shesgreen, *Engravings by Hogarth* (New York: Dover Publications; 1974).

[19]   Engravings Copyright Acts of 1735 and 1767. See C Seville, *Literary Copyright Reform in Early Victorian England: The Framing of the 1842 Act* (Cambridge: CUP; 2011); M. Rose, 'Technology and Copyright in 1735: The Engravers Act' (2005) 21(1) *The Information Society* 63–66. Also see JJ Lowndes, *A Historical Sketch of the Law of Copyright* (London: Saunders and Benning; 1840) 84.

[20]   1798 Act – passed to prevent the pirating of busts etc. See also Seville (n 19).

[21]   *Sayre v Moore* (1785): 'in the case of prints, no doubt different men may take engravings from the same picture, but one cannot copy the engravings of another'.

[22]   Ibid.

[23]   Section 5, Engravings Copyright Act 1735.

[24]   Section 35, Copyright Act 1911.

artist's own personal touch.[25] This is interesting, as the development of artistic works portrays a desire for identical replicas in the eighteenth century whilst the nineteenth century and the turn of the twentieth century required artists to move away from faithful reproduction, to works representing the author's own skill, labour, effort and judgement as reflected in UK case law throughout the years since then.[26] In fact, section 2(1)(iii) of the Copyright Act 1911 states that copyright in an artistic work shall not be infringed:

> [w]here the author of an artistic work is not the owner of the copyright therein, the use by the author of any mould, cast, sketch, plan, model, or study made by him for the purpose of the work, provided that *he does not thereby repeat or imitate the main design of that work* (emphasis added).

The Copyright Act 1956 included an entire section devoted to the subject matter of artistic works. Whilst the 1956 Act retained protection for 'engravings' as clarified in the 1911 Act, the definition was broadened to include paintings and drawings, irrespective of artistic quality as well as photographs which had been excluded under 'engravings' under the 1911 Act.[27] As such, the 1956 Act saw a broadening of the term 'artistic work' to include subject matter which had not been included before. One other aspect of the 1956 Act was the lengthening of the copyright term to 50 years from 28 years. In particular, section 3(4)(a) went on to clarify the term of protection for artistic works as 50 years from the end of the calendar year in which the author died. Where the engraving had not been published before the death of the author, the copyright would continue to subsist until the end of the period of 50 years from the end of the calendar year in which it was first published.[28]

Finally, the modern copyright Act – the Copyright, Designs and Patents Act 1988 (CDPA 1988) – broadens the meaning of artistic works even further. Section 4(1) of the Act defines an artistic work as a 'graphic work, photograph, sculpture or collage, irrespective of artistic quality...or a work of architecture

---

[25] *Infopaq International A/S v Danske Dagblades Forening* Case C-5/08 [2010] FSR 20. See also A. Rahmatian, 'Originality in UK Copyright Law: The Old "Skill and Labour" Doctrine Under Pressure' (2013) 44(1) *International Review of Intellectual Property and Competition Law* 4–34.

[26] *Hedderwick v Griffin* (1841) 3 D, 383; *Thomas v Turner* (1886) 23 ChD 292; *Walter v Lane* [1900] AC 539; *University of London Press v University Tutorial Press* [1916] 2 Ch 601; *Macmillan and Co Ltd v Cooper* (1924) 40 TLR 186; *Hogg v Toye and Co* [1935] Ch. 497. These cases established that for copyright to exist 'labour' must portray some sort of 'individuality and independency' where the pre-existing work is developed and embellished in some way.

[27] Section 3(1) Copyright Act 1956.

[28] Section 3(4)(a) Copyright Act 1956.

being a building or a model for a building or artistic craftsmanship'.[29] A sculpture is defined as including a 'cast or model made for purposes of sculpture'[30] – which appears to be a circular definition – whilst a 'work of artistic craftsmanship' is not further defined. Signalling a clear move away from the days of the 1735 and 1767 Acts, the 1988 Act states that an artistic work can be infringed by making a 3D copy of a 2D object and vice versa.[31]

However, section 51 of the CDPA 1988 is of much relevance to the present discussion and in fact limits the scope of section 17(3). Section 51 of the CDPA 1988 states that 'it is not an infringement of any copyright in a design document or model recording or embodying a design for anything other than an artistic work or a typeface to make an article to the design or to copy an article made to the design'. To clarify, it is not copyright in the 2D or 3D design itself but copyright in the *design document or model embodying a design* that is affected by this section.[32] This section, incorporating both the design document and the 3D model into a single section, is worthy of further consideration in the context of the present discussion and will be evaluated further in Section 4 of this chapter. Before doing so, the chapter will first explore the protection of a CAD design document and thereafter will question whether it has a place in copyright law.

3.   CAD DESIGN FILES: ELIGIBILITY AND PROTECTION UNDER COPYRIGHT LAW

Computers play a critical role in the 3D printing process. Without instructions from a computer, a 3D printer simply will not work. The functioning of a 3D printer therefore depends on it being 'fed' a well-designed electronic design file, which could be a CAD file, that tells it where to place the raw material. In fact, 'a 3D printer without an attached computer and a good design file is as useless as an iPod without music'.[33]

Therefore, every object produced by a 3D printer begins its design process with a CAD-based digital object design file. 'The object design file is similar

---

[29]   Section 4(1)(a)–(c) CDPA 1988.
[30]   Section 4(2) CDPA 1988.
[31]   Section 17(2), (3) CDPA 1988.
[32]   This section was interpreted in the case of *Lucasfilm Ltd & others v Ainsworth and another* [2011] 3 WLR 487. The Court, favouring the defendant in this case, argued that the Stormtrooper helmets created by the defendant were not an infringement of Lucasfilm's *Star Wars* films. 'It was the Star Wars film that was the work of art that Mr. Lucas and his company created … the helmet was utilitarian, in the sense that it was an element in the process of production of the film', *per* Lord Walker at [44].
[33]   Lipson and Kurman (n 7) 12.

to the architectural blueprints for a building or the sewing pattern for a dress – it is a digital 3D model which the printer uses to build the object using the specifications defined in the design.'[34] However, can these CAD files be protected?

In accordance with copyright law, where creators initiate and design an 'original' creative work, the copyright will rest with the first creator.[35] Where this involves a CAD file, questions of eligibility of protection arise. Matt Simon argues that even if it is determined that 3D design files are capable of being protected by copyright, for example, issues arise when considering items such as food, living cells, and organs for which 3D printing is used.[36] He opines that copyright protection 'cannot exist for…scientific progress because that is protected solely by patent law'.[37] As such, the uncertainty surrounding the protection of CAD design files has been captured in a number of academic commentaries.[38] These arguments stem from the question whether CAD design files containing machine-readable instructions can be perceived as 'data', based on the fact that they provide instructions. Or should they attract literary copyright protection, based on the fact that they encompass preparatory design

---

[34]   SM Santoso, BD Horne and SB Wicker, 'Destroying by Creating: Exploring the Creative Destruction of 3D Printing Through Intellectual Property' (2013) available at www.truststc.org/education/reu/13/Papers/HorneB_Paper.pdf.

[35]   Section 1(1)(a) Copyright, Designs and Patents Act 1988 (as amended) (hereinafter CDPA 1988). There is no express requirement of 'originality' as such in relation to films, sound recordings, broadcasts and typographical arrangements of published editions although copyright does not exist in such works which have been copied from previous sound recordings, broadcasts or published editions. See section 1(1)(b) CDPA 1988. See also *University of London Press v University Tutorial Press* [1916] 2 Ch 601.

[36]   M Simon, 'When Copyright Can Kill: How 3D Printers Are Breaking the Barriers Between "Intellectual Property" and the Physical World' (Spring 2013) 3(1) *Pace Intellectual Property Sports and Entertainment Law Forum* 59–97, available at http://digitalcommonspace.edu/pipself/vol3/iss1/4.

[37]   Ibid, at 71.

[38]   B Rideout, 'Printing the Impossible Triangle: The Copyright Implications of Three-Dimensional Printing' (2011) 5(1) *Journal of Business Entrepreneurship & Law* 161–180; D Mendis, '"Clone Wars"': Episode II The Next Generation – The Copyright Implications relating to 3D Printing and Computer-Aided Design (CAD) Files' (2014) 6(2) *Law, Innovation and Technology* 265–281; M Antikainen and D Jongsma, 'The Art of CAD: Copyrightability of Digital Design Files' in R Ballardini, M Norrgård and J Partanen, 3D Printing, *Intellectual Property and Innovation: Insights from Law and Technology* (Alphen aan den Rijn: Kluwer Law International BV; 2017) ch 1. For further insight into copyright law, from a US point of view, see also M Weinberg, 'What's the Deal with Copyright and 3D Printing' (2013) available at www.publicknowledge.org/news-blog/blogs/whats-the-deal-with-copyright-and-3d -printing; M Weinberg, 'It Will be Awesome If They Don't Screw It Up: 3D Printing, Intellectual Property and the Fight Over the Next Great Disruptive Technology' (2010) available at www.publicknowledge.org/news-blog/blogs/it-will-be-awesome-if-they -dont-screw-it-up-3d-printing.

work leading to the development of a computer program which can result from it at a later stage?

Therefore, the question is one of the protection of software and computer programs; that is, can a digital file arising from a CAD-based program be protected under copyright law? The section below attempts to shed some light on this question through a consideration of case law drawn from the Court of Justice of the European Union (CJEU) and the UK.

3.1   Protection of Software and Computer Programs: an Overview

Recital 7 of the EU Software Directive defines computer programs as follows:

> For the purpose of this Directive, the term 'computer program' shall include programs in any form including those which are incorporated into hardware. This term also includes preparatory design work leading to the development of a computer program provided that the nature of the preparatory work is such that a computer program can result from it at a later stage.[39]

An analysis of the above quote establishes that:

> the protection is…bound to the program code and to the functions that enable the computer to perform its task. This implies that there is no protection for elements without such functions (that is, graphical user interface (GUI), or 'mere data') and which are not reflected in the code (that is, functionality itself is not protected, since there could be a different code that may be able to produce the same function).[40]

In other words, copyright protection will attach to the *expression of the computer code* (source code) and will not extend to the functionality of the software (object code).

However, Waelde et al argue that the fact that object code is incapable of copyright protection is no longer sustainable.[41] Yet, it is this point which has

---

[39]   Directive 2009/24/EC of the European Parliament and of the Council of 23 April 2009 on the legal protection of computer programs, Rec (7).

[40]   *SAS Institute Inc. v World Programming Ltd.* (C-406/10) [2012] 3 CMLR 4; [2013] Bus LR 941. See also P Guarda, 'Looking For a Feasible Form of Software Protection: Copyright or Patent, Is That the Question?' [2013] 35(8) *European Intellectual Property Review* 445–454 at 447.

[41]   C Waelde, A Brown, S Kheria and J Cornwell, *Contemporary Intellectual Property: Law and Policy* (4th edn) 64–65. This argument succeeded in the Australian case of *Apple Computers Inc v Computer Edge Pty Ltd* [1986] FSR 537. In New Zealand, the object code achieved copyright as a translation of the source code: *IBM Corp v Computer Imports Ltd* [1989] 2 NZLR 395.

given rise to much debate as reflected in various articles and commentaries[42] as emerging technologies tend to blur the line between source and object code.

The issue of the status of computer programs was considered in *Bezpečnostní*[43] and *SAS Institute Inc. v World Programming Ltd.*[44] In *Bezpečnostní*, the CJEU stated, following the principles expressed in *Infopaq*,[45] that notwithstanding the position under the Software Directive, the ordinary law of copyright could protect the graphic user interface of a computer program.[46] In *SAS Institute Inc.*, the CJEU concluded (unsurprisingly) that functionality, language and data file formats are not protected by copyright under the Software Directive since they do not constitute forms of expression. However, the Court suggested that the *programming language and data file formats* 'might be protected, as works, by copyright under [the Copyright] Directive...if they are their author's own intellectual creation',[47] clearly drawing on the decision of *Bezpečnostní.*[48]

Its consideration in the UK High Court and Court of Appeal highlighted issues with the CJEU decision. For example, the decision does not answer the question as to whether copyright protection might extend to underlying elements of the program, such as its programming languages and the format of data files, under the Copyright Directive. Lewison LJ in the Court of Appeal

---

[42]   Rideout (n 38)161–180; A Daly, *Socio-Legal Aspects of the 3D Printing Revolution* (London: Palgrave Macmillan; 2016) ch 4; TY Ebrahim, '3D Printing, Digital Infringement and Digital Regulation' (2016) 14(1) *Northwestern Journal of Technology and Intellectual Property* 37–74; M Rimmer, 'The Maker Movement: Copyright Law, Remix Culture and 3D Printing' (2017) 41(2) *The University of Western Australia Law Review* 51–84; M Antikainen and D Jongsma, 'The Art of CAD: Copyrightability of Digital Design Files' in Ballardini et al (eds) (n 38) ch 12.

[43]   *Bezpečnostní Softwarová Asociace – Svaz Softwarové Ochrany v Ministerstvo Kultury* (C-393/09) [2011] ECDR 3.

[44]   *SAS Institute Inc. v World Programming Ltd.* (n 40).

[45]   *Infopaq International A/S v Danske Dagblades Forening* (n 25).

[46]   *Bezpečnostní Softwarová Asociace – Svaz Softwarové Ochrany v Ministerstvo Kultury* (n43) at paras 35 and 38.

[47]   *SAS Institute Inc., v World Programming Ltd.* (n 40) at, para 39. The CJEU also stated that 'keywords, syntax, commands and combinations of commands, options, defaults, and iterations consisting of words, figures or mathematical concepts which, considered in isolation are not, as such, an intellectual creation of the author ... It is only through the choice, sequence and combination ... that the author may express his creativity in an original manner and achieve a result, namely the user manual for the program, which is an intellectual creation' (paras 66–67).

[48]   *Bezpečnostní Softwarová Asociace – Svaz Softwarové Ochrany v Ministerstvo Kultury* (n 43) at paras 35 and 38. See also K Toft, 'The Case of SAS Institute Inc., v World Programming Ltd' [2014] 20(2) *Computer and Telecommunications Law Review* 59–62 at 60.

stated that the language used by the CJEU was at times 'disappointingly compressed, if not obscure'.[49]

According to Toft, the CJEU case law gives 'developers the freedom to reproduce the functionality of software in the knowledge they cannot be pursued for copyright infringement ... the same cannot be said for the initial software developer'.[50]

3.2 Protection of CAD-based Design Files: Protection Through Copyright Law and Unregistered Design Rights?

In the UK, the Copyright, Designs and Patents Act 1988 (as amended) states that a computer program and its embedded data, for example, is recognised as a literary work under copyright law.[51] Applying the current law to the 3D printing context, it can be established that a computer program encompasses a CAD-based object design file within its definition and is therefore capable of copyright protection in the UK as a literary work. In two previous articles, Bradshaw et al[52] and Mendis,[53] applying the law to object design files, clarified that a CAD file is an original work of authorship, which may be protected by literary copyright in the same manner as other types of computer software. Further support for this view can be found in *Autospin (Oil Seals) Ltd. v Beehive Spinning*,[54] where Laddie J makes reference, *obiter*, to three-dimensional articles being designed by computers and states that 'a literary work consisting of computer code represents the three-dimensional article'.[55]

However, it can also be argued that these CAD files simply contain machine-readable instructions for purposes of 3D printing a physical object. If so, should these CAD files be perceived as 'data', based on the fact that they provide instructions – or can they in fact be considered a copyright work, potentially under the subject matter of literary and/or artistic works?[56]

---

[49]   *SAS Institute Inc., v World Programming Ltd.* (n 40) at [5].
[50]   Toft (n 48) 62.
[51]   Section 3(1)(b), (c) CDPA 1988 (as amended).
[52]   Bradshaw et al (n 17) 24.
[53]   Mendis (n 17) 63.
[54]   *Autospin (Oil Seals) Ltd. v Beehive Spinning* [1995] RPC 683.
[55]   Ibid at 698. See also *Nova v Mazooma Games Ltd.* [2007] RPC 25. Jacob LJ, referring to the Software Directive 2009/24/EC implemented by CDPA 1988, confirmed that for purposes of copyright, the program and its preparatory material are considered to be one component as opposed to two.
[56]   D Mendis, 'In Pursuit of Clarity: the Conundrum of CAD and Copyright – Seeking Direction Through Case Law', [2018] 40(11) European Intellectual Property Review, 694–705.

A number of cases drawn from the UK, such as *Abraham Moon & Sons Ltd v Andrew Thornber and Others*,[57] *Brigid Foley Ltd v Ellott and Others*[58] and *Anacon Corp v Environmental Research Technology*,[59] lend support to the argument of a CAD file being considered a literary and artistic copyright work, despite the fact that it contains instructions for printing an end-product. For example, in the case of *Abraham Moon & Sons Ltd v Andrew Thornber and Others*, Judge Birss QC held that a ticket which did not portray any illustrations and contained two pages of written instructions – that is, having only words and numbers without any illustration – could be regarded as an artistic (graphical) work as well as a literary work.[60] Adding further support to this view, the case of *Anacon Corp v Environmental Research Technology* held that an electronic circuit diagram, containing symbols and instructions, was a literary work.

Guidance for the protection of a design document, containing a design, can also be drawn from unregistered design rights and in particular section 226 of the UK's CDPA 1988. This section provides some clarity as to the eligibility and protection of design documents in the context of CAD files. It states that '[t]he owner of design right in a design has the exclusive right to reproduce the design for commercial purposes (a) by making articles to that design, or (b) by making a design document recording that design for the purpose of enabling such articles to be made'.

As such, section 226 explicitly defines 'a design document' as being any record of a design, whether in the form of a drawing, a written description, a photograph, data stored in a computer or otherwise.[61] Accordingly it could be submitted that a CAD file could fit within the definition of a design document since it is essentially a computer file or data comprising the record of a three-dimensional object. If so, can a CAD file be infringed by the resulting end-product it produces?

This question was explored in the case of *Brigid Foley Ltd v Ellott and Others*. In this case, Megarry V-C explored the copyright status of 3D products arising from design documents and their standing as artistic works. In questioning whether the resulting products were capable of infringing a design document, Megarry V-C held that a 3D product prototype arising from a design document does not infringe the design document.[62] A similar decision was delivered by Judge Birss in the case of *Abraham Moon*. In this case the judge

---

[57]   [2012] EWPCC 37.
[58]   [1982] RPC 433.
[59]   [1994] FSR 659.
[60]   *See also Mitchell v BBC* [2011] EWPCC 42 at 25.
[61]   Section 263(1) CDPA 1988.
[62]   [1982] RPC 433; *per* Megarry V-C at 434.

explained that 'once made, a fabric would not look the same as it did on a CAD system even if one was used. With CAD, it would not be possible to feel the fabric, which is an important part of the process.'[63]

In other words, and according to the above case law, it can be argued that a design document and the resulting end-product are two separate works of creation, which attract their own separate copyright.

In concluding this part of the discussion and in reflecting on the status of a CAD-based object design file, from the EU/UK perspective, it is clear that some questions arise as to its eligibility and protection. At the same time, UK case law sheds some light and guidance on the protection of design files, which carry instructions and symbols. However, to be protected as a copyright work, a CAD file also has to demonstrate sufficient originality. Where a 3D digital model is not initiated by the creator but instead is created from scanning an existing object or modifying an existing object found on an online platform, then meeting the originality requirement under copyright law will be challenging, as discussed below.

4.   MODIFYING AN OBJECT DESIGN FILE: IMPLICATIONS FOR COPYRIGHT LAW

In considering whether a scanned 3D digital model of an artistic work is capable of copyright protection, it must first be pointed out that scanning a work which is protected by copyright constitutes copying,[64] requiring permission to avoid infringement.[65] In particular, if a 'substantial part' has been taken from another creator in designing a 3D model, then 'it makes no difference that a different medium is used (once the object has been scanned), or that the infringing work is derived indirectly from the original work, such as where an intermediary has given verbal instructions which are used by a third party to recreate the work'.[66] Thus, making an exact replica of a work that is protected by copyright, or taking a substantial part of the protected work, will infringe copyright.

However, in the 3D printing context, some interesting questions arise. For example, does a design file *embodying* a physical object infringe copyright where the design file is modified? Ultimately, a design file is a vessel for carrying the physical 3D object and such questions are worthy of consideration. Additionally, 3D scanning and printing allows recreation and restoration of

---

[63]   [2012] EWPCC 37 at para 46.
[64]   *Infopaq International A/S v Danske Dagbaldes Forening* (n 25) at [24].
[65]   Section 4 of this chapter is partly adapted from Mendis (n 38).
[66]   Ibid.

ancient works, which can now be scanned, reverse-engineered and printed, thereby creating a 'new' work. This leads to the following question: what is the copyright status of 'works' which have been restored and reconstituted through the mechanism of scanning, when in copyright or out of copyright? The case of *Sawkins v Hyperion Records*[67] provides some direction here. For example, the performance score of Lalande's music in *Sawkins* was considered an original work irrespective of the fact that it was *derived* from the original music in which copyright had expired. However, the performance score would have been original if it had been created when Lalande's original music was still under copyright protection.[68]

The Supreme Court of Israel in the *Dead Sea Scrolls* case[69] came to a similar ruling to that of *Sawkins* and shed further light on the issue. The Court held that Professor Qimron's reconstitution of the 2,000-year-old Dead Sea Scrolls was an original work for purposes of copyright. Qimron therefore owned copyright in the deciphered text as a literary work in the same way Sawkins owned a musical copyright in the performing editions.

Ong supports the view that copyright can subsist in re-creative works which have been scanned from out-of-copyright works on the basis that skill and judgement has been exercised in the re-creation of such works. He argues that copyright should not only 'incentivise' works which are 'materially altered' from the pre-existing work. He states that it could be in the public interest for authors to make identical replicas of antecedent works which are of major cultural significance or extremely inaccessible or both.[70]

This view is also supported by the cases of *Antiquesportfolio*[71] and *Painer*.[72] In *Antiquesportfolio* photographs of antiques were held to be copyright works, taking into account the positioning of the object, the angle at which it was taken, the lighting and the focus, which culminated in exhibiting particular

---

[67]   *Sawkins v Hyperion Records Ltd.* [2005] EWCA Civ 565.

[68]   P Torremans (ed), *Copyright Law: A Handbook of Contemporary Research* (Cheltenham: Edward Elgar Publishing; 2009) 32–38. See also A Rahmatian, 'The Concepts of "Musical Works" and "Originality" in UK Copyright Law – *Sawkins v Hyperion* as a Test Case' [2009] 40(5) *International Review of Intellectual Property and Competition Law* 560–591.

[69]   *Eisenmann v Qimron* 54(3) PD 817. See also M Birnhack, 'The Dead Sea Scrolls Case: Who is an Author?' [2001] 23(3) *European Intellectual Property Review* 128–133; T Lim, H MacQueen and C Carmichael (eds), *On Scrolls, Artefacts and Intellectual Property* (Sheffield Academic Press; 2001).

[70]   B Ong, 'Originality From Copying: Fitting Recreative Works into the Copyright Universe' (2010) 2 *Intellectual Property Quarterly* 165–199 at 174.

[71]   *Antiquesportfolio.com Plc v Rodney Fitch & Co. Ltd.* [2001] FSR 23.

[72]   *Painer v Standard Verlags GmbH* (C-145/10) [2012] ECDR 6 (ECJ (3rd Chamber).

qualities including the colour, features and details of the items. The Court stated that such elements could all be matters of aesthetic or even commercial judgement, albeit in most cases at a very basic level[73] but sufficient to demonstrate a degree of skill for copyright to exist in the photographs.[74]

At the same time, CJEU cases, notably *Infopaq International A/S v Danske Dagblades Forening*,[75] *Painer v Standard Verlags GmbH*[76] and most recently *Football Dataco Ltd v Yahoo! UK Ltd*,[77] concluded that a 'copyright work' should demonstrate the 'own intellectual creation of its author',[78] thereby placing the emphasis on the right form of authorial input as opposed to the category of copyright works.

Applying the above-discussed cases to scanned 3D models, it can be deduced that such objects will draw a new copyright on the basis of the skill, effort and judgement which will be expended in the reverse-engineering process. Application of European 'authorial input' – as seen in cases such as *Infopaq* discussed above – will, however, require the personal touch of the creator (rather than being verbatim or a replica) before such 3D scanned models can attract new copyright. As such, it could be argued that making creative choices – such as selecting particular views of a physical object when a 3D digital model is created through scanning an object – is sufficient to make the 3D digital model an 'intellectual creation of the author reflecting his personality and expressing his free and creative choice'[79] in its production.

Yet, it is clear that where a work is 'copied' without authorisation, this will constitute an infringement of copyright. As Bradshaw et al point out, 'trafficking in copies of a manufacturers' official 3DPDFs (3D object design files) [*sic*] for spare parts would be illegitimate'.[80] This highlights the issues which can surface from sharing 3D design files on online platforms without the consent of the copyright owner or licence holder, which can be modified numerous times by using online tools.[81]

---

[73] *Antiquesportfolio.com Plc v Rodney Fitch & Co. Ltd.* (n 71) para 36.
[74] Ibid, at para 37.
[75] (C-5/08) [2010] FSR 20.
[76] (C-145/10) [2012] ECDR 6 (ECJ (3rd Chamber).
[77] (C-604/10) [2012] Bus. L.R. 1753.
[78] Case C-5/08 *Infopaq International A/S v Danske Dagblades Forening* (n 25). See also Rahmatian (n 25).
[79] *Painer v Standard Verlags GmbH* (n 72) at para 99.
[80] Bradshaw et al (n 17) 25.
[81] D Mendis and D Secchi, *A Legal and Empirical Study of 3D Printing Online Platforms and an Analysis of User Behaviour* (London: UK Intellectual Property Office; 2015) available at https://www.gov.uk/government/publications/3d-printing -research-reports.

A Commissioned project for the UK Intellectual Property Office (UKIPO), published in 2015, concluded that the increase in scanning devices, together with the proliferation of online tools with their ability to modify third-party design files, could prove problematic in the 3D printing world for those wanting to protect their IP.[82] This issue is exacerbated by the uncertainty surrounding protection of design files, as discussed above. Therefore, as 3D printing and 3D scanning devices continue to grow, a review of the IP framework will be needed to provide much-needed certainty for key stakeholders in this field.[83]

5.   CONCLUSION

This chapter considered protection of 3D models, 3D design files and the copyright status of such design files embodying a physical object, and the copyright status where such a file is modified. In the first part of the chapter, the author drew a line through history in exploring the development of artistic works in protecting engravings, sculptures and 3D models – from the perspective of the UK – and provided guidance on the protection of 3D models.

Thereafter, the discussion focused on the eligibility and protection of CAD design files and in focusing on EU and UK laws concluded that a CAD-based design file may be protected under copyright in the UK. At the same time, recent CJEU cases have left a number of questions unanswered. However, the territorial nature of copyright law coupled with the international nature of online platforms and CAD-based design files shared therein could lead to uncertainty and complex issues in the future. Therefore, clearer guidance is needed about the status of CAD-based design files.

The third part of the chapter deliberated on the implications for copyright law as a result of scanning and modification through the use of online tools. This was considered by drawing on a line of decisions from *Walter v Lane* to *Interlego AG v Tyco Industries Inc. and Others, Antiquesportfolio.com Plc v Rodney Fitch & Co. Ltd., Sawkins v Hyperion Ltd.* and *Eisenmann v Qimron*. Based on these cases, the chapter suggested that copyright could subsist in scanned objects provided skill, labour, judgement and effort are employed in re-creating those objects or by making creative choices such as selecting particular views of the physical object to reflect the creator's personality and express the creator's free and creative choices as required by European case

---

[82]   Ibid.

[83]   The author is currently leading a project for the European Commission exploring the Intellectual Property Implications for the Development of Industrial 3D printing, which aims to identify gaps and challenges surrounding the IP framework.

law. However, the chapter also outlined that 3D digital models of works of artistic craftsmanship manufactured on an industrial scale (functional) will not attract copyright. In other words, copyright law as it stands today does not lend very much support to rightholders who may find it difficult to construct a case against those who scan and reverse-engineer their products.

Taken together, these points reflect uncertainty and fragmentation of the various practices in the 3D printing and 3D scanning spheres, which in turn can have a negative impact on the IP framework. Such fragmentation could also lead to 'the law being shaped in different legal regimes, in different ways, resulting in a lack of certainty for creators and users and incompatibility of rights and working conditions across common technological systems'.[84] These implications demonstrate a clear need for reconsideration and review of the IP law framework.[85]

As time goes by, more shops and online platforms will provide for 3D designs which can be printed in the convenience of one's home. Yet, these entitlements should be balanced against the rights of IP rightholders. In September 2018, proposed reforms to European copyright law in relation to the regulation of intermediaries was adopted through Article 13 of the Copyright Directive.[86] Article 13, also known as the 'upload filter', requires all platforms to check for copyright infringement on uploaded content. This suggestion has been met with much criticism by various stakeholders as it would significantly curtail freedom of expression and lead to censorship.[87]

Therefore, as 3D printing continues to grow, it will certainly give rise to opportunities as well as further challenges for intellectual property and copyright law.[88] In view of this, it will be sensible to review the existing IP framework and – in the context of this chapter – the copyright framework in a holistic manner. For example, adopting new business models which allow for the secure streaming of 3D CAD files via an Application Programming

---

[84]   D Mendis, J Nielsen, D Nicol and P Li, 'The Co-Existence of Copyright and Patent Laws to Protect Innovation – A Case Study of 3D Printing in UK and Australian Law' in R Brownsword, E Scotford and K Yeung (eds), *The Oxford Handbook of Law, Regulation and Technology* (Oxford: OUP; 2017) 468.

[85]   Mendis and Secchi (n 81) 43–45.

[86]   Proposal for a Directive of the European Parliament and of the Council on copy-right in the digital market COM/ 2016//0593 final, available at https://eur-lex.europa.eu/legal-content/EN/TXT/?uri=CELEX:52016PC0593. Proposed reforms to the EU Copyright Directive, including Article 13 was adopted on 12 September 2018.

[87]   https://juliareda.eu/eu-copyright-reform/.

[88]   See, European Parliament, Committee on Legal Affairs, Three-Dimensional Printing, a Challenge in the Fields of Intellectual Property Rights and Civil Liability 26 June 2018. On 3 July 2018, this own-initiative report by Joelle Bergeron was adopted by the European Parliament.

Interface (API) could be one option.[89] This would allow the build instructions to be sent directly to a selected printer, which in turn will print out the number of objects purchased. Another option could be for manufacturers to license 3D files more widely. This would avoid locking the manufacturer into an agreement through a system such as a one-stop-shop for (spare) parts.[90] Therefore, in looking ahead to the future, solutions such as these should be explored, whilst time is still on the side of the policymaker, before 3D printing will do for physical objects what MP3 files did for music and film.[91]

---

[89]   Mendis and Secchi (n 81) 44–45
[90]   Ibid.
[91]   Mendis (n 17) 165–169.

10. Different aspects of trade mark confusion with respect to distribution of CAD files in the era of 3D printing

Taina Pihlajarinne and Max Oker-Blom

1.   INTRODUCTION

When discussing online content production and distribution, 3D printing (3DP) represents an emerging technology that has the potential to rise to one of the important generators of the next industrial revolution. From a business point of view there are clearly many advantages of 3DP since it makes the manufacturing process much more efficient.[1] The development of 3DP technology will, however, create many kinds of challenges related to intellectual property rights, many of which are of a fundamental nature. The implications for copyright and design law are discussed in Chapter 9 of this volume by Dinusha Mendis.

In this present chapter, a closer look is taken at 3DP, with particular focus on trade mark confusion in Europe when distributing computer-aided design files (CAD files) for 3DP purposes via Internet platforms. Mere dissemination of a file that includes instructions for a trademarked product cannot be counted as trade mark infringement under current doctrines.[2] However, when CAD files

---

[1]   First of all it is much more flexible than standard manufacturing based on moulding. Products can easily be customized. Setting up a production system is much simpler. Instead of having to assemble different parts, the required product can be produced in one single process. 3DP allows more complexity. In addition 3DP can use multiple jets, eg to lay down different materials at the same time. See L Wallach Kloski and N Kloski, *Make: Getting Started with 3D Printing* (Maker Media, Inc 2016) 119.

[2]   This is because the file does not include a trade mark in visible form. Software merely including a description of how a trademarked product can be produced does not constitute trade mark use at all. However, since unlawful dissemination of design files can be the most detrimental for the origin function of a trade mark, it is possible that the premises of what kind of actions are counted as trade mark use will need careful reassessment. See further, T Pihlajarinne: 'Non-traditional Trademark Infringement in the

are disseminated via platforms or the printed products are subsequently used, trade mark confusion can arise. Trade mark use in the context of dissemination of CAD files might amount to infringing use only if other criteria are fulfilled (for instance, if a trademark is used commercially, that is to say, sold for a fee for example). It is not entirely clear, however, when and how the confusion takes place and whether this technology has a more profound impact on how a trade mark's origin function and trade mark confusion will be understood in the future. Confusion might not yet be a big problem in these contexts: rather, it is a rising problem. This is because the principle of confusion can be seriously challenged only after 3DP is in a state of maturity, that is to say, it is a part of consumers' everyday life.[3]

This chapter focuses on two situations with the potential for highly interesting touchstones for the principle of confusion in the future. First, initial confusion when the consumer searches for CAD files, a confusion which is, however, revealed before an act of purchase. Second, post-sale confusion in the mind of other consumers when they see a printed item being used. Providing independent status for the doctrines of initial interest confusion and post-sale confusion would indicate a remarkable extension to the traditional actual confusion-based European approach. This chapter analyses whether there will be a need for such an extension.

The perspective is on possible fragmentation of trade mark confusion due to this new technology, which might occur if initial interest confusion and post-sale confusion were to receive a standalone position in Europe instead of their current marginal recognition. The point of view is basically anchored in EU law, with some US aspects, however.

2.   3D PRINTING

The most common type of consumer 3DP, as is well known, is thought to be fused deposition modelling (FDM).[4] This involves creating objects by adding material in successive layers, building up the object layer by layer over time. A thin strand of filament feeds into a part of the printer called an extruder, which melts the plastic at a very high temperature. The instructions to the printer come from a digital file sent from a computer.[5] The digital files or 3D

3D Printing Context' in R-M Ballardini, M Norrgård and J Partanen (eds), *3D Printing, Intellectual Property and Innovation. Insights from Law and Technology* (Kluwer Law International 2017) 303, 313–314.

[3]   On development of consumer 3DP, see J Tuomi, S Chekurov and J Partanen, '3D Printing History, Principles and Technologies' in Ballardini et al (eds) (n 2) 1, 30.

[4]   Eg, Kloski and Kloski (n 1) XI.

[5]   ibid.

models can be created by using CAD modelling software programs. Mass production, creating economies of scale, is still a challenge, but so-called 3DP farms are today available.[6]

CAD files are mostly disseminated via Internet platforms. 'Platforms are a prominent feature in the highly digitized twenty-first century markets, and additive manufacturing will be no exception.'[7] This prediction, or rather statement, made two years ago, is even more relevant today. For example, viewing the various categories on the Thingiverse platform speaks for itself.[8] Over 400 000 designs of objects are available for printing. CAD files can easily be shared online and reproduction of a design comes by pressing a button.[9] Services include, for instance, platforms where users can share and upload files for free and commercial services where files are sold for users.

3. THE PRINCIPLE OF CONFUSION

3.1 The Essence of Confusion

Trade mark confusion is one of the basic pillars of trade mark law. A very straightforward, general definition of confusion is that use of similar signs causes the average consumer to be misled about the origin of goods or services. The notion of confusion has great intrinsic ability for flexibility and adaptability. While it is not an absolute requirement for trade mark infringements (for instance, protection of trade marks with a reputation and double identity protection), in all cases confusion is, however, (more or less) relevant. Therefore, trade mark confusion could be described as a principle that can be applied to a greater or lesser degree. Building blocks based on principles provide trade mark law with an intrinsic ability to adapt when faced with technological challenges – as a contrast to copyright law, which is based more on narrow concepts.[10] Legal fragmentation caused by various methods of content distribution

---

[6] R D'Aveni, 'The 3D Printing Revolution' (2015) Harvard Business Review, May, 40, 44. See also I Silverman, 'Optimising Protection: IP Rights in 3D Printing' (2015) 1 EIPR 5, 5.

[7] D'Aveni (n 6) 47.

[8] The following categories are mentioned on the Thingiverse website: 3D Printing, Art, Fashion, Gadgets, Hobby, Household, Learning, Models, Tools, and Toys and Games.

[9] See, eg, Silverman (n 6), 5.

[10] See for more on this intrinsic flexibility of the principle of trade mark confusion T Pihlajarinne, 'Should We Bury the Concept of Reproduction – Towards Principle-based Assessment in Copyright Law?' (2017) 8 International Review of Intellectual Property and Competition Law 953, 953–976.

may be perceived in the area of trade mark confusion due to a broad range of applicable approaches depending on methods of distribution.

The principle of confusion is tightly linked with the ultimate aim of trade mark protection, which is to offer information for consumers by facilitating the choice between goods and services from different origins. Therefore, trade marks are indicators of desired quality for consumers. In an economic sense, by reducing search costs, trade marks contribute to economic efficiency.[11] In the case of overprotection, protection turns out to be an impediment to competition. For instance, if exclusivity is extended to situations where competitors are comparing products or only offering options, protection hinders consumers from receiving relevant information. This might have harmful effects on markets.[12] Additionally, the feasible scope of confusion should be assessed by whether or not protection promotes this target.

3.2   The Doctrine of Confusion in the EU and the USA

3.2.1   General framework
In Europe, assessment of trade mark confusion has traditionally been based on actual confusion. In this case, confusion exists when a consumer is confused as to the origin of goods or services when making an act of purchase. If understood as an exclusive approach, in cases where a consumer discovers the confusion before an act of purchase, or if other consumers confuse the origin of a product when they subsequently see it being used, there is no trade mark infringement. Under this doctrine, the level of deception only has legal relevance if it directly affects the final purchase. The reason behind this might be an assumption that pre-sale confusion or post-sale confusion are not particularly relevant problems from a search cost standpoint. Additionally, in its pure form, this way of assessing confusion seems to be based on great respect for consumers' freedom of choice.

---

[11]   See, eg, WM Landes and RA Posner, *The Economic Structure of Intellectual Property Law* (The Belknap Press of Harvard University Press 2003) 168; N Economides, 'The Economics of Trademarks' (1988) 78 Trademark Reports 523, 525. See also SL Dogan and M Lemley, 'A Search-costs Theory of Limiting Doctrines in Trade Mark Law' in GB Dinwoodie and MD Janis (eds), *Trademark Law and Theory. A Handbook of Contemporary Research* (Edward Elgar Publishing 2008) 65, 65–94.

[12]   In general, see SL Dogan and M Lemley: 'Trademarks and Consumer Search Costs on the Internet. A Working Paper', August 2004, available at http://ssrn.com/abstract=560725, 1, 1–2.

Confusion in its various categories can potentially be assessed when interpreting the following provisions of the EU Trademark Directive:

- the so-called double identity rule[13] (article 10.2 a: both trade marks and goods/services are identical);
- the likelihood of confusion rule[14] (article 10.2 b: identical or similar trade marks and identical or similar goods/services, if a likelihood of confusion exists on the part of the public including the likelihood of association between the sign and the trade mark);
- protection for trade marks with a reputation (article 10.2 c: identical or similar trade marks irrespective of whether goods or services are identical or similar; use of the sign takes unfair advantage of, or is detrimental to, the distinctive character or the repute of a trade mark that has a reputation in the Member States).[15]

The wording of these articles leaves open the question of when confusion should take place and whose confusion is relevant: the buyer's or someone else's. Therefore, the final interpretation is made by the Court of Justice of the European Union (CJEU). The position of actual confusion is well established. However, some interesting cracks can be found in its strong surface as we will explain further.

In the USA, in contrast, assessment of confusion has partly detached itself from the premise of actual confusion. Already from at least the 1940s there has been a tendency among courts in the USA to extend the traditional concept of

---

[13]   The CJEU has stressed that only use that is detrimental to the functions of a trade mark, especially to the origin function, is an infringement under the double identity rule. Eg, the following judgments of the ECJ: *Arsenal Football Club plc v. Reed*, C-206/01; *Anheuser-Busch v. Budějovický Budvar*, C-245/02, para 59; *Adam Opel AG v. Autec Ag.*, C-48/05. Such a use is not, however, necessary, since the CJEU has stated that use that is detrimental to the investment function could also be infringing under this rule. See cases *L'Oréal SA, Lancome parfums et beauté & Cie SNC and Laboratoire Garnier & Cie v. Bellure NV, Malaika Investments Ltd and Starion International Ltd*, C-487/07 and *Interflora Inc. Interflora British Unit v. Marks & Spencer et al.*, C-323/09.

[14]   The CJEU has stated in cases *SABEL BV and Puma AG, Rudolf Dassler Sport*, C-251/95 and *Marca Mode CV and Adidas AG, Adidas Benelux BV*, C-425/98 that mere association is not in itself a sufficient ground for concluding that there is a likelihood of confusion.

[15]   Protection includes cases where confusion is created but it is not, however, restricted to them. It is only required that the public makes a connection between the sign and the mark. See *Adidas-Salomon AG, Adidas Benelux BV v. Fitnessworld Trading Ltd*, C-408/01.

actual confusion.[16] The 'initial interest confusion' – or 'pre-sale confusion'[17] –
doctrine was applied in the USA for the first time in the 1970s. The likelihood
of confusion, as meant in the Lanham Act, has been interpreted to cover initial
interest confusion.[18] The Lanham Act of 1946 referred to purchasers where
the plaintiff subsequently had to prove that the infringing mark was 'likely to
cause confusion or mistake or to deceive purchasers as to the source of origin
of such goods'.[19] In the latter Act the language 'as to the source of origin' was
deleted. Some, but not all, courts interpreted this as encompassing all sorts
of confusion, that is, confusion as to affiliation, sponsorship or association.
This was referred to as sponsorship confusion.[20] These interpretations were
confirmed in 1988. The 1988 amendment to the Lanham Act thus codified the
liberalized interpretation given by many courts.[21] The reference to 'purchasers'
was omitted in the 1962 Lanham Act, which opened the gate for the post-sale
confusion doctrine.[22]

Particularly since 1962, when the amended Lanham Act came into force,
a conceptual expansion has taken place. During that development, both initial

---

[16] AM McCarthy, 'The Post-sale Confusion Doctrine: Why the General Public
Should Be Included in the Likelihood of Confusion Inquiry' (1999) 6(1) Fordham Law
Review 3337, 3337–3369.

[17] On the initial interest confusion doctrine, B.J Maynard, 'The Initial Interest
Confusion Doctrine and Trademark Infringement on the Internet', in 57 *Wash & Lee
Law Review* (2000), 1301, 1303–1353; S Maniatis, 'Trade Mark Use on the Internet' in
Phillips, Jeremy and Simon, Ilanah (eds) *Trade Mark Use*, OUP 2005, 269; A Blythe,
'Initial interest confusion: attempting to define its current status within European trade
mark law', 38 EIPR (2016), 201, 201–207.

[18] It was applied for the first time in the US Court of Appeals, Second
Circuit in *Grotrian, Helfferich, Schulz, Th. Steinweg Nachf. v. Steinway & Sons*,
Defendant-Appellee. 9 July 1975. See, eg, also cases US Court of Appeals, Second
Circuit, *Mobil Oil Corporation v. Pegasus Petroleum Corporation*, 4 May 1987 and US
District Court, N.D. Iowa, Cedar Rapids Division, *Green Products Co. v. Independence
Corn by-Products Co*, 25 September 1997. See further, eg, A Deutsch, 'Concealed
Information in Web Pages: Metatags and U.S. Trade Mark Law' (2000) 31(7/8)
International Review of Intellectual Property and Competition Law 845, 864.

[19] McCarthy (n 16) 3346.

[20] ibid, 3348.

[21] ibid 3349.

[22] It is claimed that there are at least two explanations for the deletion of the
reference to 'purchasers' from the Lanham Act in 1962. One is that since 'purchaser'
was not mentioned elsewhere in the Act it had to be omitted here as well – a technical
change, in other words. The other interpretation is that Congress wanted to eliminate
the restriction on those whose confusion matters. McCarthy (n 16) 3350. There are reasonable arguments for the latter view, ie, to expand confusion to concern 'the general
public'.

interest and post-sale confusion doctrines have established their independent position in the USA.[23]

3.2.2   The current position of the initial interest confusion doctrine

According to the initial interest confusion doctrine, a risk of confusion exists when the average consumer is misled about the origin of goods or services when choosing them, but the confusion is revealed before the final purchase. In these cases, a sign is used in order to attract the consumer's interest. The most evident application of the doctrine is in cases of reputed trade marks since they have a capacity to be used as bait.

The different ways to use trade marks in digital contexts are often by their nature such that they cause initial confusion.[24] Initial confusion, however, might often be discovered before the actual purchase. Therefore, the potential of initial interest confusion has increased due to the diversification of methods for distributing trademarked goods. However, the rise of the initial interest confusion doctrine blurs the limits between protection from actual confusion and protection of a sign's independent goodwill.

The initial interest confusion doctrine has gained an important role in one specific situation, namely when assessing trade mark confusion in a domain name context. Its role is strongly established in specific domain name conflict resolution schemes, within the Uniform Domain Name Dispute Resolution Policy (UDRP), for instance.[25] However, many examples in European case

---

[23]   Eg, according to Dogan and Lemley, initial interest confusion 'has morphed into a standalone doctrine whose criteria bear little relationship to a traditional likelihood of confusion claim', Dogan and Lemley (n 12) 4–5.

[24]   Similarly, A Blythe, 'Confusion Online: Does the Test for Trade Mark Confusion on the Internet Differ From That Applied to Infringement in Other Spheres?' (2014) 36(9) EIPR 563, 563.

[25]   This approach is underlined, eg, in the UDRP decisions *Arthur Guinness Son & Co. (Dublin) Limited v. Dejan Macesic*, D2000-1698 and *Kirkbi AG v. Michele Dinoia*, D2003-0038. Application of the initial interest confusion doctrine is explicitly mentioned, eg, in the UDRP decisions *CBS Broadcasting Inc., f/k/a CBS Inc v. Nabil Zaghloul* D2004-0988; *Joseph Dello Russo MD v. Michelle Guillaumin*, D2006-1627; and *Actelion Pharmaceuticals, Ltd v. Hackard & Holt*, D2007-0838. According to the WIPO Overview of WIPO Panel Views on Selected UDRP Questions, most WIPO/UDRP decisions represent this particular view. However, the panels do not in every case apply the initial interest doctrine totally strictly or without exceptions. Some panels have, eg, taken into account the type of goods or services offered on the site and the use of the plaintiff's trade mark there. Eg, in the UDRP case *Expedia Inc. v. European Travel Network*, D2000-0137 and *Busy Body, Inc. v. Fitness Outlet Inc.*, D2000-0127 the panel concluded that similarity of the goods offered influenced assessment of confusion between the trade mark and the domain name. In *Weber-Stephen Products Co. v. Armitage Hardware*, D2000-0187 the domain name holder aimed at

law indicate that the doctrine is also relevant when traditional trade mark legislation is applied to domain name conflicts.[26] In applying the doctrine for trade mark use to domain names, assessment of confusion is based solely on the comparison between the domain name and the trade mark. The fact that the Internet user probably discovers the confusion after opening the site does not remove liability for trade mark infringement. In addition, the distinctiveness of a protected sign and the degree of a sign's reputation as well as the annexation of a domain name related to the actions of, for instance, a trade mark proprietor may have relevance in the assessment.[27] Additionally, beyond the domain name context, some case law has emanated from European countries embracing the construction.[28]

---

creating an impression of a commercial connection between the domain name holder and the trade mark holder on the site. This influenced the assessment.

[26] Eg, in the Norwegian Supreme Court case 7.11.2004, *Volvo Personbiler Norge AS v. Ole Bjørn Gryving Hoppestad* the site included a clause stating that the domain name holder as a reseller of Volvo goods does not have any connection with the proprietor of the 'Volvo' trade mark. The trade mark proprietor was considered to have legitimate reason to oppose trade mark use since the domain name created an impression of a commercial connection. However, in the case the fact that the conflicting domain name was used for marketing the same or similar goods as those for which the trade mark was registered made it less complicated to decide. In the English legal literature there are also some indications of a rather flexible interpretation of similarity between goods and services when domain name grabbing is concerned. See L Bently and B Sherman, *Intellectual Property Law* (OUP 2009) 724–725.

[27] For application of the initial interest confusion doctrine in domain name dispute resolution in general, see, eg, T Pihlajarinne, 'Protection of Trade Marks When Used as Domain Names. Towards an Inevitable Fragmentation in Trade Mark Protection' (2010) 5 *Nordiskt Immateriellt Rättsskydd* 416, 426–429. For the doctrine specifically in the UDRP procedure, see A Kur, *UDRP* (Max-Planck-Institute for Foreign and International Patent, Copyright and Competition Law 2001) 23–24 and from a perspective of the alternative dispute resolution mechanism for .eu domain names, see D Kipping, *Das Recht der .eu-Domains* (Carl Heymanns Verlag 2008) 31–32.

[28] For instance, in the Northern Ireland Court of Appeal case, *BP Amoco PLC v. John Kelly Ltd & Anor* [2001] NICA 3 (2nd February 2001) the plaintiff, which ran a chain of petrol stations, used entirely green-coloured signs, protected by registered trade marks, in front of the stations. The defendant used similar coloured signs outside of its petrol stations. The court concluded that the defendant had infringed the trade mark. The court stated that a motorist might perceive the defendant's sign from a distance as the mark of the BP company when driving at speed on the road, and therefore prepare to turn off into the station. Therefore, there was a likelihood of confusion even if the driver would discover the confusion when getting closer to the petrol station. In the case *Och-Ziff Management Europe Ltd v. Och Capital LLP*, the High Court of Justice, Chancery Division, 20 October 2010, the plaintiff, OCH-Ziff Management, alleged that the defendant had infringed trade marks 'OCH-ZIFF' and 'OCH' for financial services. The sign was used in a window of the defendant's office, on website and in the domain name, and as suffixes to email addresses. The court concluded that

In a European context, initial interest confusion could, in principle, be regarded as being detrimental to a trade mark's origin function when applying the Trademark Directive article 10.2(a), or cause the likelihood of confusion meant by article 10.2(b).[29] Potential for initial interest confusion protection can also be found in EU unfair competition law. Article 4 f–g of Directive 2006/114/EC concerning misleading and comparative advertising includes elements of initial interest confusion protection.[30] The CJEU has not made any explicit statements on the doctrine so far. However, one could refer to the *Interflora* case[31] on using trade marks as ad words, that is to say, displaying advertisements based on keywords corresponding to a trade mark proprietor's trade mark, to include a statement with a slight indication of a reserved interpretation.[32]

---

the creation of initial interest confusion indicated confusing similarity as meant in the Trademark Directive (article 5.1(b)).

[29]   Blythe suggests that initial interest confusion could be applied as part of the protection of trade marks with a reputation conferred by the Directive article 10.2(c), since it includes a strong element of taking unfair advantage of the reputation of another's trade mark. Blythe (n17) 205–207.

[30]   Comparative advertising is permitted as far as the comparison is concerned when the conditions set in article 4 are met. Article 4 g, according to which 'it does not present goods or services as imitations or replicas of goods or services bearing a protected trade mark or trade name' might indirectly protect trade marks from initial interest confusion. The same concerns article 4 f, which requires that no unfair advantage is taken of the reputation of a trade mark, trade name or other distinguishing marks of a competitor of the designation of origin of competing products.

[31]   In this case the court stated that the use might adversely affect the trade mark's origin function if the advertising does not enable reasonably well-informed and reasonably observant Internet users, or enables them only with difficulty, to ascertain whether the goods or services originate from the trade mark proprietor or from an undertaking that it has an economic link with, or from a third party. On the question whether the use is detrimental for the advertising function, the court stated that 'the mere fact that the use, by a third party, of a sign identical with a trade mark in relation to goods or services identical with those for which that mark is registered obliges the proprietor of that mark to intensify its advertising in order to maintain or enhance its profile with consumers is not a sufficient basis, in every case, for concluding that the trade mark's advertising function is adversely affected. In that regard, although the trade mark is an essential element in the system of undistorted competition which European law seeks to establish, its purpose is not, however, to protect its proprietor against practices inherent in competition.'

[32]   By contrast, in the USA there has been stronger support in applying the doctrine also to using trade marks in metatags. In the US Court of Appeals, Ninth Circuit case, *Brookfield Communications Inc. v. Westcoast Entertainment Corporation*, 22 April 1999, the court deemed trade mark use in metatags as infringing use of a trade mark on the basis of initial interest confusion. Also in US Court of Appeals, Ninth Circuit *Playboy Enterprises, Inc. v. Netscape Communications Corp.*, 14.1.2004 a keyed

All in all, in Europe the doctrine is relevant only in discrete situations, but in some of them the role could be described as dominant (domain name cases). At this moment, it does not have a broader, independent, general role in European trade mark law.

3.2.3 The current position of the post-sale confusion doctrine

The rationale of post-sale confusion is to prevent other consumers, as potential purchasers, from being affected by a low-quality product when they see it being used, and as a consequence make a negative assessment of the trade mark proprietor's products. A relative phenomenon is 'status confusion', which refers to a situation where, due to confusingly similar products, a trade mark loses its high-status image due to loss of scarcity. The consequence is that consumers' willingness to pay a high price for a trademarked product might be reduced. Post-sale confusion can lead potential buyers to choose a competitor's product instead.[33] The idea of protection from post-sale confusion is to secure the investment in the trade mark. Therefore, one might claim that it is not a matter of confusion at all,[34] or at least that it blurs the limit between confusion protection and protection of a sign's independent goodwill, in exactly the same way as initial interest confusion.

The post-sale confusion doctrine has a relatively established position in the USA.[35] In her article, McCarthy refers to the language of the amended Lanham Act, comments on the Act and court practice as well as the lack of subsequent action by Congress. She concludes by noting that the courts, which have adopted an expansive view of the relevant population '... reason that the revision reveals Congress's intent to prohibit confusion of non-purchasers in a post-sale setting'.[36] We are thus speaking of an independent post-sale confusion concept, that is, one with respect to which courts decide '...if third parties are misled by being confronted with items put to their intended use after pur-

---

banner advertisement was considered as causing initial confusion. See also, for instance Deutsch (n 18) 865.

[33] See J. Grace, 'The End of Post-Sale Confusion: How Consumer 3D Printing Will Diminish the Function of Trademarks' (2014) 28(1) Harvard Journal of Law & Technology 263, 271–272.

[34] CD Powell, 'We all Know It's a Knock Off – Re-Evaluating the Need for the Post-Sale Confusion Doctrine in Trademark Law' (2012) 14 North Carolina Journal of Law & Technology 1, 24.

[35] The landmark case was *Ferrari S.P.A Esercizio v. Roberts* 944 F.2d 1235, 1244–1245 (6th Cir. 1991). Also in a number of counterfeit cases concerning, eg, watches and bags, the courts have relied on the post-sale confusion concept: see Powell (n 34) 17–24.

[36] McCarthy (n 16) 3368.

chase'.[37] However, she conditions her conclusion by referring to the possible facts in the case involved. This is of course not surprising in a common-law country such as the USA, taking into account that not all courts seem to have accepted an expansive interpretation.[38]

While post-sale confusion in the USA is regarded as an independent concept, this is not the case in Europe. In EU trade mark law it has been argued that post-sale confusion has an affirmative, ancillary function only.[39] In *Arsenal v. Reed*, C-206/01, a case concerning double identity, that is, a case regarding which both the mark and goods are considered identical, the court – on the basis of an abstract comparison – concluded that actual confusion had taken place. The court's view – that consumers who had not seen the notice in Mr Reed's stall outside the football stadium indicating that the goods did not constitute official Arsenal FC products, could also be confused, that is, post-sale confusion – has been regarded only as confirming the abstract comparison.[40]

In a subsequent decision by the CJEU concerning *Anheuser Busch v. Budějovický Budvar* C-245/02, post-sale confusion has been argued as achieving a more independent role.[41] Here the court is talking about the impression conveyed by a third party to consumers that a material link in trade exists between the goods of that party and the undertaking from which the goods in question originate and which are sold by that third party. The court furthermore states that it has to be shown that those consumers who have left the point of sale are also likely to interpret the sign as designating the undertaking from which the third party's goods originate.

The level of attention required by the public and competition has also been taken into account when assessing the independence of post-sale confusion, in the light of two later cases decided by the CJEU. In *Picasso/Picaro* C-361/04, it seems to be clear that even though post-sale confusion might occur, where high-priced goods and goods with a technological character, such as vehicles, are involved, confusion has to be assessed with the actual purchase in mind. Post-sale confusion lacks relevance, depending on the character of the goods, namely in situations like *Picasso/Picaro*, which concerns the well-known painter and a car.

---

[37] ibid, 3350.
[38] The courts have been reluctant to apply the doctrine in such cases, eg, where the trade mark is not very visible for others when the product is used. Powell (n 34) 22–23.
[39] See eg, Anette Kur and Martin Senftleben, *European Trade Mark Law* (OUP 2017) 318–322.
[40] ibid, 319. Cf Andreas Breitschaft, 'The Future of the Passing-off Action in the Law Against Unfair Competition – An Evaluation from a German Perspective' (2010) 32(9) EIPR 427, 427–436, where he argues for adopting a post-sale confusion concept.
[41] See especially para 60.

In terms of competition, the decision in *Viking Gas v. Kosan Gas* C-46/10[42] indicates that even though the labels attached by Viking Gas to Kosan Gas bottles when refilling them could be construed as causing post-sale confusion, this was not the case. The court argued that consumers in this sector were aware of the absence of any connection between the re-filler and the original producer.

From these cases at least two conclusions can be drawn. First, we are talking about quite traditional situations concerning traditional consumer goods and services. The question therefore remains whether the need arises to apply EU trade mark law differently, that is, more extensively, in a digitized environment. Second, interestingly enough, the *Picasso/Picaro* and the *Viking Gas* cases indicate just that, namely that the character of the goods and the situation have to be taken into account. Of course it can also be argued somewhat more conservatively, as Kur and Senftleben do, that post-sale confusion in the EU is an ancillary concept only.[43] However, one systematic argument is that by introducing an independent concept of post-sale confusion the requirement regarding tarnishing – namely that the trade mark affected is a mark with a reputation – would be watered down.[44] Therefore, one option is that post-sale confusion is considered relevant only in connection with trade marks with a reputation.

4.   TRADE MARK CONFUSION AND 3DP

4.1   Actual Confusion in a 3DP Context

At this moment, the probability of creation of actual confusion in the context of 3DP is relatively low. The current situation is that selling official CAD files is not yet a common part of trade mark holders' business, and files are mostly utilized only by users that are informed of the special characteristics and platforms of 3DP. Therefore, users are presumably aware that files are not

---

[42]   The case was based on articles 5 (in general) and 7 of the Trademark Directive 89/104.

[43]   Cooper Dreyfuss also presents a critical viewpoint towards the post-sale confusion doctrine when she suggests that it would be no more harmful than the bad impression a consumer gets from seeing an original product which has been mistreated. R Cooper Dreyfuss 'Reconciling Trademark Rights and Expressive Values: How to Stop Worrying and Learn to Love Ambiguity' in Dinwoodie and Janis (n 11) 261, 275. However, these two situations are not fully comparable, since post-sale confusion due to 3DP could in the future be systematic as opposed to seeing mistreated products occasionally. In addition, post-sale confusion could be a part of free-riding on a rival's goodwill whereas a mistreated product is not an action by a competitor.

[44]   Kur and Senftleben (n 39) 321–322.

commercially connected to trade mark holders. This might change in the future if trade mark proprietors change their business models.

4.2   Initial Interest Confusion in a 3DP Context

So-called initial interest confusion may find new situations to be applied in a 3DP context, on account of confusion created by CAD files. However, the ways and circumstances of distributing CAD files on platforms are highly diverse. For instance, some files are free while others are sold for a fee – and trade mark use can be counted as an infringement only when a trade mark is used in commerce. There is also a great variety as to what kind of information is given, for instance, how a trade mark is displayed, and whether information is available on who created the file. There might be a disclaimer stating that no licence is given by the trade mark holder – and the disclaimer might naturally be represented in various ways. In some cases this information might not be very easily perceivable for users since, for example, the text might appear in small letters in the corner of the site, whereas in some cases there is no such clause at all.

However, very often the site includes a photo of the 3D printed item besides other information on the item. While that is not always the case, a trade mark might be affixed to the printed product, and this might be visible in the photo. This is typical of scale models that are offered for 3DP – toy models which are copies of a real car or a motorcycle, for instance, in reduced scale. An essential feature of scale models is that they are expected to be exactly similar to their originals in every single detail.

To illustrate, a buyer that looks at small pictures of printed products on the platform can make an initial assumption that the file is licensed. In such a case, the user might discover the confusion when further exploring the file or the information attached thereto. It is possible, however, that the user might decide to buy it anyway. Of course, the possibility of such confusion depends on the circumstances in each case. From a broader perspective, among trade mark proprietors, the future level of maturity of the business model of selling CAD files will have an impact on how easily initial confusion is created. Another crucial issue is how informed a particular user – or users in general in the 3DP era – will be regarding the nature and characteristics of disseminated files and different platforms. This might have an influence on the need to protect trade mark proprietors from initial interest confusion.

And if a risk of such confusion exists, to what extent should a trade mark holder be protected from this? In that context, it might provide guidance to compare the interest to equivalent interests in other new situations of trade mark infringements emerging due to technical development, such as domain names, where the initial interest confusion doctrine has made a breakthrough as the primary method of assessing confusion. The ultimate reasons for the success of initial interest confusion lie in a domain name's nature as a web address and in its technical characteristics. First, domain names must be registered and naturally it is not possible to register and use more than one identical domain name. While several top-level domains[45] are available, some have more commercial potential than others. Therefore, when domain names are considered, a trade mark proprietor's own possibility to use a trade mark in respect of one form of utilization – a domain name – has special relevance. Application of the initial interest confusion doctrine safeguards that special need.[46]

On the other hand, one could claim that the initial interest confusion doctrine also serves as a tool for reducing consumers' search costs. But how relevant are search costs overall on the Internet? As explained above, by reducing search costs, trade marks contribute to economic efficiency[47] and therefore, there should be an infringement only in cases where use is disruptive in the sense of search cost theory. Digitalization in general has reduced consumers' search costs. Therefore, the harm caused by trade mark confusion is also smaller since it is only a matter of a few clicks to start a new search after a consumer finds out that a product is not the trade mark proprietor's. But this does not imply that search costs would lack relevance on the Internet. What is important is that the role of trade marks has changed: they are tools for navigation, helping users to find products and producers to find buyers.[48]

When considering traditional shops and marketing in a traditional environment, a trade mark proprietor usually has more space to take initiatives to involve consumers with a trade mark, for instance by active marketing. On the Internet, in contrast, while active marketing is fully possible, the first step is, however, more often in consumers' hands: they usually start their shopping on the Internet by making searches by using general words of trade mark products. Protection that prevents disrupting crucial navigation tools as information links and free-riding on their goodwill might, to some extent, be relevant from the search cost perspective. Trade mark protection should prevent finding genuine trademarked products from turning into trying to find a needle in a haystack. However, the exclusivity conferred by trade marks should not serve as an impediment to offering alternatives for consumers. Therefore,

---

[45]   The top-level domain is usually the last part of the domain name, such as .com, .net or .eu. They are divided into two groups: country-code top-level domains and general top-level domains.

[46]   See further on the reason for adopting the initial interest confusion doctrine in the domain name context Pihlajarinne (n 27) 428–429.

[47]   See n 11.

[48]   Cooper Dreyfuss (n 43) 265.

initial interest argumentation should be accepted only in restricted cases with special interests.

As mentioned before, in the current situation where basically no CAD files are offered by rightholders and where users of 3DP might consist of informed users only, users might be fully aware that the files are most probably not commercially connected to trade mark holders. Therefore, there is a relatively low probability of causing such initial confusion as would be detrimental enough. But in the not-so-distant future the situation might change – if 3DP reaches such a stage of establishment that it is a part of a typical Internet user's life and business models are developed so that the files perceived by users could be potentially either legal or illegal. However, even in this situation users might, in the end, be informed about the special characteristics of platforms and files if, for instance, distribution channels are divided between those offering legal files and others offering illegal files. In that case, there would no special reasons for widening the applicability of the initial interest confusion doctrine to cases involving 3DP files. Users might usually be aware of the fact that many of the items they find on certain platforms, for instance using search words corresponding to a trade mark, are not licensed. It is more probable that they will assume that the files they find by using this method have only some similar characteristics to a trade mark proprietor's products.

When comparing with a domain name context, the nature of domain names as addresses – due to which parallel use of identical domain names is not possible – is a special reason behind acceptance of the initial interest confusion doctrine. This is essentially different when considering the future scenario of 3DP and information provided in the context of CAD files. Even trade marks utilized as search engine ad words might be more detrimental for trade mark proprietors compared to future CAD file dissemination. This is because ad words are tools for redirecting traffic – traffic consisting of search engine users, that is to say, most ordinary Internet users. As a part of a competition on ad words, multiple advertisers can buy the same ad word and the one who pays the most usually succeeds in getting its link to appear in the most prominent position.[49] Still, a full comparison cannot be made to the effect of registering a trade mark proprietor's domain name as described above since while ad words play an important role, they do not share the position of domain names as unique Internet addresses for essential building blocks. However, as explained above, the CJEU has not been eager to stretch the applicability of the initial interest confusion doctrine to ad words, and therefore it will not easily accept similar arguments regarding 3DP files.

---

[49]   See Blythe (n 24) 564.

Solely creating initial interest confusion would not, in normal cases, cause relevant disruptions for trade marks' ability to reduce search costs.[50] However, there might be a reason to apply the doctrine in such exceptional cases where a trade mark is used in a highly visible way and solely as misleading bait, and all the initial information provided clearly suggests that the file is official – and just after the act of sale the confusion is revealed.

4.3   Post-sale Confusion in a 3DP Context

3DP might create pressure to open the doors for extending the scale of confusion to situations of post-sale confusion. This is because 3DP will probably increase situations where, due to the use of unauthorized 3D printed trademarked products, other consumers – except the one who has printed the item – might get a false impression that those goods originate from the trade mark proprietor. Therefore, the position of post-sale confusion might need re-evaluation in the 3D era in Europe. One option would be that the development of 3DP could change the position of the post-sale confusion doctrine into a direction of having an independent position instead of serving only as an ancillary concept.

However, in the existing phase of digitization it seems that currently there is no need to expand the concept of post-sale confusion regarding CAD files intended for 3DP. The situation might change, however, and consequently post-sale confusion may emerge as an independent concept to support protection of trade marks which have not quite reached the requirements for a mark with a reputation. This depends, among other things, on the technological development of 3DP – will it be used in 'every' home instead of traditional buying or ordering goods on the Internet? At present it is also unclear to what degree companies will change their business models to accompany this development, that is, whether they will start supplying 3D printers and material for printing besides ready-made goods.

An extreme scenario would be, first, that if consumers in general become very familiar with 3DP, they might not be genuinely confused when seeing printed products being used. This is because they would assume that products being printed by 3DP techniques do not originate from a trade mark owner.

---

[50]   Cooper Dreyfuss states that '[o]n the internet, this claim of "initial interest confusion" is based on the notion that being drawn to a rival website is like getting off at the wrong exit from a highway, finding a rival's store, and deciding it isn't "worth the trouble to continue searching". Courts have not, apparently, noticed that clicking on a second website is nothing like getting back to the car, starting it up, locating a highway entrance, finding a new exit, searching the "right" store, stopping a car and getting out.' Cooper Dreyfuss (n 43), 275.

That would mean disruption of the position of a trade mark as a badge of origin. This scenario is, however, far-reaching, and it would have the potential to come true only if 3DP becomes the mainstream method for ordinary people to acquire products. And, second, where products were mainly printed only by using illegal CAD files, that would, in fact, indicate trade mark proprietors' complete failure to update their business models. The situation would mean that the rationale behind post-sale confusion would no longer be valid.[51] This scenario is not very probable, however.

Quality control aspects are of utmost importance when considering the issue of post-sale confusion in the future. If one contemplates the development of sales outlets, the development is from physical stores to Internet purchase and delivery and – with 3DP – to production at home. We are thus moving away from assessing trademarked goods physically or on the net to the originality of CAD files. Does this affect search costs, that is, the impression the consumer gets, of the trade mark? Arguably, the consumer is able to make a real quality assessment only when the goods have been printed. In addition, if the producer is unable to control the quality of the goods, then post-sale confusion might also be relevant as a separate means of defending the trademarked goods in question. But, as indicated, if producers change their business model by themselves supplying printers and materials, this might not be necessary.

5.   CONCLUSIONS

Technical evolution is diversifying the ways of utilizing trade marks and, consequently, assessment of confusion is also inclined to become more complex than before. Therefore, regarding European trade mark law there is also a growing pressure towards a more flexible and more extensive interpretation of confusion. The question is thus how much fragmentation should be tolerated in this respect.

Currently, there exists no urgent need to extend the application of either initial interest confusion or post-sale confusion doctrines in general in EU trade mark law or in a 3DP context. But, as stated, this might change. At that stage of 3DP development, it seems that applying initial interest confusion could be more realistic, taking into account its established position with respect to domain names, than applying post-sale confusion. But even if fundamental changes occur in 3DP business models and consumer behaviour, applying the initial interest confusion doctrine should not be mainstream but be limited to special cases.

---

[51]   Grace (n. 33) 283–284.

The emergence of a need to expand protection in the direction of post-sale confusion in the era of 3DP would be an indication of trade mark proprietors' failure to update their business models. On the other hand, in the case of such failure being total, the help that the post-sale confusion doctrine could offer to trade mark proprietors might prove very restricted due to erosion of a trade mark's position as a badge of origin.

PART IV

Digital Single Market, Competition and
Regulation

11. Digital Single Market, digital content and consumer protection – critical reflections

Katri Havu

1. INTRODUCTION

Consumption of digital content such as movies, music or e-books forms a significant part of European consumers' daily lives. The Digital Single Market (DSM) agenda of the European Commission seeks to release the untapped potential of e-commerce and online business models and addresses supply of digital content to consumers as part of the programme.[1]

A proposal for a directive concerning consumer contract rules in the context of the supply of digital content was presented by the European Commission in 2015 together with a proposal covering online and distance sales of tangible goods.[2] The proposal materials note that even though consumer law has been partially harmonized in the EU, important aspects of consumer transactions

---

[1] See further, eg, European Commission, 'A Digital Single Market Strategy for Europe' (Communication) COM(2015) 192 final.

[2] European Commission, 'Proposal for a directive on certain aspects concerning contracts for the supply of digital content' COM(2015) 634 final; European Commission, 'Proposal for a directive on certain aspects concerning contracts for the online and other distance sales of goods' COM(2015) 635 final. See also European Commission, 'Impact Assessment – Accompanying the document Proposals for Directives (1) on certain aspects concerning contracts for the supply of digital content and (2) on certain aspects concerning contracts for the online and other distance sales of goods' (Staff Working Document) SWD(2015) 274 final/2; European Commission, 'Digital Contracts for Europe' (Communication) COM(2015) 633 final. The proposal concerning sales of goods has subsequently been amended (2017). With respect to the supply of digital content, the 2015 directive proposal is the only complete proposal available at the time of writing this chapter (writing completed in March 2018). The legislation-drafting process and inter-institutional negotiations are in progress, and there is no final directive text yet. See, eg, European Parliament, Legislative Observatory, Procedure file 2015/0287(COD) Contracts for the supply of digital

and contracts in particular are still regulated by diverging national regimes. This may be a cause of insecurity and caution for consumers and deter e-commerce.[3] Thus the proposed consumer contract rules address and fully harmonize 'in a targeted way the key mandatory rights and obligations of the parties to a contract' for the supply of digital content and sale of goods,[4] covering, in particular, conformity with the contract, hierarchy and exercise of remedies, and the consumer's right to terminate the contract.[5]

Moreover, the DSM agenda entails several other initiatives and proposals touching upon the position or protection of consumers of digital content. For instance, matters related to portability of digital content have been addressed.[6] Further, ceasing unjustified geo-blocking is on the agenda.[7] Additionally, the European Commission has communicated that the position and behaviour of online platforms will be scrutinized.[8] Competition concerns of the DSM include geo-blocking and platform issues but also extend beyond these and have been studied recently.[9] European Commission guidance on treatment of unfair commercial practices has been updated to better take into account the challenges of digital markets.[10] Enforcement of consumer law is being strengthened and better adapted to the digital age.[11]

---

content (2018) http://www.europarl.europa.eu/oeil/popups/ficheprocedure.do?lang=en &reference=2015/0287(OLP)#tab-0, accessed 18 March 2018.

[3] See, eg, COM(2015) 633 final, at 2–7, 9; COM(2015) 634 final, at 2–3, 16–18; SWD(2015) 274 final/2, at 10–11, 13–16, 40–42, 49.

[4] See COM(2015) 633 final, at 3.

[5] See COM(2015) 633 final, at 3, 5–6; COM(2015) 634 final, at 3, 11–13, 19–22.

[6] See, in particular, Regulation (EU) 2017/1128 on cross-border portability of online content services in the internal market [2017] OJ L168/1.

[7] See, in particular, European Commission, 'Proposal for a Regulation on addressing geo-blocking and other forms of discrimination based on customers' nationality, place of residence or place of establishment within the internal market and amending Regulation (EC) No 2006/2004 and Directive 2009/22/EC' COM(2016) 289 final. Additionally, geo-blocking is addressed as a competition concern, see, eg, n 9.

[8] See, eg, European Commission, 'Online Platforms and the Digital Single Market, Opportunities and Challenges for Europe' (Communication) COM(2016) 288 final; European Commission, 'Online Platforms – Accompanying the document Communication on Online Platforms and the Digital Single Market' (Staff Working Document) SWD(2016) 172 final. See also European Commission, 'Commission publishes mid-term review of the 2015 Digital Single Market strategy' (Fact Sheet, 10 May 2017, MEMO/17/1233).

[9] See, in particular, European Commission, 'Final Report on the E-commerce Sector Inquiry' COM(2017) 229 final.

[10] See European Commission, 'Guidance on the Unfair Commercial Practices Directive' (Staff Working Document) SWD(2016) 163 final.

[11] See, eg, COM(2015) 192 final, 5. After this chapter was written (final version completed in March 2018), the European Commission published, in April 2018, a new

This chapter addresses the position of consumers of digital content in the light of DSM proposals and initiatives. Particular attention is paid to the planned directive concerning consumer contract rules in the context of supply of digital content (Digital Content Directive, DCD). The future directive appears to entail problematic choices as regards the presented rules themselves as well as remaining legal complexity and fragmentation. Moreover, the bigger picture of the DSM strategy and its initiatives affecting the position of consumers is also fragmentary. Additionally, several major legal challenges to the DSM remain at least partially unresolved.

2.   PROPOSED CONSUMER CONTRACT RULES ON THE SUPPLY OF DIGITAL CONTENT

2.1   Brief Overview

The planned DCD is meant to alleviate problems related to current and potential future divergence between national regimes[12] and to remedy the absence of clear, uniform contractual rights in terms, for instance, of faulty content.[13] Further, how to classify digital content contracts has not been always clear. This may have caused ambiguities in EU Member States regarding, for instance, the applicability of certain consumer protection rules.[14]

The proposal for the DCD is to be read as a part of other DSM initiatives and against the backdrop of EU law regimes concerning copyright and data protection.[15] The main contents of the contemplated legislation may be described as follows: Article 2 of the DCD includes definitions of central concepts. The definition of digital content is broad, with the intention of being 'future-proof', and encompasses (a) data produced and supplied in digital form, such as video, applications, digital games and other software; (b) a service allowing creation, processing or storage of data in digital form, where such data is provided by the consumer; and (c) a service allowing sharing of – and other interaction with – data in digital form provided by other users of the service. Thus, in addition

---

legislation proposal package ('New Deal for Consumers'). The package includes proposals on representative actions for the protection of the collective interests of consumers and on enforcement and modernization of EU consumer protection rules.

[12]   For discussion on national regimes applicable to digital content contracts, see, eg, P Giliker, 'Regulating Contracts for the Supply of Digital Content: The EU and UK Response' in TE Synodinou et al (eds), *EU Internet Law: Regulation and Enforcement* (Springer International Publishing 2017) 101, 101–103, 114–124.

[13]   COM(2015) 634 final, 2–3; SWD(2015) 274 final/2, 13–16.

[14]   See COM(2015) 634 final, 5–6.

[15]   COM(2015) 634 final, 4.

to covering, for instance, web-streamed movies, the concept of digital content also includes data in cloud storage services and social media.[16]

According to Article 3, the proposed rules cover the supply of all types of digital content. Also included is digital content supplied in exchange for (personal and other) data provided by consumers. The proposed DCD is intended to cover only business-to-consumer transactions.[17] The proposed rules are meant to apply to a durable medium (such as a CD or DVD) incorporating digital content where the durable medium has been used exclusively as a carrier of digital content.[18] Article 3 further clarifies that the proposed DCD is without prejudice to the EU rules on data protection. Moreover, Article 3 sets out that the directive does not affect national laws with respect to matters not regulated by the instrument, such as national rules providing for obligations of the consumer to the supplier, or regulating the qualification, formation or validity of contracts.

Article 4 notes the full-harmonization nature of the proposed directive. Full harmonization signifies that there is no room for national manoeuvre as regards how strict or lenient the final rules are. However, with respect to matters not covered by the proposed directive, Member States are free to adopt their own solutions.[19]

Articles 5–10 of the proposed DCD discuss supply of digital content and address conformity with the contract. As a main rule, digital content should be supplied instantly after conclusion of the contract (Article 5). In order to conform with the contract, digital content must, *inter alia*, be of 'the quantity, quality, duration and version and…possess functionality, interoperability and other performance features such as accessibility, continuity and security, as required by the contract including in any pre-contractual information', and 'be fit for any particular purpose for which the consumer requires it and which the consumer made known to the supplier'. Digital content supplied over a period of time must be in conformity with the contract throughout the duration of the contract, while the version of digital content supplied must be the most recent version available at the time of concluding the contract (Article 6).

---

[16]   See also COM(2015) 634 final, 11, and, eg, recs 11 and 29.
[17]   See also COM(2015) 634 final, 11, and the definition of 'supplier' in Art 2.
[18]   See also European Commission, 'Amended proposal for a Directive of The European Parliament and of the Council on certain aspects concerning contracts for the online and other distance sales of goods, amending Regulation (EC) No 2006/2004 of the European Parliament and of the Council and Directive 2009/22/EC of the European Parliament and of the Council and repealing Directive 1999/44/EC of the European Parliament and of the Council' COM(2017) 637 final, Art 1 and rec 13.
[19]   See also COM(2015) 634 final, recs 9–10, and at 12.

Lack of conformity of digital content resulting from incorrect integration into the consumer's hardware and software should, according to the proposal, amount to lack of conformity of the digital content itself if the reasons for incorrect integration are related to the supplier (Article 7). Digital content must be clear of third-party rights, including intellectual property rights (Article 8). The burden of proof regarding conformity (whether the digital content conforms at the time of delivery) is on the supplier, unless the consumer's digital environment is not compatible with the digital content. This reversal of the burden of proof is not limited in time, which the proposal materials justify by noting that digital content is not subject to wear and tear.[20] The supplier is liable to the consumer if the content fails to conform to the contract or if content was not supplied at all (Article 10).

Articles 11–16 discuss remedies, their hierarchy (order of use), and to some extent their practical implications. The consumer can terminate the contract immediately if the supplier fails to supply the digital content altogether (Article 11). Article 12 sets out that in case of lack of conformity with the contract, the consumer would primarily be entitled to have the digital content brought into conformity with the contract. In a second step, the consumer would be entitled to have the price reduced or the contract terminated if the lack of conformity relates to main performance features. Article 14 establishes the consumer's right to damages in the case of economic damage to the digital environment (digital content and hardware) of the consumer.[21] Article 17 provides the supplier with a right of redress against earlier links in the contractual chain in the case of liability to the consumer due to failure to supply or lack of conformity.

2.2   Further Remarks on the Proposed Rules

Only some selected further notes on the proposed rules may be presented in this concise chapter.

Matters related to the substantive scope of the proposed DCD have been discussed in a critical fashion. Without repeating this discussion too much, it may be noted, for example, that the distinction between digital content and tangible goods with 'insignificant' incorporated digital content[22] has been perceived as prone to create ambiguities concerning the applicability of the future directive and also otherwise problematic – incorporated digital content may de facto form a central component of many contemporary devices such as cars.[23]

---

[20]   See COM(2015) 634 final, Art 9, rec 43, and at 12.
[21]   See also COM(2015) 634 final, rec 44, and at 13.
[22]   See COM(2015) 634 final, Art 3, rec 12.
[23]   See, eg, G Spindler, 'Contracts for the Supply of Digital Content – Scope of Application and Basic Approach – Proposal of the Commission for a Directive on

The amended proposal for the directive applicable to sales of goods excludes from the scope of the future directive tangible mediums 'incorporating digital content where the tangible medium has been used exclusively as a carrier for the supply of the digital content to the consumer' (Article 1). Even the final text of the DCD will probably be coherent with this approach (thus remaining partially problematic).[24] It can be pointed out that although the division of labour between the directive on goods and the DCD is of significance and interesting, a notable part of consumer transactions are in any case likely to be such that it is easy to conclude which of the future directives applies.

Conformity of digital content with the contract is addressed in the DCD proposal by a lengthy provision (Article 6) that nevertheless places significant emphasis on contract terms and pre-contractual information. This kind of approach leaves power for suppliers: they can significantly regulate their own responsibilities. Reasonable expectations concerning digital content are not central, that is, the provision does not primarily focus on objective general standards and justified expectations as to quality, but underlines the signifi-cance of contract terms.[25] This choice has been criticized for not promoting consumer protection and, for example, for making it possible to exclude the consumer's right to updates or patches even though the digital content would likely require these.[26] The provision on conformity may be seen as particularly problematic because the full-harmonization nature of the DCD precludes more consumer-friendly solutions in national laws.[27] In any case, enacting an effective and clear provision on conformity is not easy. As noted by commen-tators,[28] reasonable expectations (based on average characteristics of similar digital content) are not a simple benchmark in the context of digital content

---

Contracts for the Supply of Digital Content' (2016) 12 European Review of Contract Law 183, 187–190; V Mak, 'The New Proposal for Harmonised Rules on Certain Aspects Concerning Contracts for the Supply of Digital Content, In-Depth Analysis' (PE 536.494, European Parliament 2016) 7–9.

[24]   See also COM(2017) 637 final, rec 13 ('This Directive should not apply to goods like DVDs and CDs incorporating digital content in such a way that the goods function only as a carrier of the digital content. However, this Directive should apply to digital content integrated in goods such as household appliances or toys where the digital content is embedded in such a way that its functions are subordinate to the main func-tionalities of the goods...'), and at 6 (noting that the amended proposal is 'consistent with the proposal for a Directive on the supply of digital content').

[25]   See COM(2015) 634 final, Art 6, recs 24–25.

[26]   See further, eg, Spindler (n 23) 198–199; R Mańko, 'Towards New Rules on Sales and Digital Content: Analysis of the Key Issues' (PE 599.359, European Parliament 2017) 12–15.

[27]   See also concerning Member States that would have to lower their consumer protection standards: Mańko (n 26) 30.

[28]   See, eg, Mak (n 23) 15–18.

contracts, as the products and services themselves are novel and very much in the process of development.

The burden of proof as to conformity of digital content with the contract (at the time of supply) is placed on the supplier.[29] Notably, the proposed DCD also stipulates that the supplier bears this reversed burden of proof 'permanently': the reversal is not bound to any time limit.[30] National limitation periods are referred to in the proposal as a possibility to secure legal certainty,[31] which signifies that general rules on prescription may in practice set time limits to claims based on non-conformity. Since these would be national and, as such, divergent, the question arises whether it would have been clearer, and more closely in accordance with the goals of harmonization, to directly set a time limit in the DCD.[32] Further, even though not including a time limit may seem beneficial for consumers, in practice it is relatively unlikely that claims concerning non-conformity (at the time of supply) would be presented a very long time after receiving digital content. Digital content is presumably often consumed relatively soon after it is received, and most of it is unlikely to be tested for the first time after several years, for example. It may be pointed out, however, that suppliers may find the rules on burden of proof with respect to conformity alarming and seek to recover the costs of potential liability in advance by setting higher prices than they would otherwise do.[33]

In cases of non-conformity with the contract, the primary remedy of the consumer is to request specific (supplementary) performance, that is, to bring the digital content into conformity with the contract, free of charge. Secondary remedies involve requesting price reduction or termination of the contract (Article 12).[34] In non-conformity situations, termination is possible if non-conformity affects main performance features.[35]

Notably, bringing digital content into conformity with the contract may signify different meanings in the context of different types of digital content, while practical possibilities to bring content into conformity may vary depending on the type of digital content. A more general remark can also be made: remedies originally designed for sales of tangible goods may simply not be well suited to the digital content context.[36] The proposed directive provides further clarification on when bringing content into conformity will be deemed

---

[29] See COM(2015) 634 final, Arts 9 and 10.
[30] See COM(2015) 634 final, recs 32, 43, and at 12.
[31] COM(2015) 634 final, rec 43.
[32] See also discussion by, eg, Mańko (n 26) 15–17, 20–21; Spindler (n 23) 213.
[33] See also, eg, Mak (n 23) 19–22.
[34] See also COM(2015) 634 final, recs 36–37, and at 12–13.
[35] COM(2015) 634 final, Art 12, recs 36–37, and at 12–13.
[36] See also, eg, Giliker (n 12) 107.

disproportionate, that is, where the costs for the supplier are unreasonable. Further, the specific performance remedy does not apply if bringing content into conformity would be impossible, illegal or significantly inconvenient for the consumer.[37] Price reduction or contract termination, being less dependent on the nature of content, are relatively simple and straightforward as remedies. According to the proposal and its fixed hierarchy of remedies, they are, nevertheless, relevant mainly in situations where the specific performance remedy is not a possible or sensible option, or the supplier chooses not to bring the content into conformity.[38]

The primacy of the new opportunity for the supplier to deliver conforming content is not necessarily particularly consumer-friendly, especially in the case of online transactions. Consumers are not well placed to discuss, possibly in a foreign language, the details and sufficiency of specific performance with suppliers who may be located in another country. As suppliers are professionals, they would not seem to be in particular need of the protection which is now given to them, at the cost of depriving the consumer of free choice between remedies.[39]

Details of remedies are not exhaustively regulated by the proposed DCD, which signifies that rules and principles of national law complement directive-based rules. This applies, for instance, to the practical consequences of termination to the extent they are not discussed in the DCD, and to the detailed conditions for exercising other remedies.[40] The question may be raised whether the EU law rules are detailed enough so as to truly secure a level playing field.[41] Nevertheless, aspects of termination and its consequences are covered by the proposed directive to a notable degree (Article 13). This is reasonable as the private law consequences of termination, in particular restitution, may be challenging to regulate in the context of supply of digital content. Here vague directive provisions could have signified remarkable divergence in rules actually applied in Member States and, hence, case outcomes.

Importantly, 'returning' digital content (restitution) may significantly differ from the obligation to return a tangible good. Some digital content, for instance an episode of a TV series, is in any case only consumed once, and any 'return' would not change the fact that the consumer used the digital content and thus

---

[37] See COM(2015) 634 final, Art 12, recs 36–37, and at 12–13.
[38] See COM(2015) 634 final, Art 12, recs 36–37, and at 12–13.
[39] For further discussion see, eg, Mańko (n 26) 25–26; E Arroyo Amayuelas, 'La Propuesta de Directiva Relativa a Determinados Aspectos de los Contratos de Compraventa en Línea y Otras Ventas de Bienes a Distancia' (2016) 3 InDret: Revista Para El Análisis Del Derecho 1, 18–19.
[40] See COM(2015) 634 final, Arts 12–13, recs 9–10, 36–40, and at 12–13.
[41] See also next section of this chapter.

received benefit. Even the proposed DCD illustrates difficulties in addressing the consequences of termination. For instance, Article 13 states that the supplier must reimburse the price or, if counter-performance consisted of data, refrain from using those data and any other information which the consumer has provided in exchange for the digital content. It also clarifies that the consumer must refrain from further use of digital content after termination.[42] These obligations are 'weak' in the sense that often it is not possible to perfectly monitor or guarantee that they are complied with.

The overview of the contemplated DCD and the brief highlights above illustrate, inter alia, that regulating consumer contracts for the supply of digital content remains challenging as the phenomenon and its specialities are still relatively novel.[43] The intention to make the forthcoming directive 'future-proof'[44] and the discernible reluctance to engage in comprehensive and detailed harmonization at this stage appear to lead to inclusion of some highly superficial or vague[45] and some relatively complex[46] provisions. Further, including several very different types of digital content in the substantive scope of the DCD is clearly prone to create problems in finding effective general provision formulations, as the situations and facts which the rules should apply to will vary markedly.[47]

Moreover, issues included in the contemplated DCD and those left out are somewhat sporadic. Perhaps this, too, evidences that the European legislator is still insecure about optimal ways to tackle this area. Interestingly, and as highlighted by some commentators, matters such as possibilities to download several copies or resell digital content, or the right to updates are not addressed by the proposed rules, even though these issues are central for the consumer.[48] From a broader perspective, it may be noted that it is debatable how much the proposed consumer contract rules are apt to enhance 'consumer confidence'

---

[42]   See also COM(2015) 634 final, at 13, and recs 38–41.

[43]   See also, eg, S Grundmann and P Hacker, 'Digital Technology as a Challenge to European Contract Law' (2017) 13 European Review of Contract Law 255, 261–262, 287–291.

[44]   See COM(2015) 634 final, eg, rec 11, and at 11.

[45]   See, eg, Art 9 concerning the burden of proof with respect to conformity; Art 14 on damages; Art 17 on the supplier's right of redress.

[46]   See, eg, Art 12 on hierarchy of remedies (even though also being partially vague); Art 13 on the effects of termination.

[47]   See for discussion on 'future-proof' legislation and including numerous types of content, eg, Mak (n 23) 7–9; Giliker (n 12) 108–109. See also Spindler (n 23) 217 regarding the 'broad scope and abstract nature' of the proposed directive.

[48]   See, eg, H Beale, 'Scope of Application and General Approach of the New Rules for Contracts in the Digital Environment, In-Depth Analysis' (PE 536.493, European Parliament 2016) 27.

or 'trust', even though this is highlighted as a goal.[49] The prospective failure to significantly affect 'consumer confidence' relates to the central role left for diverging national laws, and complexity and fragmentation of the legal landscape. These issues are further explored below.

3. PROPOSED CONSUMER CONTRACT RULES: RELATIONSHIP TO OTHER EU AND MEMBER STATE LAW

The relationship between the proposed DCD and the rules on sales of goods has already been touched upon above. Moreover, the proposed DCD excludes from its scope certain areas that are subject to particular EU legislation, for example gambling, financial services and healthcare.[50] It is also otherwise obvious that even though the scope of application of the future DCD is broad, the future directive entails general consumer contract law on digital content transactions, not highly specific rules applicable to particular areas or different situations. It is underlined in the proposal materials that the proposal supplements earlier EU law on consumer rights (where, in particular, pre-contractual information requirements and the right of withdrawal have already been legislated upon)[51] and on unfair terms in consumer contracts.[52] Additionally, the E-Commerce Directive[53] is mentioned as related legislation.[54]

The absence of EU law regulating central contract law issues in supplying digital content to consumers, and the fact and risk of divergence of national regimes, are underlined as the main justifications for enacting the DCD.[55] Indeed, the proposed directive would signify harmonization of certain essential aspects of supplying digital content.

---

[49]   The European Commission underlines that uniform and clear new EU rules encourage cross-border transactions. See, eg, COM(2015) 633 final, 2–7, 9. For critical discussion on achieving a boost in 'consumer confidence', see K Havu, 'The EU Digital Single Market from a Consumer Standpoint: How Do Promises Meet Means?' (2017) 9 Contemporary Readings in Law and Social Justice 146, 164–166.

[50]   See COM(2015) 634 final, Art 3, and at 11.

[51]   See Directive (EU) 2011/83 on consumer rights, amending Council Directive 93/13/EEC and Directive 1999/44/EC and repealing Council Directive 85/577/EEC and Directive 97/7/EC [2011] OJ L304/64.

[52]   See Directive (EEC) 93/13 on unfair terms in consumer contracts [1993] OJ L95/29.

[53]   Directive (EC) 2000/31 on certain legal aspects of information society services, in particular electronic commerce, in the Internal Market [2000] OJ L178/1.

[54]   See COM(2015) 634 final, at 3–4.

[55]   See, eg, COM(2015) 633 final, at 3–4; COM(2015) 634 final, at 3.

Nevertheless, many issues are not covered by the directive proposal or are only mentioned in passing. This raises the question whether the problem of possibly diverging national regimes is adequately addressed. Central aspects of consumer contracts, such as formation and validity, are left for diverging national laws (and sporadic previous EU law). The DCD would not establish a self-sufficient EU law body of consumer contract rules, but would be a mere piece in the puzzle of EU and national law.[56] Relevant EU law remains scattered in various pieces of legislation.[57]

Furthermore, the supply of digital content in business-to-business relationships falls outside the scope of the DCD[58] and is subject to potentially notably diverging national regimes – an aspect which may slow down the development of cross-border commerce contrary to the goals of the planned directive. Moreover, it has been pointed out that the relationship between the directive proposal and the new General Data Protection Regulation is problematic.[59]

Some further remarks can be presented with respect to the proposed rules and their intertwinement with national laws. The proposed rules discuss conformity with the contract and remedies in case of non-conformity in a relatively detailed manner.[60] Consequences of termination are discussed as regards, in particular, restitution. In any case, the proposed rules are not exhaustive.[61] Significant room for divergence is visible with respect to damages issues touched upon in the DCD. Article 14 sets out a consumer's right to damages

---

[56]   The fact that the DCD does not meet its full harmonization goal, implications, and the bigger picture of consumer (contract) law harmonization in the EU has been discussed by this author in more detail in Havu (n 49).

[57]   See also, eg, Giliker (n 12) 114.

[58]   The DCD is consumer law harmonization based on Art 114 of the Treaty on the Functioning of the EU. Promoting the functioning of the internal market and simplifying the legal landscape as seen from the business standpoint are central in the proposal materials. See, eg, COM(2015) 634 final, Arts 1, 3, 4, and at 5–6, 11–12.

[59]   Regulation (EU) 2016/679 on the protection of natural persons with regard to the processing of personal data and on the free movement of such data, and repealing Directive 95/46/EC (General Data Protection Regulation) [2016] OJ L119/1. See Grundmann and Hacker (n 43) 287–291.

[60]   COM(2015) 634 final, Arts 6–16.

[61]   COM(2015) 634 final, see, eg, Arts 11–13, 3, and recs 10, 36–40. See also the discussion in the two previous sections of this chapter. For further discussion on termination, see B Fauvarque-Cosson, 'The New Proposal for Harmonised Rules for Certain Aspects Concerning Contracts for the Supply of Digital Content (Termination, Modification of the Digital Content and Right to Terminate Long Term Contracts), In-Depth Analysis' (PE 536.495, European Parliament 2016) eg, 11–12.

but notes that national laws should provide complementing, specific details.[62] The damages provision in the DCD itself is interesting:

> The supplier shall be liable to the consumer for any economic damage to the digital environment of the consumer caused by a lack of conformity with the contract or a failure to supply the digital content. Damages shall put the consumer as nearly as possible into the position in which the consumer would have been if the digital content had been duly supplied and been in conformity with the contract.[63]

The provision limits the relevant damage to economic damage to the digital environment. Vitally, this type of damage may not be the most relevant in the context of mundane digital content transactions. Further, harms that could, from the standpoint of the consumer, be more central – for example dissatisfaction, inconvenience or other non-material harm, or costs related to obtaining functioning content from elsewhere – are not covered. The very limited Article 14 actually underlines the fact that the proposed directive does not set out any general right to damages. Additionally, the provision, together with the full-harmonization nature of the contemplated directive, appears to signify that national rules may not provide for any broader liability.[64]

It can be further noted that Article 17 sets out a seller's right to pursue remedies against earlier links in the contractual chain in the case of liability towards the consumer (right of redress). Nonetheless, '(t)he person against whom the seller may pursue remedies and the relevant actions and conditions of exercise, shall be determined by national law'. This signifies that a great part of the actual subject matter of the right of redress is left for national systems to provide. In practice, therefore, the sellers' possibilities for succeeding in obtaining redress from the earlier links of the distribution chain may vary notably from one Member State to another. The sellers take into account the prevailing circumstances in each country, and their conduct towards consumers is potentially affected.

All in all, the proposal for the DCD only covers and 'fully harmonizes' some aspects of consumer contracts. Even after enacting the DCD, the whole of relevant law would be formed by rules from different sources. Additionally, what kind of national solutions are in accordance with partially vague EU law could be ambiguous. Especially if the option of presenting preliminary ruling

---

[62]   COM(2015) 634 final, Art 14.
[63]   COM(2015) 634 final, Art 14(1).
[64]   See COM(2015) 634 final, recs 9–10. See also discussion by, eg, Mańko (n 26) 27.

requests to the Court of Justice of the EU (CJEU) is overlooked, diverging parallel interpretations could prevail.[65]

Further, it can be noted that the proposed rules on the consequences of termination, on restitution and on damages liability intervene relatively far into traditionally highly national areas of law, but as individual, specific 'spikes' of EU law, which still rely significantly on complementing Member State systems. EU law thus contains sporadic rules that override earlier national law, but surrounding these rules, national norms remain central.[66] The division of labour between EU law(-based rules) and complementing national law does not appear to be based on any specific reasoning that would explain why some details are harmonized at the EU level while others are not. Absent such a clear rationale, it might also be challenging to recognize, while dealing with concrete court cases, which parts of legislation or which particular details should be interpreted in accordance with EU law methods. Essential aspects of applying EU law include noting, for example, the indirect effect of directives, and taking into account the constantly developing case law of the CJEU.[67]

4.   THE POSITION OF CONSUMERS OF DIGITAL CONTENT: THE BIG PICTURE

Many other DSM initiatives and proposals also affect the position of consumers of digital content. Below, some brief, selected remarks are presented with respect to different kinds of legal matters.

The progress already achieved as regards portability of digital content is welcome but it should also be borne in mind that portability matters are only one aspect of the entire spectrum of digital content issues of the EU DSM. Additionally, the Portability Regulation and its drafts have also been criticized, inter alia, for not exhaustively resolving central problems, not fully including all types of content, and for being vague in defining a temporary visit to another country.[68]

---

[65]   See also discussion by, eg, M Lehmann, 'A Question of Coherence: The Proposals on EU Contract Rules on Digital Content and Online Sales' (2016) 23 Maastricht Journal of European and Comparative Law 752, 764–770, 774.

[66]   See also, eg, Mańko (n 26) 30.

[67]   See also Lehmann (n 65) 765–770, 774. See further earlier similar reflections by Smits (concerning the unsuccessful 2008 proposal for a directive on consumer rights: European Commission, 'Proposal for a Directive of the European Parliament and of the Council on Consumer Rights' COM(2008) 614 final): J Smits, 'Full Harmonization of Consumer Law? A Critique of the Draft Directive on Consumer Rights' (2010) 18 European Review of Private Law 5.

[68]   Regulation (EU) 2017/1128 on cross-border portability of online content services in the internal market [2017] OJ L168/1. For discussion see, eg, J Althoff, 'EU

Geo-blocking, which is further discussed in Chapters 12–14, is being targeted with particular legislation and as a competition concern. Especially as regards geo-blocking as a potential competition restriction and alternatives to geo-blocking practices, further inquiries are still needed and final solutions seem to be relatively far away.[69] The findings of the European Commission's e-commerce sector inquiry highlight that geo-blocking should be addressed on a case-by-case basis, paying particular attention to specific circumstances and reasons behind geo-blocking in the digital content business.[70] Particular factors include licensing matters and copyright law. This implies that the entire legal landscape remains complex and in flux.

Online platforms may, for instance, impose unfair trading conditions on their contract partners and de facto regulate possibilities of undertakings to access broad consumer groups and the infrastructure necessary for serving them.[71] These practices affect consumer choice and the entire dynamics of the markets. Studying the role and behaviour of platforms is desirable and takes place under the DSM agenda, but concrete final solutions and plans as regards platforms are still to be seen. The European Commission has thus far formulated its policy approach and listed key areas for further assessment.[72]

Different competition concerns of the DSM are highly relevant from the standpoint of consumers of digital content. Contract-based geo-blocking practices, price discrimination and refusal to supply customers (unilateral geo-blocking) are examples of potential competition restrictions, as are other

---

Council's Approach to Cross-Border Portability of Online Content Services' (2016) 27 Entertainment Law Review 269; G Campus, 'Recent developments on the EU Proposal for a Regulation on cross-border portability' (Kluwer Copyright Blog, 19 December 2016) http://kluwercopyrightblog.com/2016/12/19/recent-developments-eu -proposal-regulation-cross-borderportability/, accessed 18 March 2018; 'Agreement reached on EU portability regulation' (Osborne Clarke, 8 February 2017) http://www .osborneclarke.com/insights/agreementreached-on-eu-portability-regulation/, accessed 18 March 2018. See also further Chapter 12 by Giuseppe Mazziotti in this volume.

[69] See COM(2016) 289 final; COM(2017) 229 final, paras 16–22, 45–48, 57–72; European Commission, 'Staff Working Document Accompanying the Document Final Report on the E-commerce Sector Inquiry' SWD(2017) 154 final, paras 414–433, 1024–1033.

[70] See, eg, COM(2017) 229 final, paras 16–22, 45–48, 57–72; SWD(2017) 154 final, paras 414–433, 1024–1033.

[71] See further, eg, A Ezrachi, 'The Ripple Effects of Online Marketplace Bans' (2017) 40 World Competition 47, 48–50.

[72] See, eg, COM(2016) 288 final; SWD(2016) 172 final. See also European Commission, 'Commission publishes mid-term review of the 2015 Digital Single Market strategy' (Fact Sheet, 10 May 2017, MEMO/17/1233); European Commission, 'Digital Single Market – Online Platforms', https://ec.europa.eu/digital-single-market/ en/policies/online-platforms, accessed 18 March 2018.

potentially abusive practices by major digital content distributors. The findings of the e-commerce sector inquiry do not directly translate into solutions for all potential competition concerns but point out areas for further assessment. Additionally, the European Commission has noted the need for targeted competition investigations.[73]

While reviewing the European Commission's guidance on applying the law to unfair commercial practices with a particular focus on digital markets is welcome,[74] the practical implications of this development depend on more general law enforcement trends. In this respect, creation of an online dispute resolution platform and updating the framework for enforcement cooperation between authorities constitute concrete steps for developing enforcement of EU consumer law and are highlighted by the DSM materials.[75] Nevertheless, the activity and resources of individual national consumer protection authorities and organizations remain central. General promotion of effective, concrete public enforcement of EU (and national) consumer law is still needed.[76] Additionally, the DSM materials themselves note a lack of enforcement of existing EU consumer law, suggesting that more active enforcement of

---

[73] See COM(2017) 229 final; SWD(2017) 154 final. See also, eg, European Commission, 'Antitrust: Commission publishes final report on e-commerce sector inquiry' (Press release, 10 May 2017, IP/17/1261).

[74] See SWD(2016) 163 final; Directive (EU) 2005/29 concerning unfair business-to-consumer commercial practices in the internal market and amending Council Directive 84/450/EEC, Directives 97/7/EC, 98/27/EC and 2002/65/EC of the European Parliament and of the Council and Regulation (EC) No 2006/2004 of the European Parliament and of the Council (Unfair Commercial Practices Directive) [2005] OJ L149/22.

[75] See, eg, COM(2015) 192 final, page 5; European Commission, 'Solving disputes online: New platform for consumers and traders' (Press release, 15 February 2016, IP/16/297); Regulation (EU) 524/2013 on online dispute resolution for consumer disputes and amending Regulation (EC) No 2006/2004 and Directive 2009/22/EC [2013] OJ L165/1; Regulation (EU) 2015/1051 on the modalities for the exercise of the functions of the online dispute resolution platform, on the modalities of the electronic complaint form and on the modalities of the cooperation between contact points provided for in Regulation (EU) No 524/2013 of the European Parliament and of the Council on online dispute resolution for consumer disputes [2015] OJ L171/1; European Commission, 'A Comprehensive Approach to Stimulating Cross-Border E-Commerce for Europe's Citizens and Businesses' (Communication) COM(2016) 320 final, 5, 9; European Commission, 'Proposal for a Regulation on Cooperation between National Authorities Responsible for the Enforcement of Consumer Protection laws' COM(2016) 283 final.

[76] For further discussion see Havu (n 49) 161–164.

previously enacted basic rules also plays a key role in improving consumer protection (as understood broadly) in the digital markets.[77]

This brief exploration of aspects of the DSM Strategy illustrates that much work remains in terms of improving the position of consumers of digital content. Different DSM initiatives are proceeding at their own pace and even relatively vital issues, such as resolving geo-blocking matters in a concrete and comprehensive manner are, at best, in progress. Moreover, the question may be raised whether more overarching approaches would yield better, more systematic and more lasting results than working individually on highly specific 'pointillist' questions – such as portability or selected aspects of consumer contracts.

5. CONCLUDING REMARKS

This chapter has addressed the position of consumers of digital content under the EU DSM Strategy. Particular attention has been paid to the proposed DCD, which seeks to harmonize certain aspects of consumer contract law focusing on digital content transactions. Additionally, some selected remarks have been presented on different aspects of the DSM agenda affecting protection of consumers.

The proposal for the DCD provides clarity and uniform rules regarding some basic aspects of consumer contracts. Nevertheless, the proposed directive appears to include sub-optimal rules and vague provisions. Moreover, the proposed DCD is far from exhaustive and only tackles selected aspects of consumer contracts, not all central contract law matters or all practical issues relevant for the consumer. Hence, national private laws are left to play a central part. The goals of harmonization are likely to be only partially achieved. Approachable and optimal EU-wide digital content markets, as well as clear and uniform applicable law, would require a more comprehensive effort.

As regards the whole of the DSM agenda, it may be noted that the position of consumers is improved but in a fragmentary manner. Further, several DSM Strategy plans that appear beneficial for consumers are still being put into effect, while concrete outcomes remain to be seen. The piecemeal nature of the DSM proposals affecting consumers, as well as the incompleteness of the legal framework and enforcement systems, signify that there is still a long way to go to a safe, fair and appealing DSM.[78]

---

[77] See, eg, COM(2015) 192 final, at 5; SWD(2015) 274 final/2, at 17, 45; COM(2016) 288 final, at 5, 10–11. SWD(2016) 172 final, at 12, 14, 21.

[78] Compare to, eg, COM(2015) 192 final, at 2–7.

12. Allowing online content to cross borders: is Europe really paving the way for a Digital Single Market?

Giuseppe Mazziotti

1. INTRODUCTION

In the context of its Digital Single Market strategy, the removal of territorial barriers in content distribution has become a priority for the European Union.[1] Smooth access to high-quality and customized content offerings is regarded as a pre-condition for the development of well-functioning markets for creative works and the re-affirmation of the function of intellectual property in the online environment. Access to copyright works on a multi-territorial basis in Europe would entail both regulatory changes and economic incentives to be given to content creators and suppliers of online services who still find it more convenient to partition markets along national borders. Despite the existence of technologically borderless platforms, markets for creative works in Europe are still highly fragmented, especially in the audiovisual sector, where copyright works are exploited locally for both commercial and cultural (or linguistic) reasons.[2] These commercial partitions and the establishment, through distinct licensing agreements, of areas of so-called 'absolute territorial exclusivity' are the main reason why geo-blocking measures are eventually implemented and prove to be very difficult to remove. In this regard, geo-blocking measures are

---

[1] European Commission (2015), 'A Digital Single Market Strategy for Europe', COM(2015) 192 final.

[2] A Renda, F Simonelli, G Mazziotti, A Bolognini and G Luchetta, 'The Implementation, Application and Effects of the EU Directive on Copyright in the Information Society', Centre for European Policy Studies (CEPS), November 2015, 58 ff.; G Mazziotti and F Simonelli, 'Another Breach in the Wall: Copyright Territoriality in Europe and Its Progressive Erosion on the Grounds of Competition Law' (2016) 18(6) *Journal of Policy, Regulation and Strategy for Telecommunications, Information and Media* 55, at 56–58.

no more than a tool to enforce contractual provisions that do not allow service suppliers to do their business outside of a given territory.[3]

This chapter analyses the function and scope of EU regulatory measures that are being adopted and implemented with a view to tackling the issue of territorial discrimination of consumers in the market for digital creative content. First, the chapter focuses on the notion of cross-border 'portability' under Regulation 2017/1128 and briefly describes what the consequences of this Regulation in the markets for online content services are expected to be.[4] Second, cross-border portability will be compared to the much broader notion of 'cross-border trade', which could have fallen within the scope of Regulation 2018/302 on geo-blocking and other forms of discrimination based on consumers' nationality, place of residence or place of establishment.[5] Third, the chapter takes into consideration the territorial anti-discrimination principle embodied in Regulation 2018/302 to point out that online content services have been expressly excluded, at least for now, from the scope of application of the Regulation. As a result, the creative sector is expected to be unaffected by the 2018 Geo-blocking Regulation. Fourth, it will be argued that copyright holders and online content exploiters might be forced or encouraged to remove certain territorial restrictions from their licensing agreements in response to antitrust investigations based on Article 101 TFEU or due to the emergence of web-based business models giving up the criterion of territoriality in determining the price and conditions of access to copyright works. In conclusion, the chapter will assess the overall impact of the new EU regulations on existing obstacles to cross-border trade, clarifying whether or not consumers can expect significant improvements in access to creative works on the Internet.

---

[3]   G Mazziotti, 'Is Geo-blocking a Real Cause for Concern in Europe?' (2016) 38(6) *European Intellectual Property Review* 366, at 368–372.

[4]   Reg (EU) 2017/1128 of the European Parliament and of the Council of 14 June 2017 on cross-border portability of online content services in the internal market, OJ L 168/1, 30.06.2017 ('Portability Regulation').

[5]   Reg 2018/302 of the European Parliament and of the Council on addressing Geo-blocking and other forms of discrimination based on customers' nationality, place of residence or place of establishment within the internal market and amending Regulation No 2006/2004 and Directive 2009/22/EC, OJ L 601, 2.3.2018, 1–15 ('Geo-blocking Regulation'). See also Chapter 13 by Vesala and Chapter 14 by Cantero in this volume.

2. THE 2017 REGULATION ON CROSS-BORDER PORTABILITY OF ONLINE CONTENT SERVICES

In June 2017, for the first time in the history of EU copyright law, the European Parliament and the Council adopted a copyright regulation on cross-border portability of online content services. This legislative act can be regarded as the very first example of 'federal' copyright law in Europe since it directly enables certain categories of consumers (travellers, tourists and other short-term migrants) to bring their online content services across borders whenever they are temporarily present in a Member State other than the Member State where they reside.[6] When the European Commission proposed its adoption, the Portability Regulation was presented as an effective remedy against geo-blocking and as a relevant step towards a goal that, with a good dose of emphasis, has been defined as the Digital Single Market.[7]

The Portability Regulation seeks to enable subscribers to portable online services obtain access to content such as music, games, films and sporting events provided in exchange for payment of money (or without payment of money, if the service provider verifies the subscriber's Member State of residence) to access and use such services not only in their own country of residence, but in all the EU Member States where they happen to be located for a limited period.[8] For example, a subscriber to an online audiovisual content supplier residing in Spain who travels for a limited period to France or Germany will have the right under the 2017 Regulation to access the same content package in Paris or Berlin, as if they were physically located in Madrid. Through what has been regarded as a legal fiction, the Regulation ensures that copyright content streamed by a subscriber in Paris or Berlin is to be considered as being streamed in Madrid.[9] This mechanism entails that a service provider who acquires the online rights to exploit certain works in a given EU country

---

[6]   Portability Regulation, Art 3, para 1.

[7]   European Commission (2015), 'Commission takes first steps to broaden access to online content and outlines its vision to modernise copyright rules', Press release, Brussels, 9.12.2015 (where Andrus Ansip, Vice-President for the Digital Single Market said: 'Seven months ago, we promised fast delivery of the Digital Single Market. Today we present our first proposals. We want to ensure the portability of content across borders. People who legally buy content – films, books, football matches, TV series – must be able to carry it with them anywhere they go in Europe. This is a real change, similar to what we did to end roaming charges …)'.

[8]   Portability Regulation, Art 1, para 1.

[9]   G Mazziotti and F Simonelli, 'Regulation on "cross-border portability" of online content services: roaming for Netflix or the end of copyright territoriality?' (2015) CEPS Commentary, available at http://ceps.eu.

(for example, Spain) will have these rights automatically extended – by mere operation of the Portability Regulation – to the EU jurisdictions where its subscribers would happen to be located on a temporary basis (in our example, France or Germany). To ensure its functioning from a legal point of view, the Portability Regulation does not specify how long the journeys or stays abroad of the beneficiaries of the new law should be. In particular, the Regulation expressly deprives copyright holders and online content service providers of the possibility of limiting, in terms of scope and/or duration, the right of European consumers to cross-border portability of their content (cf. Article 7). Rather, the Regulation grants that right by creating an obligation for providers of online content services to verify the Member State of residence of their subscribers by means of verification showing a clear link between the consumer and an EU Member State.[10] As briefly pointed out above, the obligation of service providers is based on a legal fiction that consists of treating content transmissions that reach the consumer in any of the EU countries as occurring – legally speaking – solely in their own EU country of residence.[11] In the same way as other EU law provisions, the Portability Regulation has the effect of avoiding application of a multiplicity of laws when a consumer travels across Europe. Moreover, the Regulation extends, for a limited period, the territorial scope of online rights licensed by the copyright holder to the EU territories where the consumer receives online content transmissions.

It is worth recalling that this is not the first time that EU law has relied on legal 'fictions' in order to limit the scope of copyright territoriality and to make application of national copyright laws compatible with the freedom to provide services within the European Union. Relevant precedents are embodied in directives that are aimed at simplifying clearance of copyright and to strengthen the freedom to provide certain services on a multi-territorial basis.[12]

---

[10] Art 5 of the Portability Regulation requires service providers to verify the Member State of residence of the subscriber by using not more than two of the following means of verification, ensuring that the means used are reasonable, proportionate and effective: (i) payment details or credit/debit card numbers; (ii) the place of installation of a set top box, decoder or similar device used for the supply of services to the subscriber; (iii) payment by the subscriber of a licence fee for other services provided in the Member State, such as public service broadcasting; (iv) an Internet or telephone service supply contract; (v) registration on local electoral rolls; (vi) payment of local taxes; (vii) a utility bill or the billing or postal address of the subscriber; (viii) a declaration by the subscriber confirming his or her address in the Member State; (ix) an Internet Protocol (IP) address check, to identify where the subscriber accesses the online content service.
[11] Portability Regulation, Art 4 (Localisation of provision of, access to and use of online content services).
[12] Audiovisual Media Services Directive, Art 2; also Directive 2007/65 of the European Parliament and of the Council of 11 December 2007 amending Council

These directives impose on the EU Member States adoption of a 'country of origin' principle that makes cross-border content exploitation such as satellite broadcasts and digital TV services subject to one single national law, as if those activities occurred just in the country where the service provider is established. An identical objective is being pursued at the EU level through an EU regulation which the European Commission proposed in September 2016 in order to facilitate clearance of copyright for online ancillary services and content re-transmissions by broadcasters and operators of services such as IP TV providers wishing to offer access to their television and radio programmes on a cross-border basis.[13] To this end, by complementing the existing Satellite and Cable Directive, the Broadcasting Regulation aims to make certain online transmissions of radio and TV broadcasts, as well as their cross-border re-transmissions, subject solely to the law of the country of origin of the broadcaster.[14]

3.   PORTABILITY VERSUS CROSS-BORDER TRADE

In spite of the potentially borderless dimension of the Internet, copyright holders still have a strong preference for concluding licensing agreements that clear or assign their rights on a strictly territorial basis. It has been shown that the creative sector finds territorially restricted licensing practices more sustainable and commercially more profitable than (still non-existing) licences of the

---

Directive 89/552/EEC on the coordination of certain provisions laid down by law, regulation or administrative action in Member States concerning the pursuit of television broadcasting activities, OJ L 322/27, 18.12.2007; and Council Directive 93/83/EEC of 27 September 1993 on the coordination of certain rules concerning copyright and rights related to copyright applicable to satellite broadcasting and cable retransmission, OJ L 248, 6.10.1993 ('Satellite and Cable Directive').

[13]   Proposal for a Regulation laying down rules on the exercise of copyright and related rights applicable to certain online transmissions of broadcasting organisations and retransmissions of television and radio programmes, COM/2016/0594 final – 2016/0284 (COD) ('Broadcasting Regulation'). Rec 8 of the Broadcasting Regulation refers to 'ancillary services' as those services offered by broadcasting organizations which have a clear and subordinate relationship to the broadcast.

[14]   Services falling within the scope of application of the Broadcasting Regulation include transmissions of radio and TV programmes simultaneously to the broadcast; services giving access, within a defined period after the broadcast, to radio and TV programmes which have previously been transmitted by the same organization (so-called 'catch-up' services); services providing access to material that enriches or otherwise expands radio and TV broadcasts (eg, previewing, reviewing).

same rights to single pan-European exploiters.[15] Especially in the audiovisual sector, professional content creation depends economically on pre-production agreements that normally restrict the licensing freedom of film producers as a result of pre-sales or assignments of the film rights to certain commercial exploiters on an exclusive territorial basis.[16] Cinematographic production, in particular, entails complex fund-raising activity in both the Hollywood studio system and in the European film sector. Hollywood studios traditionally assign their copyright to a distributor or licence their rights by territory, by linguistic version and, less frequently, on a regional basis. These pre-production arrangements give rise to 'windowed' releases (defining content exploitation through pay-TV broadcasts, DVDs and free-to-air broadcasts after release in cinemas) whose ultimate end is to place a movie in the best competitive position in order to cover the production costs and to gain profits. For European film productions, in contrast, given the subsidies granted at national level by governments and other public bodies, limitations or barriers to online exploitation might easily derive from administrative regulations applicable to funding or co-production agreements with public institutions such as public broadcasters, which might be reluctant or commercially unable to make their movies available for EU-wide online exploitation.[17]

Territorial licensing in the audiovisual sector might also be viewed as a necessity on the basis of Europe's culturally and linguistically diverse audiences and the fact that, commercially speaking, content adaptation through dubbing and subtitles (together with other forms of content versioning) is still indispensable in four of the five biggest markets in Europe: (Germany, France, Italy and Spain).[18]

Finally, it is undeniable that copyright territoriality and persisting divergences between national systems on elements – such as the definition of authorship and contract law provisions applicable to the transfer and management of copyright by authors and performers – end up encouraging country-by-country licensing schemes.[19]

The narrow scope of the Portability Regulation and the legal mechanism the Regulation relies upon clearly show that the main goal of the new law is to ensure consumer protection in the market for online content services. In

---

[15] European Parliament, 'Combating Consumer Discrimination in the Digital Single Market: Preventing Geo-blocking and Other Forms of Geo-Discrimination' (2016) DG for Internal Policies, Study for the IMCO Committee, 17–18.

[16] G Mazziotti, 'Copyright in the Digital Single Market' (2013) Centre for European Policy Studies (CEPS), Brussels, available at http://ceps.eu, 52–54.

[17] ibid, 53.

[18] Renda et al (n 2) 63.

[19] European Parliament (n 15) 17–18; Mazziotti (n 3) 368.

no way does the Regulation impact on the freedom of copyright holders and online content exploiters to give their licensing agreements a strictly territorial dimension and to partition digital markets along national borders. Nothing in this Regulation restricts the implementation of geo-blocking measures. Geo-blocking, in this regard, has the function of limiting access to protected works to a national or a linguistically homogeneous audience and of enabling price discrimination between different EU countries where consumers have different purchasing power. The only aim of the Regulation is to protect access by European residents to territorially restricted content services by ensuring that their temporary presence abroad does not impair their enjoyment of the content services they legitimately access at home.

By presupposing the national dimension of online content markets and the existence of territorial restrictions, the 2017 Regulation inevitably confers legitimacy on the implementation of geo-blocking measures. The Regulation creates a temporary exception to the principle of copyright territoriality and to the strictly national dimension of online content markets by granting consumers a short-term right to access their services on a cross-border basis. This time-limited exception has nothing to do with the broader concept of cross-border trade in online copyright works. Cross-border trade would take place if consumers residing in Europe were enabled, on a permanent basis, to access online services that are offered in a Member State other than their home country. For instance, one could effectively speak of cross-border trade if a consumer residing in Spain or Portugal were allowed to subscribe to an online service giving access to a selection of content that is targeted at and offered on an exclusive basis to audiences based in Germany or Ireland.

Recent cases analysed by European institutions have shown that cross-border trade is still far from materializing because of well-established licensing practices aimed at creating areas of absolute territorial exclusivity for services giving access to sporting events and audiovisual works.[20] Under standard licensing agreements copyright holders explicitly restrict their licensees from selling access to copyright content outside of the territories where they are granted exclusive rights of commercial exploitation. In a case regarding pay-per-view TV services, a Greek broadcaster had acquired from the Premier League exclusive rights to broadcast UK football matches while undertaking to prevent the public from receiving the broadcasts outside of Greece. In another case regarding the pay-per-view TV market, agreements concluded by major

---

[20]   Joined Cases C-403/08 *Football Association Premier League* v *QC Leisure and Others* and C-429/08 *Karen Murphy* v *Media Protection Services Ltd*, Judgment, 4 October 2011 (*Premier League*); European Commission, 'Commission sends statement of objections on cross-border provision of pay-TV services available in UK and Ireland, Press release', Brussels, 23.07.2015 (*Sky UK*).

US film producers (Disney, NBC Universal, Paramount Pictures, Sony, 20th Century Fox and Warner Bros) with the largest European pay-TV broadcasters contractually restricted licensees such as Sky UK from enabling EU consumers based in other Member States to access (both online and via satellite) the pay-TV services which Sky provided in the UK and Ireland. Despite their partitioning effects on the Internal Market, in neither of these cases did the Court of Justice (in *Premier League*) or the European Commission (acting as European antitrust authority) have the opportunity to clarify whether licensing agreements giving rise to areas of absolute territorial exclusivity entail a violation of EU competition law (Article 101 TFEU). In particular, in *Premier League* the Court of Justice was asked to assess whether a licensing agreement could restrict the cross-border supply of cards and decoding devices giving access to the Greek TV content package to commercial users (UK-based bar and restaurant owners) wishing to take advantage of the lower Greek subscription price. The Court held that the territorial exclusivity sought by the Premier League with regard to its content in Europe was legitimate but it should not have enjoyed absolute protection so as to end up restricting cross-border trade in physical goods that made content transmissions technically accessible. As we will see, especially as far as online content distribution is concerned, this conclusion might be interpreted as a relevant limit created by EU competition law for content owners and content suppliers to give areas of territorial exclusivity an absolute character.

4.   REGULATION AGAINST TERRITORIAL DISCRIMINATION IN ELECTRONIC COMMERCE

From the perspective on cross-border trade described above, a recently adopted EU regulation on geo-blocking is designed to set out the conditions and to identify the sectors in which services will have to be made accessible to consumers located in a Member State other than the one where the trader is established or where it is actively promoting its business. To this end, the 2018 Geo-blocking Regulation embodies general provisions aimed at prohibiting traders from blocking or limiting customer access, through the use of technological measures, to the trader's online interfaces (websites, mobile device applications), goods or services for reasons related to the customers' nationality, place of residence or place of establishment.[21] The Regulation also prohibits traders from discriminating among consumers on the grounds of their residence or nationality for reasons related to payment methods accepted

---

[21]   Geo-blocking Regulation, Arts 3 and 4.

by the trader.[22] The entry into force of this Regulation in December 2018 will be particularly relevant for traders and consumers to better understand what forms of territorial discrimination and geo-blocking measures will have to be regarded as permissible in the domain of electronic commerce, notwithstanding the goal of a Digital Single Market.

While clarifying the sectors and services for which geo-blocking and other forms of territorial discrimination of consumers should still be viewed as legitimate, the Geo-blocking Regulation ensures that obligations and duties established under EU and/or national laws with regard to certain products and services are not easily circumvented or eluded through cross-border online sales. Through such exclusions, the Regulation clarifies that in sectors where legal requirements or forms of regulation are still to be enforced at national level, consumers cannot resort to foreign traders to skip national regulatory control or the territorial enforcement of mandatory rules.[23] Moreover, the Regulation does not interfere with the principle of freedom of contract and the freedom of enterprises to limit their businesses when cross-border trade of their products or services would raise disproportionate costs deriving from regulatory constraints such as diverging national tax rules and other obstacles to cross-border sales such as delivery costs.

The main criterion the Geo-blocking Regulation relies upon in order to map the sectors where no geo-blocking measure will be allowed in the future is the distinction between justified and unjustified forms of territorial discrimination.[24] The Regulation re-states and extends the pre-existing non-discrimination principle laid down under Article 20 of Directive 2006/123 (the so-called 'Services' Directive), whose prescriptive force is now strengthened by its incorporation into an EU-wide regulation whose enforcement will be supervised by national authorities and facilitated by judicial initiatives that consumers and their associations will be able to undertake.[25]

---

[22]   Geo-blocking Regulation, Art 5.

[23]   If there was no interface between the Geo-blocking Regulation and legal requirements established at national level, a resident of, eg, Sweden would be enabled to buy and receive stocks of wine and spirits from online stores operating in Italy or France and delivering these goods to a EU Member State where such sale would elude existing legal restrictions in the marketing of these products.

[24]   Art 1 of the Geo-blocking Regulation (Objective and scope) makes it clear that the purpose of the regulation is to prevent unjustified Geo-blocking and other forms of discrimination based, directly or indirectly, on customers' nationality, place of residence or place of establishment, including certain situations where consumer discrimination cannot be justified under Art 20(2) of Directive 2006/123/EC.

[25]   Art 7 of the Geo-blocking Regulation (Enforcement) requires each Member State to designate a body or bodies responsible for adequate and effective enforcement of the Regulation.

The Geo-blocking Regulation provides that blocking access to websites and applications as well as redirecting customers on the grounds of their nationality or place of residence or establishment is generally forbidden, unless such practices are put in place to comply with legal requirements imposed by EU or national rules. The requirements and mandatory national rules which are still regarded as a legitimate exception to the principle of territorial non-discrimination of consumers are identified by reference to Article 2(2) of the 2006 Services Directive.[26] In terms of electronically supplied services giving access to copyright works, the 2018 Geo-blocking Regulation excludes all of them from its scope of application in a twofold way. First, the Regulation maintains and re-states the exclusion of audiovisual services laid down in the 2006 Services Directive. Second, the Regulation expressly excludes the generality of copyright works that was added under Article 1 to the original text proposed by the European Commission.[27]

Consistently with the main goal of the 2017 Portability Regulation, exclusion of copyright works from the principle of territorial non-discrimination of consumers indirectly endorses the legitimacy of contractual practices ensuring commercial exploitation and online enforcement of copyright along strictly national borders. Interestingly, the Internal Market and Consumer Protection (IMCO) Committee of the European Parliament discussed limited inclusion of copyright works in the scope of the Geo-blocking Regulation and approved a few amendments in April 2017 that would have made non-audiovisual copyright content fall within the scope of the Regulation under certain conditions.[28] Those amendments provided that the Regulation would outlaw territorial discrimination of consumers if requests for access to an online content service came from a Member State where the service provider had acquired the rights to exploit a given piece of content or a given package or repertoire. This different approach was eventually dropped in the final version of the Regulation, with the consequence that online content suppliers of non-audiovisual copyright works can still price-discriminate among consumers residing in different

---

[26] Art 2(2) of the 'Services' Directive refers to non-economic services of general interest, transport services, audiovisual services, retail financial services, electronic communications services and networks, gambling, healthcare and certain social services.

[27] European Commission, Proposal for a regulation of the European Parliament and of the Council on addressing Geo-blocking and other forms of discrimination based on customers' nationality, place of residence or place of establishment within the internal market and amending Regulation (EC) No 2006/2004 and Directive 2009/22/EC, COM(2016) 289 final, Brussels, 25.5.2016.

[28] European Parliament, IMCO Committee, 'e-Commerce: Ending unjustified Geo-blocking across the EU', Press release, Brussels, 25.04.2017, available at http://www.europarl.europa.eu.

countries.[29] The final version of the 2018 Geo-blocking Regulation merely confers on the Commission the task of evaluating a possible extension of the scope of the Regulation to copyright works two years after its entry into force.[30]

5.   WHAT WOULD MAKE ONLINE CONTENT DISTRIBUTION EFFECTIVELY CROSS-BORDER?

As we have seen, none of the above-mentioned EU law measures is designed to challenge the legitimacy of agreements concluded by copyright holders and service suppliers aimed at creating areas of absolute territorial exclusivity in online content distribution. Even though the 2017 Portability Regulation and the upcoming Broadcasting Regulation are designed to give content distribution a potentially pan-European dimension, their respective rules constitute exceptions to the principles of territoriality justified by the intent to grant an access right, for a limited period, to travellers and short-term migrants within the EU and a simplified licensing mechanism for broadcasters willing to provide some ancillary services on a cross-border basis. Both of these regulations presuppose – as upheld by the provisions of the Geo-blocking Regulation – fragmentation of the EU into rigidly territorial content markets.

That said, one might wonder how a Digital Single Market might develop in the creative sector, at least in the near future. As has been pointed out, the present situation of fragmentation might evolve in the absence of regulatory intervention at the EU level if Article 101 TFEU – which outlaws agreements having the effect of partitioning the 'Common Market' – was effectively enforced in the online environment.[31] So far, however, the territorially restricted content services under scrutiny have not concerned web-based delivery. The *Premier League* and *SKY UK* cases entailed cross-border access to TV services offered by a provider based in Member State A to commercial users (*Premier League*) or consumers (*Sky UK*) residing in Member State B. Even though none of these cases helped clarify how the national dimension of copyright can be reconciled with the purpose of creating unified digital

---

[29]   It should be borne in mind that inclusion of services giving access to audiovisual works was never taken into consideration because of inclusion of such services in the list of sectors identified under Art 2(2) of Directive 2006/123/EC.

[30]   Geo-blocking Regulation, Art 9, para 2. See also Chapter 13 by Vesala in this volume (future extension of the scope of the Geo-Blocking Regulation).

[31]   A Renda, F Simonelli, G Mazziotti and G Luchetta, 'Policy Options for Improving the Functioning and Efficiency of the Digital Single Market in the Field of Copyright' (2015) Centre for European Policy Studies, available at http://ceps.eu, 10; Mazziotti (n 3) 374.

markets, both the situations scrutinized at the EU level showed the potential of competition law enforcement for the liberalization of cross-border trade. These two cases evidenced that in the audiovisual sector (which includes the supply of sports content) standard contractual provisions prevent licensees from selling their TV content packages outside of the territories (Greece and the UK, respectively) where they had obtained an exclusive licence from the copyright owners. Moreover, agreements of this kind normally embody contractual clauses obliging content producers such as the major US film studios to include equivalent restrictions in the licensing agreements they conclude with pay-TV broadcasters based in other EU countries. This means that standard licensing agreements restrict so-called 'passive sales', which are deemed to occur in response to unsolicited requests from consumers who are not located where the sale of a good or service has been actively promoted or advertised.[32]

To understand the relevance and the potential of passive sales in the online environment, one should consider that the physical distance of consumers from the country of origin of a content seller counts much less in online markets than in physical markets.[33] This means that, despite the lack of exposure of consumers to marketing campaigns and commercial promotions of a content service in a given Member State, consumers residing in another Member State could be increasingly interested in having access to a 'foreign' content service after having looked for it and located it through a simple web search.[34] As we have seen, passive sales are currently restricted under standard licensing agree-

---

[32] It must be recalled that the European Commission considers the restriction of passive sales as falling within the notion of hard-core antitrust restrictions, which fall outside of the scope of application of the block exemption regulation on vertical restraints: Commission Regulation No 330/2010 of 20 April 2010 on the application of Article 101(3) TFEU to categories of vertical agreements and concerted practices, OJ L 102/1, 23.4.2010, Art 4(c).

[33] As pointed out in the relevant literature, in online markets the role of physical distance between consumers and the place where digital content is made available to the public has sharply diminished: E Gomez and B Martens, 'Language, Copyright and Geographic Segmentation in the EU Digital Single Market for Music and Film', European Commission, Joint Research Centre, JRC Technical Reports (2015) 12.

[34] As emphasized in Mazziotti and Simonelli (n 2) 61, the Commission has confirmed that vertical agreements preventing online passive sales should be found anti-competitive by object: European Commission, 'Commission Notice, Guidelines on Vertical Restraints', OJ C 130, 19.05.2010, 1. The authors point out that, according to the Commission guidelines, online sales should generally be considered a form of passive rather than active sale because it is the customer who takes the initiative to visit a given website. The fact that a website and its contents are automatically indexed on search engines or comparison websites places customers – without territorial distinctions – in a position to access and request the goods and services of an online trader also outside of its territory of operation and business.

ments, which oblige service providers not to sell their services to consumers located outside of a given territory. From an economic point of view, this absolute territorial exclusivity has been justified on the assumption that the supply of audiovisual and TV content – for both cultural and commercial reasons – has been mostly a prerogative of broadcasters and providers of pay-per-view TV services, whose audiences are mostly confined within national borders. This exclusivity has been strengthened by extension of the scope of licensing agreements to clearance of online rights, which allow pay-TV broadcasters to make the same contents simultaneously available to their subscribers via web-based deliveries and encrypted TV content transmissions made accessible through decoding devices. In this scenario, pay-TV service providers have extended their services to the online environment and started competing with on-demand web-based services such as those offered by Netflix and Amazon. The main difference between the business models of these digital content services is that online supply of audiovisual content is just a complement to the core business of pay-TV services, which rely on the functioning of decoding devices and different packages of content strictly defined on territorial grounds. For content suppliers such as Netflix, Amazon or Apple, in contrast, online distribution is their core business since their services are provided only online. Unlike the current business models of pay-TV service providers, the content distribution strategies of web-based suppliers inevitably entail simultaneous consumer access to the same works in a multiplicity of countries.[35] The increasing success and popularity of purely web-based on-demand platforms suggest that, in the near future, online content distribution might no longer rely on territoriality as the main criterion to build up online content markets.[36] The acquisition of exploitation rights on a multi-territorial or pan-European basis

---

[35] It should be borne in mind that the EU is extending media law obligations to the domain of video-on-demand content providers such as Netflix through an amendment to Directive 2010/13 (Audiovisual Media Services Directive). The fact that these companies will be obliged, as a matter of cultural policy, to promote production and access to European works is a factor that might discourage unification of the same online content packages on a multi-territorial or pan-European basis.

[36] In spite of the simultaneous availability of large amounts of copyright works in all EU countries, a recent study focusing on Apple's iTunes store showed that, in 2015, because of geographical restrictions implemented by Apple, less than half of all songs and music albums were available in all of the national music stores: see Gomez and Martens (n 33). The study also found that – because of commercial strategies that draw on drivers of content demand such as language and home market bias – music availability was somewhere between 73 and 82 per cent of what it could have been in an unrestricted 'Digital Single Market' where all music content would be available in all Member States. The situation was worse for digital movies, whose simultaneous availability was estimated at 40 per cent of the whole amount of content made available by iTunes.

and/or vertical integration between production and supply of creative content (as evidenced by increasingly relevant audiovisual works produced directly by Netflix) show that purely web-based business models might trigger erosion of today's territoriality of markets.

If the logic of multi-territorial access to creative works might progressively replace the criterion of territoriality on the grounds of pure market and technological developments, what should be the role of regulatory intervention in the EU in order to allow or facilitate cross-border trade in the content sector? As pointed out above, the modest scope of EU regulations on cross-border portability and certain web-based broadcasting services as well as the attempt by the Geo-blocking Regulation to preserve the territoriality of markets, especially in the audiovisual sector, show that there is an effort to reaffirm copyright territoriality as a tool enabling each Member State to protect the logic of fair remuneration within its own cultural policy framework.[37] It is therefore distinctly unclear, in the existing legislative framework, whether the absolute character of areas of territorial exclusivity should be regarded as a hard-core restriction of competition and whether passive sales should be liberalized in purely web-based content distribution models. The 2018 Geo-blocking Regulation clearly leaves copyright holders and online content suppliers with the freedom to restrict passive sales in their contractual agreements. The Geo-blocking Regulation clearly provides that its entry into force should leave unaffected agreements restricting passive sales concerning transactions falling outside of the scope of the prohibitions laid down in the Regulation.[38] In this regard, the explicit exclusion of the audiovisual sector and of other electronically supplied copyright works from the realm of services subject to the principle of territorial non-discrimination entails that the present contractual restrictions of passive sales will remain untouched. Moreover, a possible extension of the scope of application of the Geo-blocking Regulation to non-audiovisual content services would be expressly limited to situations where content suppliers own online exploitation rights for both the country where their services are offered and the country where a consumer seeks to access those services. Last but not least, inclusion of the audiovisual sector in the list of services for which territorial restrictions should be regarded as legitimate means that online distribution of audiovisual works – which are the most affected by the issue of geo-blocking – will continue to be shaped on strictly territorial grounds. Even though Article 101 TEFU has a constitutional dimension that prevails

---

[37] This is exactly what the European Parliament claimed in its Resolution of 9 July 2015 on the implementation of Directive 2001/29/EC on the harmonisation of certain aspects of copyright and related rights in the information society, 2014/2256(INI), paras 6 and 7. See also Chapter 14 by Cantero in this volume (territoriality issues).
[38] Geo-blocking Regulation, Art 6.

over the provisions of secondary EU law such as the 2018 Geo-blocking Regulation, it would be difficult for the European Commission, acting as the EU antitrust authority, to claim a breach of EU competition law in cases where the contractual partition of online markets along national borders is expressly authorized, if not encouraged, by EU lawmakers. As things stand, therefore, a Digital Single Market in the creative content sector is likely to materialize mostly as a result of commercial decisions and the predominance of territorially unrestricted models of online content distribution over the strictly national distribution models of pay-TV service providers.

6.   CONCLUSION

It seems evident that unified markets will be very hard (or impossible) to develop in so far as the attempt to foster cross-border trade through territorial anti-discrimination covers a relatively small range of online activities, such as cross-border transmissions reaching travellers and short-term migrants within the EU and web-based ancillary services of radio and TV broadcasters. Even though EU lawmakers might reconsider their decision to exclude the creative content sector and all types of copyright works from the realm of services whose trade should not be territorially subject to discrimination and geo-blocking, such reconsideration is likely not to touch upon the audiovisual sector. This chapter has shown that, in spite of regulatory changes implemented in 2017 and 2018, with so much emphasis at a political level, territorial fragmentation will persist in the European Union as a result of legislative and contractual constraints that inevitably keep certain activities and businesses within national (or, in the best case scenario, regional) borders. This chapter has argued that adoption and enforcement of EU regulations on portability, broadcasting and geo-blocking will not help develop the Digital Single Market because of their relatively modest scope in terms of exceptions to copyright territoriality. As this chapter has shown, there is an objective risk that these new regulatory interventions might slow down – instead of facilitating – the process of integration of digital markets at the European level through the codification of cases and situations of justified geo-blocking that presuppose the uncontested dominance of national interests and sovereign powers over the ambition (and the rhetoric) of single markets, especially in the online environment.[39] Considering the state of the art, it is also unrealistic that, at least in the near future, the EU might take a step forward and decide to unify

---

[39]   Such uncontested predominance of national interests was emphasized by the European Parliament, Resolution of 9 July 2015 on the implementation of Directive 2001/29/EC, (n 37) paras 6 and 7.

its copyright system. This would occur if a regulation were adopted to replace national copyright systems with an EU-wide copyright code or – alternatively – through an additional (and parallel) layer of regulation and enforcement for copyright holders wishing to exploit their works on a genuinely pan-European basis.[40] The fact that the easiest and most effective solution to encourage formation of digitally unified markets was not even taken into consideration by policymakers shows that territorial restrictions and geo-blocking measures are still viewed as essential tools for guaranteeing correct enforcement of (still diverging) national laws and cultural policies. The purpose of preserving the integrity of culturally and linguistically diverse markets, especially in the audiovisual sector, has clearly prevailed over the logic of making copyright content available within digital Europe without legal and technical barriers.

---

[40]   Such a regulatory intervention was presented to the Legal Affairs Committee of the European Parliament as the optimal (although still politically unrealistic) solution to the problem of market fragmentation and online copyright enforcement in the EU by Renda et al (n 31) 17–18.

13. Achieving a Digital Single Market for online distribution of content: when would extending the Geo-blocking Regulation be justified?

Juha Vesala[1]

1.   INTRODUCTION

The European Commission has made efforts to create a Digital Single Market (DSM) in which goods and services are offered online throughout the European Union (EU). As regards online distribution of content, these include legislative action in copyright and internal market law as well as enforcement measures in competition law. These efforts are now starting to bear fruit as legislative proposals have been – or are close to being – adopted.

Despite ambitious aims, the policies adopted fall short of realizing EU-wide distribution of copyright-protected content online. This is partly because a key regulation seeking to address unjustified geo-blocking does not fully apply to services featuring audiovisual or copyright-protected content. Additionally, the other pieces of legislation – adopted and proposed – do not generally enable or require cross-border provision of copyright-protected content to new customers. However, the Geo-blocking Regulation provides for a review as to whether its scope should be expanded to fully cover audiovisual and copyright-protected content. Expansion could accomplish EU-wide supply of content but raises complicated questions, particularly about its impact on content creation.

This chapter examines whether extending the Geo-blocking Regulation to cover copyright-protected and audiovisual content would achieve EU-wide distribution and seeks to determine when it would be justified. In principle,

[1]   Excellent research assistance by Tone Knapstad is gratefully acknowledged. This chapter has been produced as part of an Academy of Finland-funded research project (#275956).

such expansion could be justified where harm to financing and creation of content can be avoided, for example by allowing territorial exclusivity for a certain period before the geo-blocking rules become fully applicable or by determining specific categories of content subject to the rules. However, in order to succeed, the extension would need to be accompanied by a country-of-origin or comparable rule to resolve copyright obstacles that could prevent provision of content in accordance with the regulation. Revision of the Geo-blocking Regulation along these lines would not be drastic as it would effectively align treatment of online content distribution with that of content distributed in tangible form and of satellite broadcasts, while recognizing the need for exclusivity of content distribution, production and financing of content.

The chapter proceeds as follows. After first laying out the possibilities to limit provision of content online territorially within the EU (Section 2), the main features of Commission measures seeking to limit the effectiveness of territorial restraints are presented (Section 3). Then the impact of measures on territorial limitations in online content distribution is examined (Section 4) and the case for extending the scope of the Geo-blocking Regulation evaluated (Section 5), followed by conclusions (Section 6).

2.   TERRITORIALLY EXCLUSIVE LICENSING OF CONTENT FOR ONLINE DISTRIBUTION

Availability of copyright-protected content online is often territorially limited within the EU. Often the reason is that content has been licensed on a territorially limited basis so that online content services are not permitted under their agreements or under copyright law to offer the service to consumers in other territories in the EU. To ensure compliance with copyright and contracts, the services often technically and practically limit sales and access solely to customers that have been determined as residing and located in licensed territories.[2]

Generally, EU and national law both allow licensing in this territorially limited scope, exclusively or non-exclusively. This means that the licensee

---

[2]   See eg Sari Depreeuw and Jean-Benoit Hubin, 'Study on the Making Available Right and Its Relationship with the Reproduction Right in Cross-Border Digital Transmissions' (2014) http://ec.europa.eu/internal_market/copyright/docs/ studies/141219-study_en.pdf, accessed 16 February 2018; Giuseppe Mazziotti, 'Is Geo-blocking a Real Cause for Concern in Europe?' (2016) 38 EIPR 365; Juha Vesala, 'Geoblocking Requirements in Online Distribution of Copyright-Protected Content: Implications of Copyright Issues on Application of EU Antitrust Law' (2017) 25 Michigan State International Law Review 595, 597–599.

can offer content within the licensed area but doing so outside of that area could infringe copyright or breach an agreement. Additionally, if licensed exclusively, neither the licensor nor any other licensee may offer that content in the licensed area because that may infringe copyright. Consequently, only an exclusive licensee is able to serve the area for which it has been licensed and no competition takes place with respect to that content within that territory.[3]

The free movement of services (Article 56 TFEU) and EU competition law (Articles 101 and 102 TFEU) do not categorically or generally preclude exclusive territorial licensing despite its possibly separating national markets and preventing competition between undertakings located in different Member States. However, arrangements to further bolster territorial exclusivity may preclude copyright protection in cross-border situations under the free movement of services rules or result in infringement of EU competition law. Combining the grant of an exclusive licence with a passive sales restraint that entirely prevents sales to other territories is an example of such an agreement that likely violates EU competition law and may also constitute an unjustified restraint of free movement of services by creating absolute territorial protection.[4] It can be lawful, though, to use arrangements such as geo-blocking if they are confined to preventing unlicensed, copyright-infringing practices by distributors.[5]

Accordingly, licensing agreements can be used to limit online distribution of copyright-protected content to a certain area of the EU in a way that is valid and protected against infractions by parties to agreements or third parties. These licensing practices may result in absence of cross-border competition and inability of consumers to access or purchase content from other territories. Indeed, in some sectors this often occurs, as discussed next.

---

[3]   ibid.

[4]   See eg Joined Cases C-403 and C-429/08 *Football Association Premier League and Others v QC Leisure and Others* EU:C:2011:631; Case C-262/81 *Coditel v Ciné-Vog Films* EU:C:1982:334. See also Pablo Ibáñez Colomo, 'Copyright Licensing and the EU Digital Single Market Strategy' in Roger D Blair and D Daniel Sokol (eds), *Handbook of Antitrust, Intellectual Property and High Technology* (CUP 2017); Mazziotti (n 2); Vesala (n 2); Jonathan D C Turner, *Intellectual Property and EU Competition Law* (2nd edn, OUP 2015). See for discussion of these issues also Chapter 12 by Mazziotti and Chapter 14 by Cantero in this volume.

[5]   See eg Pablo Ibáñez Colomo, 'The Commission Investigation into Pay TV Services: Open Questions' (2014) 5 Journal of European Competition Law & Practice 531; Vesala (n 2).

3.   COMMISSION INITIATIVES TO PROMOTE ONLINE DISTRIBUTION OF CONTENT WITHIN THE EU

The Commission has observed that licensing practices of undertakings can hinder realization of a DSM for digital content and competition within that market. Especially in distribution of premium content – such as sports, television series and movies – territorially exclusive licensing practices are often used with the result that supply and access are limited to a certain area.[6] This may unjustifiably limit trade, competition and access within the EU in ways that may not be desirable for economic integration, competition or other goals of the EU.

To address unjustified private and public obstacles preventing the emergence of an EU-wide market for online content services, the Commission is tackling specific problems in several areas of law, as outlined next.

3.1   Copyright Law: Exclusive Rights and Their Limitations

Within copyright law, the Commission has proposed a directive on copyright in the DSM[7] that seeks to enable (1) text and data mining,[8] (2) online educational activities[9] and (3) preservation of works by cultural heritage institutions[10] by means of exceptions and limitations allowing these activities without a licence and partly also unrestrained by agreements.[11] These mandatory limitations/exceptions would reduce uncertainty caused by the scope and optionality of existing limitations and exceptions.[12]

Additionally, the proposed directive would task collective management organizations with granting licences to cultural heritage institutions for certain uses beyond the exception/limitation in cross-border situations as well.[13] The directive also seeks to promote cross-border supply of audiovisual content

---

[6]   Commission, 'Final report on the E-commerce Sector Inquiry' COM(2017) 229 final, paras 50–52.

[7]   Proposal for a Directive on copyright in the Digital Single Market, COM(2016) 593 final (Proposed Directive on Copyright in DSM).

[8]   ibid art 3.

[9]   ibid art 4.

[10]   ibid arts 7–8.

[11]   ibid art 3(2).

[12]   ibid p. 2.

[13]   ibid arts 7–8.

by a proposed mechanism to help on-demand services negotiate licensing agreements.[14]

While the proposal seeks to promote these activities within and across borders,[15] it would not significantly affect online content services offered commercially as the activities targeted are mostly non-commercial and the means used as regards commercial activities, such as facilitation of negotiations, are moderate.

3.2   Internal Market Legislation: Exercise of Copyright and Distribution Practices

The Commission has also proposed regulations that seek to address obstacles that stem from exercise of copyright and conduct of undertakings involved in distribution of content. First, the Commission has proposed a regulation that would localize provision of online services ancillary to broadcasts at the place of establishment of the broadcasting organization.[16] This would allow broadcasters to offer ancillary online services – such as catch-up and simulcast services – in all other EU Member States, as that would be deemed to occur where the organization has its place of establishment.[17] However, the scope of that possibility has narrowed during the legislative process so that only some broadcasts may ultimately end up being covered.[18] In addition to the country-of-origin rule, the proposed regulation would subject retransmissions

---

[14]   ibid art 10.

[15]   ibid p. 2 and recs 3 and 5.

[16]   Commission, Proposal for a Regulation of the European Parliament and of the Council laying down rules on the exercise of copyright and related rights applicable to certain online transmissions of broadcasting organisations and retransmissions of television and radio programmes, COM(2016) 594 final (Commission Proposal for a Broadcast Transmissions Regulation), art 2.

[17]   ibid rec 10.

[18]   European Parliament, 'Report on the proposal for a regulation of the European Parliament and of the Council laying down rules on the exercise of copyright and related rights applicable to certain online transmissions of broadcasting organisations and retransmissions of television and radio programmes (COM(2016)0594 – C8-0384/2016 – 2016/0284(COD))' (1st reading) A8-0378/2017 (27 November 2017); European Council Presidency, 'Proposal for a Regulation of the European Parliament and of the Council laying down rules on the exercise of copyright and related rights applicable to certain online transmissions of broadcasting organisations and retransmissions of television and radio programmes – Presidency compromise proposal with a view to agreeing on a General Approach' ST 15479 2017 INIT (8 December 2017).

of broadcasts to collective management. This would permit broadcasts to be retransmitted online in other EU Member States by using certain technologies.[19]

Second, a regulation on portability of online content services has now entered into force.[20] The regulation entitles subscribers to online content services to access services while temporarily present in an EU Member State other than the one in which they habitually reside and purchased the subscription.[21] Additionally, this regulation localizes relevant copyright activity in providing and accessing services in a single Member State – that is, the one which the subscription covers – so that providing portability elsewhere in the EU does not constitute copyright infringement.[22]

Finally, a regulation against unjustified geo-blocking was recently adopted and becomes applicable in late 2018.[23] The regulation will secure access by consumers to goods and services offered online as well as online interfaces, such as web shops, listing them for sale by banning discrimination based on consumer nationality or place of residence.[24] In effect, this introduces mandatory EU-wide distribution on non-discriminatory terms in the specified situations. However, the regulation currently does not apply to audiovisual services, and its key provision against discrimination in general conditions of access only applies to online services whose main purpose is other than provision of access to copyright-protected content.[25] This means that most online content

---

[19] Commission Proposal for a Broadcast Transmissions Regulation (n 16) art. 3. Both of the above measures would, in particular, extend beyond the existing EU rules currently limited to satellite broadcast and cable retransmissions. Council Directive 93/83/EEC of 27 September 1993 on the Coordination of Certain Rules Concerning Copyright and Rights Related to Copyright Applicable to Satellite Broadcasting and Cable Retransmission [1993] OJ L248/15.

[20] Council and Parliament Regulation 2017/1128 on cross-border portability of online content services in the internal market [2017] OJ L168/1 (Portability Regulation). See for more extensive discussion Chapter 12 by Mazziotti and Chapter 14 by Cantero in this volume.

[21] ibid art 3.

[22] ibid art 4. This benefit is also available voluntarily to online content service providers that are not required to offer portability. Art 6.

[23] European Parliament and Council Regulation (EU) 2018/302 of 28 February 2018 on addressing unjustified geo-blocking and other forms of discrimination based on customers' nationality, place of residence or place of establishment within the internal market and amending Regulations (EC) No 2006/2004 and (EU) 2017/2394 and Directive 2009/22/EC [2018] OJ L60I/1 (Geo-blocking Regulation). See for more details Chapter 12 by Mazziotti and Chapter 14 by Cantero in this volume.

[24] ibid arts 3 and 4.

[25] ibid arts 1(3) and 4(1)(b); European Commission, 'Impact assessment accompanying the document proposal for a regulation of the European Parliament and of the Council on addressing geo-blocking and other forms of discrimination based on place' SWD (2016) 173 final, 5.

distribution – as it typically features audiovisual or copyright-protected content – is not affected. The regulation does provide, though, for a Commission review of whether these limitations should be scrapped.[26]

3.3   Competition Law: Licensing and Distribution Agreements

Besides legislative measures, the Commission seeks to address cross-border issues in online distribution through its competition law powers. The Commission has carried out a sector inquiry into e-commerce which examined practices that may threaten competition in online distribution. As regards online distribution of content, territorial restraints, such as those requiring geo-blocking, may in particular raise concerns.[27]

The Commission has also initiated antitrust investigations into potentially problematic territorial restraints in online content distribution.[28] The most significant case concerns agreements on satellite and online distribution of pay-TV content that require distributors to refrain from sales to and access from non-licensed areas. The Commission's position in the case is that these restrictions are presumptively unlawful passive sales or other 'by object' restrictions and are unjustified by efficiencies or otherwise.[29] This position would mean that licensing agreements could not require distributors to refrain from passively selling and offering content services to non-licensed areas in the EU, leaving the decision to the distributor.

Several other investigations are pending that could clarify to what extent territorial restraints and differentiation are acceptable in online distribution. One concerns whether requiring consumers to purchase access codes – sold separately in Member States for playing video games offered online – amounts

---

[26]   Geo-blocking Regulation (n 23) art 9.

[27]   Commission, 'Final report on the E-commerce Sector Inquiry' COM(2017) 229 final, paras 65–67.

[28]   See for an overview eg Lars Kjølbye, Alessio Aresu and Sophia Stephanou, 'The Commission's E-Commerce Sector Inquiry – Analysis of Legal Issues and Suggested Practical Approach' (2015) 6 Journal of European Competition Law and Practice 465.

[29]   Commission, 'Antitrust: Commission investigates restrictions affecting cross border provision of pay TV services' (Press release) IP/14/15 (13 January 2014); *Cross-border access to pay-TV* (Case AT:40023) Commission Decision 2016/C 437/04 [2016] OJ C437/25. One undertaking has entered into a commitment decision removing such clauses from agreements (*Cross-border access to pay-TV* (Case AT:40023) cited earlier in this footnote) but the investigation is ongoing with respect to other undertakings and an action against the commitment decision is pending before the General Court ('Case T-873/16: Action brought on 8 December 2016 – Groupe Canal + v European Commission' [2017] OJ C38/50).

to unlawful partitioning of the market.[30] The other ongoing investigations deal with online distribution of products other than copyright-protected content but will likely have implications for online content distribution.[31]

4.   IMPACT OF COMMISSION MEASURES ON TERRITORIAL EXCLUSIVITY IN ONLINE DISTRIBUTION

These Commission measures would limit the possibilities and effects of exclusive territorial licensing outlined in Section 2.[32] The measures would promote EU-wide supply by removing copyright liability where covered by proposed exceptions/limitations[33] or localization rules of portability[34] or broadcast transmissions regulation,[35] by requiring EU-wide supply in cases of geo-blocking and portability duties[36] and by limiting the effectiveness of agreements that limit cross-border supply.[37] When covered by the rules, a rightholder would thus no longer be able contractually to require distributors to limit access to

---

[30]   Commission, 'Antitrust: Commission opens three investigations into suspected anticompetitive practices in e-commerce' (Press release) IP/17/201 (2 February 2017).

[31]   Commission, 'Antitrust: Commission opens formal investigation into distribution of clothing company Guess' (Press release) IP/17/1549 (6 June 2017); Commission, 'Antitrust: Commission opens formal investigations into Nike's, Sanrio's and Universal Studios' licensing and distribution practices' (Press release) IP/17/1646 (14 June 2017).

[32]   See for discussion on the legal implications on territoriality of the initiatives eg Alain Strowel, 'From Content Portability to Data Portability: When Regulation Overlaps with Competition Law and Restrictions Can Be Justified by Intellectual Property' (2016) 2 Competition Law and Policy Debate 63; Thomas Riis and Jens Schovsbo, 'The Borderless Online User – Carving Up the Market for Online and Streaming Services' in Paul Torremans (ed), *Copyright Law: A Handbook of Contemporary Research* (2nd edn, Edward Elgar Publishing 2017); Giuseppe Mazziotti and Felice Simonelli, 'Another Breach in the Wall: Copyright Territoriality in Europe and its Progressive Erosion on the Grounds of Competition Law' (2016) 18 Journal of Policy, Regulation and Strategy for Telecommunications, Information and Media 55; Dimitrios Doukas, 'The Sky Is Not the (Only) Limit: Sports Broadcasting Without Frontiers and the Court of Justice: Comment on Murphy' (2012) 37 European Law Review 605; Juha Vesala, 'Regulation Complementing EU Competition Law in the Digital Economy: Impact of the Proposed Digital Single Market Rules on Online Distribution Practices' in Björn Lundqvist and Michal Gal (eds), *Competition Law For the Digital Economy* (Edward Elgar Publishing) (forthcoming).

[33]   Proposed Directive on Copyright in DSM (n 7) arts 3, 4 and 7–8.

[34]   Portability Regulation (n 20) art 4.

[35]   Commission Proposal for a Broadcast Transmissions Regulation (n16) art 2.

[36]   Portability Regulation (n20) art 3; Geo-blocking Regulation (n23) art 4(1)(b).

[37]   Portability Regulation (n 20) art 7; Geo-blocking Regulation (n 23) art 6.

content on a territorial basis or by asserting copyright, and it would even be unlawful for distributors to do so independently.[38]

However, the impact of the rules on provision of online content services is limited because the new requirements and possibilities hardly ever apply to provision of online content services. First and foremost, although the obligation under the Geo-blocking Regulation to provide electronically supplied services in a non-discriminatory manner could realize EU-wide distribution of content by mandating provision of services to any consumer regardless of their location or residence, even so most online content services will not be affected since audiovisual and copyright-dominant services are not covered by this requirement.[39] For example, online services featuring movies, television series, music, e-books and sports broadcasts are not subject to this requirement.

Second, while removing copyright obstacles from engaging in certain cross-border activities in providing access, the Portability Regulation does not enable provision or sales of online content services to new customers in other EU Member States – the duty and right to offer portability only concerns existing subscribers. Moreover, while the proposed broadcast transmissions regulation would allow distributors to offer EU-wide access to ancillary online content services – such as allowing catch-up of television series – to both existing and new customers, at the current stage of the legislative process the most sought-after types of broadcasts – such as sports broadcasts, licensed television series and movies – have been excluded from the scope of this rule.[40] Additionally, the regulation would not oblige broadcasters to offer access or free them from contractual restraints. Broadcasters could therefore be prevented by agreements or could independently decide not to offer cross-border

---

[38]　See eg Portability Regulation (n 20) arts 3 and 7; Geo-blocking Regulation (n 23) arts 4(1)(b) and 6; Vesala (n 32).

[39]　Geo-blocking Regulation (n 23), arts 1(3) and 4(1)(b). See also Vesala (n 32). See for these and other limitations also Chapter 12 by Mazziotti and Chapter 14 by Cantero in this volume.

[40]　European Parliament, 'Report on the proposal for a regulation of the European Parliament and of the Council laying down rules on the exercise of copyright and related rights applicable to certain online transmissions of broadcasting organisations and retransmissions of television and radio programmes (COM(2016)0594 – C8-0384/2016 – 2016/0284(COD))' (n18); European Council Presidency, 'Proposal for a Regulation of the European Parliament and of the Council laying down rules on the exercise of copyright and related rights applicable to certain online transmissions of broadcasting organisations and retransmissions of television and radio programmes – Presidency compromise proposal with a view to agreeing on a General Approach' (n18).

or EU-wide access even when possible.[41] These regulations would therefore not significantly promote EU-wide sales and supply of content to new customers.[42]

Additionally, the Commission's competition law efforts to condemn passive sales or territorial restraints have limited the potential to accomplish EU-wide supply of content. A key reason here is that distributors would rarely be entitled or obliged under competition law to provide content beyond the scope of their licences. Even when contractual restraints requiring distributors to limit supply territorially are restrictive of competition, limiting the territorial scope of licences under copyright law remains possible under EU competition law.[43] Unless the free movement of services or the previously discussed regulations eliminate copyright infringement (which they only exceptionally do),[44] distributors may thus still be prevented or deterred from providing content outside the licensed territories as that likely infringes copyright. Even if copyright infringement did not prevent provision of content beyond the territorial scope of the licence, distributors do not necessarily choose to do so but may for various reasons prefer not to compete throughout the EU.[45] EU competition law generally does not require distributors, even dominant ones, to offer online content services throughout the EU.[46]

5.   A CASE FOR EXTENDING THE GEO-BLOCKING REGULATION TO AUDIOVISUAL AND COPYRIGHT-PROTECTED CONTENT?

As explained above, efforts by the Commission to promote EU-wide and cross-border provision of online content do not realize EU-wide provision of and access to online content services. The situation could be different if the

---

[41]   Commission Proposal for a Broadcast Transmissions Regulation (n 16) rec 11.

[42]   See also Vesala (n 32); Chapter 12 by Mazziotti and Chapter 14 by Cantero in this volume.

[43]   See above Sections 2 and 3.3. For a more optimistic view of ability of competition law to resolve the issues see Chapter 12 by Mazziotti in this volume.

[44]   See above Sections 2 and 4; Vesala (n 2) 612–616.

[45]   See eg European Commission, 'Impact assessment accompanying the document proposal for a regulation of the European Parliament and of the Council on addressing geo-blocking and other forms of discrimination based on place' SWD (2016) 173 final, 15–16.

[46]   Vesala (n 32). Moreover, the introduction of specific internal market regulations adds to the complexity and fragmentation of the rules that in competition law govern the exercise of copyright and distribution practices. In addition, uncertainty and potential for conflicts is increased by the fact that competition law and geo-blocking rules can be enforced by different Member State authorities. This is despite similar practices and even identical concepts (eg 'passive sales' restraints) being involved. ibid.

Geo-blocking Regulation had fully covered online content services featuring audiovisual and copyright-protected content. Nonetheless, the Geo-blocking Regulation does provide for Commission review of whether the scope of the regulation should be expanded by lifting these limitations.[47] The forthcoming review raises the question whether fully subjecting online content services to the Geo-blocking Regulation would achieve EU-wide distribution and under what circumstances it would be warranted.

5.1   Consequence of Extending Coverage of the Geo-blocking Regulation

Extending the Geo-blocking Regulation to fully cover services featuring audiovisual and copyright-protected content would result in online content ser-vices being obliged to offer their services across the EU without discriminating directly or indirectly on the basis of consumer nationality or place of residence. In their general conditions of access, service providers would not be permitted to refuse sales or supply on these grounds or to apply different prices.[48] This would in principle allow consumers in the EU to access and purchase content offered by online content services operating anywhere in the EU.

However, extending the scope of the regulation alone would not prevent content suppliers and service providers from limiting supply and access terri-torially. First, if the extension of the ban against discrimination is limited to situations where the distributor has the necessary rights – an option primarily to be considered in the Commission review[49] – it would still be possible to prevent EU-wide supply by granting territorially limited licences to separate distributors, as then no distributor would have the requisite licences to offer content in other, non-licensed parts of the EU. By dividing rights among sepa-rate legal entities, the geo-blocking rules could thus be evaded and might even be intentionally circumvented.

Second, even if the extension were not conditioned upon service provid-ers having the necessary licences, the duty to engage in non-discriminatory EU-wide supply still might not apply if a distributor does not have a licence covering the entire EU. That is, where EU law – or national law compliant with EU law – prevents provision of services, the ban against discrimination in general sales conditions does not apply.[50] Therefore, online content services might not be required to offer their services to unlicensed EU Member States

---

[47]   Geo-blocking Regulation (n 23) art 9(2).
[48]   ibid art 4(1)(b).
[49]   ibid art 9 and attached Statement by the Commission.
[50]   ibid art 4(5).

when doing so violates national copyright legislation which in the relevant aspects is presumptively compliant with EU law due to being extensively harmonized by EU legislation. Thus content suppliers might be able to maintain territorial exclusivity by limiting licences territorially. To overcome this would require provision for a country-of-origin rule or a comparable mechanism to resolve copyright issues raised when service providers supply content outside licensed territories within the EU.[51]

Even if these copyright issues were resolved, applying geo-blocking fully to online content services would not eliminate territorial exclusivity entirely as semi- and de facto exclusivity could still be achieved. First, it would remain possible under the regulation, as well as EU competition law, to limit active sales of online content services.[52] Thus online content services operating in different Member States could be limited to competing only by means of passive sales outside their explicitly licensed territories, without engaging in active marketing and sales efforts. The stricter stance against passive sales under the regulation than under EU competition law[53] does not considerably change the status quo because passive sales restrictions are rarely permitted in EU competition law.[54] Second, content suppliers, by tailoring the content offered, would be able to achieve partial, de facto territorial differentiation and exclusivity where content consumption preferences are territorial. For instance, by only providing audio and subtitles in a certain language, a service may only be attractive in areas where that language is used.[55]

Accordingly, extending the Geo-blocking Regulation to cover audiovisual and copyright-protected content alone would not realize EU-wide provision of content services. A country-of-origin or similar rule would be required to ensure that copyright does not prevent distributors from offering online content services throughout the EU. This would bring legal and commercial

---

[51]   The existing or proposed rules do not do so except for very limited circumstances. See above, Section 4.

[52]   Geo-blocking Regulation (n 23) art 6 and rec 26; Commission Regulation (EU) No. 330/2010 of 20 April 2010 on the application of Article 101(3) of the Treaty on the Functioning of the European Union to categories of vertical agreements and concerted practices [2010] OJ L102/1, art 4(b)(b)(i) (Vertical Block Exemption Regulation); *Cross-border access to pay-TV* (Case AT:40023) Commission Decision (n 29).

[53]   Geo-blocking Regulation (n 23) art 6.

[54]   See eg Commission, 'Guidelines on Vertical Restraints' [2010] OJ C130/1, para 61 (passive sales can be lawful for two years, for instance, when necessary for introduction of a new product).

[55]   OXERA and O&O 'The impact of crossborder access to audiovisual content on EU consumers' (May 2016)   https://www.oxera.com/Latest-Thinking/Publications/Reports/2016/The-impact-of-cross-border-access-to-audiovisual-c.aspx,   accessed   16 May 2018, 66–67.

conditions close to those governing physical goods, online services not featuring copyright-protected content, and satellite broadcasts of content. In particular, this would mean that once content is offered online in the EU, consumers could acquire and access it from anywhere in the EU without suppliers being permitted to block access or limit passive sales or to discriminate in sales conditions.

5.2   Circumstances Possibly Meriting Extension in Terms of Economic Welfare

Extending the scope of the Geo-blocking Regulation, accompanied by a country-of-origin or comparable rule, could enable EU-wide supply of online content services by enabling and requiring online content distributors to offer their services within the entire EU. However, whether and when that would be desirable in terms of its economic effects raises complex questions.[56] In particular, mandating EU-wide supply could harm the expected rewards of content production, or subvert the mechanisms used to finance production of content, such as presales of exclusive territorial licences, or to efficiently distribute content. Limiting the possibilities and effects of territorially exclusive licensing could in these ways impair production and supply of new content and thus ultimately also harm consumers by means – or in terms – of reduced content production, availability or competition.

However, the threats are not omnipresent and inevitable but could be avoided under some circumstances and conditions, as discussed below.

5.2.1   Conditions allowing maintenance of financing and incentives to create

In circumstances where harm to content creation is avoided, expanding geo-blocking could promote consumer welfare by improving availability of content and enhancing competition between online content services.

This seems possible at least in principle as audiovisual and copyright-protected content are currently already being distributed without territorial exclusivity. First, territorially exclusive licensing and distribution is not used in all categories of copyright-protected content within the EU, but mostly

---

[56]   See eg European Commission, 'Impact assessment accompanying the document proposal for a regulation of the European Parliament and of the Council on addressing geo-blocking and other forms of discrimination based on place' SWD (2016) 173 final; J. Scott Marcus and Georgios Petropoulos 'Extending the scope of the geo-blocking prohibition: An economic assessment' (In-depth analysis) IP/A/IMCO/2016-15 (February 2017).

in the audiovisual sector and for premium content.[57] Second, EU legislation already provides for EU-wide distribution of copyright-protected and audiovisual content embodied in tangible products such as books and DVDs, and in satellite broadcasts.[58] Third, premium audiovisual and copyright-protected content, such as television series, is already being acquired and made available online – even globally – by some online services.[59]

In any event, territorial exclusivity might not be necessary perpetually. Temporal windows of exploitation are frequently used in licensing, so that the most profitable uses are licensed before other less profitable distribution methods are offered. Providing for EU-wide provision only after the period of exclusivity in which most revenue is typically reaped, say 12–24 months, thus might not significantly undermine expected revenues or incentives to create as only a minor part of revenues would be denied the premium of territorial exclusivity and price differentiation.[60] However, while expected rewards might not be significantly affected, the impact of such an approach to production models and financing arrangements needs closer scrutiny. In principle, avoiding a negative impact on rewards could allow those arrangements in modified form, but eliminating exclusivity can also increase transaction costs as more

---

[57] See eg Commission, 'Final report on the E-commerce Sector Inquiry' COM(2017) 229 final, paras 65–66; European Commission, 'Impact assessment accompanying the document proposal for a regulation of the European Parliament and of the Council on addressing geo-blocking and other forms of discrimination based on place' SWD (2016) 173 final, 100–101; Georgios Alaveras, Estrella Gomez-Herrera and Bertin Martens, 'Geo-blocking of Non Audio-visual Digital Media Content in the EU Digital Single Market' (2017) JRC Digital Economy Working Paper, https://ec.europa.eu/jrc/sites/jrcsh/files/jrc106520.pdf accessed 14 February 2018; Marcus and Petropoulos (n 56) 26–28.

[58] European Parliament and Council Directive 2001/29/EC of 22 May 2001 on the harmonisation of certain aspects of copyright and related rights in the information society [2001] OJ L167/10, art 4(2) (providing for exhaustion of distribution rights); Council Directive 93/83/EEC of 27 September 1993 on the coordination of certain rules concerning copyright and rights related to copyright applicable to satellite broadcasting and cable retransmission [1993] OJ L248/15 (country of origin rule applicable to satellite broadcasts); Joined Cases C-403 and C-429/08 *Football Association Premier League and Others v QC Leisure and Others* EU:C:2011:631 (free movement and competition law limitations on satellite broadcast services).

[59] See eg Emily Steel, 'In Quest for Global Presence, Netflix Acquires Rights to 3 More Shows', *New York Times* (28 September 2015); Netflix Media Center, https://media.netflix.com/en/only-on-netflix#/new?page=1, accessed 16 May 2018 (listing titles currently distributed globally).

[60] Marcus and Petropoulos (n 56) 12 and 47–49.

complex arrangements might be needed or could make workable arrangements impossible if arrangements alternative to exclusivity are not effective.[61]

When considering the necessity of exclusivity for maintaining incentives to create and for achieving efficient cooperation, it should be noted that even fully applying the Geo-blocking Regulation to online content services would not entirely preclude territorial exclusivity.[62] While the regulation would effectively establish a right for consumers to – at least passively – purchase and access services, agreements and practical arrangements could still be used to achieve semi- or de facto exclusivity. First, EU-wide exclusive licensing to a single distributor would be possible, allowing for the benefits of exclusivity to copyright holders and the distributor. The premium from exclusivity (but not necessarily for territorial price differentiation[63]) could thus still be obtained. Second, the Geo-blocking Regulation and other relevant rules would allow active sales restraints, thus enabling limitation of active marketing and sales efforts to a particular territory, and only allow passive sales to other areas.[64] Third, content and services could be tailored to specific languages, cultures and other preferences so as to achieve corresponding territorial exclusivity.[65] Consumers may prefer familiar, domestic service providers for several reasons, such as being able to obtain customer support in their own languages.[66] Moreover, exclusivity and differentiation based on other than geographic factors can be used as alternatives.[67]

---

[61]   See eg Gregor Langus, Damien Neven and Sophie Poukens, 'Economic Analysis of the Territoriality of the Making Available Right in the EU' (March 2014) http://ec .europa.eu/internal_market/copyright/docs/studies/1403_study1_en.pdf, accessed 16 May 2018, 62.

[62]   See on necessity of territorial exclusivity for various economic benefits eg Langus, Neven and Poukens (n 61) 54–63, 76–77 and 105–118. As comparison, active sales restraints are in other circumstances deemed sufficient for achieving some types of efficiencies in the case of exclusive distribution and only, eg, in order to launch new products does the Commission accept restrictions of passive sales. Vertical Block Exemption Regulation (n 52) art 4(b)(i); Commission, 'Guidelines on Vertical Restraints' (n 54) paras 61 and 107. However, allowing only passive sales could be detrimental when consumers can easily find content online. See, eg, Marcus and Petropoulos (n 56) 47; Langus, Neven and Poukens (n 61) 105.

[63]   The Geo-blocking Regulation (n 23) art 4(1)(b) would ban discrimination in prices and other conditions of access.

[64]   ibid art 6 and rec 26.

[65]   See, eg, OXERA and O&O (n 55) 66–67.

[66]   See, eg, Marcus and Petropoulos (n 56) 17.

[67]   These include, eg, dynamic or personalized pricing. See, eg, Inge Graef, 'Algorithms and Fairness: What Role for Competition Law in Targeting Price Discrimination Towards End Consumers?' (2017) https://ssrn.com/abstract=3090360, accessed 14 February 2018.

Finally, it is not clear that not serving a territory – or doing so only after a considerable delay – is always in the interest of copyright holders. To illustrate, copyright holders lose revenue by not selling content to consumers who are willing to pay but who may resort to illegal sources or pay less if accessing content only later, for example, for free on television. Therefore, facilitating access might in some circumstances increase the rewards of copyright holders by better meeting demand and alleviating the effects of piracy.[68] Content producers are not necessarily privately able to achieve a desirable outcome as setting up a system featuring semi-exclusivity akin to the Geo-blocking Regulation can be complicated, and coordinating cross-border competition between distributors could raise competition law concerns.[69] The Geo-blocking Regulation could thus in some circumstances overcome transaction costs and competition law issues that prevent socially desirable arrangements from being attained privately.

Accordingly, it appears possible to achieve EU-wide supply of online content services in a way that does not significantly threaten production and distribution of content. Instead of entirely excluding copyright-protected and audiovisual content from the key provisions of the Geo-blocking Regulation, it seems possible to delineate standards that better reflect the need of exclusivity for incentives, financing and cooperation arrangements.[70] Negative effects could be avoided by allowing territorial exclusivity for a certain period before the geo-blocking rules become fully applicable, defining categories of content or distribution methods to which the duties apply, or with more nuanced rules to assess the need for exclusivity in particular situations.[71] However, determining the circumstances and conditions under which the Geo-blocking Regulation should fully apply requires extensive analysis of the sectors concerned to dispel the various threats to incentives, financing and cooperation posed by reduced territorial exclusivity. Another challenge, examined next, is

---

[68] See, eg, Marcus and Petropoulos (n 56) 11 and 35–43. The economic potential of unmet demand for audiovisual content has been estimated to be in the range of hundreds of millions of euros, ibid 11–12; PLUM Consulting, 'The economic potential of cross-border pay-to-view view and listen audiovisual media services' (2012) http://ec.europa.eu/internal_market/media/docs/elecpay/plum_tns_final_en.pdf, accessed 16 May 2018, 9–10. An industry-funded study, though, estimates that producer revenues would fall by billions if territorial exclusivity were abolished. OXERA and O&O (2016) (n 55) 4–6.

[69] Langus, Neven and Poukens (n 61) 107.

[70] For an overview see, eg, ibid 54–63.

[71] Categorizations of content based on their nature and production origin have been introduced during the legislative process into the proposed rules governing broadcast transmissions. See legislative documents cited above (n 40).

that the benefits of mandating EU-wide supply are not always unambiguously positive.

5.2.2   Potential benefits of mandating EU-wide supply of content

Justifying extension of the scope of the Geo-blocking Regulation would, in addition to excluding major negative effects, require creation of sufficient economic or other benefits. Extending the scope may in particular expand availability of content and otherwise benefit consumers.[72] From a static perspective, competition between online distributors would be increased as services operating in other EU territories became competitors and a broader catalogue of content became available to consumers due to complementary selections of content.

However, the static perspective can be deceptive. This is because changes to the legal framework are likely to alter licensing and distribution practices.[73] Reducing territorial exclusivity would likely prompt undertakings involved in content production and distribution to consider alternative ways of protecting their interests. For instance, content producers could favour exclusive EU-wide licensing to fewer distributors, and withdraw content from some territories or distribution channels if they become accessible throughout the EU.[74] These reactions can limit the extent to which benefits are achieved and may result in outcomes that are not ideal from competition policy and consumer welfare perspectives.

While availability of content is the main reason why consumers desire cross-border access to content,[75] enabling cross-border access does not guarantee increased availability. If online distribution methods easily accessible to consumers throughout the EU, such as online catch-up services, are exposed to the Geo-blocking Regulation, content suppliers could withdraw content from them and favour distribution channels, such as cable television, in which cross-border access is not as convenient.[76] For example, it might remain impossible to access a popular TV series currently offered without payment online in another Member State, as the series could be removed from these types of services if the Geo-blocking Regulation becomes applicable.

As regards competitive effects, it is not obvious either that expanding the scope of the Geo-blocking Regulation enhances competition between online distributors. First, when content is licensed exclusively for the entire EU –

---

[72]   See on the potential benefits, eg, Marcus and Petropoulos (n 56) 60–62; Alaveras, Gomez-Herrera and Martens (n 57).

[73]   Langus, Neven and Poukens (n 61) 118.

[74]   OXERA and O&O (n 55) 5 and 58–74.

[75]   Alaveras, Gomez-Herrera and Martens (n 57) 6–7.

[76]   ibid 8; OXERA and O&O (n 55) 66–74.

which would be an attractive licensing strategy for copyright holders in order to capture the maximum value of content[77] – only a single undertaking would still supply that content. This scenario would not give rise to more competition with respect to content. Second, it is not clear whether companies would compete more effectively when licensing is explicitly EU-wide or due to the Geo-blocking Regulation effectively resulting in that situation. On the one hand, competition could be less effective if fewer undertakings can afford to obtain EU-wide licences and the market could ultimately become more concentrated if national level distributors are marginalized.[78] On the other hand, undertakings could compete more vigorously on the EU level as stakes are higher and resources to compete greater. Facilitating acquisition of EU-wide licences could also reduce barriers to entry.[79]

Accordingly, the impact on availability of content and competition of mandating EU-wide supply of content might not be as unequivocally positive when examined from a dynamic perspective. This is not to say that promoting EU-wide supply of content online would not be desirable; on the contrary, increased access, competition and efficiency appear plausible and appreciable in many scenarios. However, in order to justify extending the Geo-blocking Regulation to audiovisual and copyright-dominant services, the likelihood of obtaining benefits should be ascertained. For example, it might not be desirable to adopt rules realizing EU-wide access to content if this results in a concentrated market or reduced selection of content available.

6.   CONCLUSIONS

The legislative and other measures that the European Commission has taken to promote EU-wide online distribution do not drastically affect online distribution of content. This is because services featuring copyright-protected or audiovisual content are not fully subject to provisions enabling and mandating EU-wide supply. For instance, it remains possible in licensing agreements to limit online distribution of content to a specific Member States and to prevent sales to and access from other Member States.

---

[77]   See eg OXERA and O&O (n 55) 59–61.

[78]   See, eg, Langus, Neven and Poukens (n 61) 112–113 (changes to the legal framework may prompt rightholders to grant fewer licences and only to larger players).

[79]   Langus, Neven and Poukens (n 61) 119 (noting that transaction costs could be reduced with certain policies but also noting that not allowing for exclusivity could increase transaction costs by increasing uncertainty). But see Chapter 14 by Cantero in this volume (arguing that even the current regime may increase the transaction costs of non-EU undertakings).

Extending the coverage of the Geo-blocking Regulation, combined with a new country-of-origin rule, could accomplish EU-wide provision of online content services. However, the circumstances where that is justified may be limited to those where harm to incentives and financing of content production can be avoided. Avoiding such harm might be possible, for example, by allowing an initial period of territorial exclusivity allowing content producers to capture most of their rewards before subjecting content to EU-wide distribution or by determining specific categories of content or specific online distribution methods to which the geo-blocking rules apply. While specifying rules specific to particular types of content or distribution methods would add to the fragmentation that subjecting online distribution of content to various fields of law already entails, it may be warranted in order to avoid negative effects on creation of content. The specifics of approaches to extending the scope of the regulation require extensive analysis in order to dispel concerns about harming content production and to ensure that sufficient benefits to access, competition and trade are achieved.

Finally, extending the scope of the Geo-blocking Regulation is not the only – or indeed necessarily the best – way to attain increased EU-wide trade, competition and availability. Instead of mandating EU-wide supply, an alternative that could be less risky to benefits associated with exclusive territorial licensing might be to facilitate EU-wide licensing and to clarify what kinds of distribution arrangements are acceptable.

14. Protecting domestic online content distribution in the EU: the impact of geo-blocking and open Internet rules on non-EU Over-The-Top players

Marta Cantero[1]

1. INTRODUCTION

Digitalization has introduced a new paradigm in the way we communicate or consume digital content and audiovisual services. The evolution of digital technologies has contributed to the instant distribution of content across borders via the Internet. Online content applications are rapidly pervading all segments of commerce and society, affecting and disrupting traditional industries in many ways. These days, we no longer watch traditional television, but rather consume online video on demand (VOD). The online distribution of content is currently dominated by the 'Tech Giants': Youtube, Amazon, iTunes, Netflix or Spotify are the most prominent examples of online content service providers. These ever-growing businesses have been characterized as Over-The-Top players (OTTs).[2] At the same time, most of these platforms are non-EU companies that operate globally.

Aware of these industry transformations and with a view to contributing to the better functioning of the internal market, the 2015 Digital Single Market (DSM) Strategy included several initiatives for improving the online distribu-

---

[1] The research leading to these results receives funding from the Academy of Finland – Finland Distinguished Professor programme (FIDiPro) [283002]: *The External Dimension of European Private Law*.

[2] The term Over-the-Top (OTT) players is used to describe online services which, to some extent, are functionally equivalent to those provided by traditional media and telecom services. More specifically, BEREC defines OTTs as 'content, a service or an application that is provided to the end user over the open Internet', see BEREC Report on OTT services, BoR (15) 142.

tion of content throughout the EU internal market.[3] While some of these legislative developments concerning online distribution of creative content within
the DSM are encountering challenges, others have been formally adopted. The
present volume addresses these legislative developments in different chapters.[4]
This chapter focuses on the current EU regulatory framework for online distribution of content with a view to illustrating the incompatibility of copyright
territoriality with the policy aims of the DSM. In this manner, it shows how
the current re-examination of the principle of territoriality, primarily aimed at
contributing to the free movement of online content in the EU, may serve secondarily to protect EU companies vis-à-vis third-country OTTs. The chapter
contends that the different legislative initiatives recently passed under the
DSM Strategy are not yet solving fragmentation problems concerning online
content distribution in the EU. Arguably, the European regulatory framework
is, at the same time, imposing significant restrictions on non-European market-
dominant online platforms supplying content services within the EU.

The chapter is organized as follows. Section 2 illustrates how copyright
territoriality stands as the main obstacle to online distribution of content in the
EU DSM. Section 3 provides an overview of the current regulatory framework.
This section first introduces the idea of how online distribution of content
in the EU does not fully take advantage of the benefits associated with free
movement of services. In the absence of free movement of online content, the
rest of the section ponders different mechanisms for bypassing copyright rules
with a view to achieving a genuine DSM. In so doing, attention is here paid
to existing and newly passed rules intended to ensure that copyright-protected
content is accessible across borders by prohibiting territorial restrictions or
safeguarding end-users' non-discriminated or prioritized access to the Internet.
Section 4 observes that some of the implications of these rules secondarily
involve protection of domestic online content service providers. These observations will lead us to conclude (Section 5) that, under current DSM initiatives,
there is a perceivable trend to protect domestic online distribution of content.

2.   'NOT AVAILABLE IN YOUR COUNTRY' – COPYRIGHT TERRITORIALITY

It is late November 2017, the prelude to Finland's 100 years of independence.
Users located in Finland are unable to watch copyright-protected music videos

---

    [3]   Communication from the Commission to the European Parliament, the Council,
the European Economic and Social Committee and the Committee of the Regions,
'A Digital Single Market Strategy for Europe', COM/2015/0192 final.
    [4]   See chapters by Kivistö, Moscon, Havu, Mazziotti and Vesala in this volume.

– including Sibelius' *Finlandia* – on YouTube, the largest online video service and second most popular website in the world. 'Not available in your country': that was the message greeting users located in Finland when trying to view music videos by any of the 30,000 Finnish recording artists and 'almost three million foreign composers, lyricists, arrangers and music publishers' represented by Teosto, the Finnish organization taking care of copyright-protected musical works. The blockage arose following lack of common ground between Teosto and Google's video platform concerning the renewal of the licensing agreement for use of music on YouTube in Finland. On the expiration of the former agreement, Teosto tried to improve the conditions concerning royalties and compensation to be paid to music authors. In response, and due to failure to reach a new licensing agreement by the expiration date of the previously existing agreement, the Google-owned platform decided to block thousands of music videos hosted on YouTube. Interestingly, the Teosto–YouTube conflict deprived users located in Finland of the possibility to access online content that could still be lawfully accessible from Internet Protocol (IP) addresses outside the Nordic country. While the situation was rapidly resolved and a new licensing agreement has now been signed, this story illustrates the operation in practice of copyright law, based on territoriality.

Similarly to any other intellectual property right, the principle of territoriality is paramount in copyright. Under territoriality, the rights associated with or derived from copyright are governed by the law of the country where they have been granted. This means that a copyright infringement or violation is subject to the law of the country in which the violation occurs. At the same time, this system of protection allows for exclusive territorial licensing. This means that, within the EU internal market, rightholders may license their rights to a single provider in each territory.

For many years, copyright in the EU has been a proportionate and justified derogation from free movement.[5] But, in times of globalization and digitalization, demands for global accessibility to copyrighted material and free flow of data are at odds with free movement and non-discrimination – the pillars of the internal market. In the case of online content, copyright stands as an objective restriction to the free online distribution of protected content. Country-by-country licensing led to a fragmented environment resulting in copyright territoriality preventing free movement of online content services.[6]

---

[5]   Dir 2000/31/EC of the European Parliament and of the Council of 8 June 2000 on certain legal aspects of information society services, in particular electronic commerce, in the Internal Market (OJ L 178, 17.7.2000, 1–16) Annex (Derogations from Article 3).

[6]   G Mazziotti, 'Is Geo-Blocking a Real Cause for Concern in Europe?', EUI Department of Law Research Paper No. 2015/43 (2015); available at SSRN: https://ssrn .com/abstract=2728675.

Given that digitalization has facilitated distribution of copyright-protected material, especially by electronic means, a re-examination of the principle is called for.

This re-examination has taken place as part of the ambitious DSM Strategy.[7] Building a DSM for Europe requires the removal of barriers to distribution of content – a genuine internal market cannot be conceived where territorial restrictions apply. In that light, current developments and initiatives are sailing towards configuring the principle of mutual recognition in copyright with a view to overcoming restrictions resulting from territorial protection. The following section pays attention to the different legislative initiatives under the DSM Strategy having an impact on the online distribution of content in the EU.

3.   THE REGULATORY FRAMEWORK FOR ONLINE CONTENT DISTRIBUTION IN THE EU

The EU DSM is set to become the online counterpart of the internal market. While the functioning of the internal market requires effective application of free movement provisions, the DSM seeks to remove barriers to online trade by ensuring access to online activities by individuals and businesses. This aspiration includes an ambitious work programme that is gradually putting in place conditions for ensuring fair competition, data and consumer protection in the online world.[8] The programme also attempts to accomplish seamless cross-border access to digital content and to electronically delivered content services by removing obstacles presented by geo-blocking and copyright.

This section outlines the operation and (un)feasibility of a potential recognition of free movement of online content under the current EU legal framework. In that light, this section also examines recent attempts to overcome territoriality by a non-discriminatory access approach consisting of portability rules preventing geo-blocking, and through open Internet rules.

3.1   Free Movement of Online Content

The transfer of internal market values to the DSM raises several questions. Perhaps the most important of these is whether the data economy would require an extension of the scope of internal market fundamental economic freedoms. Arguably, the DSM demands a new category of economic freedom accompanying goods, services, capital and labour: free movement of online content. Access to digital content can be considered the fuel of the DSM. Aware of this,

---

[7]   Digital Single Market Strategy (n 3).
[8]   ibid.

the European Commission is currently pushing for free movement of data as the fifth freedom.[9] Thus, free movement of data stands as a necessary condition for the twenty-first-century EU as a means to unleash the potential of the data economy. Indeed, the free flow of personal data has already materialized in the General Data Protection Regulation (GDPR).[10]

The topic is not new. With the arrival of the Internet and the possibility of providing services remotely and by electronic means,[11] determining the applicable legal regime for cross-border transactions among individuals entered into a new, and more complex, dimension. The emergence of information society services benefited from free movement to provide services but also required translation of analogue-free movement of services to the online realm. The e-Commerce Directive, currently under review, enabled such translation by mirroring free movement to provide services online and the removal of obstacles to cross-border provision of such services in the EU internal market.[12] However, the e-Commerce Directive itself establishes a derogation – in the case of copyright – from the freedom to provide information society services across borders.[13]

The digital entertainment and media sectors have dramatically increased over recent years. Yet, in these markets, copyright acts as a prevailing barrier to cross-border access to international digital entertainment and, in particular, as an obstacle to portability of content services (such as Netflix or Spotify)

---

[9] EU Presidency, 'Vision Paper on the Free Movement of Data Executive Summary', https://www.eu2017.ee/sites/default/files/inline-files/EU2017_FMD_vis ionpaper_summary_0.pdf. See also National Board of Trade Sweden, 'Data Flows. A Fifth Freedom for the Internal Market?', December 2016, available at https://www.kommers.se/Documents/dokumentarkiv/publikationer/2016/Publ-Data-flows.pdf.

[10] Reg (EU) 2016/679 of the European Parliament and of the Council of 27 April 2016 on the protection of natural persons with regard to the processing of personal data and on the free movement of such data, and repealing Dir 95/46/EC (OJ L 119, 4.5.2016, 1–88).

[11] Information Society services as defined in Dir 98/34/EC of the European Parliament and of the Council of 22 June 1998 laying down a procedure for the provision of information in the field of technical standards and regulations and of rules on information society services and in Dir 98/84/EC of the European Parliament and of the Council of 20 November 1998 on the legal protection of services based on, or consisting of, conditional access. Art 1, Dir (EU) 2015/1535 of the European Parliament and of the Council of 9 September 2015 laying down a procedure for the provision of information in the field of technical regulations and of rules on Information Society services.

[12] Art 3, Dir 2000/31/EC of the European Parliament and of the Council of 8 June 2000 on certain legal aspects of information society services, in particular electronic commerce, in the Internal Market (OJ L 178, 17.7.2000, 1–16).

[13] ibid, Annex.

when they have been subscribed to in a different Member State. The increase in demand for online content services pressed the European Commission to commit to the creation of a pan-European copyright regime that would make copyright more compatible with free movement of the services required for the functioning of an effective DSM.[14] In this manner – and with a view to modernizing copyright in the age of the digital revolution and to increasing online distribution of content across the DSM – several legislative proposals have been put forward, including regulation of contracts for supply of digital content and digital services to consumers,[15] a new framework for audiovisual media services[16] and for copyright in the DSM,[17] a review of the Satellite and Cable Directive,[18] online cross-border TV and radio broadcasts, and the introduction of cross-border portability of online content services in the internal market.[19]

This volume as a whole focuses on the online distribution of content. Yet it is necessary to distinguish between digital content and online content services. As recently defined by Regulation (EU) 2017/1128 on cross-border portability of online content services in the internal market,[20] an 'online content service' refers to a service in the sense of Article 57 of the Treaty on the Functioning of the European Union (TFEU). Such a service can be an audiovisual media service[21] or a 'service the main feature of which is the provision of access to, and the use of, works, other protected subject-matter or transmissions of broadcasting organisations, whether in a linear or an on-demand manner'.[22] The

---

[14] A Digital Single Market Strategy for Europe, SWD(2015) 100 final. For a further analysis, see Chapter 13 by Vesala in this volume.

[15] Proposal for a Directive of the European Parliament and of the Council on certain aspects concerning contracts for the supply of digital content, COM/2015/634 final.

[16] Proposal for a Directive amending Directive 2010/13/EU on the coordination of certain provisions laid down by law, regulation or administrative action in Member States concerning the provision of audiovisual media services in view of changing market realities, COM/2016/0287 final – 2016/0151 (COD).

[17] COM/2016/0593 final – 2016/0280 (COD).

[18] Council Directive 93/83/EEC of 27 September 1993 on the coordination of certain rules concerning copyright and rights related to copyright applicable to satellite broadcasting and cable retransmission (OJ L 248, 6.10.1993, pp. 15–21).

[19] Reg (EU) 2017/1128 of the European Parliament and of the Council of 14 June 2017 on cross-border portability of online content services in the internal market (OJ L 168, 30.6.2017, 1–11).

[20] ibid.

[21] As defined in point (a) of Art 1 of Dir 2010/13/EU on the coordination of certain provisions laid down by law, regulation or administrative action in Member States concerning the provision of audiovisual media services (OJ L 95, 15.4.2010, 1–24).

[22] See Art 2, EU Regulation on cross-border portability of online content services (n 19).

service must be lawfully provided online to subscribers on agreed terms, and in their Member State of residence. On the other hand, pursuant to the proposed Directive on contracts for the supply of digital content, 'digital content' means (a) data produced and supplied in digital form, such as video, audio, applications, digital games and any other software, (b) a service allowing the creation, processing or storage of data in digital form, where such data is provided by the consumer, and (c) a service allowing sharing of and any other interaction with data in digital form provided by other users of the service.[23]

As seen above, online distribution of content across borders is constrained by copyright principles. By contrast, and following the definitions provided above, online distribution of content must be understood as a beneficiary of free movement of services. However, copyright-protected content is subject to geographical restrictions – protected by exclusive territorial licensing rules. National or territorial copyright systems make it harder for content distributors to export, or for the consumer to purchase, online content services from distributors located in another Member State. This is to say that geographical restrictions based on copyright prevent free distribution of copyright-protected content. Further, the principle of territoriality in copyright protection also clashes with the non-discrimination principle on grounds of nationality as enshrined in Article 18(1) TFEU.

Nevertheless, distribution of online content usually takes place *inter partes*. In this regard, it has been accepted that the horizontal and direct application of Treaty provisions on free movement and non-discrimination ought to be only prudently granted.[24] From this perspective, removal of barriers preventing the free flow of digital content and online distribution of content services within the EU has required the adoption of EU secondary legislation. However, while a generic prohibition of discrimination based on nationality or place of residence is conceded in the Services Directive,[25] differences in access directly justified by objective criteria may constitute a derogation from non-discrimination.[26] Accordingly, the effective creation of a DSM requires striking the difficult balance between free movement and copyright rules.

---

[23] Art 2, Proposal for a Directive of the European Parliament and of the Council on certain aspects concerning contracts for the supply of digital content, COM/2015/0634 final – 2015/0287 (COD).

[24] N Reich, 'Free Movement v. Social Rights in an Enlarged Union: the Laval and Viking Cases Before the European Court of Justice' (2008) 9 *German Law Journal* 125; H Schepel, 'Constitutionalising the Market, Marketising the Constitution, and to Tell the Difference: On the Horizontal Application of the Free Movement Provisions in EU Law' (2012) 18(2) *European Law Journal* 177–200.

[25] Art 20(1), Dir 2006/123/EC of the European Parliament and of the Council of 12 December 2006 on services in the internal market (OJ L 376, 27.12.2006).

[26] ibid, Art 20(2).

The question arises as to how to deliver effective access to and use of online content services without sidelining copyright.

Articulating a peaceful and proportionate relationship between copyright protection and free movement has been a constant in efforts by the EU legislator. Recently passed EU rules aimed at preventing geo-blocking and ensuring an open Internet are steps taken in that direction.

3.2   Streaming Across Borders by Removing Geo-blocking

Geo-blocking is a practice consisting of denying access to websites, products or services from other Member States. The key element of this type of barrier to trade is that the restriction takes place by reason of the geographic location of the consumer, in other words, geo-discrimination. This discrimination is manifested in differentiated access to the best prices or sales conditions compared to nationals or residents. Yet such restrictions are not always voluntary. In some instances, these territorial limitations are based on objective criteria, such as differences in treatment resulting from taxation or public interest regulation. In that light, putting an end to unjustified geo-blocking for consumers wishing to buy products or services online within the EU has been one of the most ambitious legislative initiatives under the DSM Strategy.[27]

Despite the increase in streaming of video and entertainment, consumers still find restrictions on access to portable content throughout the EU. Consumers cannot temporarily use their subscriptions when they are located in a different Member State from that where the services were contracted. This could be considered discrimination on the basis of place of residence. While in some instances this is due to copyright (or more broadly intellectual property) territoriality, this discrimination can also take place as a result of market partition business practices as well as intended and temporary exclusive licensing. Yet, as mentioned above, since these restrictions are regularly of a contractual nature that results from the actions of private parties (mainly in the form of licensing agreements), the removal of discriminatory barriers preventing free movement requires adoption of secondary and specific legislation.

Recently passed rules addressing geo-blocking could contribute to preventing territorial or geographical discrimination in the online distribution of content. Regulation (EU) 2018/302 on addressing unjustified geo-blocking ('Geo-blocking Regulation') aims at preventing unjustified geo-blocking and

---

[27]   Proposal for a Regulation on addressing geo-blocking and other forms of discrimination based on customers' nationality, place of residence or place of establishment within the internal market and amending Regulation (EC) No 2006/2004 and Directive 2009/22/EC, COM/2016/0289 final – 2016/0152 (COD).

other forms of discrimination based, directly or indirectly, on the customer's nationality, place of residence or place of establishment, including by further clarifying certain situations where different treatment cannot be justified on the basis of legitimate derogations from free movement.[28] However, the EU Geo-blocking Regulation excludes from its scope of application 'audio-visual services, including cinematographic services, whatever their mode of production, distribution and transmission, and radio broadcasting'.[29] In a controversial move, and although subject to review of the scope by 2020, the final text also excluded application of geo-blocking banning rules to copyrighted material, most notably that provided by video streaming platforms.[30]

In view of this exclusion, the removal of geographical barriers to free movement of online content distribution services was left to the complementary rules included in the proposed Directive on contracts for the supply of digital content[31] and the recently adopted EU Regulation on cross-border portability of online content services in the internal market.[32] The latter imposes an obligation on the provider of the service to allow cross-border access at no additional cost for the subscriber.[33] This obligation came into effect on 1 April 2018. The aim is to temporarily remove geographical barriers imposed by copyright territoriality operating in the provision of online content services. In this manner, cross-border portability temporarily removes copyright restrictions.

In sum, it has been argued that the cross-border portability Regulation incorporates the formula introduced with the *Murphy* ruling[34] to the EU legal framework, amounting to a virtual extension of the 'exhaustion doctrine'.[35] However, while *Murphy* circumvents restrictions imposed by copyright rules, the Regulation on cross-border portability of content curbs the effects derived from that ruling by incorporating the rules on the consumer's country of

---

[28] Reg (EU) 2018/302 of the European Parliament and of the Council of 28 February 2018 on addressing unjustified geo-blocking and other forms of discrimination based on customers' nationality, place of residence or place of establishment within the internal market and amending Regulations (EC) No 2006/2004 and (EU) 2017/2394 and Directive 2009/22/EC (OJ L 601, 2.3.2018, 1–15).

[29] ibid, Art 1(3).

[30] ibid, Art 1(5).

[31] n 22.

[32] n 18.

[33] ibid, Art 3.

[34] Joined Cases C-403/08 and C-429/08, *Football Association Premier League Ltd and Others v QC Leisure and Others* and *Karen Murphy v Media Protection Services Ltd* ('*Murphy*') EU:C:2011:631.

[35] See P Ibáñez Colomo, 'Copyright Licensing and the EU Digital Single Market Strategy' in Roger D Blair and D Daniel Sokol (eds), *Handbook of Antitrust, Intellectual Property and High Technology* (CUP, 2016).

residence.[36] Moreover, despite the temporary cross-border access obligation, certain constraints remain as to full abolition of geo-blocking for online content.

First, the temporary cross-border access obligation only applies in the case of services provided against payment of money.[37] This formula also includes situations where payment is indirectly made to the provider of online content. By way of example, this would be the case where the subscription is part of a package of electronic communications, such as telephony and Internet. Payment of a mandatory fee for public broadcasting services does not fall under the category of payment of money for an online content service.[38] This clears doubts about the vertical direct effect of Treaty provisions on free movement, which would set aside territorial restrictions in the case of public broadcasting services online. In this manner, the EU legislator excludes the possibility of lifting geographical restrictions on public broadcasting. By contrast, in the case of online content services provided without payment of money, the decision on the possibility of enabling cross-border access is left to the provider of the service.[39] This would be the case for streaming content in freely accessible websites, such as use of YouTube or freemium Spotify subscriptions. However, in such cases, the effect of the temporary access obligation under the EU cross-border portability Regulation is different. Pursuant to the portability Regulation, temporary use of services across borders, such as freemium Spotify, would be left to the decision of the provider, while in the case of YouTube, users of the service may not necessarily be subscribers to the service.

Second, the obligation only ensures cross-border access to services subscribed to at home, that is, in the subscriber's Member State of residence.[40] The EU Regulation on cross-border portability of online content specifies that the access obligation concerns access to the 'same content'. However, it is very difficult to determine whether the 'same content' here refers to services as such (access to the platform) or to an identical platform catalogue. Using a practical example: does the obligation require the possibility to access HBO UK – and therefore the HBO UK catalogue – with an HBO Nordic subscription, or the HBO Nordic catalogue? In view of the wording of the Regulation, it seems that the latter would prevail; that is, the subscriber must be able to access the content of the HBO Nordic catalogue in the UK by making use of their home

---

[36]   G Monti and G Coelho, 'Geo-Blocking between Competition Law and Regulation' (2017) *Competition Policy International*.

[37]   n 27, Art 2.

[38]   ibid, see Rec 18.

[39]   Regulation on cross-border portability (n 19) Art 6.

[40]   ibid, Art 1.

subscription abroad. This means, however, that, where catalogue differences exist, consumers will not be able to subscribe to online content services not available in their home country unless otherwise access to local content is voluntarily offered by the online content service provider.

Apart from these newly introduced rules, competition law may also function as a safety net for preserving free movement and non-discrimination among private parties. Competition rules play a role in preventing geographical restrictions when they not only affect free movement, but also restrict competition (Article 101 TFEU).[41] In this light, it is necessary to examine whether competition law accounts for situations where geo-blocking restrictions on copyrighted content should be lifted. The European case law is clear on prohibition of discriminatory restrictions on distribution in a bricks-and-mortar marketplace as well in online distribution. Territorial restrictions on offline distribution of content have generally been found to be incompatible with Article 101 TFEU.[42] Similarly, restrictions on Internet sales would be incompatible with Article 101(1) TFEU. This is consistent with Article 4(b) of Regulation 330/2010, which provides that export bans are blacklisted, and therefore agreements included in this provision cannot benefit from the block exemption and only exceptional circumstances could justify an export ban.[43] However, this contrasts with the recent judgment in *Coty Germany*, where the Court of Justice of the European Union (CJEU) considered that selective distribution systems which restrict third-party platforms for the Internet sale of contract goods can appear to be lawful in relation to Article 101(1) TFEU.[44] In doing so, the CJEU in this case seems to temper the way in which competition law can constrain online distribution.[45] Nevertheless, online

---

[41]   W Cornish, D Llewelyn and T Aplin, *Intellectual Property: Patents, Copyright, Trade Marks and Allied Rights* (8th edn, Sweet & Maxwell, 2003). C Stothers, *Parallel Trade in Europe: Intellectual Property, Competition and Regulatory Law* (Hart Publishing, 2007). Joined Cases 56 and 58–64, *Établissements Consten S.à.R.L. and Grundig-Verkaufs-GmbH v Commission of the European Economic Community*, Judgment of the Court of 13 July 1966.

[42]   Case 19/77, *Miller International Schallplatten GmbH v Commission of the European Communities*, ECLI:EU:C:1978:19.

[43]   Commission Reg (EU) No 330/2010 of 20 April 2010 on the application of Art 101(3) of the Treaty on the Functioning of the European Union to categories of vertical agreements and concerted practices.

[44]   C-230/16, *Coty Germany*, ECLI:EU:C:2017:941, paras 52–57.

[45]   Perhaps due to the fact that online distribution would fall under the category of selling arrangements. In view of this, since *Keck* (C-267/91), the Court – although not unambiguously – seems to be more permissive with selling arrangements than with product rules. See E Spaventa, 'Leaving Keck Behind? The Free Movement of Goods After the Rulings in Commission v Italy and Mickelsson and Roos' (2009) 35(6) *European Law Review* 914–932.

distribution of licensed copyright content works somewhat differently. In the case of copyrighted works the CJEU has conceded that exclusive licences do not necessarily restrict competition, where justified.[46] The circumstances and policy considerations operating as a justification in *Coditel* may not operate in distribution of music via iTunes, which would not justify the restriction.[47] This view would be in line with the more radical approach evidenced in *Murphy*. However, regulatory fragmentation still imposes restrictions on the online distribution of content.[48]

Accordingly, real free movement of online content services, where consumers could benefit from retail pricing arbitrage, would have to be found elsewhere, such as within open Internet provisions.

3.3   Distributing Online Content in an Open Internet

Provision of electronic communications services is impacted by open Internet rules that affect the way in which consumers access content and applications.[49] The successful development of Tech Giants and OTTs in the online distribution of content industry is partially due to the openness and non-discriminatory access to the Internet. Global access to the World Wide Web (WWW) and to all the applications that run on it have favoured a situation where these companies could operate globally. However, Internet Service Providers (ISPs) are in charge of controlling access to the Internet and hence can exert control over online distribution of content. Thus, where dominant market players exist (and the Internet is known for that), competitive access to content will be undermined without open Internet.

Open Internet, also known as network neutrality, has been a highly controversial and much-debated issue over the last decade in the EU[50] – the discussion is somewhat older on the other side of the Atlantic.[51] Unsurprisingly, regulating net neutrality stands as a significant regulatory issue concerning the

---

[46]   Case 262/81, *Coditel v Ciné Vog Films*, ECLI:EU:C:1982:334.

[47]   M Maduro, G Monti and G Coelho, 'The Geo-blocking Proposal: Internal Market, Competition Law and Regulatory Aspects: Study for the IMCO Committee' (2017) IP/A/IMCO/2016-14; PE 595.362.

[48]   For a further analysis, see Chapter 12 by Mazziotti in this volume.

[49]   N Economides, 'Net Neutrality, Non-Discrimination and Digital Distribution of Content Through the Internet' (2008) *NYU Stern School of Business* EC-07-09.

[50]   M Cave and P Crocioni, [Special Section on Net Neutrality] 'Does Europe Need Network Neutrality Rules?' (2007) 1(1) *International Journal of Communication* 11. A Renda, 'I Own the Pipes, You Call the Tune: The Net Neutrality Debate and Its (Ir) relevance for Europe' (2008) Centre for European Policy Studies (CEPS).

[51]   AD Thierer, '"Net Neutrality": Digital Discrimination Or Regulatory Gamesmanship in Cyberspace?' Cato Institute, Policy Analysis no. 507.

regulation and governance of the Internet. In the absence of open Internet or net neutrality rules, ISPs may prioritize Internet traffic by establishing 'tolls' for Internet access by end-users. While it is not easy to define net neutrality, it can be described in very simple terms as non-discriminatory treatment of bits of information that flow through electronic communications networks; put differently, all Internet traffic has to be treated equally.[52]

As seen above, online geo-blocking restrictions by reason of copyright have so far been legitimate limitations to free movement of online distribution of licensed content. Likewise, blocking, throttling or discrimination of online content, applications and services also function as a barrier to content distribution. In this manner, legislation ensuring non-discriminatory access to the Internet may serve to safeguard competitive access to online content and contribute to free movement and portability of online content services.

In the absence of net neutrality rules, telecoms operators can freely distribute traffic. Some of these providers also supply content services. This has significant consequences for competition. On the one hand, dominant digital platforms could use their market power to pay telecoms network operators in exchange for speeding data for the use of Netflix, for example. On the other hand, ISPs can prioritize or even exempt their own streaming video and music services from data counts; that is, applying a price zero to data associated with those services. This practice is known as 'zero rating'. Accordingly, the question is then how can open Internet rules play a role in the way content services are provided? Regulatory choices range from regulating the Internet as a public utility to establishing certain contractual rules that would guarantee non-discriminatory access.

Although never really overcome, the debate on net neutrality has been reinvigorated following a recent decision by the US Federal Communications Commission (FCC) to put an end to regulation of the Internet as a public utility;[53] that is, revoking the net neutrality rules introduced by the Obama administration.[54] By contrast, the EU's regulatory solution involved establishing a contractual obligation on ISPs to ensure high-quality non-discriminatory Internet access services.[55]

---

[52] For a further analysis, see Chapter 15 by Honkkila in this volume.

[53] Federal Communications Commission FCC 17-166.

[54] Federal Communications Commission (13 April 2015) 'Protecting and Promoting the Open Internet – A Rule by the Federal Communications Commission on 04/13/2015' Federal Register.

[55] Reg (EU) 2015/2120 of the European Parliament and of the Council of 25 November 2015 laying down measures concerning open internet access and amending Directive 2002/22/EC on universal service and users' rights relating to electronic com-

4.   ONLINE DISTRIBUTION OF CONTENT IN THE EU BY THIRD-COUNTRY OTT PLAYERS

This section provides an overview of how EU rules on geo-blocking (and cross-border portability) as well as EU net neutrality rules (open Internet) accidentally serve purposes other than putting an end to the fragmentation of the internal market. Both EU and non-EU online content providers are equally exposed to the disadvantages associated with this fragmentation. However, while the examination above has revealed that the newly introduced rules do not entirely solve the fragmentation problem, the following analysis suggests that they may well serve to protect EU content services providers and content creators vis-à-vis non-EU Tech Giants. First, the prohibition of geo-blocking practices and more specifically the establishment of a system for cross-border portability involve the supremacy of a potential EU-wide exhaustion principle over the internationally recognized principle of copyright territoriality. Second, open Internet rules can be used to prevent eventual third-country dominant digital platforms in the EU from leveraging their market power to pay telecoms network operators for prioritizing access to their services.

4.1   Preventing Geo-blocking Involves a New Licensing Approach

As seen above, copyright territoriality is compatible with the prohibition of geo-blocking practices as copyright-protected content falls outside the scope of the EU Geo-blocking Regulation. However, the EU Regulation on cross-border portability temporarily lifts territorial restrictions imposed by reason of copyright. This system entails mutual recognition of copyright so that copyright-protected works can be temporarily accessed from non-licensed territories within the EU.

Conventionally, licensing agreements are unilaterally negotiated by the parties under freedom of contract. In practice, however, establishing a sort of 'EU-wide exhaustion principle' leaves no room for online content services providers and content creators to individually negotiate licensing agreements in each Member State. Pursuant to Article 7(1) of the EU Regulation on cross-border portability:

> Any contractual provisions, including those between providers of online content services and holders of copyright or related rights or those holding any other rights in the content of online content services, as well as those between such providers and their subscribers, which are contrary to this Regulation, including those which

---

munications networks and services and Reg (EU) No 531/2012 on roaming on public mobile communications networks within the Union (OJ L 310, 26.11.2015, 1–18).

prohibit cross-border portability of online content services or limit such portability to a specific time period, shall be unenforceable.

Thus, Article 7(1) now precludes the possibility of negotiating licensing agreements that do not respect the provisions contained in the Regulation in an attempt to safeguard its effectiveness. Moreover, even in situations where the parties agree on a choice of law different from the EU framework, Article 7(2) provides that the Regulation applies irrespective of the law applicable to contracts concluded between providers of online content services and holders of copyright or related rights or those holding any other rights in the content of online content services, or to contracts concluded between those providers and their subscribers.

How can this arrangement protect EU content services providers vis-à-vis non-EU Tech Giants? The answer can be found in the following scenario. Allowing temporary non-discriminatory and cross-border access to online content in the EU may impact online content providers' businesses by preventing the establishment of technological geo-blocking solutions. This prohibition would involve rightholders having to litigate on a case-by-case basis instead of automatic copyright enforcement facilitated by technology.[56] This solution is not only inefficient,[57] but can also discourage participation by third-country content service providers in the European market as they would not be able to partition the market according to their business needs.

4.2 Open Internet Favours Competition but Restricts Freedom of Contract

Preserving an open Internet is crucial to development of online content services providers. The global accessibility of the Internet has favoured a small set of providers dominating the content distribution industry. Data from Internet usage in North America shows that more than half of the downstream Internet traffic at peak hours (primetime) is dominated by online content applications and services provided by non-EU Tech Giants such as Netflix (35.15%), YouTube (17.53%), and Amazon Video (4.26%).[58] The European market is dominated by non-EU online content services providers. In Europe, data from 2015 shows that real-time entertainment amounted to up to a total

---

[56] MJ Schmidt-Kessen, 'EU Digital Single Market Strategy, Digital Content and Geo-Blocking: Costs and Benefits of Partitioning EU's Internal Market' (2018) *Columbia Journal of European Law* (forthcoming).

[57] ibid. See also Chapter 12 by Mazziotti in this volume.

[58] Data from *Sandvine Global Internet Phenomena Report – 2016*.

of 43.3 per cent of peak downstream traffic.[59] Although no specific data is provided, the dominant players in the EU are similar to those dominating the American market.[60] This reinforces the significance of real-time entertainment (streaming) as a channel for online content distribution.

For some, net neutrality means rejecting freedom of contract.[61] Open Internet rules serve to prevent these non-EU content services from paying telecoms network operators for prioritizing access to their services – in the case at hand, open Internet. Consequently, given that dominant content service providers are non-European, open Internet provisions could function as a protectionist tool to shield domestic online content service providers and EU content creators from aggressive (and non-competitive) practices by non-EU OTT players.

5.   CONCLUSIONS

This chapter has provided an overview of the key legislative developments and initiatives of the DSM with a view to improving online distribution of content, focusing on measures aimed at preventing geo-blocking and those related to safeguarding the open Internet. The EU DSM has not yet fully exploited its potential. In the meantime, existing regulatory hurdles have not yet been out-flanked – most prominently those arising in connection with copyright. This sits at odds with the spirit of the EU DSM, which aims at improving access by consumers and businesses to digital goods and services across Europe. In par-ticular, the chapter has found that the current EU regulatory environment does not provide a consistent framework for regulating online content services and that the limitations to freedom of contract introduced by different regulatory initiatives concerning geo-blocking and open Internet do not fully contribute to improving online distribution of content within the DSM. Wider concerns include the inability of free movement rules to entirely overcome territorial restrictions.

It is vitally important to not lose sight of the fact that the DSM is currently at the very early stages of its development. However, this chapter finds that, apart from putting in place a genuine internal market for the digital ecosystem, existing regulatory initiatives represent a significant move towards protecting the European online content industry. This protectionist trend is consistent

---

[59]   BEREC, Desk Research on the demand side of Internet use, Annex 1 to BoR 15(65).

[60]   A recent study finds that, in the EU, Amazon Video is the market leader with a viewer share of 30.4% followed by Netflix with 21.4% while Sky Go and Sky Ticket jointly reach 15.3% and Maxdome 8.6%. This data is not conclusive. Source: Goldmedia VOD ratings, July–September 2017.

[61]   Thierer (n 51).

with the approach introduced in audiovisual and media sector-specific policy. The newly reviewed Audiovisual Media Services Directive (AVMSD) will introduce a formula requiring a 30 per cent European content threshold for audiovisual platforms providing VOD subscriptions. This means that at least 30 per cent of the content offered by companies such as Amazon Video, Netflix, or iTunes will have to be 'made in Europe'.[62] In this manner, by fuelling competition, the DSM could contribute to shielding EU online content service providers and producers vis-à-vis third-country dominant Tech Giant platforms.

---

[62] Proposal for a Directive on the coordination of certain provisions laid down by law, regulation or administrative action in Member States concerning the provision of audiovisual media services in view of changing market realities (n 16). See Art 13. The original proposal attempted to achieve a more level playing field in the promotion of European works by obliging on-demand services to reserve at least a 20% share for European works in their catalogues and to ensure adequate prominence of those works. The text – passed by the European Parliament and recently approved by the Council – has increased that share up to 30%.

15. The Internet access provider's commercial practices under the EU rules on open Internet

Olli Honkkila

1.   INTRODUCTION

1.1   Net Neutrality

The success of the Internet has often been credited to its openness. Both big and small content and application providers have experienced low barriers to entry to the Internet's open platform. As a result, creation has flourished, leading to a multitude of innovative services.[1] However, the openness of the Internet cannot and should not be taken for granted – several factors may affect how open the Internet is as a platform, thus affecting online distribution of content and services. In particular, as noted by Cantero in Chapter 14 above, the role of Internet access service providers (IAPs, often also referred to as Internet service providers, ISPs) continues to be a highly debated issue both in the EU and globally as the ability of ISPs to manage traffic in their networks has led to a number of policy concerns. Unlike in the early days of the truly decentralised Internet, ISPs are equipped to prioritise, slow down or even block delivery of specific content in their networks.[2]

A demand to impose restrictions on ISPs to protect the openness of the Internet is often referred to as 'net neutrality' or 'network neutrality', a concept

---

[1]   Eg, L Belli, 'Net Neutrality, Zero-rating and the Minitelisation of the Internet' (2017) 2 *Journal of Cyber Policy* 96; L Daigle, 'On the Nature of the Internet' (2015) Global Commission on Internet Governance Paper Series No 7, 6, https://www .cigionline.org/sites/default/files/gcig_paper_no7.pdf, accessed 9 May 2018.

[2]   For an overview of traffic management techniques: L Belli, 'End-to-End, Net Neutrality and Human Rights' in L Belli and P De Filippi (eds), *Net Neutrality Compendium: Human Rights, Free Competition and the Future of the Internet* (Springer 2016).

coined by Tim Wu.[3] While there is no single accepted definition of net neutrality, it can be described as the principle of equal treatment of network traffic.[4] Net neutrality concerns aspects of both the relationships between ISPs and providers of content and applications and the relationships between ISPs and citizens/consumers. Hahn and Wallsten explain that net neutrality 'usually means that broadband service providers charge consumers only once for Internet access, don't favor one content provider over another, and don't charge content providers for sending information over broadband lines to end users'.[5]

The debate over net neutrality has been multidimensional, including economic, technical and social arguments. The proponents of net neutrality argue that ISPs should not have the power to act as gatekeepers to information and decide which applications and services succeed or to restrict people from exercising their fundamental rights, such as the rights to privacy and freedom of expression.[6] Hence, they have advocated special regulation to ensure nondiscriminatory access to the Internet – arguing for at least similar treatment between similar applications and services.[7]

In contrast, opponents of net neutrality consider that differential treatment of even similar applications and services can be beneficial and fear that net neutrality would stifle the development of broadband Internet. According to this view, competition between ISPs is sufficient to ensure unhindered development of the Internet ecosystem and any anti-competitive behaviour should be dealt with through a case-by-case approach under general competition law.[8]

---

[3]   T Wu, 'Network Neutrality, Broadband Discrimination' (2003) 2 Journal of Telecommunications and High Technology Law 141–79.

[4]   See J S Marcus, 'Network Neutrality Revisited: Challenges and Responses in the EU and in the US', a study requested by the European Parliament Committee on the Internal Market and Consumer Protection (IP/A/IMCO/2014-02 2014 PE 518.751) http://www.europarl.europa.eu/RegData/etudes/STUD/2014/518751/IPOL_STU(2014)518751_EN.pdf, accessed 9 May 2018, 18–21.

[5]   R Hahn and S Wallsten, 'The Economics of Net Neutrality' (2006) 3(6) The Economists' Voice, Article 8, 1.

[6]   Eg Wu (n 3); M A Lemley and L Lessig, 'The End of End-to-End: Preserving the Architecture of the Internet in the Broadband Era' (2000) 48 UCLA Law Review 925; Belli (n 2).

[7]   B van Schewick, 'Network Neutrality and Quality of Service: What a Nondiscrimination Rule Should Look Like' (2015) 67(1) Stanford Law Review 1, 83; Belli (n 1) 104.

[8]   C Yoo, 'Network Neutrality and the Economics of Congestion' (2006) 94 Georgetown Law Journal 1849; T W Hazlett and J D Wright, 'The Law and Economics of Network Neutrality' (2012) 45 Indiana Law Review 767; A Renda, 'Antitrust, Regulation and the Neutrality' (2015) CEPS Special Report, No 104.

In considering these opposing views, it must be noted that there is no consensus in the economic literature regarding the economics of net neutrality.[9] Moreover, even fundamental rights are not absolute and the rights of all end-users (including content and application providers) and ISPs need to be balanced.[10]

1.2　　　Open Internet rules of the EU

After a lengthy debate, partly motivated by the desire to prevent legal fragmentation caused by national legislation of Member States,[11] in April 2016 the EU adopted rules for safeguarding open Internet access in the form of Regulation 2015/2120[12] ('the Regulation'). In addition, further guidance has been provided by the Body of European Regulators for Electronic Communications (BEREC), which has published guidelines[13] 'On the Implementation by National Regulators of the European Net Neutrality rules' ('BEREC Guidelines').

The scope and purpose of the Regulation is set out in Article 1, according to which the Regulation 'establishes common rules to safeguard equal and non-discriminatory treatment of traffic in the provision of Internet access services and related end-users' rights'.[14] Recital 1 adds that the Regulation 'aims

---

[9]　　Eg Greenstein, Peitz and Valletti, who point out that the economic literature examining net neutrality is young and warn that little support exists for the claims of the most extreme supporters and opponents of net neutrality; S Greenstein, M Peitz and T Valletti, 'Net Neutrality: A Fast Lane to Understanding the Trade-offs' (2016) 30(2) Journal of Economic Perspectives 127, 129.

[10]　　A J Carillo, 'Having Your Cake and Eating It Too? Zero-Rating, Net Neutrality, and International Law' (2016) 19 Stanford Technology Law Review 364, 371; Belli (n 2) 14.

[11]　　Reg 2015/2120 Rec 3.

[12]　　Reg (EU) 2015/2120 laying down measures concerning open internet access and amending Directive 2002/22/EC on universal service and users' rights relating to electronic communications networks and services; Reg (EU) No 531/2012 on roaming on public mobile communications networks within the Union (Reg 2015/2120) [2015] OJ L 310.

[13]　　BEREC, 'Guidelines on the Implementation by National Regulators of European Net Neutrality Rules' (BoR (16) 127). These Guidelines are based on Art 5(3) of Reg 2915/2120. While the recommendations in the BEREC Guidelines are non-binding, national regulatory authorities should take them into utmost account when supervising the Regulation. This is based on Art 3(3) of Reg (EC) No 1211/2009 establishing the Body of European Regulators of Electronic Communications and the Office [2015] L 337 and Rec 19 of Reg 2015/2120.

[14]　　Reg 2015/2120 includes a definition for an internet access service but not for an end-user. Art 2(2) defines an internet access service as 'a publicly available electronic communications service that provides access to the internet, and thereby connectivity

to protect end-users and simultaneously to guarantee the continued functioning of the Internet ecosystem as an engine of innovation'.

To meet these rather high-level and vague goals, Article 3(1) sets end-user choice as one of the governing principles of the Regulation.[15] Moreover, the Regulation clearly establishes *ex ante* obligations for ISPs regarding the technical treatment of Internet traffic (traffic management). As a starting point, the Regulation requires ISPs to treat all traffic equally, but it does allow differential treatment of traffic based on objective technical quality requirements (Art 3(3)). This means that blocking, slowing down or other ways of discriminating between Internet traffic in ISP networks cannot be based purely on commercial considerations.

In contrast, the Regulation is less clear on the commercial treatment of Internet traffic, such as pricing specific traffic differentially from other traffic. Article 3(2) provides that

> [a]greements between end-users and the providers of internet access services on commercial and technical conditions and the characteristics of internet access service such as price, data volumes or speed, and any commercial practices conducted by providers of internet access services, shall not limit the exercise of the rights of end-users laid down in paragraph 1.[16]

Article 3(2) and the accompanying recitals do not fully succeed in clarifying how the rights of end-users need to be taken into account in the contractual relationship between end-users and ISPs as well as in the unilateral practices of ISPs. The question is: how much can an ISP influence end-users without limiting their right to choose how they access or distribute content and services online?

In particular, the legitimacy of a specific commercial practice referred to as 'zero-rating' has been widely debated. Zero-rating is a practice where an ISP offers a specific application (or service) or category of applications that do not count towards any data cap in place on the Internet access service or that

---

to virtually all end points of the internet, irrespective of the network technology and terminal equipment used'. In the BEREC Guidelines the term 'end-user' is considered to include both individuals and businesses (BEREC Guidelines para 4).

[15] According to Art 3(1) '[E]nd-users shall have the right to access and distribute information and content, use and provide applications and services, and use terminal equipment of their choice, irrespective of the end-user's or provider's location or the location, origin or destination of the information, content, application or service, via their internet access service'.

[16] In this chapter the term 'commercial practices' refers both to agreements between parties and unilateral practices.

are free to use even without a data plan.[17] In some Member States, National Regulatory Authorities (NRAs) have already investigated zero-rating services with varying results.[18]

The conflicting views on how the, arguably high-level and principle-based, Regulation should be interpreted regarding commercial treatment of Internet traffic can be summarised as follows:

1. Commercial differentiation of traffic is, as such, prohibited based on Article 3(3) of the Regulation, which requires ISPs to treat all traffic equally when providing an Internet access service.
2. Commercial practices should be assessed case by case, *ex post* using competition law principles.
3. Commercial practices should be assessed case by case, *ex post* but not relying purely on competition law principles. Guidance (*ex ante*) on how to assess commercial practices can be given in order to contribute to consistent application of the Regulation.

This chapter will examine these different interpretations of Regulation 2015/2120, including the recommendations of BEREC and their role in practice.

2.   INTERPRETATION 1: COMMERCIAL DISCRIMINATION OF TRAFFIC IS, AS SUCH, PROHIBITED BASED ON ARTICLE 3(3)

2.1   Prohibition of Price Differentiation in Dutch Law

Before Regulation 2015/2120 was adopted in the EU, some Member States had already adopted national network neutrality legislation. One of these early adopters was the Netherlands, which amended its Telecommunications Act 1998 (Telecommunicatiewet, 'TW') in June 2012 by adopting specific net neutrality rules. Article 7.4a(3), which was annulled in July 2018,[19] of the TW addressed commercial practices, requiring providers of Internet access services not to make the level of tariffs for Internet access services dependent on the services and applications that are offered or used via these services.

---

[17]   For an overview of different zero-rating practices: Carillo (n 10) 372–383.

[18]   BEREC, 'Report on the implementation of Regulation (EU) 2015/2120 and BEREC Net Neutrality Guidelines', BoR (17) 240, 8–10.

[19]   The annulment of Article 7.4a(3) was announced in Staatsblad (24 May 2018), 2018, nr. 142. The annulment has become effective on 1 July 2018, which was published in Staatsblad (29 June 2018), 2018, nr. 207.

The District Court of Rotterdam confirmed in *Vodafone v ACM*[20] that the prohibition on price differentiation practices laid down in Article 7.4a(3) of the TW also included zero-rating. In August 2014 the Netherlands Authority for Consumers and Markets (ACM) had banned Vodafone Libertel B.V. (Vodafone) from offering a zero-rated video streaming application called HBO Go. Vodafone had offered zero-rated use of HBO Go in combination with Vodafone Red, a bundle of mobile services including a mobile Internet access service. The zero-rating of the HBO Go application meant that usage of that application did not count towards the data cap included in the Vodafone Red plan.[21]

The District Court pointed out that Article 7.4a(3) of the TW prevented ISPs from making the price of their Internet access service depend on the services the end-users can use as this might influence end-users when they make their choice between different Internet-based services.[22] The District Court ruled that zero-rated offering of the HBO Go application was an illegal price differentiation prohibited in Dutch law.[23]

Considering these national circumstances, it is not surprising that the Dutch government was active in the drafting process of the Regulation and ended up voting against it in the Council of the European Union. According to the Dutch government, the reason for this was that the Regulation lacked a clear ban on price differentiation. At the time, the Dutch government stated that as a result of the final text of the Regulation, the Netherlands would be obliged to withdraw the ban on price differentiation from its national net neutrality rules.[24]

However, after some further consideration the Dutch government came to the opposite conclusion and decided to keep the prohibition on price differentiation in its national legislation. In a letter[25] to the Dutch Parliament, the Dutch

---

[20] *Vodafone Libertel B.V v de Autoriteit Consument en Markt* (ACM), 4 February 2016, Rechtbank Rotterdam (ECLI:NL:RBROT:2016:810).

[21] ibid, at 2.1.

[22] ibid, at 3.3.

[23] ibid, at 3.4.

[24] Draft regulation of the European Parliament and of the Council laying down measures concerning the European single market for electronic communications and to achieve a connected continent, and amending directives 2002/20/EC, 2002/21/EC and 2002/22/EC and regulations (EC) No 1211/2009 and (EU) No 531/2012 (First Reading) (29 September 2015, 12279/15 ADD 1 REV 1).

[25] H G J Kamp, Minister of Economic Affairs, 'Nota naar aanleiding van het verslag voorstel van wet tot wijziging van de Telecommunicatiewet ter uitvoering van de netneutraliteitsverordening' (Kamerstuk 34 379) 23 March 2016, https://www.rijksoverheid.nl/documenten/kamerstukken/2016/03/23/nota-naar-aanleiding-van-verslag-over-wetsvoorstel-uitvoering-netneutraliteitsverordening, accessed 9 May 2018.

government argued that price differentiation is not allowed under Regulation 2015/2120, even though it is not explicitly prohibited. The Dutch government claimed that the national prohibition of price differentiation can be maintained to clarify primarily the first subparagraph of Article 3(3) of the Regulation, which requires ISPs to treat all traffic equally when providing Internet access services.[26]

This interpretation was soon rejected by the District Court of Rotterdam. In April 2017 the District Court ruled in *T-Mobile v ACM*[27] that, without any doubt, Regulation 2015/2120 does not contain a categorical ban on price discrimination.[28] The court based its view on the legislative history of the Regulation and the structure of Article 3(3) of the Regulation.[29] These arguments will be discussed next.

2.2   Price Differentiation is Not Categorically Prohibited in Regulation 2015/2120

While the U-turn by the Dutch government was rather surprising, it was not entirely without merit. The first subparagraph of Article 3(3) requires ISPs to 'treat all traffic equally'. Generally, there is no reason to assume that the term 'treatment' could only refer to technical – but not commercial – treatment of traffic, including price differentiation. In fact, in the USA the Federal Communications Committee (FCC) has referred to zero-rating as one form of favourable treatment of traffic. According to the FCC,

> where an edge provider [the FCC refers to providers of content and applications as 'edge providers'] attempts to purchase favorable treatment for its traffic (such as through zero rating), that treatment would be experienced by the BIAS subscriber (such as through an exemption of the edge-provider's data from a usage limit) and the impact on the BIAS subscriber, if any, would be assessed under Title II.[30]

However, as pointed out by the Dutch Court, the structure of Article 3(3) suggests that the scope of the requirement in its first subparagraph to treat all traffic equally is limited to technical treatment of traffic. Article 3(3) has no reference to non-technical commercial practices, whereas the second and third

---

[26]   ibid, at 6–7.
[27]   *T-Mobile Netherlands B.V. v ACM*, 24 April 2017, Rechtbank Rotterdam (ECLI: NL:RBROT:2017:2940).
[28]   ibid at 6.7.
[29]   ibid at 6.5.
[30]   Federal Communications Committee (2015) Report and Order on Remand, Declaratory Ruling, and Order on the Matter of Protecting and Promoting the Open Internet (GN Docket No. 14-28) para 339.

subparagraphs of Article 3(3) only cover issues relating to traffic management measures, establishing a framework for assessing such measures.

Moreover, there are strong reasons to believe that the intention of the Council and the European Parliament, as co-legislators of the Regulation, was to apply Article 3(3) only to technical treatment of traffic and not to impose a per se prohibition on price differentiation. The initial conclusion of the Netherlands – that the ban on price discrimination needs to be removed from their national legislation – reflects this intention of the co-legislators.[31] It is also clear that the European Commission (EC) does not share the view that the Regulation prohibits, as such, all types of price differentiation of traffic in the provision of Internet access services. According to a fact sheet published by the EC, national authorities are required to monitor and assess commercial practices such as zero-rating and to intervene if necessary.[32] Hence, the EC clearly considers that the principle of equal treatment of traffic set out in Article 3(3) is limited to the technical treatment of traffic.

As a conclusion, while the language of the Regulation allows some room for interpretation, it is quite clear that the purpose of the Regulation is not to prohibit per se any commercial practices, such as zero-rating. Instead, such practices should be assessed on a case-by-case approach under Article 3(2) of the Regulation, whereas application of Article 3(3) is limited to assessing the technical treatment of traffic. It must be noted that an assessment of technical treatment of traffic based on Article 3(3) may, of course, also be a part of the assessment of any agreements or commercial practices covered by Article 3(2) of the Regulation.

3. INTERPRETATION 2: AN ASSESSMENT BASED ON COMPETITION LAW PRINCIPLES

3.1 Arguments for a Dominant Role of Competition Law Principles

Even before Regulation 2015/2120 was adopted, many commentators argued that there was no need for special net neutrality legislation and that competition rules were sufficient to prevent abuses of market power.[33] First, agreements between the ISP and a content provider will need to be compatible with

---

[31] See n 25.

[32] European Commission, 'Roaming charges and open Internet: questions and answers' (Fact sheet, 30 June 2015, MEMO/15/5275) http://europa.eu/rapid/press-release_MEMO-15-5275_nl.htm, accessed 9 May 2018.

[33] See n 8.

Article 101 of the Treaty on the Functioning of the European Union[34] (TFEU), which prohibits agreements and concerted practices that are restrictive of competition. Second, certain behaviour could potentially be prohibited under Article 102 of the TFEU, which prohibits abuse of a dominant market position. For example, denying prioritisation from some content providers while granting it to others could potentially be considered as a refusal to deal or applying dissimilar conditions to equivalent transactions.[35] However, it is worth noting that under EU law even a dominant firm has an obligation to deal only in specific circumstances: the product or service needs to be indispensable for the customer requesting it and refusal is liable, or likely, to eliminate all effective competition in the market.[36]

Since adoption of Regulation 2015/2120 one of the key questions has been the relationship between the Regulation and general EU competition law, in particular as to the role of competition law principles, if any, in assessing the commercial practices of IAPs under Article 3(2). During the consultation process for the BEREC Guidelines, several ISPs argued that assessment of commercial practices under Article 3(2) of the Regulation should be done *ex post* based on competition law principles. This interpretation is based mainly on the language of Recital 7 of the Regulation, which provides high-level guidance on how to assess agreements and commercial practices. The claim of many ISP stakeholders is that Recital 7 borrows its concepts from competition law – concepts such as references to the scale of a practice, materiality in reduction of the end-user's choice, reduction of choice in practice, and the requirement to take market positions into account. Therefore, according to this view, assessment of commercial practices should be based on an effect-based test carried out in line with well-established EU competition law principles.[37]

---

[34] Consolidated Version of the Treaty on the Functioning of the European Union [2010] OJ C83/47; Reg (EU) 2015/2120 laying down measures concerning open internet access and amending Directive 2002/22/EC on universal service and users' rights relating to electronic communications networks and services; Reg (EU) No 531/2012 on roaming on public mobile communications networks within the Union (Reg 2015/2120) [2015] OJ L310.

[35] See, eg, P Larouche, 'Network Neutrality: The Global Dimension' in M Burri and T Cottier (eds), *Trade Governance in the Digital Age* (Cambridge University Press 2012) 113.

[36] Case C-418/01 *IMS Health GmbH & Co. OHG v NDC Health GmbH & Co. KG* [2004] ECR I-5039 and Case T-201/04, *Microsoft Corp v Commission* [2007] EU:T: 2007:289.

[37] Eg, Telia Company, 'Reply to BEREC public consultation on the Net Neutrality Guidelines', 12 July 2016, http://berec.europa.eu/eng/document_register/ subject_matter/berec/public_consultations/6216-contribution-by-telia-to-the-public -consultation-on-berec-guidelines-on-the-implementation-by-national-regulators-of -european-net-neutrality-rules, accessed 9 May 2018, 4–7.

3.2 Article 3(2) – More Than a Reference to Competition Law

In Regulation 2015/2120 the impact on end-users' choice is a key factor both in prohibiting restrictive traffic management measures (Recital 11) and in assessing whether agreements or commercial practices result in undermining the essence of the end-users' rights (Recital 7). As regards agreements and commercial practices, Recital 7 refers to situations where such practices, by reason of their scale, lead to a situation where end-users' rights are materially reduced in practice. Recital 7 also states that the respective market positions of the parties involved should be taken into account, among other things.

Recital 11 explains that protection from blocking or other restrictive measures not falling within the justified exceptions is required because of their negative impact on end-user choice and innovation. Unlike in competition law, there is no question that the requirements for equal technical treatment of traffic laid down in Article 3(3) apply to all ISPs, regardless of their market power. In other words, some restrictive technical measures which could be compatible with competition law might not be compatible with the Regulation, according to which the practices of an ISP can have a negative effect on end-users' choice regardless of the ISP's market power.

Considering the argument that Article 3(2) requires assessment of commercial practices to be based on competition law principles, it is remarkable that the Regulation makes no reference to competition law, either in the Articles or in the recitals. This lack of clear references to competition law in Regulation 2015/2120 raises doubts about the suggested dominant role of the principles of competition law in the assessment of commercial practices under the Regulation. As Lenaerts and Gutiérrez-Fons point out, 'no provision of EU laws should be redundant'.[38] If the co-legislators of the Regulation had intended that commercial practices should be assessed purely based on competition law principles, why not clearly state so? Why is assessment of commercial practices under Article 3(2) built around the end-user's choice instead of including direct reference to competition law?

Comparing situations where a commercial practice could have a similar effect to technical blocking or some other restrictive measure illustrates how protecting end-users' rights should be interpreted consistently under the different Articles of the Regulation. As some commentators have pointed out, it is true that the effects of commercial practices may be less obvious compared

---

[38] K Lenaerts and J A Gutiérrez-Fons, 'To Say What the Law of the EU Is: Methods of Interpretation and the European Court of Justice' (2014) 20(2) Columbia Journal of European Law 3, 14.

to the effects of technical restrictions, such as blocking.[39] However, both technical and commercial measures have the potential to render a service or application effectively unusable. For example, according to research published in 2014 by Digital Fuel Monitor, some mobile network operators in the EU have zero-rated their own online video services and have thus included practically unlimited use of those services in the monthly subscription fee of the mobile data service. In contrast, in some cases monthly data caps allowed users to use competing video services, such as Netflix, for no more than two hours a month.[40]

If the effect of a commercial practice is de facto the same as, or considerably similar to, one resulting from a restrictive technical measure not falling within the justified exemptions provided in Article 3(3), the Regulation gives no reason to conclude that the two cases should be treated differently. The references in Recital 7 to the scale of a commercial practice and the market positions of the parties involved are hardly sufficient to draw the conclusion that commercial practices should be assessed purely based on general competition law principles.

Taking these considerations into account, it is unsurprising that even the EC, which largely contributed to the inclusion of the reference to market positions in Recital 7, does not share the view that assessment of commercial practices under Article 3(2) of Regulation should be based solely on competition law principles. The answer given by the EC to the European Parliament summarises well the relationship between the Regulation and competition law:

> *The...Regulation includes three safeguards* to protect end-users from possible negative effects of commercial agreements or practices, including zero-rating: a) They cannot limit end-users's right to access and distribute content, applications and services of their choice via the Internet; b) All commercial agreements and practices, including zero rating, have to comply with the principle of equal and non-discriminatory treatment of all traffic, which cannot be derogated from unilaterally or contractually; c) National regulatory authorities are empowered and obliged to ensure, through monitoring and enforcement action, that the rights of end-users are not impaired, including the rights of providers of content, services and applications. These safeguards ensure a future-proof approach that allows regulators to adapt to new practices, rather than just addressing the practices of today. Regulators and courts will analyse zero-rating and other practices on their merits, case-by-case,

---

[39] F Marini-Balestra and R Tremolada, 'The EU Debate on Net Neutrality: What About Zero-rating?' 21(5) Computer and Telecommunications Law Review 115, 116.

[40] Rewheel, 'Neelie Kroes's Specialized Services are a giant Net Neutrality loophole' (Rewheel/Digital Fuel Monitor premium research note, 27 October 2014) www.dfmonitor.eu/downloads/Neelie_Kroes_Specialized_Services_are_a_giant_net_neutrality_loophole_HIGHLIGHTS.pdf, accessed 9 May 2018.

in their specific national circumstances, to ensure that the objective of effective end-user choice is not undermined in practice.
In addition, competition law, which is enshrined in the Treaty, *is directly applicable* and may be enforced as needed (emphasis added).[41]

The EC could not have been more explicit about the distinct and complementary roles of Regulation 2015/2120 and competition law. The aim of competition law is not to ensure consumer choice – as Petit notes, the Court of Justice of the European Union implicitly affirmed in *Post Danmark*[42] that as a result of competition consumers may end up with only one supplier.[43] Moreover, even in competitive markets all or the majority of ISPs could have incentives to discriminate against some, or certain types of, applications and services.[44] Unlike an assessment based on competition law, assessment of commercial practices under Article 3(2) of Regulation 2015/2120 needs to take into account the emphasis given in the Regulation to the rights of end-users and the continued functioning of the Internet ecosystem as an engine of innovation.[45]

As a conclusion, stakeholders who support a dominant role for competition law (principles) seem to find little room for other criteria in the assessment of commercial practices under Article 3(2). However, this is too narrow an interpretation of the role of the Regulation. While assessment of the competitive situation may be an integral part of assessing commercial practices under Article 3(2) of the Regulation, the safeguards provided in the Regulation to protect end-users' rights require a broader approach than an assessment based solely on competition law principles. Depending on the circumstances, these

---

[41]   Gunther Oettinger, EU Commissioner for Digital Economy and Society, 'Answer given by Mr Oettinger on behalf of the Commission' (European Parliament, 15 January 2016) www.europarl.europa.eu/sides/getAllAnswers.do?reference=E-2015-014462& language=EN, accessed 9 May 2018.
[42]   Case C-209/10, *Post Danmark A/S v Konkurrencerådet* [2012] ECLI:EU:C: 2012:172.
[43]   N Petit, 'Intel, Leveraging Rebates and the Goals of Article 102 TFEU' (2015) 11(1) European Competition Journal 26, 62.
[44]   See Belli (n 2) 22; A Cooper and I Brown, 'Net Neutrality: Discrimination, Competition, and Innovation in the UK and US' (2015) 15(1) ACM Transactions on Internet Technology, Article 2: J Holopainen 'Verkkoneutraliteettisääntelyn tavoitteet Suomessa, EU:ssa ja Yhdysvalloissa (2017) 5 Lakimies 627, 646.
[45]   B van Schewick, 'Comments on BEREC Guidelines on the Implementation by National Regulators of European Net Neutrality Rules', BoR (16) 94 (Contribution to the public consultation on BEREC Guidelines on the Implementation by National Regulators of European Net Neutrality Rules (18 July 2016) 13), http://berec.europa.eu/ eng/document_register/subject_matter/berec/public_consultations/6304-contribution -by-stanford-to-the-public-consultation-on-berec-guidelines-on-the-implementation -by-national-regulators-of-european-net-neutrality-rules, accessed 9 May 2018.

safeguards may be triggered even in situations where the parties involved lack the market power required for application of either Articles 101 or 102 of the TFEU. As Marsden points out, net neutrality is not only about economics and technology, and 'communication policy is about fundamental rights of citizens as well as public welfare for consumers'.[46] Openness of access to the Internet depends on technical, economic and social aspects, and assessment of social aspects may require different analytical tools than assessment of the competitive situation.[47] This is the approach adopted by BEREC in its guidelines, which will be discussed next.

4.   INTERPRETATION 3: ASSESSING COMMERCIAL PRACTICES *EX POST* BUT WITH THE HELP OF (*EX ANTE*) GUIDANCE – THE APPROACH ADOPTED BY BEREC

4.1   Comprehensive Case-by-case Assessment of Commercial Practices

In August 2016 BEREC published 'Guidelines on the Implementation by the National Regulators of European Net Neutrality Rules'.[48] These guidelines are not binding but constitute recommendations, which NRAs are required to take into maximal account.[49]

The BEREC Guidelines clearly point out that Article 3(2) of Regulation 2015/2120 needs to be interpreted together with the other provisions of the Regulation. In addition to the provisions in Article 3 and the related recitals, assessment of commercial practices based on Article 3(2) should, according to the BEREC Guidelines, take into account the aim of the Regulation to 'safeguard equal and non-discriminatory treatment of traffic' (Article 1) and to 'guarantee the continued functioning of the internet ecosystem as an engine of innovation' (Recital 1).[50]

BEREC considers that not every factor affecting end-users' choice necessarily limits the exercise of end-users' rights under Article 3(1) and accordingly urges NRAs to consider to what extent the choice available to end-users is

---

[46]   C Marsden, *Net Neutrality: Towards a Co-Regulatory Solution* (Bloomsbury Academic 2010) 20.

[47]   Eg, K S Rahman, 'Private Power, Public Values: Regulating Social Infrastructure in a Changing Economy' (2018) 39(5) Cardozo Law Review, https://ssrn.com/abstract =2986387, accessed 9 May 2018 and Marsden (n 46).

[48]   n 13.

[49]   ibid.

[50]   BEREC Guidelines para 43.

restricted by the commercial practices of the ISP.[51] In paragraph 46 of the Guidelines, BEREC concludes that a comprehensive case-by-case assessment of commercial and technical conditions may be required, taking into account in particular the following factors:

- The goals of the Regulation. Commercial practices should not be used to circumvent these aims.
- The respective market positions of the involved ISPs and CAPs (content and application providers). According to BEREC, these market positions should be analysed in line with competition law principles. BEREC makes a difference between 'strong' and 'weak' market positions, finding that, all else being equal, a limitation of the exercise of the end-user rights is more likely to arise in the former situation.
- The effects on both consumer and business customer end-user rights and whether the end-user choice is reduced in practice. BEREC considers that this assessment should include, among other things, the effect of the commercial practice on the range and diversity of content and applications. Moreover, in footnote 12, BEREC adds that '[T]his may also concern the effect on freedom of expression and information, including media pluralism'. According to BEREC, the assessment should also encompass 'whether the end-user is incentivised to use, for example, certain applications' and 'whether the IAS subscription contains characteristics which materially reduce end-user choice'.
- The effects on CAPs end-user including, among other things, the effect on diversity of content and applications and the harms to competition. According to BEREC, NRAs should assess 'whether the continued functioning of the Internet ecosystem as an engine of innovation is impacted, for example, whether it is the ISP that picks winners and losers, and on the administrative and/or technical barriers for CAPs to enter into agreements with ISPs'.
- As the last two factors BEREC presents the scale of the practice and the presence of alternatives – regarding both the alternative offers and/or competing ISPs to choose from.

According to BEREC, the presence of one or more of these factors may limit the exercise of end-users' rights under Article 3(2).[52] This raises the question how these different and potentially conflicting factors should be evaluated in practice. For example, what if the end-user is strongly incentivised to use a certain application but both the ISP and the CAP have a 'weak' market

---

[51]   ibid para 45.
[52]   ibid para 47.

position? Can the market position of the parties or the scale of the practice be irrelevant in some circumstances?

Clearly, some of these factors are not alone – without the presence of any other factor – capable of limiting end-users' rights as provided in Article 3(1). Clearly more than the presence of a 'strong' market position is required, while the scale of a practice or the limited availability of alternative offers is alone not enough for such a finding. The BEREC Guidelines do not, however, provide more guidance on the methodology of assessment but instead provide further considerations on specific commercial practices.

4.2   BEREC Considerations Regarding Specific Commercial Practices

In the Guidelines, BEREC provides examples of commercial practices and evaluates the likelihood of those practices being acceptable under the Regulation. According to BEREC, some of these practices would be – or would likely be – acceptable or, compared to another commercial practice, would 'more likely' be either acceptable or prohibited.[53] BEREC also identifies circumstances where a commercial practice limits or is likely to limit the exercise of end-users' rights.[54]

First, in the Guidelines BEREC provides examples of commercial practices which would be or would likely be acceptable under the Regulation. For example, BEREC concludes that when data volumes (or speed characteristics) are applied equally to all applications (application-agnostic), end-users' rights are likely to be unaffected.[55]

Second, BEREC provides relative comparisons between the effects of different commercial practices. As regards price differentiation of data traffic, BEREC concludes that the impact may be different depending on whether price differentiation concerns a whole class[56] of applications or individual applications within a class. BEREC considers that price differentiation applied to classes of applications is more likely to just influence end-users than to limit the exercise of their rights defined in Article 3(1) of the Regulation.[57] In contrast, according to BEREC, price differentiation between individual applications within a class of applications affects competition within that class. Therefore, it may be more likely to undermine the goals of the Regulation than price differentiation between classes of applications.

---

[53]   ibid, eg, paras 35 and 42.
[54]   ibid, eg, paras 38 and 48.
[55]   ibid para 35.
[56]   BEREC seems to use the terms 'class' and 'category' interchangeably.
[57]   BEREC Guidelines para 39.

Third, BEREC identifies two situations where a commercial practice is 'likely' to limit the exercise of end-users' rights. BEREC first acknowledges that agreements and commercial practices may in some circumstances have an effect similar to technical blocking of access. BEREC considers such cases to likely infringe Article 3(1) and 3(2).[58] BEREC also considers that applying a higher price to data associated with a specific application or class of application is 'likely to limit the exercise of end users' rights because of the potentially strong disincentive created to the use of the application(s) affected, and consequent restriction of choice'.[59] Hence, drawing the above-mentioned distinction between practices concerning individual applications and classes of applications may not, according to BEREC, always be relevant when assessing price differentiation practices.

Fourth, BEREC identifies some practices that would limit the exercise of end-users' rights set out in Article 3(1). BEREC concludes that technical practices which infringe Article 3(3) limit, at least typically, the exercise of end-users' rights and thus constitute an infringement of Article 3(1) and 3(2).[60] Moreover, the BEREC Guidelines do not allow commercial practices circumventing the obligations laid down in Article 3(3). For example, according to BEREC, zero-rating offers where all other than zero-rated applications are blocked (or slowed down) once the data cap is reached would infringe Article 3(3) first and third subparagraphs.[61] BEREC also considers that contractually banning the use of specific content or applications or categories thereof would limit end-users' rights. BEREC refers to this practice as an offering of 'sub-internet service'. BEREC gives banning the use of VoIP (voice over the Internet) as an example of a practice it would consider as an offer of a sub-Internet service.[62]

In summary, in the Guidelines BEREC distinguishes between 'influencing' or 'incentivising' and 'limiting' choice. On the one hand, BEREC recognises that there are multiple ways to influence people without necessarily limiting their choices. On the other hand, BEREC finds that an Internet access service subscription may have characteristics which materially reduce end-user choice. In other words, BEREC considers that some commercial practices could limit the exercise of end-users' rights irrespective of the market positions of the parties or the scale of the practice. However, apart from practices involving technical preferential treatment or banning the use of certain services contrac-

---

[58] ibid para 48 first bullet.
[59] ibid para 48 second bullet.
[60] ibid para 37.
[61] ibid para 41.
[62] ibid para 38.

tually, BEREC refrains from drawing any definitive conclusions regarding commercial practices.

4.3   The Role of the BEREC Guidelines in Practice

The non-binding BEREC Guidelines provide a general framework, a starting point on what technical, economic and social factors should be included in case-by-case assessment. However, the fact that BEREC does not provide theoretical justifications or guidance about the methodology for assessment raises questions about how these guidelines can be taken into account in practice.

In some Member States the NRAs have, either formally or informally, investigated zero-rating services. In some of these cases, NRAs have focused solely on the technical treatment of traffic based on Article 3(3) of the Regulation. For example, the Swedish Post- and Telecom Authority ('PTS'), found that two zero-rated services by Telia Company resulted in unlawful traffic management because when the data cap in place was reached all other services and applications except the zero-rated ones were blocked.[63] In another example from Austria, the Telekom-Control-Kommission requested A1 Telekom Austria AG ('A1') to remove the bandwidth and picture resolution limitations ('traffic shaping') A1 had imposed on the zero-rated Free Stream video streaming service.[64]

There are also cases where NRAs have assessed zero-rating services based on Article 3(2) of the Regulation. In their assessments the NRAs have taken into account, or at least attempted to do so, multiple factors, such as the amount of data available for other than zero-rated services and the market positions. Interestingly, the NRAs have had differences in their approaches, especially regarding the significance of whether or not all providers of the respective zero-rated category of applications (in these cases music or video services) can participate in the zero-rating scheme. In the Netherlands ACM considered the zero-rated service of T-Mobile to be in line with the Regulation, due to its being open to all publicly available music-streaming services that met certain technical criteria, regardless of their market positions.[65] However, zero-rating just a single application has also been considered not to limit end-users' rights under the Regulation. The Belgian Institute for Postal Services and Telecommunications ('BIPT') found in an informal report that there were no grounds to intervene in a zero-rating plan offered by Proximus, where

---

[63]   Swedish Post- and Telecom Authority, DNR 16-545 and 15-5474, 24 January 2017, pp. 7–8. At the time of writing this decision is still under appeal.
[64]   Telekom-Control-Kommission (18.12.2017 - R 5/17).
[65]   ACM: ACM/DTVP/2017/205487_OV, para 76.

just a single application, chosen by the end-user from a preselected group of popular applications, was zero-rated.[66] One of the main arguments of BIPT was that no decrease in the range and diversity of content and applications had been observed since the launch of the zero-rating service.[67] This view has been, justifiably, criticised as only taking into account the (very) short-term observable – but not the long-term potential – effects on the range and diversity of applications.[68]

These differences illustrate a lack of detailed guidance on the methodology for assessment of commercial practices in the BEREC Guidelines. The line between 'influencing' and 'limiting' end-users' choice remains blurry and more work is clearly needed to develop analytical tools. This has been recognised by NRAs, who are seeking evidence-based approaches to assessing commercial practices under Article 3(2). For example, in a press release the Swedish NRA – PTS – noted that market developments should be followed over time and that there is a need for 'continuous work in order to identify and assess several factors affecting competition and the availability of access to an open internet'.[69] Moreover, BEREC has further analysed existing tools and has proposed a template for NRAs to use voluntarily in their investigations.[70] However, the template mostly contributes to coordinating how investigations are conducted but does not provide more guidance on how different commercial practices should be assessed.

5.   CONCLUSION

Article 3(1) of Regulation 2015/2120 sets end-users' choice as one of the governing principles of the Regulation. One of the safeguards protecting end-users' rights is provided in Article 3(2) of the Regulation, which requires that any commercial practice conducted by an Internet access service must not limit the exercise of end-users' rights laid down in Article 3(1).

---

[66]   Belgian Institute for Postal Services and Telecommunications, 'Report Regarding the Analysis of Zero-rating of Apps in the Proximus Offers' (30 January 2017) www .bipt.be/public/files/en/22099/Report_Zero_rating_Proximus.pdf, accessed 9 May 2018.

[67]   ibid para 99.

[68]   Dennis Brouwer, 'Zero-rating and Net Neutrality in the European Union: What Legal Approach Should the EU Legislator Adopt with Respect to Zero-rating Offers Where Applications Do Not Count Towards the Data Cap of the Consumer?' (Masters Thesis, Tilburg University 2017) 42.

[69]   PTS, 'Operators shall treat internet traffic equally according to a draft decision from PTS' (Press Release, 7 December 2016).

[70]   BEREC, 'Report on tools and methods used to identify commercial and technical practices for the implementation of article 3 of Regulation 2015/2120' (BoR (17) 241).

There are, however, multiple ways to influence people without necessarily limiting their choices – advertising is one example. On the other
hand, some commercial practices may have characteristics which materially
reduce end-users' choice irrespective of the market positions of the parties
involved.[71] Therefore, Article 3(2) of the Regulation does not authorise any
per se prohibitions of commercial practices but requires a case-by-case assessment. However, there are no reasons to conduct a case-by-case assessment
solely based on competition law principles. The safeguards provided in the
Regulation to protect end-users' rights require a broader approach than an
assessment based solely on competition law principles.

The obvious question therefore is: what should an assessment of commercial
practices under the Regulation then be based on? The BEREC Guidelines do
not provide a complete answer to this question, but instead provide a general
framework taking into account a wide range of technical, economic and social
factors. The BEREC Guidelines reflect the fact that access to the Internet has
become in many ways a crucial infrastructure for end-users, including business
end-users, to fully exercise their fundamental rights and freedoms, such as
freely disseminating information and ideas.[72] Yet even fundamental rights and
freedoms, including freedom of expression, are not absolute and the different
factors in each case need to be balanced against each other.[73]

As a conclusion, the new open Internet access framework in the EU was
at least partly motivated by the aim to prevent legal fragmentation between
Member States. However, due to their wide scope, the rules regarding the
assessment of commercial practices under Article 3(2) of the Regulation do not
easily fit in any traditional category of law, such as competition or consumer
law. As a result, this kind of legal fragmentation causes challenges to the
efficient enforcement of these rules. To meet these challenges NRAs need to
gather more empirical data on user behaviour and to further develop analytical
tools to assess commercial practices under Article 3(2) of the Regulation.
Assessment should not be based only on – arguably short-term – economic
factors but should take into account the Internet's vital role for culture and
democracy in the long term.[74] In its core, the Internet has been and can continue to be a technology of abundance and not scarcity. As pointed out by
Schejter and Yemini, 'the promise of the Internet does not lie in its support of

---

[71]   See eg BEREC Guidelines para 48.
[72]   See Belli (n 1) and L C Audibert and A D Murray, 'A Principled Approach to
Network Neutrality' (2016) 13 SCRIPTed – A Journal of Law, Technology & Society
118, 120.
[73]   Carillo (n 10) 414.
[74]   Audibert and Murray (n 72) 119.

large businesses, but in the opportunities it provides for those who could not have had a say in technologies of content scarcity'.[75]

Maxwell suggests that lessons could be learned from regulators for audiovisual media services and environmental protection authorities.[76] Indeed, such cooperation has already been welcomed by some of these authorities.[77] Additionally, applying behavioural economics could provide useful tools for NRAs to better understand the decision-making process of end-users and the cognitive biases affecting their decision-making.[78]

If the effect of a commercial practice is the same as or considerably similar to one resulting from a prohibited technical restriction, Regulation 2015/2120 gives no reason to treat these two cases differently. Regarding zero-rating of applications and services, market data on actual user behaviour is needed to determine the extent that zero-rating affects the use of non-zero-rated applications and services. NRAs should, among other things, investigate whether ISPs are artificially framing the choice of limited access to the Internet to make it seem superior to full access to the Internet. In particular, if use of other services is very low compared to use of zero-rated services, especially use of applications and services similar to zero-rated ones, the zero-rating practice in question may limit the exercise of end-users' rights as set out in Article 3(1) of the Regulation.

---

[75] A M Schejter and M Yemini, 'Justice, and Only Justice, You Shall Pursue: Network Neutrality, the First Amendment and John Rawls's Theory of Justice' (2007) 14 Michigan Telecommunications and Technology Law Review 137, 171.

[76] Winston Maxwell, 'DSM Watch: Hogan Lovells partner discusses net neutrality at BEREC forum' (Global Media and Communications Watch, 26 October 2016) www.hlmediacomms.com/2016/10/26/dsm-watch-hogan-lovells-partner-discusses-net -neutrality-at-berec-forum/, accessed 9 May 2018.

[77] See, for example, Die Medienanstalten, 'BEREC Guidelines on Net Neutrality: Position of the German Media Authorities' (Contribution to the public consultation on BEREC Guidelines on the Implementation by National Regulators of European Net Neutrality Rules,18 July 2016) http://berec.europa.eu/eng/document_register/subject _matter/berec/public_consultations/6292-contribution-by-german-media-authorities -to-the-public-consultation-on-berec-guidelines-on-the-implementation-by-national -regulators-of-european-net-neutrality-rules, accessed 9 May 2018.

[78] For an overview of behavioural economics, see K Mathis and A D Steffen, 'From Rational Choice to Behavioural Economics' in K Mathis (ed), *European Perspectives on Behavioural Law and Economics. Economic Analysis of Law in European Legal Scholarship* (Springer 2015). For a more comprehensive analysis see, eg, C Jolls, C R Sunnstein and R Thaler, 'A Behavioral Approach to Law and Economics' (1998) 50 Stanford Law Review 1471.

PART V

Concluding Remarks

16. Concluding remarks

Taina Pihlajarinne, Juha Vesala and Olli Honkkila

The digital evolution – or revolution – has been having profound implications on the distribution of content online. New legal issues are constantly arising as companies and consumers seize the opportunities afforded by advances in technology. For instance, consumers have gravitated from watching live television towards watching television via mobile devices. This has given rise to legal issues relating to ability to access services abroad and across Member State borders, as well as to the ability of content service providers to enable this to be done lawfully. Naturally these developments have also attracted reactions from the EU and national policymakers.

The previous chapters in this book establish a highly topical snapshot of the current state of the law affecting online distribution of content within the European Union. The analyses also illustrate the obstacles still remaining and pinpoint new problems raised by new legislative, administrative and judicial developments.

1. FIRST STEPS TOWARDS A DIGITAL SINGLE MARKET FOR CONTENT

Several chapters of this book highlight that the measures in the Digital Single Market (DSM) package – both those proposed and those so far adopted – are not sufficient to attain the ambitious objectives involved in establishing a DSM. Mazziotti, Cantero and Vesala note in their chapters that the new Geo-blocking and Portability Regulations have only limited impact on online content distribution within the EU. They note the limited scope of application in particular of the Geo-blocking Regulation and the limited impact of the Portability Regulation, and each in their chapters identifies other remaining obstacles to EU-wide online content sales and accessibility. As to consumer rights, Havu finds that the DSM package offers consumers only partial improvement for their protection. She criticizes the DSM proposal's piecemeal nature affecting consumers and raises the question whether longer-lasting results could be achieved by more overarching approaches. Kivistö and Moscon also identify various problems that prevent the proposed Directive on copyright in the DSM from meeting its objective of promoting cross-border activities online.

Nonetheless, the challenges involved in establishing a DSM for digital content and content services need to be recognized. The diverging interests alone make progress difficult. The first steps taken towards improved EU-wide distribution of content constitute a promising seed for further improvements. For instance, cross-border access to online content services already subscribed has been improved by the Portability Regulation; and the Geo-blocking Regulation provides for a review of whether its rules should be extended to online content services (Mazziotti, Cantero and Vesala). However, the new Regulations also introduce inconsistencies in the legal framework (Cantero) and may impede integration of the market by recognizing the territoriality and justifiability of geo-blocking practices (Mazziotti). The limited improvements now accomplished may also act as a catalyst for subsequent legislation to further promote online distribution of content throughout the EU.

2.   FRAGMENTATION OF APPROACHES TO ONLINE DISTRIBUTION OF CONTENT

The chapters in this book illustrate that regulation of online distribution of content is becoming increasingly fragmented. This process can occur in various ways. First, similar situations may be treated differently within the same field of law due to some distinguishing factor, such as the technology or product concerned. These technology- or product-specific fragmentation issues are identified in terms of EU copyright legislation (Kivistö), specific rules related to the proposed protection of press publications (Moscon), different approaches in copyright and trademark law as regards linking, AI-produced creations and 3D-printing technologies (Pihlajarinne; Ballardini, Roos and He; Mendis; Pihlajarinne and Oker-Blom), and specialized rules applied to online services depending on their nature (Vesala and Mazziotti).

Second, fragmentation is caused by different legal systems with diverging approaches within a particular area of regulation. These can be observed in approaches to copyright enforcement – which vary by Member State (Weckström Lindroos) – and 3D-printing (Mendis). Indeed, in many cases the emergence of fragmented practices between different Member States has been a major motivator for creating EU-level legislation, such as in the case of net neutrality (Honkkila) and protection of press publishers (Moscon). However, adopted (or proposed) solutions at the EU level may sometimes be partial and ambiguous, as in the proposed Digital Content Directive (Havu) or the Directive on copyright in the DSM (Kivistö), which can lead to diverging national interpretations that introduce fragmentation.

Finally, fragmentation may take place across various areas of law when the same issue is regulated by several areas of law. As an illustration, online distribution of content can be affected simultaneously by copyright protection, exercise of copyright and licensing practices by copyright law, fundamental freedoms of the EU, internal market legislation, EU competition law and sector-specific regulations (Mazziotti, Cantero, Vesala, Honkkila). For example, new regulations and competition law address similar issues in supply of copyright-protected online content in potentially problematic ways.

While distinctions may be warranted between technologies or types of content or other creations (eg AI-generated outputs), or while differing objectives of regulation can justify the use of separate instruments, at the same time fragmentation can be problematic. Fragmentation makes compliance with legislation more costly, thus raising prices and preventing desirable activities, such as cross-border trade. The rules can also undermine or conflict with the objectives of other rules in undesirable ways. Administration and enforcement by separate administrative and judicial bodies also reduces predictability. It would therefore be desirable to reduce – or at least avoid – increasing fragmentation. While some types of fragmentation may be reduced by the measures this book examines, other kinds of fragmentation appear likely to increase.

3.   FROM TERRITORIAL TO OTHER FRAGMENTATION

Territorial fragmentation of intellectual property rights and other legislation is a problem that the DSM strategy seeks to address. Technological development creates fragmented practices and in turn fragmentation both of rights and of the legal framework in general. Hence, in many cases legal intervention may seem a compelling means of creating uniformity. However, the dilemma is that attempts to address fragmentation caused by different approaches adopted by EU Member States to address issues introduced by advances in technology at national level may bring about increased legal fragmentation.

Legal intervention may therefore, for instance, accelerate fragmentation of rules if differentiated ways of assessment or *sui generis*-type rules are adopted in order to accommodate the special circumstances in each technology. Regulation may thus splinter into many small pieces instead of creating and developing uniform general legal principles applicable to all technologies. This can be problematic because technology-specific rules generate casuistic approaches that might not be capable of resolving problems caused by future technical developments.

To illustrate, Kivistö's view of the proposed Directive on copyright in the DSM as 'a set of utmost complex and controversial copyright-related problems ... put together to form clusters of provisions with no apparent systemic interrelations or thematic proximity' causes serious concerns as to coherence of legal rules and principles. EU copyright seems to be on track to becoming increasingly complex and fragmented in terms of the rationale, subject-matter and scope of protection as well as enforcement mechanisms.

Moscon further illustrates fragmentation relating to the proposed related right of press publishers. As an alternative to the proposed right, Moscon advocates safeguarding press publishers' interests by a holistic approach through four especially important tools: copyright law, *sui generis* database protection, competition law and trademark law. As for the fragmented treatment of linking in the case law of the Court of Justice of the European Union (CJEU), Pihlajarinne suggests that more nuanced standards by the CJEU on linking as a copyright issue might also help address the problems of press publishers that the proposed press publisher's right seeks to tackle. According to Mezei, a balanced approach to digital exhaustion can be achieved by legal and technical means, in a legal context governed by various legal instruments at international, EU and national levels.

New technologies will soon raise problems that need to be addressed within the EU in order to avoid fragmentation. For instance, Mendis demonstrates that the EU copyright system will probably have to be re-assessed due to 3D printing. Additionally, as illustrated by Ballardini, Roos and He, no uniform concept as yet covers the meaning of 'author', a problem soon to be exacerbated by increased generation of works by AI. This might lead to multiple definitions of authorship being adopted in EU copyright.

Moreover, fragmentation caused by adopting technology-specific rules instead of resorting to general legal principles can generate casuistic approaches that might not be capable of resolving problems caused by future technical developments. As noted by Pihlajarinne and Oker-Blom in their chapter dealing with the application of trademark law to 3D printing, this kind of legal fragmentation might also occur within the application of flexible principles such as the principle of confusion in trademark law.

As regards fragmentation of approaches in different areas of law, the new and proposed rules applying to online distribution of content provide an example of fragmentation, with, for instance, copyright protection and its exercise via licensing having become subject to separate copyright and internal market legislation as well as EU treaty provisions (Vesala and Mazziotti). According to Mazziotti, the logic of territoriality in the new legislation can undermine EU-wide provision of copyright-protected content. In her chapter, Cantero argues that inconsistencies and limitations on freedom of contract in regulations relating to geo-blocking and the open internet introduce fragmentation that particularly impedes non-EU companies. Honkkila notes that tensions, differences and uncertainties remain as to principles that should govern net neutrality regulation. Additionally, Weckström Lindroos illustrates the complexity involved in accommodating copyright, procedural and data protection interests in enforcing copyright.

It can be concluded that technological development has led to fragmentation of rights and other rules governing online distribution of content within the EU, as discussed above. However, fragmentation is not always problematic. As law constantly evolves, some flexibility at the national level may be warranted to test new concepts, such as the new usage cases of extended collective licensing in Finland (Alén-Savikko and Knapstad). Moreover, in order to avoid harming incentives to create content, content- or technology-specific approaches under the Geo-blocking Regulation may be justified (Vesala). Fragmentation may also be useful in revealing 'silent national legal cultures in decision-making', as noted by Weckstöm Lindroos. This may in turn, according to Weckstöm Lindroos, allow an approach based more on the fundamental values embedded in the legal system instead of relying on piecemeal sectoral regulation. Moreover, Weckstöm Lindroos notes, for instance, that if local democratic and constitutional values influence liability for copyright infringement, this would lead rightholders not to bring suit in forums with high compensation cultures.

However, as discussed above, fragmentation might be harmful if it leads to a lack of coherence since legislation and judicial and administrative approaches in a particular area are split into segments. Fragmented rules, reflecting a particular stage of technical development, might not prove as sustainable during future development of technology and digital services. Avoiding the negative effects of legal fragmentation is therefore crucial to achieving the aims of digital single markets in the EU. Might it be possible to create much-needed coherence by resorting more to general legal principles, or at least ascertain that new, specific rules are sufficiently connected to these principles?

Index

alternative dispute resolution
  proposed DSM Directive 20
Amazon 75, 77, 200, 223
  Video 237, 239
Anheuser Busch v. Budějovický Budvar
  163
Antiquesportfolio.com Plc v Rodney
  Fitch & Co. Ltd 148–9
Apple 43, 75, 200
  iTunes 68, 70, 77, 200, 223, 234,
    239
Arsenal v. Reed 163
artificial intelligence (AI) 27, 37–8, 39,
    117–20, 134–5, 262, 263
  copyright law and authors 120–121,
    264
    'author' in European law 122–4
    interpretation by CJEU 124–6
  patent law and inventor 126–7
    EPO and national case law
      127–9
  theory of evolution 129–30
    modernist school 133–4
    revolutionary school 130–132,
      134
    romantic school 132–3, 134
audiovisual sector/works 101, 123, 124,
    125, 188, 228, 259
  European content threshold 239
  extended collective licensing 93
  Geo-blocking Regulation 197, 201,
    209–10, 212, 231
  extending 204–22
  Italy: sports rights 47
  proposed DSM Directive
    out-of-commerce works 13
    video-on-demand platforms
      14–15, 24, 207–8
  territorial licensing 193, 194–5,
    198–200, 201, 202, 203
Australia 51, 95
  exhaustion, doctrine of 63
Austria
  A1 Telekom Austria AG 256
  press publishers 44
authors and copyright 193
  artificial intelligence *see separate*
    entry

behavioural economics 259
Belgium
  Institute for Postal Services and
    Telecommunications (BIPT)
    256–7
  press publishers 45
Berne Convention 30, 31
  author 122–3
  exclusivity 88–9
  extended collective licensing 88–91
  formalities, ban on 88, 89–90
  national treatment 88, 89
  news protection 41, 50, 52–3, 57
  three-step test 88, 90–91

BestWater International GmbH v. Michael Mebes and Stefan Potsch 33
Bezpečnostní 144
biases, cognitive 259
BitTorrent technology 108–12
blockchain technology 77
Body of European Regulators for Electronic Communications (BEREC) 242, 244
Guidelines 242, 248, 252–7, 258
Brexit 138
broadcasting 21, 55–6, 57, 80, 81–4, 85, 92–3, 94, 95, 217, 220, 228
country of origin 192
offer ancillary online services in other Member States 192, 208–9, 211, 212–13
public 232
territorial licensing 193, 194–5, 198–200, 207, 210, 231
burden of proof
Finnish Market Court (MAO): technology and 106–12
proposed Digital Content Directive 176, 178
business models 25, 31, 36, 172
exhaustion, doctrine of 65, 72, 73, 74
extended collective licensing 80
news aggregators 16
press publishers 16, 43, 57, 59, 60, 61
social media 16
territoriality of markets 189, 200, 201
3D printing 151–2, 165, 167, 168, 169, 170

Canada
extended collective licensing 92
Capital Records v. ReDigi 68–70

case law of CJEU 63, 83, 106–7, 184
authors and copyright law 124–6
competition law 233–4, 251
computer programs 65–8, 144–5
confidentiality of communications 113
cross-border trade 194–5, 198–9
digital exhaustion
UsedSoft 65–8, 74
digitisation of out-of-print books 86–7
linking and copyright 25, 31, 32–6, 38–9, 264
3D printing 144–5, 149, 150–151
trade marks 157, 161, 163–4, 167
CDs 73, 77, 175
censorship 151
civil law systems 56, 100, 103, 122, 123
code is law, law is code or law is law 97, 98, 99–106
Coditel 234
cognitive biases 259
collective management organisations (CMOs)
extended collective licensing 88–9, 90, 91, 92, 96
broadcasting 84, 85, 92, 94
Nordic 80
multi-territorial licensing 94
proposed DSM Directive 85, 207
out-of-commerce works 12–13, 23–4
common law systems 56, 62, 122, 123
competition law 185–6, 189, 195, 198–9, 201–2, 206, 210–211, 213, 215, 219, 233–4, 263
net neutrality 241
open Internet rules of EU 244, 247–52, 258
press publishers 42, 52, 53–4, 55, 57, 58, 59, 60–61
computer-generated works 38, 133

computer programs 65–8
  author 123, 124, 125
  copyright protection 143–5
  Directive 2009/24/EC 8, 9, 11, 66–7,
      123, 124, 143, 144, 145
  patentable subject-matter 131
consumer protection, digital content and
      DSM 172–4, 187, 226, 261
  big picture 184–7
  portability of digital content 193–4
  proposed consumer contract rules
      187, 228, 231, 262
    definition of digital content
        174–5, 229
    further remarks 176–81
    future-proof 174, 180
    limitation periods 178
    other EU and Member State
        law 181–4
    overview 174–6
    remedies 173, 176, 178–80,
        182–3, 184
contact information of Internet service
      users *see* enforcement of
      copyright and data protection
Copyright Treaty, WIPO 30–31, 32, 122,
      123
  exhaustion, doctrine of 64, 65, 71,
      73, 78
  idea/expression dichotomy 52
Coty Germany 233
country-of-origin rule 94, 192, 208,
      215–16, 222
cultural heritage 82
  Europeana project 87
  proposed DSM Directive 11, 12, 13,
      85, 207

data
  free movement of 227
  fundamental digital resources 60
data protection 174, 175, 182, 226, 265

enforcement of copyright and *see*
      separate entry
databases 125
  sui generis right 49–50, 57, 58, 59,
      61
degradation of digital content 75
democracy 99–100, 103, 109, 258, 265
Denmark
  extended collective licensing 82, 91
design rights, UK 146
Directive 93/83/EEC, Satellite and Cable
      84, 85, 124, 192, 209, 217, 228
Directive 96/9/EC, Database 8, 9, 10, 11,
      49–50, 124
Directive 2000/31/EC, E-commerce 18,
      71, 101, 181, 225, 227
Directive 2001/29/EC, InfoSoc 8, 9, 10,
      11, 15, 16, 22, 23, 31, 32, 35, 41,
      45, 65, 71, 83, 85, 86–7, 90, 101,
      125, 144, 201, 202, 217
Directive 2004/48/EC, Enforcement of
      IPRs 58–9
Directive 2006/114/EC, Misleading and
      Comparative Advertising 161
Directive 2006/115/EC, Rental and
      Lending 41, 124
Directive 2009/24/EC, Software 8, 9, 11,
      66–7, 123, 124, 143, 144, 145
Directive 2012/28/EU, Orphan Works
      16, 22, 85
Directive 2014/26/EU, CRM 12, 85
Directive 2015/2436, Trademark 157,
      161
Directive, proposed Digital Content
      172–83, 187, 228, 229, 231, 262
Directive, proposed DSM 5–6, 24, 211,
      228, 261–2, 263–4
  access to content, wider
    audiovisual works on VoD
        platforms 14–15, 24,
        207–8

out-of-commerce works 12–14,
22, 23–4
adapting exceptions
cultural heritage, preservation
of 11, 207
digital and cross-border
teaching 9–11, 207
text and data mining 8–9, 23–4,
207
background and general framework
6–7
collective licensing 86
cultural heritage 11, 12, 13, 85
marketplace for copyright,
well-functioning
certain uses of protected
content 18–19
fair remuneration: authors and
performers 19–21, 24
rights in publications 15–17,
25–6, 38–9, 40–41,
45–50, 61
some considerations on 21
choice of instrument 21–2
grand visions and high-quality
legislation 22–3
to induce or to impose 23–4
domain names 159–60
DVDs 73, 77, 175, 193, 217

e-books 65, 71, 212
education
proposed DSM Directive: digital
and cross-border teaching
activities 9–11, 207
enforcement of consumer law 186–7
enforcement of copyright and data
protection 97–9, 115, 262, 264–5
code is law, law is code or law is
law 97, 98, 99–106
contact information, release of 98,
107, 109, 113–15

law in action: silent legal culture
98, 115
cultural fundamental values
112–15
legal fundamental values
106–12
engineering projects 56–7
England
copyright 29
environmental protection 259
European Broadcasting Union (EBU)
92–3
European Parliament 5, 46, 47, 131, 247
Internal Market and Consumer
Protection (IMCO)
Committee 197
European Patent Convention (EPC) 126,
127
Europeana project 87
evidence
Finnish Market Court (MAO):
illegal file-sharing 97, 98–9,
107–12
exhaustion, doctrine of 34–5, 62–5, 231,
264
balanced approach for digital 76–8
blockchain technology 77
Capital Records v. ReDigi 68–70
fate of digital
constructive realism 72–8
traditional positivism 70–72
forward-and-delete technology 73,
75, 76, 77, 78
goods-versus-service dichotomy
71–2
pros and cons 72–6
unique ID number 76, 77–8
UsedSoft case 65–8, 74
expression, freedom of 26, 28, 33, 36,
151, 241, 253, 258
extended collective licensing and online
distribution 79–81, 95–6

EU developments around ECL
84–6, 96
international legal framework
88–92, 96
promises and problems 92–5
recent use cases from Finland 81–4,
92, 93, 94, 265

Facebook 43
fair remuneration 201
authors and performers 63
bestseller clause 20
proposed DSM Directive
19–21, 24
file-sharing, illegal *see* enforcement of
copyright and data protection
films/film sector 193, 207, 212
Filmspeler 33–5
financial services 181, 197
Finland 224–5
extended collective licensing 80,
81–4, 88, 92, 93, 94, 265
Market Court (MAO): illegal
file-sharing *see* enforcement
of copyright and data
protection
first sale doctrine *see* exhaustion,
doctrine of
Football Dataco 125, 149
France 193
patent law and inventor 128
press publishers 44–5, 49
sporting events, organisers of 46–7
free movement of data 227
free movement of online content 226–30,
231, 234, 235
free movement of services 63, 65, 100,
206, 213, 224, 225, 226, 227, 228,
229
free-riding 25, 27–8, 44
fundamental values *see* enforcement of
copyright and data protection

gambling 181, 197
general legal principles 263, 264, 265
geo-blocking 173, 185, 187, 188–9, 261,
264, 265
country-of-origin rule 208, 215–16,
222
cross-border online content
distribution 198–202
extending coverage of Regulation
204–22
consequences 214–16
economic welfare 216–21
financing and incentives to
create 216–20
potential benefits 220–221
and open Internet rules: impact
on non-EU Over-The-Top
players 223–39
copyright territoriality 224–6
free movement of online
content 226–30, 231,
234, 235
freedom of contract 236–7, 238,
264
new licensing approach 236–7
open Internet 234–5, 237–8
streaming across borders
230–234
portability of digital content and
194, 197, 198
Regulation 195–8, 201–2, 209,
230–231, 236, 262
copyright works 197–8, 201,
202, 209–10, 212
extending to cover
copyright-protected
and audiovisual content
204–22
Germany 193
exhaustion, doctrine of 62–3
extended collective licensing

out-of-commerce works 86
patent law and inventor 128
press publishers 44, 48–9
Google 43, 225
*GS Media BV v. Sanoma Media
Netherlands BV et al.* 33–5

healthcare 181, 197
*Hewlett-Packard Belgium SPRL v.
Reprobel SCRL* 17
hyperlinks 27, 28, 33

idea/expression dichotomy 52
Infopaq 124–5, 144, 149
information society service providers
(ISSPs) 18–19, 24
Instagram 43
Interflora 161
Internet service providers (ISPs) 101,
234–5
commercial practices under EU
rules of open Internet
240–259
net neutrality 240–242
Israel
Dead Sea Scrolls case 148
Italy 193
audio-visual sports rights 46
press publishers 44–5, 48–9, 59
unfair competition 59
iTunes 68, 70, 77, 200, 223, 234, 239
*ITV Broadcasting et al v TV Catch Up
Ltd* 83

Japan
exhaustion, doctrine of 63
jurisdiction 98, 103
shopping 20

Kohler, Joseph 62

law is law, code is law or law is law 97,
98, 99–106

liability and access to contact
information 97–9, 115, 262,
264–5
cease-and-desist letters 107, 111,
114, 115
code is law, law is code or law is
law 97, 98, 99–106
compensation 98, 108, 109, 110,
112–13, 114–15
contact information, release of 98,
107, 109, 113–15
contextual solution-seeking
regulation 102, 109
international law 103–4, 105
law in action: silent legal culture
98, 115
cultural fundamental values
112–15
legal fundamental values
106–12
modern approach to law 105
presumptive contextualism 102,
106, 115
questions of fact and questions of
law 109, 110, 111
standing 114
linking and copyright 25–7, 38–9, 262,
264
artificial intelligence (AI) 27, 37–8,
39
diversity of linking and legitimate
interests 27–9
future 37–8
illegal material linked 35
implied licence 34–5
key copyright concepts: historical
developments 29–32
new public 31, 33
possible solution 36
two lines of cases 32–6

media archives

extended collective licensing 81–2, 96
media pluralism 253
Messenger 43
multi-territory licensing 87, 94
Murphy 125, 194, 231, 234
musical works 48, 212
    iTunes 68, 70, 77, 200, 223, 234, 239
    online marketplace for digital used music
        Capital Records v. ReDigi 68–70
mutual recognition 226, 236

nation state 102–5
neighbouring/related rights 40–41, 87
    international law 55
    press publishers *see separate entry*
    sporting events, organisers of 41, 46–7
    systematic approach for 56–7
neoliberalism 104
net neutrality *see* open Internet
Netflix 200, 201, 223, 227, 237, 239
Netherlands
    exhaustion, doctrine of 63
    net neutrality 244–7, 256
network personal video recorder (NPVR) services
    extended collective licensing 81, 82–4, 88, 93, 94, 96
New Zealand
    exhaustion, doctrine of 63
news aggregators 16, 25–6, 27–9, 38–9
    artificial intelligence (AI) 37–8
news publishers *see* press publishers
non-discrimination 225, 229, 234
    net neutrality 235, 241, 242
    Services Directive 196, 229
    territorial *see* geo-blocking
non-EU Over-The-Top players 223

    impact of geo-blocking and open Internet rules 223–39
Nordic extended collective licensing *see* extended collective licensing and online distribution
Norway
    extended collective licensing 91, 94

Obama, Barack 235
open Internet
    BEREC Guidelines 242, 248, 252–7, 258
    and geo-blocking: impact on non-EU Over-The-Top players 223–39
    copyright territoriality 224–6
    free movement of online content 226–30, 231, 234, 235
    freedom of contract 236–7, 238, 264
    new licensing approach 236–7
    open Internet 234–5, 237–8
    streaming across borders 230–234
    net neutrality 240–242, 262
    rules of EU: Reg 2015/2120 242–4, 257–9, 264
    interpretation 1: treat all traffic equally 244–7
    interpretation 2: assessment based on competition law principles 244, 247–52
    interpretation 3: assessing commercial practices *ex post* (*ex ante* guidance) 244, 252–7
OpenBazaar 77
optimists, term 74
Orwell, George 74
out-of-commerce works 86–7

Germany 86
Poland 86
proposed DSM Directive 12–14, 22, 23–4
Over-The-Top players, non-EU 223
   impact of geo-blocking and open Internet rules on 223–39

Painer 125, 148, 149
patent law 142
   and inventor *see* artificial intelligence
peer-to-peer (P2P) technology 108–12
performers 19–20, 55–6, 193
photographs 56, 124, 148–9
Picasso/Picaro 163, 164
Poland
   extended collective licensing out-of-commerce works 86
polycentricity 100
portability of digital content 173, 184, 187, 189, 190–192, 202, 209, 211, 212, 228, 231–3, 261, 262
   geo-blocking 194, 197, 198
   non-EU Tech giants 236–7
   portability versus cross-border trade 192–5
Post Danmark 251
Premier League 125, 194–5, 198–9, 206, 217, 231
press publishers 8, 15–17, 25–6, 40–42, 60–61, 262, 264
   business model 16, 43, 57, 59, 60, 61
   Commission's proposal
      case study 46–7
      content 45–6
      sui generis database protection 49–50
      undefined subject matter of protection 47–50

competition law and intellectual property 42, 52, 53–4, 55, 57, 58, 59, 60–61
   conflict of interests 58
   holistic approach 58–60, 61
   international law 57–8, 60
      Berne Convention 50, 52–3, 57
      neighbouring rights 55–6
      news stories and investments of press publishers 51–2
      premise 50
      taxonomy of rights 55–6, 58
   multifaceted background 42–5
      low-quality content 42, 43
   news aggregators 16, 25–6, 38–9
      artificial intelligence 37–8
      diversity of linking 27–9
   systematic approach for neighbouring rights 56–7
privacy 241
protectionism 238–9
public inerest 230
public-private partnerships 9

related rights *see* neighbouring/related rights
Reprobel 17
research organisations
   text and data mining 8–9, 23–4
Rome Convention 41, 55, 56
rule of law 99

SAS Institute Inc. v. World Programming Ltd 144
Sawkins v Hyperion Records 148
second-hand markets and doctrine of exhaustion 34–5, 62–5
   balanced approach 76–8
   Capital Records v. ReDigi 68–70
   constructive realism 72–8
   forward-and-delete technology 73, 75, 76, 77, 78

traditional positivism 70–72
unique ID number 76, 77–8
UsedSoft case 65–8, 74
silent national legal cultures *see* liability
        and access to contact information
smart contracts
    digital exhaustion doctrine 77
smartphones
    news consumption 43
social media
    freedom of speech 28
    press publishers 16, 42–3
Soulier and Doke 86–7
sound recordings 48, 55–6, 57
sovereignty 102–4
Spain 193
    press publishers 44, 49
specific performance 178–9
sporting events 212
    organisers 41, 46–7
    territorial licensing 194–5, 198–9,
        207
Spotify 223, 227, 232
Svensson et al v. Retriever Sverige AB
        32–3, 34
Sweden
    Post and Telecom Authority (PTS)
        256, 257
    press publishers 44
Switzerland
    exhaustion, doctrine of 63

T-Mobile v. ACM 246
taxation 230
teaching practices
    proposed DSM Directive: digital
        and cross-border 9–11, 207
telecommunications sector 100–101
term optimists 74
territorial restrictions *see* geo-blocking
text and data mining

proposed DSM Directive 8–9, 23–4,
    207
theatrical sketches 56
theories justifying IPRs 129–30
    and IPR regulation of AI 130–134
3D printing and copyright 136–8,
    150–152, 262, 264
    CAD design files 138, 141–3,
        145–7, 151–2
        protection of software and
            computer programs
            143–5
    changing landscape of artistic works
        in UK 139–41
    modifying object design file 147–50
3D printing and trade marks 153–5,
    169–70, 262, 264
    confusion
        essence of 155–6
        EU and USA 156–64
        3DP and trade mark 164–9
    initial confusion 154, 158–9, 169
        current position 159–62
        3DP context 165–8
    post-sale confusion 154, 158–9,
        169–70
        current position 162–4
        3DP context 168–9
trade marks 262
    press publishers 48, 58, 60, 61
    3D printing and distribution of CAD
        files *see* 3D printing and
        trade marks
trade secrecy 132
transaction costs 20
    cultural heritage institutions 11, 87
    extended collective licensing 81, 84,
        93, 96
    out-of-commerce works 12
    territorial exclusivity 217–18, 219
transparency

fair remuneration for authors and
performers
proposed DSM Directive
20–21, 24
treaty interpretation 50
TRIPS (Trade-Related Aspects of
Intellectual Property Rights)
Agreement 122, 123
exhaustion, doctrine of 63–4
extended collective licensing 88, 90
idea/expression dichotomy 52
neighbouring rights 55
three-step test 90

unfair competition 52, 55, 57, 59, 161,
226
United Kingdom
Brexit 138
computer-generated works 38, 133
England: copyright 29
extended collective licensing 86
patent law and inventor 128
3D printing and copyright 136–8,
150–152
CAD design files 138, 141–7,
151–2
changing landscape of artistic
works 139–41
modifying object design file
147–50
originality 147, 148–9
unregistered design rights 146
United States 30
exhaustion, doctrine of 62–3
Capital Records v. ReDigi
68–70
extended collective licensing 92

Federal Communications
Commission (FCC) 235, 246
film sector 193
net neutrality 235
news protection 51–2
patents 126, 131
trade marks 157–9, 162–3
zero-rating 246
UsedSoft 65–8, 74

VCAST Limited v RTI SpA 83
video games 210–211
videograms 57
Vienna Convention on the Law of
Treaties (VCLT) 50
Viking Gas v. Kosan Gas 164
Vodafone v. ACM 245

WhatsApp 43
World Intellectual Property Organization
(WIPO) 30, 55
Copyright Treaty 30–31, 32, 122,
123
exhaustion, doctrine of 64, 65,
71, 73, 78
idea/expression dichotomy 52
Performances and Phonograms
Treaty 55, 56
exhaustion, doctrine of 64, 65,
71

YouTube 223, 225, 232, 237

zero-rating 235, 243–4, 247, 250, 255,
256, 259
Austria 256
Belgium 256–7
Netherlands 245, 256
Sweden 256
United States 246